LIVES OF THE POETS
[COWLEY TO PRIOR]

BY

SAMUEL JOHNSON

Dolphin Books
Doubleday & Company, Inc.
Garden City, New York

Printed in the United States of America

ADVERTISEMENT

The Booksellers having determined to publish a body of English Poetry, I was persuaded to promise them a Preface to the Works of each Author; an undertaking, as it was then presented to my mind, not very extensive or difficult.

My purpose was only to have allotted to every Poet an Advertisement, like those which we find in the French *Miscellanies*, containing a few dates and a general character; but I have been led beyond my intention, I hope by the honest desire of giving useful pleasure.

In this minute kind of History, the succession of facts is not easily discovered; and I am not without suspicion that some of Dryden's works are placed in wrong years. I have followed Langbaine, as the best authority for his plays, and, if I shall hereafter obtain a more correct chronology, will publish it; but I do not yet know that my account is erroneous.

Dryden's *Remarks on Rymer* have been somewhere printed before. The former edition I have not seen. This was transcribed for the press from his own manuscript.

As this undertaking was occasional and unforeseen, I must be supposed to have engaged in it with less provision of materials than might have been accumulated by longer premeditation. Of the later writers at least I might, by attention and inquiry, have gleaned many particulars, which would have diversified and enlivened my *Biography*. These omissions, which it is now useless to lament, have been often supplied by the kindness of Mr. Steevens and others; and great assistance has been given me by Mr. Spence's *Collections*, of which I consider the communication as a favour worthy of public acknowledgment.

CONTENTS

LIVES OF THE POETS

[COWLEY TO PRIOR]

ABRAHAM COWLEY
1618–1667

Birth and Parentage—Genius—Educated at Westminster and Cambridge—His learned Puerilities—His *Mistress*—His Compliance with the Times—His Latin Poetry—His *Davideis*—His Love of Solitude—Death and Burial in Westminster Abbey—The Metaphysical Poets—Pindarism—Works and Character.

The Life of Cowley, notwithstanding the penury of English biography, has been written by Dr. Sprat, an author whose pregnancy of imagination and elegance of language have deservedly set him high in the ranks of literature; but his zeal of friendship, or ambition of eloquence, has produced a funeral oration rather than a history: he has given the character, not the life of Cowley; for he writes with so little detail, that scarcely anything is distinctly known, but all is shown confused and enlarged through the mist of panegyric.

Abraham Cowley was born in the year 1618. His father was a grocer, whose condition Dr. Sprat conceals under the general appellation of a citizen; and, what would probably not have been less carefully suppressed, the omission of his name in the register of St. Dunstan's parish gives reason to suspect that his father was a sectary. Whoever he was, he died before the birth of his son, and consequently left him to the care of his mother, whom Wood represents as struggling earnestly to procure him a literary education, and who, as she lived to the age of eighty, had her solicitude rewarded by seeing her son eminent, and, I hope, by seeing him fortunate, and partaking his prosperity. We know at least, from Sprat's account, that he always acknowledged her care, and justly paid the dues of filial gratitude.

In the window of his mother's apartment lay Spenser's *Fairy Queen*, in which he very early took delight to read, till, by feeling the charms of verse, he became, as he relates, irrecoverably a poet. Such are the accidents which, sometimes remembered, and perhaps sometimes forgotten, produce that particular designation of mind, and propensity for some certain science or employment, which is commonly called genius. The true genius is a mind of large general powers, accidentally determined to some particular direction. Sir Joshua Reynolds, the great painter of the present age, had the first fondness for his art excited by the perusal of Richardson's treatise.

By his mother's solicitation he was admitted into Westminster School, where he was soon distinguished. "He was wont," says Sprat, "to relate that he had this defect in his memory at that time, that his teachers never could bring it to retain the ordinary rules of grammar."

This is an instance of the natural desire of man to propagate a wonder. It is surely very difficult to tell anything as it was heard, when Sprat could not refrain from amplifying a commodious incident, though the book to which he prefixed his narrative contained its confutation. A memory admitting some things and rejecting others, an intellectual digestion that concocted the pulp of learning, but refused the husks, had the appearance of an instinctive elegance, of a particular provision made by nature for literary politeness. But in the author's own honest relation the marvel vanishes: "He was," he says, "such an enemy to all constraint, that his master never could prevail on him to learn the rules without book." He does not tell that he could not learn the rules, but that, being able to perform his exercises without them, and being an "enemy to constraint," he spared himself the labour.

Among the English poets, Cowley, Milton, and Pope might be said "to lisp in numbers"; and have given such early proofs, not only of powers of language, but of comprehension of things, as to more tardy minds seems scarcely credible. But of the learned puerilities of Cowley there is no doubt, since a volume of his poems was not only written but printed in his thirteenth year, containing, with other poetical compositions, *The Tragical History of Pyramus and Thisbe*, written when he was ten years old; and *Constantia and Philetus*, written two years after.

While he was yet at school he produced a comedy called *Love's Riddle*, though it was not published till he had been some time at Cambridge. This comedy is of the pastoral kind, which requires no acquaintance with the living world, and therefore the time at which it was composed adds little to the wonders of Cowley's minority.

In 1636 he was removed to Cambridge, where he continued his studies with great intenseness; for he is said to have written, while he was yet a young student, the greater part of his *Davideis*—a work of which the materials could not have been collected, without the study of many years, but by a mind of the greatest vigour and activity.

Two years after his settlement at Cambridge he published *Love's Riddle*, with a poetical dedication to Sir Kenelm Digby, of whose acquaintance all his contemporaries seem to have been ambitious, and *Naufragium Joculare*, a comedy written in Latin, but without due attention to the ancient models; for it is not loose verse, but mere prose. It was printed with a dedication in verse to Dr. Comber, master of the college; but having neither the facility of a popular nor the accuracy of a learned work, it seems to be now universally neglected.

At the beginning of the civil war, as the Prince passed through Cambridge in his way to York, he was entertained with a representation of the *Guardian*, a comedy, which Cowley says was neither written nor acted, but rough-drawn by him, and repeated by the scholars. That this comedy was printed during his absence from his country, he appears to have considered as injurious to his reputation; though, during the suppression of the theatres, it was sometimes privately acted with sufficient approbation.

In 1643, being now Master of Arts, he was, by the prevalence of the Parliament, ejected from Cambridge, and sheltered himself at St. John's College in Oxford, where, as is said by Wood, he published a satire, called *The Puritan and*

the Papist, which was only inserted in the last collection of
his works, and so distinguished himself by the warmth of his
loyalty, and the elegance of his conversation, that he gained
the kindness and confidence of those who attended the King,
and amongst others of Lord Falkland, whose notice cast a lustre on all to whom it was extended.

About the time when Oxford was surrendered to the Parliament, he followed the Queen to Paris, where he became
secretary to the Lord Jermyn, afterwards Earl of St. Alban's,
and was employed in such correspondence as the royal cause
required, and particularly in ciphering and deciphering the letters that passed between the King and Queen—an employment
of the highest confidence and honour. So wide was his province
of intelligence that, for several years, it filled all his days and
two or three nights in the week.

In the year 1647 his *Mistress* was published; for he imagined, as he declared in his preface to a subsequent edition,
that "poets are scarce thought freemen of their company without paying some duties, or obliging themselves to be true to
love."

This obligation to amorous ditties owes, I believe, its original to the fame of Petrarch, who, in an age rude and uncul-
tivated, by his tuneful homage to his Laura, refined the manners of the lettered world, and filled Europe with love and
poetry. But the basis of all excellence is truth: he that professes love ought to feel its power. Petrarch was a real lover,
and Laura doubtless deserved his tenderness. Of Cowley, we
are told by Barnes, who had means enough of information,
that, whatever he may talk of his own inflammability, and the
variety of characters by which his heart was divided, he in reality was in love but once, and then never had resolution to
tell his passion.

This consideration cannot but abate, in some measure, the
reader's esteem for the work and the author. To love excellence is natural; it is natural likewise for the lover to solicit
reciprocal regard by an elaborate display of his own qualifications. The desire of pleasing has in different men produced
actions of heroism, and effusions of wit; but it seems as reasonable to appear the champion as the poet of an "airy

nothing," and to quarrel as to write for what Cowley might have learned from his master Pindar to call the "dream of a shadow."

It is surely not difficult, in the solitude of a college or in the bustle of the world, to find useful studies and serious employment. No man needs to be so burthened with life as to squander it in voluntary dreams of fictitious occurrences. The man that sits down to suppose himself charged with treason or peculation, and heats his mind to an elaborate purgation of his character from crimes which he was never within the possibility of committing, differs only by the infrequency of his folly from him who praises beauty which he never saw, complains of jealousy which he never felt, supposes himself sometimes invited and sometimes forsaken, fatigues his fancy and ransacks his memory for images which may exhibit the gaiety of hope or the gloominess of despair, and dresses his imaginary Chloris or Phyllis sometimes in flowers fading as her beauty, and sometimes in gems as lasting as her virtues.

At Paris, as secretary to Lord Jermyn, he was engaged in transacting things of real importance with real men and real women, and at that time did not much employ his thoughts upon phantoms of gallantry. Some of his letters to Mr. Bennet, afterwards Earl of Arlington, from April to December in 1650, are preserved in *Miscellanea Aulica*, a collection of papers published by Brown. These letters, being written like those of other men whose minds are more on things than words, contribute no otherwise to his reputation than as they show him to have been above the affectation of unseasonable elegance, and to have known that the business of a statesman can be little forwarded by flowers of rhetoric.

One passage, however, seems not unworthy of some notice. Speaking of the Scotch treaty then in agitation:

"The Scotch treaty," says he, "is the only thing now in which we are vitally concerned; I am one of the last hopers, and yet cannot now abstain from believing that the agreement will be made: all people upon the place incline to that opinion. The Scotch will moderate somewhat of the rigour of their demands; the mutual necessity of an accord is visible, the King is persuaded of it, and all mankind, but two or three mighty tender consciences about him. And to tell you the truth (which I take to be an argument above all the rest), Virgil has told me something to that purpose."

This expression from a secretary of the present time would be considered as merely ludicrous, or at most as an ostentatious display of scholarship; but the manners of that time were so tinged with superstition, that I cannot but suspect Cowley of having consulted on this great occasion the Virgilian lots, and to have given some credit to the answer of his oracle.

Some years afterwards, "business," says Sprat, "passed of course into other hands"; and Cowley, being no longer useful at Paris, was in 1656 sent back into England, that, "under pretence of privacy and retirement, he might take occasion of giving notice of the posture of things in this nation."

Soon after his return to London, he was seized by some messengers of the usurping powers, who were sent out in quest of another man; and, being examined, was put into confinement, from which he was not dismissed without the security of a thousand pounds given by Dr. Scarborough.

This year [1656] he published his Poems, with a preface, in which he seems to have inserted something, suppressed in subsequent editions, which was interpreted to denote some relaxation of his loyalty. In this preface he declares that "his desire had been for some years past, and did still vehemently continue, to retire himself to some of the American plantations, and to forsake this world for ever."

From the obloquy which the appearance of submission to the usurpers brought upon him, his biographer has been very diligent to clear him, and indeed it does not seem to have lessened his reputation. His wish for retirement we can easily believe to be undissembled: a man harassed in one kingdom, and persecuted in another, who, after a course of business that employed all his days and half his nights in ciphering and deciphering, comes to his own country and steps into a prison, will be willing enough to retire to some place of quiet and of safety. Yet let neither our reverence for a genius, nor our pity for a sufferer, dispose us to forget that, if his activity was virtue, his retreat was cowardice.

He then took upon himself the character of physician, still, according to Sprat, with intention "to dissemble the main design of his coming over"; and, as Mr. Wood relates, "complying with some of the men then in power (which was much taken notice of by the royal party), he obtained an order to be created doctor of physic, which being done to his mind (whereby he gained the ill-will of some of his friends), he went into France again, having made a copy of verses on Oliver's death."

This is no favourable representation, yet even in this not much wrong can be discovered. How far he complied with the men in power is to be inquired before he can be blamed. It is not said that he told them any secrets, or assisted them by intelligence, or any other act. If he only promised to be quiet, that they in whose hands he was might free him from confinement, he did what no law of society prohibits.

The man whose miscarriage in a just cause has put him in the power of his enemy may, without any violation of his integrity, regain his liberty or preserve his life by a promise of neutrality: for the stipulation gives the enemy nothing which he had not before; the neutrality of a captive may be always secured by his imprisonment or death. He that is at the disposal of another may not promise to aid him in any injurious act, because no power can compel active obedience. He may engage to do nothing, but not to do ill.

There is reason to think that Cowley promised little. It does not appear that his compliance gained him confidence enough to be trusted without security, for the bond of his bail was never cancelled; nor that it made him think himself secure, for at that dissolution of government which followed the death of Oliver he returned into France, where he resumed his former station, and stayed till the Restoration.

"He continued," says his biographer, "under these bonds till the general deliverance": it is therefore to be supposed that he did not go to France and act again for the King without the consent of his bondsman; that he did not show his loyalty at the hazard of his friend, but by his friend's permission.

Of the verses on Oliver's death, in which Wood's narrative seems to imply something encomiastic, there has been no appearance. There is a discourse concerning his government, indeed, with verses intermixed, but such as certainly gained its author no friends among the abettors of usurpation.

A doctor of physic, however, he was made at Oxford, in December, 1657; and in the commencement of the Royal Society, of which an account has been given by Dr. Birch, he appears busy among the experimental philosophers with the title of Dr. Cowley.

There is no reason for supposing that he ever attempted practice; but his preparatory studies have contributed something to the honour of his country. Considering botany as necessary to a physician, he retired into Kent to gather plants; and, as the predominance of a favourite study affects all subordinate operations of the intellect, botany in the mind of Cowley turned into poetry. He composed in Latin several books on plants, of which the first and second display the qualities of herbs, in elegiac verse; the third and fourth, the beauties of flowers, in various measures; and the fifth and sixth, the uses of trees, in heroic numbers.

At the same time were produced, from the same university, two great poets, Cowley and Milton, of dissimilar genius, of opposite principles, but concurring in the cultivation of Latin poetry, in which the English, till their works and May's poem appeared, seemed unable to contest the palm with any other of the lettered nations.

If the Latin performances of Cowley and Milton be compared (for May I hold to be superior to both), the advantage seems to lie on the side of Cowley. Milton is generally content to express the thoughts of the ancients in their language; Cowley, without much loss of purity or elegance, accommodates the diction of Rome to his own conceptions.

At the Restoration, after all the diligence of his long service, and with consciousness not only of the merit of fidelity, but of the dignity of great abilities, he naturally expected ample preferments; and, that he might not be forgotten by his own fault, wrote a Song of Triumph. But this was a time of such general hope, that great numbers were inevitably disappointed, and Cowley found his reward very tediously delayed. He had been promised, by both Charles I. and II., the mastership of the

Savoy; "but he lost it," says Wood, "by certain persons, enemies to the Muses."

The neglect of the Court was not his only mortification: having, by such alteration as he thought proper, fitted his old comedy of the *Guardian* for the stage, he produced it [8th Dec. 1661] under the title of *Cutter of Coleman-street*. It was treated on the stage with great severity, and was afterwards censured as a satire on the King's party.

Mr. Dryden, who went with Mr. Sprat to the first exhibition, related to Mr. Dennis, "that, when they told Cowley how little favour had been shown him, he received the news of his ill success not with so much firmness as might have been expected from so great a man."

What firmness they expected, or what weakness Cowley discovered, cannot be known. He that misses his end will never be as much pleased as he that attains it, even when he can impute no part of his failure to himself; and when the end is to please the multitude, no man, perhaps, has a right, in things admitting of gradation and comparison, to throw the whole blame upon his judges, and totally to exclude diffidence and shame by a haughty consciousness of his own excellence.

For the rejection of this play it is difficult now to find the reason: it certainly has, in a very great degree, the power of fixing attention and exciting merriment. From the charge of disaffection he exculpates himself in his preface, by observing how unlikely it is that, having followed the royal family through all their distresses, "he should choose the time of their restoration to begin a quarrel with them." It appears, however, from the Theatrical Register of Downes the prompter, to have been popularly considered as a satire on the royalists.

That he might shorten this tedious suspense, he published his pretensions and his discontent in an ode called *The Complaint*, in which he styles himself the *melancholy* Cowley. This met with the usual fortune of complaints, and seems to have excited more contempt than pity.

These unlucky incidents are brought, maliciously enough, together in some stanzas, written about that time, on the choice of a laureat; a mode of satire by which, since it was

first introduced by Suckling, perhaps every generation of poets
has been teased.

> Savoy-missing Cowley came into the court,
>   Making apologies for his bad play:
> Every one gave him so good a report,
>   That Apollo gave heed to all he could say:
> Nor would he have had, 'tis thought, a rebuke,
>   Unless he had done some notable folly;
> Writ verses unjustly in praise of Sam Tuke,
>   Or printed his pitiful Melancholy.

His vehement desire of retirement now came again upon
him. "Not finding," says the morose Wood, "that preferment
conferred upon him which he expected, while others for their
money carried away most places, he retired discontented into
Surrey."

"He was now," says the courtly Sprat, "weary of the vexations and formalities of an active condition. He had been perplexed with a long compliance to foreign manners. He was
satiated with the arts of a court; which sort of life, though
his virtue had made it innocent to him, yet nothing could
make it quiet. Those were the reasons that moved him to
forego all public employments, and follow the violent inclination of his own mind, which, in the greatest throng of his
former business, had still called upon him, and represented to
him the true delights of solitary studies, of temperate pleasures, and of a moderate revenue below the malice and flatteries of fortune."

So differently are things seen! and so differently are they
shown! but actions are visible, though motives are secret. Cowley certainly retired; first to Barn-elms, and afterwards to
Chertsey, in Surrey. He seems, however, to have lost part of
his dread of the *hum of men*. He thought himself now safe
enough from intrusion, without the defence of mountains and
oceans; and instead of seeking shelter in America, wisely went
only so far from the bustle of life as that he might easily find
his way back, when solitude should grow tedious. His retreat
was at first but slenderly accommodated; yet he soon obtained,
by the interest of the Earl of St. Alban's and the Duke of

Buckingham, such a lease of the Queen's lands as afforded him an ample income.

By the lover of virtue and of wit it will be solicitously asked if he now was happy. Let them peruse one of his letters accidentally preserved by Peck, which I recommend to the consideration of all that may hereafter pant for solitude.

> "*To Dr. Thomas Sprat.*
>
> "Chertsey, 21 May, 1665.
>
> "The first night that I came hither I caught so great a cold, with a defluxion of rheum, as made me keep my chamber ten days; and, two after, had such a bruise on my ribs with a fall, that I am yet unable to move or turn myself in my bed. This is my personal fortune here to begin with. And, besides, I can get no money from my tenants, and have my meadows eaten up every night by cattle put in by my neighbours. What this signifies, or may come to in time, God knows; if it be ominous, it can end in nothing less than hanging. Another misfortune has been, and stranger than all the rest, that you have broke your word with me, and failed to come, even though you told Mr. Bois that you would. This is what they call *monstri simile*. I do hope to recover my late hurt so farre within five or six days (though it be uncertain yet whether I shall ever recover it) as to walk about again. And then, methinks, you and I and the Dean might be very merry upon St. Anne's Hill. You might very conveniently come hither the way of Hampton town, lying there one night. I write this in pain, and can say no more: *Verbum sapienti*."

He did not long enjoy the pleasure or suffer the uneasiness of solitude, for he died at the Porch-house in Chertsey in 1667, in the forty-ninth year of his age.

He was buried with great pomp near Chaucer and Spenser; and King Charles pronounced, "That Mr. Cowley had not left behind him a better man in England." He is represented by Dr. Sprat as the most amiable of mankind; and this posthumous praise may safely be credited, as it has never been contradicted by envy or by faction.

Such are the remarks and memorials which I have been able to add to the narrative of Dr. Sprat, who, writing when the feuds of the civil war were yet recent, and the minds of either party were easily irritated, was obliged to pass over many transactions in general expressions, and to leave curiosity often unsatisfied. What he did not tell, cannot however now be known. I must therefore recommend the perusal of his work, to which my narration can be considered only as a slender supplement.

Cowley, like other poets who have written with narrow views, and, instead of tracing intellectual pleasures in the mind of man, paid their court to temporary prejudices, has been at one time too much praised, and too much neglected at another.

Wit, like all other things subject by their nature to the choice of man, has its changes and fashions, and at different times takes different forms. About the beginning of the seventeenth century appeared a race of writers that may be termed the *metaphysical poets*, of whom, in a criticism on the works of Cowley, it is not improper to give some account.

The metaphysical poets were men of learning, and to show their learning was their whole endeavour; but, unluckily resolving to show it in rhyme, instead of writing poetry they only wrote verses, and very often such verses as stood the trial of the finger better than of the ear; for the modulation was so imperfect, that they were only found to be verses by counting the syllables.

If the father of criticism has rightly denominated poetry τέχνη μιμητική, *an imitative art*, these writers will, without great wrong, lose their right to the name of poets, for they cannot be said to have imitated anything; they neither copied nature for life, neither painted the forms of matter, nor represented the operations of intellect.

Those, however, who deny them to be poets, allow them to be wits. Dryden confesses of himself and his contemporaries, that they fall below Donne in wit, but maintains that they surpass him in poetry.

If wit be well described by Pope, as being "that which has

been often thought, but was never before so well expressed," they certainly never attained, nor ever sought it; for they endeavoured to be singular in their thoughts, and were careless of their diction. But Pope's account of wit is undoubtedly erroneous: he depresses it below its natural dignity, and reduces it from strength of thought to happiness of language.

If by a more noble and more adequate conception that be considered as wit which is at once natural and new, that which, though not obvious, is, upon its first production, acknowledged to be just; if it be that which he that never found it wonders how he missed, to wit of this kind the metaphysical poets have seldom risen. Their thoughts are often new, but seldom natural; they are not obvious, but neither are they just; and the reader, far from wondering that he missed them, wonders more frequently by what perverseness of industry they were ever found.

But wit, abstracted from its effects upon the hearer, may be more rigorously and philosophically considered as a kind of *discordia concors*; a combination of dissimilar images, or discovery of occult resemblances in things apparently unlike. Of wit, thus defined, they have more than enough. The most heterogeneous ideas are yoked by violence together; nature and art are ransacked for illustrations, comparisons, and allusions; their learning instructs, and their subtlety surprises; but the reader commonly thinks his improvement dearly bought, and, though he sometimes admires, is seldom pleased.

From this account of their compositions it will be readily inferred that they were not successful in representing or moving the affections. As they were wholly employed on something unexpected and surprising, they had no regard to that uniformity of sentiment which enables us to conceive and to excite the pains and the pleasure of other minds: they never inquired what, on any occasion, they should have said or done, but wrote rather as beholders than partakers of human nature; as beings looking upon good and evil, impassive and at leisure; as Epicurean deities, making remarks on the actions of men, and the vicissitudes of life, without interest and without emotion. Their courtship was void of fondness, and their lamentation of sorrow. Their wish was only to say what they hoped had been never said before.

Nor was the sublime more within their reach than the pathetic; for they never attempted that comprehension and expanse of thought which at once fills the whole mind, and of which the first effect is sudden astonishment, and the second rational admiration. Sublimity is produced by aggregation, and littleness by dispersion. Great thoughts are always general, and consist in positions not limited by exceptions, and in descriptions not descending to minuteness. It is with great propriety that subtlety, which in its original import means exility of particles, is taken in its metaphorical meaning for nicety of distinction. Those writers who lay on the watch for novelty could have little hope of greatness; for great things cannot have escaped former observation. Their attempts were always analytic; they broke every image into fragments; and could no more represent, by their slender conceits and laboured particularities, the prospects of nature, or the scenes of life, than he who dissects a sunbeam with a prism can exhibit the wide effulgence of a summer noon.

What they wanted however of the sublime, they endeavoured to supply by hyperbole; their amplification had no limits; they left not only reason but fancy behind them; and produced combinations of confused magnificence, that not only could not be credited, but could not be imagined.

Yet great labour, directed by great abilities, is never wholly lost: if they frequently threw away their wit upon false conceits, they likewise sometimes struck out unexpected truth; if their conceits were far-fetched, they were often worth the carriage. To write on their plan, it was at least necessary to read and think. No man could be born a metaphysical poet, nor assume the dignity of a writer, by descriptions copied from descriptions, by imitations borrowed from imitations, by traditional imagery, and hereditary similes, by readiness of rhyme, and volubility of syllables.

In perusing the works of this race of authors, the mind is exercised either by recollection or inquiry; either something already learned is to be retrieved, or something new is to be examined. If their greatness seldom elevates, their acuteness often surprises; if the imagination is not always gratified, at least the powers of reflection and comparison are employed; and in the mass of materials which ingenious absurdity has thrown together, genuine wit and useful knowledge may be sometimes found buried perhaps in grossness of expression, but useful to those who know their value; and such as, when they are expanded to perspicuity, and polished to elegance, may give lustre to works which have more propriety though less copiousness of sentiment.

This kind of writing, which was, I believe, borrowed from Marino and his followers, had been recommended by the example of Donne, a man of a very extensive and various knowledge; and by Jonson, whose manner resembled that of Donne more in the ruggedness of his lines than in the cast of his sentiments.

When their reputation was high, they had undoubtedly more imitators than time has left behind. Their immediate successors, of whom any remembrance can be said to remain, were Suckling, Waller, Denham, Cowley, Cleveland, and Milton. Denham and Waller sought another way to fame, by improving the harmony of our numbers. Milton tried the metaphysic style only in his lines upon Hobson the Carrier. Cowley adopted it, and excelled his predecessors, having as much sentiment and more music. Suckling neither improved versification, nor abounded in conceits. The fashionable style remained chiefly with Cowley; Suckling could not reach it, and Milton disdained it.

Critical remarks are not easily understood without examples; and I have therefore collected instances of the modes of writing by which this species of poets, for poets they were called by themselves and their admirers, was eminently distinguished.

As the authors of this race were perhaps more desirous of being admired than understood, they sometimes drew their conceits from recesses of learning not very much frequented by common readers of poetry. Thus Cowley on *Knowledge*:

> The sacred tree midst the fair orchard grew;
> The phœnix Truth did on it rest,

> And built his perfum'd nest,
> That right Porphyrian tree which did true logic show.
> Each leaf did learned notions give,
> And th' apples were demonstrative:
> So clear their colour and divine,
> The very shade they cast did other lights outshine

On Anacreon continuing a lover in his old age:

> Love was with thy life entwin'd,
> Close as heat with fire is join'd,
> A powerful brand prescrib'd the date
> Of thine, like Meleager's fate,
> Th' antiperistasis of age
> More inflam'd thy amorous rage.
> *Elegy upon Anacreon.*

In the following verses we have an allusion to a Rabbinical opinion concerning Manna:

> Variety I ask not: give me one
> To live perpetually upon.
> The person Love does to us fit,
> Like manna, has the taste of all in it.

Thus Donne shows his medicinal knowledge in some encomiastic verses:

> In every thing there naturally grows
> A balsamum to keep it fresh and new,
> If 't were not injur'd by extrinsique blows;
> Your birth and beauty are this balm in you.
> But you, of learning and religion,
> And virtue, and such ingredients, have made
> A mithridate, whose operation
> Keeps off, or cures what can be done or said.
> DONNE, *To the Countess of Bedford.*

Though the following lines of Donne, on the last night of the year, have something in them too scholastic, they are not inelegant:

This twilight of two years, not past nor next,
    Some emblem is of me, or I of this,
Who, meteor-like, of stuff and form perplext,
    Whose what and where in disputation is,
    If I should call me anything, should miss.
I sum the years and me, and find me not
    Debtor to th' old, nor creditor to th' new;
That cannot say, my thanks I have forgot,
    Nor trust I this with hopes; and yet scarce true
    This bravery is, since these times show'd me you.
        DONNE, *To the Countess of Bedford.*

Yet more abstruse and profound is Donne's reflection upon
man as a microcosm:

If men be worlds, there is in every one
Something to answer in some proportion
All the world's riches: and in good men, this
Virtue, our form's form, and our soul's soul is.

Of thoughts so far-fetched, as to be not only unexpected but
unnatural, all their books are full.

    To a Lady, who made posies for rings
They, who above do various circles find,
Say, like a ring th' æquator heaven does bind.
When heaven shall be adorn'd by thee,
(Which then more heaven than 'tis, will be,)
'Tis thou must write the poesy there,
For it wanteth one as yet,
Though the sun pass through 't twice a year,
The sun, who is esteem'd the god of wit.
        COWLEY.

The difficulties which have been raised about identity in
philosophy, are by Cowley with still more perplexity applied
to love:

Five years ago (says story) I lov'd you,
For which you call me most inconstant now:
Pardon me, madam, you mistake the man;

For I am not the same that I was then;
No flesh is now the same 'twas then in me,
And that my mind is chang'd yourself may see.
The same thoughts to retain still, and intents,
Were more inconstant far: for accidents
Must of all things most strangely inconstant prove,
If from one subject they t' another move:
My members then, the father members were
From whence these take their birth, which now are here.
If then this body love what th' other did,
'Twere incest, which by nature is forbid.

Inconstancy.

The love of different women is, in geographical poetry, compared to travels through different countries:

> Hast thou not found each woman's breast
>   (The land where thou hast travelled)
> Either by savages possest,
>   Or wild, and uninhabited?
> What joy could'st take, or what repose,
> In countries so uncivilis'd as those?
>
> . . . . . .
>
> Lust, the scorching dog-star, here
>   Rages with immoderate heat;
> Whilst Pride, the rugged Northern Bear
>   In others makes the cold too great.
> And where these are temperate known,
> The soil's all barren sand, or rocky stone.

COWLEY, *The Welcome.*

A lover, burnt up by his affection, is compared to Egypt:

> The fate of Egypt I sustain,
>   And never feel the dew of rain
> From clouds which in the head appear;
>   But all my too much moisture owe
>   To overflowings of the heart below.

COWLEY, *Sleep.*

The lover supposes his lady acquainted with the ancient laws of augury and rites of sacrifice:

> And yet this death of mine, I fear,
> Will ominous to her appear:
>   When, sound in every other part,
>   Her sacrifice is found without an heart.
>   For the last tempest of my death
>   Shall sigh out that too, with my breath.
>   COWLEY, *The Concealment.*

That the chaos was harmonised, has been recited of old; but whence the different sounds arose remained for a modern to discover:

> Th' ungovern'd parts no correspondence knew;
> An artless war from thwarting motions grew;
> Till they to number and fixt rules were brought.
> Water and air he for the tenor chose;
> Earth made the base; the treble, flame arose.
>   COWLEY.

The tears of lovers are always of great poetical account; but Donne has extended them into worlds. If the lines are not easily understood, they may be read again:

>   On a round ball
>   A workman, that hath copies by, can lay
>   An Europe, Afric, and an Asia,
> And quickly make that, which was nothing, All.
>   So doth each tear,
>   Which thee doth wear,
> A globe, yea would, by that impression grow,
> Till thy tears mixt with mine do overflow
> This world, by waters sent from thee my heaven dissolved so.
>   *A Valediction of Weeping.*

On reading the following lines, the reader may perhaps cry out—*Confusion worse confounded*:

Here lies a she sun, and a he moon there,
  She gives the best light to his sphere,
  Or each is both, and all, and so
They unto one another nothing owe.
DONNE, *Epithalamion on the Count Palatine, etc.*

Who but Donne would have thought that a good man is a telescope?

Though God be our true glass through which we see
All, since the being of all things is he,
Yet are the trunks, which do to us derive
Things in proportion fit, by perspective
Deeds of good men; for by their living here,
Virtues, indeed remote, seem to be near.

Who would imagine it possible that in a very few lines so many remote ideas could be brought together?

Since 'tis my doom, Love's undershrieve,
    Why this reprieve?
Why doth my she advowson fly
    Incumbency?
To sell thyself dost thou intend
    By candle's end,
And hold the contract thus in doubt,
    Life's taper out?
Think but how soon the market fails,
Your sex lives faster than the males;
And if to measure age's span,
The sober Julian were th' account of man,
Whilst you live by the fleet Gregorian.
CLEVELAND, *To Julia to expedite her Promise.*

Of enormous and disgusting hyperboles, these may be examples:

By every wind that comes this way,
  Send me at least a sigh or two,
Such and so many I'll repay
  As shall themselves make winds to get to you.
                                        COWLEY.

In tears I'll waste these eyes,
   By Love so vainly fed;
So lust of old the Deluge punished.
                              COWLEY.

All arm'd in brass, the richest dress of war,
   (A dismal glorious sight,) he shone afar.
The sun himself started with sudden fright,
To see his beams return so dismal bright.
                              COWLEY.

An universal consternation:

   His bloody eyes he hurls round, his sharp paws
   Tear up the ground; then runs he wild about,
   Lashing his angry tail and roaring out.
   Beasts creep into their dens, and tremble there:
   Trees, though no wind is stirring, shake with fear;
   Silence and horror fill the place around;
   Echo itself dares scarce repeat the sound.
                              COWLEY.

Their fictions were often violent and unnatural.

                Of his Mistress bathing
   The fish around her crowded, as they do
   To the false light that treacherous fishes show,
   And all with as much ease might taken be,
         As she at first took me:
         For ne'er did light so clear
         Among the waves appear,
   Though every night the sun himself set there.
                              COWLEY.

The poetical effect of a lover's name upon glass:

         My name engrav'd herein
      Doth contribute my firmness to this glass;
         Which, ever since that charm, hath been
      As hard as that which grav'd it was.
DONNE, A *Valediction of my Name in the Window.*

Their conceits were sentiments slight and trifling.

On an inconstant Woman

He enjoys thy calmy sunshine now,
 And no breath stirring hears,
In the clear heaven of thy brow
 No smallest cloud appears.
He sees thee gentle, fair, and gay,
And trusts the faithless April of thy May.
    COWLEY, *in imitation of Horace.*

Upon a paper written with the juice of lemon, and read by the fire:

So, nothing yet in thee is seen,
But when a genial heat warms thee within,
A new-born wood of various lines there grows;
 Here buds an A, and there a B,
 Here sprouts a V, and there a T,
And all the flourishing letters stand in rows.
    COWLEY.

As they sought only for novelty, they did not much inquire whether their allusions were to things high or low, elegant or gross; whether they compared the little to the great, or the great to the little.

Physic and Chirurgery for a Lover

Gently, ah gently, madam, touch
 The wound which you yourself have made;
That pain must needs be very much,
 Which makes me of your hand afraid.
Cordials of pity give me now,
 For I too weak for purgings grow.
    COWLEY, *Counsel.*

The World and a Clock

Mahol, th' inferior world's fantastic face
Thro' all the turns of matter's maze did trace,
Great Nature's well-set clock in pieces took;
On all the springs and smallest wheels did look
Of life and motion, and with equal art
Made up again the whole of every part.
    COWLEY, *Davideis,* book i.

A coal-pit has not often found its poet; but that it may not want its due honour, Cleveland has paralleled it with the sun:

> The moderate value of our guiltless ore
> Makes no man atheist, nor no woman whore;
> Yet why should hallow'd vestal's sacred shrine
> Deserve more honour than a flaming mine?
> These pregnant wombs of heat would fitter be,
> Than a few embers, for a deity.
> Had he our pits, the Persian would admire
> No sun, but warm 's devotion at our fire:
> He'd leave the trotting whipster, and prefer
> Our profound Vulcan 'bove that waggoner.
> For wants he heat, or light? or would have store,
> Of both? 'tis here: and what can suns give more?
> Nay, what's the sun but, in a different name,
> A coal-pit rampant, or a mine on flame?
> Then let this truth reciprocally run,
> The sun 's heaven's coalery, and coals our sun.
>   CLEVELAND, *News from Newcastle*.

> *Death, a Voyage*
>   No family
> E'er rigg'd a soul for heaven's discovery,
> With whom more venturers might boldly dare
> Venture their stakes, with him in joy to share.
>   DONNE.

Their thoughts and expressions were sometimes grossly absurd, and such as no figures or licence can reconcile to the understanding.

> *A Lover neither dead nor alive*
> Then down I laid my head,
> Down on cold earth; and for a while was dead.
> And my freed soul to a strange somewhere fled;
>   "Ah, sottish soul," said I,
>   When back to its cage again I saw it fly;
>   "Fool to resume her broken chain,
>   And row her galley here again!
>   Fool to that body to return

Where it condemn'd and destin'd is to burn!
  Once dead, how can it be,
Death should a thing so pleasant seem to thee,
That thou should'st come to live it o'er again in me?"
                              COWLEY, *The Despair*.

A Lover's Heart, a hand grenado

Wo to her stubborn heart, if once mine come
  Into the self-same room,
    'Twill tear and blow up all within,
Like a grenado shot into a magazine.
Then shall Love keep the ashes, and torn parts,
  Of both our broken hearts:
    Shall out of both one new one make;
From her's th' allay; from mine, the metal take.
                              COWLEY, *The Given Heart*.

The poetical propagation of light:

The prince's favour is diffus'd o'er all,
From which all fortunes, names, and natures fall;
Then from those wombs of stars, the bride's bright eyes,
  At every glance a constellation flies
And sowes the court with stars, and doth prevent
  In light and power, the all-ey'd firmament:
First her eye kindles other ladies' eyes,
  Then from their beams their jewels lustres rise;
And from their jewels torches do take fire,
And all is warmth, and light, and good desire.
                                        DONNE.

They were in very little care to clothe their notions with
elegance of dress, and therefore miss the notice and the praise
which are often gained by those who think less, but are more
diligent to adorn their thoughts.

That a mistress beloved is fairer in idea than in reality, is
by Cowley thus expressed:

Thou in my fancy dost much higher stand
Than women can be plac'd by Nature's hand;
And I must needs, I'm sure, a loser be,
To change thee, as thou'rt there, for very thee.
                              COWLEY, *Against Fruition*.

That prayer and labour should co-operate, are thus taught by Donne:

> In none but us are such mixt engines found,
> As hands of double office; for the ground
> We till with them; and them to heaven we raise:
> Who prayerless labours, or, without this, prays,
> Doth but one half, that's none.

By the same author, a common topic, the danger of procrastination, is thus illustrated:

> —— That which I should have begun
> In my youth's morning, now late must be done;
> And I, as giddy travellers must do,
> Which stray or sleep all day, and having lost
> Light and strength, dark and tir'd, must then ride post.
> DONNE, *To M. B. B.*

All that man has to do is to live and die: the sum of humanity is comprehended by Donne in the following lines:

> Think in how poor a prison thou didst lie;
> After enabled but to suck and cry.
> Think, when 'twas grown to most, 'twas a poor inn,
> A province pack'd up in two yards of skin,
> And that usurp'd, or threaten'd with a rage
> Of sicknesses, or their true mother, age.
> But think that death hath now enfranchis'd thee;
> Thou hast thy expansion now, and liberty;
> Think, that a rusty piece discharg'd is flown
> In pieces, and the bullet is his own,
> And freely flies: this to thy soul allow,
> Think thy shell broke, think thy soul hatch'd but now.
> DONNE, *The Progress of the Soul.*

They were sometimes indelicate and disgusting. Cowley thus apostrophises beauty:

> —— Thou tyrant, which leav'st no man free!
> Thou subtle thief, from whom nought safe can be!
> Thou murtherer, which hast kill'd, and devil which would'st
> damn me!
> COWLEY, *Beauty.*

Thus he addresses his mistress:

> Thou who, in many a propriety,
> So truly art the sun to me,
> Add one more likeness, which I'm sure you can,
> And let me and my sun beget a man.
>
> <div align="right">COWLEY, <i>The Parting</i>.</div>

Thus he represents the meditations of a lover:

> Though in thy thoughts scarce any tracts have been
> So much as of original sin,
> Such charms thy beauty wears as might
> Desires in dying confest saints excite.
>   Thou with strange adultery
> Dost in each breast a brothel keep;
>   Awake, all men do lust for thee,
> And some enjoy thee when they sleep.
>
> COWLEY.

The true Taste of Tears

> Hither with crystal vials, lovers, come,
>   And take my tears, which are love's wine,
> And try your mistress' tears at home;
>   For all are false, that taste not just like mine.
>
> <div align="right">DONNE, <i>Twickenham Garden</i>.</div>

This is yet more indelicate:

> As the sweet sweat of roses in a still,
> As that which from chaf'd musk-cat's pores doth trill,
> As the almighty balm of th' early East;
> Such are the sweat drops of my mistress' breast.
> And on her neck her skin such lustre sets,
> They seem no sweat drops, but pearl coronets:
> Rank, sweaty froth thy mistress' brow defiles.
>
> <div align="right">DONNE, <i>Elegie VIII</i>.</div>

Their expressions sometimes raise horror, when they intend perhaps to be pathetic:

> As men in hell are from diseases free,
>   So from all other ills am I,

> Free from their known formality:
> But all pains eminently lie in thee.
> COWLEY, *The Usurpation*.

They were not always strictly curious, whether the opinions from which they drew their illustrations were true; it was enough that they were popular. Bacon remarks, that some falsehoods are continued by tradition, because they supply commodious allusions.

> It gave a piteous groan, and so it broke:
> In vain it something would have spoke:
> The love within too strong for 't was,
> Like poison put into a Venice-glass.
> COWLEY, *The Heartbreaking*.

In forming descriptions, they looked out, not for images, but for conceits. Night has been a common subject which poets have contended to adorn. Dryden's *Night* is well known; Donne's is as follows:

> Thou seest me here at midnight, now all rest:
> Time's dead low-water; when all minds divest
> To-morrow's business, when the labourers have
> Such rest in bed, that their last church-yard grave,
> Subject to change, will scarce be a type of this,
> Now when the client, whose last hearing is
> To-morrow, sleeps; when the condemned man,
> Who, when he opes his eyes, must shut them then
> Again by death, although sad watch he keep,
> Doth practise dying by a little sleep,
> Thou at this midnight seest me.

It must be however confessed of these writers, that if they are upon common subjects often unnecessarily and unpoetically subtle, yet where scholastic speculation can be properly admitted, their copiousness and acuteness may justly be admired. What Cowley has written upon Hope shows an unequalled fertility of invention:

> Hope, whose weak being ruin'd is,
> Alike if it succeed, and if it miss;

Whom good or ill does equally confound,
And both the horns of Fate's dilemma wound;
    Vain shadow! which dost vanquish quite,
    Both at full noon and perfect night!
    The stars have not a possibility
    Of blessing thee;
If things then from their end we happy call,
'Tis Hope is the most hopeless thing of all.
    Hope, thou bold taster of delight,
    Who, whilst thou should'st but taste, devour'st it quite!
    Thou bring'st us an estate, yet leav'st us poor,
    By clogging it with legacies before!
    The joys which we entire should wed,
    Come deflower'd virgins to our bed;
Good fortunes without gain imported be,
    Such mighty custom's paid to thee:
For joy, like wine kept close, does better taste,
If it take air before its spirits waste.

                COWLEY, *Against Hope*.

To the following comparison of a man that travels, and his wife that stays at home, with a pair of compasses, it may be doubted whether absurdity or ingenuity has the better claim:

    Our two souls therefore, which are one,
        Though I must go, endure not yet
    A breach, but an expansion,
        Like gold to airy thinness beat.
    If they be two, they are two so
        As stiff twin-compasses are two;
    Thy soul the fixt foot, makes no show
        To move, but doth, if th' other do.
    And though it in the centre sit,
        Yet, when the other far doth roam,
    It leans, and hearkens after it,
        And grows erect, as that comes home.
    Such wilt thou be to me, who must
        Like th' other foot obliquely run.
    Thy firmness makes my circle just,
        And makes me end, where I begun.
    DONNE, A *Valediction forbidding Mourning*.

In all these examples it is apparent, that whatever is improper or vicious is produced by a voluntary deviation from nature in pursuit of something new and strange; and that the writers fail to give delight, by their desire of exciting admiration.

Having thus endeavoured to exhibit a general representation of the style and sentiments of the metaphysical poets, it is now proper to examine particularly the works of Cowley, who was almost the last of that race, and undoubtedly the best.

His *Miscellanies* contain a collection of short compositions, written, some as they were dictated by a mind at leisure, and some as they were called forth by different occasions; with great variety of style and sentiment, from burlesque levity to awful grandeur. Such an assemblage of diversified excellence no other poet has hitherto afforded. To choose the best, among many good, is one of the most hazardous attempts of criticism. I know not whether Scaliger himself has persuaded many readers to join with him in his preference of the two favourite odes, which he estimates in his raptures at the value of a kingdom. I will however venture to recommend Cowley's first piece, which ought to be inscribed *To my Muse*, for want of which the second couplet is without reference. When the title is added, there will still remain a defect; for every piece ought to contain in itself whatever is necessary to make it intelligible. Pope has some epitaphs without names; which are therefore epitaphs to be let, occupied indeed for the present, but hardly appropriated.

The ode on Wit is almost without a rival. It was about the time of Cowley that *Wit*, which had been till then used for *Intellection*, in contradistinction to *Will*, took the meaning, whatever it be, which it now [1779] bears.

Of all the passages in which poets have exemplified their own precepts, none will easily be found of greater excellence than that in which Cowley condemns exuberance of wit:

> Yet 'tis not to adorn and gild each part,
> That shows more cost than art.
> Jewels at nose and lips but ill appear;

Rather than all things wit, let none be there.
  Several lights will not be seen,
  If there be nothing else between.
Men doubt, because they stand so thick i' th' sky,
If those be stars which paint the galaxy.

COWLEY, *Ode: Of Wit.*

In his verses to Lord Falkland, whom every man of his time was proud to praise, there are, as there must be in all Cowley's compositions, some striking thoughts, but they are not well wrought. His elegy on Sir Henry Wotton is vigorous and happy, the series of thoughts is easy and natural, and the conclusion, though a little weakened by the intrusion of Alexander, is elegant and forcible.

It may be remarked, that in this elegy, and in most of his encomiastic poems, he has forgotten or neglected to name his heroes.

In his poem on the death of Hervey, there is much praise, but little passion, a very just and ample delineation of such virtues as a studious privacy admits, and such intellectual excellence as a mind not yet called forth to action can display. He knew how to distinguish, and how to commend the qualities of his companion; but when he wishes to make us weep, he forgets to weep himself, and diverts his sorrow by imagining how his crown of bays, if he had it, would *crackle* in the *fire.* It is the odd fate of this thought to be worse for being true. The bay-leaf crackles remarkably as it burns; as therefore this property was not assigned it by chance, the mind must be thought sufficiently at ease that could attend to such minuteness of physiology. But the power of Cowley is not so much to move the affections, as to exercise the understanding.

The *Chronicle* is a composition unrivalled and alone: such gaiety of fancy, such facility of expression, such varied similitude, such a succession of images, and such a dance of words, it is in vain to expect except from Cowley. His strength always appears in his agility; his volatility is not the flutter of a light, but the bound of an elastic mind. His levity never leaves his learning behind it; the moralist, the politician, and the critic, mingle their influence even in this airy frolic of genius. To such a performance Suckling could have brought the gaiety, but not the knowledge; Dryden could have supplied the knowledge, but not the gaiety.

The verses to Davenant, which are vigorously begun, and happily concluded, contain some hints of criticism very justly conceived and happily expressed. Cowley's critical abilities have not been sufficiently observed: the few decisions and remarks which his prefaces and his notes on the *Davideis* supply, were at that time accessions to English literature, and show such skill as raises our wish for more examples.

The lines from Jersey are a very curious and pleasing specimen of the familiar descending to the burlesque.

His two metrical disquisitions *for* and *against* Reason are no mean specimens of metaphysical poetry. The stanzas against Knowledge produce little conviction. In those which are intended to exalt the human faculties, reason has its proper task assigned it; that of judging, not of things revealed, but of the reality of revelation. In the verses *for* reason is a passage which Bentley, in the only English verses which he is known to have written, seems to have copied, though with the inferiority of an imitator.

> The Holy Book like the eighth sphere does shine
>   With thousand lights of truth divine,
> So numberless the stars that to the eye
>   It makes but all one galaxy:
> Yet Reason must assist too; for in seas
>   So vast and dangerous as these,
> Our course by stars above we cannot know
>   Without the compass too below.

After this says Bentley:

> Who travels in religious jars,
> Truth mix'd with error, shade with rays,
> Like Whiston wanting pyx or stars,
> In ocean wide or sinks or strays.

Cowley seems to have had, what Milton is believed to have wanted, the skill to rate his own performances by their just value, and has therefore closed his *Miscellanies* with the verses upon Crashaw, which apparently excel all that have gone before them, and in which there are beauties which common authors may justly think not only above their attainment, but above their ambition.

To the *Miscellanies* succeed the *Anacreontiques*, or paraphrastical translations of some little poems, which pass, however justly, under the name of Anacreon. Of those songs dedicated to festivity and gaiety, in which even the morality is voluptuous, and which teach nothing but the enjoyment of the present day, he has given rather a pleasing than a faithful representation, having retained their sprightliness, but lost their simplicity. The Anacreon of Cowley, like the Homer of Pope, has admitted the decoration of some modern graces, by which he is undoubtedly more amiable to common readers, and perhaps, if they would honestly declare their own preceptions,—to far the greater part of those whom courtesy and ignorance are content to style the learned.

These little pieces will be found more finished in their kind than any other of Cowley's works. The diction shows nothing of the mould of time, and the sentiments are at no great distance from our present habitudes of thought. Real mirth must be always natural, and nature is uniform. Men have been wise in very different modes; but they have always laughed the same way.

Levity of thought naturally produced familiarity of language, and the familiar part of language continues long the same; the dialogue of comedy, when it is transcribed from popular manners and real life, is read from age to age with equal pleasure. The artifice of inversion, by which the established order of words is changed, or of innovation, by which new words or meanings of words are introduced, is practised, not by those who talk to be understood, but by those who write to be admired.

The *Anacreontiques* therefore of Cowley give now all the pleasure which they ever gave. If he was formed by nature for one kind of writing more than for another, his power seems to have been greatest in the familiar and the festive.

The next class of his poems is called *The Mistress*, of which it is not necessary to select any particular pieces for praise or censure. They have all the same beauties and faults, and nearly in the same proportion. They are written with exuberance of wit, and with copiousness of learning; and it is truly asserted by Sprat, that the plenitude of the writer's knowledge flows in upon his page, so that the reader is commonly surprised into some improvement. But, considered as the verses of a lover, no man that has ever loved will much commend them. They are neither courtly nor pathetic, have neither gallantry nor fondness. His praises are too far sought, and too hyperbolical, either to express love, or to excite it; every stanza is crowded with darts and flames, with wounds and death, with mingled souls, and with broken hearts.

The principal artifice by which *The Mistress* is filled with conceits is very copiously displayed by Addison. Love is by Cowley, as by other poets, expressed metaphorically by flame and fire; and that which is true of real fire is said of love, or figurative fire, the same word in the same sentence retaining both significations. Thus, "observing the cold regard of his mistress's eyes, and at the same time their power of producing love in him, he considers them as burning-glasses made of ice. Finding himself able to live in the greatest extremities of love, he concludes the torrid zone to be habitable. Upon the dying of a tree, on which he had cut his loves, he observes, that his flames had burnt up and withered the tree."

These conceits Addison calls "mixed wit"; that is, wit which consists of thoughts true in one sense of the expression, and false in the other. Addison's representation is sufficiently indulgent. That confusion of images may entertain for a moment; but being unnatural, it soon grows wearisome. Cowley delighted in it, as much as if he had invented it; but, not to mention the ancients, he might have found it full-blown in modern Italy. Thus Sannazaro:

> Aspice quam variis distringar Lesbia curis!
>   Uror, et heu! nostro manat ab igne liquor;
> Sum Nilus, sumque Ætna simul; restringite flammas
>   O lacrimæ, aut lacrimas ebibe flamma meas.

One of the severe theologians of that time censured him as having published *a book of profane and lascivious verses*. From the charge of profaneness, the constant tenor of his life, which seems to have been eminently virtuous, and the general tendency of his opinions, which discover no irreverence of religion, must defend him; but that the accusation of lasciviousness is unjust, the perusal of his works will sufficiently evince.

Cowley's "Mistress" has no power of seduction: "she plays round the head, but reaches not the heart." Her beauty and absence, her kindness and cruelty, her disdain and inconstancy, produce no correspondence of emotion. His poetical account of the virtues of plants, and colours of flowers, is not perused with more sluggish frigidity. The compositions are such as might have been written for penance by a hermit, or for hire by a philosophical rhymer who had only heard of another sex; for they turn the mind only on the writer, whom, without thinking on a woman but as the subject for his task, we sometimes esteem as learned, and sometimes despise as trifling, always admire as ingenious, and always condemn as unnatural.

The Pindaric Odes are now to be considered; a species of composition which Cowley thinks Pancirolus might have counted *in his list of the lost inventions of antiquity,* and which he has made a bold and vigorous attempt to recover.

The purpose with which he has paraphrased an Olympique and Nemæan Ode is by himself sufficiently explained. His endeavour was, not to show *precisely what Pindar spoke, but his* [way and] *manner of speaking.* He was therefore not at all restrained to his expressions, nor much to his sentiments; nothing was required of him, but not to write as Pindar would not have written.

Of the Olympique Ode the beginning is, I think, above the original in elegance, and the conclusion below it in strength. The connection is supplied with great perspicuity, and the thoughts, which to a reader of less skill seem thrown together by chance, are concatenated without any abruption. Though the English ode cannot be called a translation, it may be very properly consulted as a commentary.

The spirit of Pindar is indeed not everywhere equally preserved. The following pretty lines are not such as his *deep mouth* was used to pour:

> [Great Rhea's son,]
> If in Olympus' top where thou
> Sitt'st to behold thy sacred show,
> If in Alpheus' silver flight,
> If in my verse thou dost delight,
> My verse, O Rhea's son, which is
> Lofty as that, and smooth as this.
> COWLEY, *2nd Olympique Ode.*

In the Nemæan Ode the reader must, in mere justice to Pindar, observe that whatever is said of *the original new moon, her tender forehead and her horns,* is superadded by his paraphrast, who has many other plays of words and fancy unsuitable to the original, as:

> The table which is free for every guest,
> No doubt will thee admit,
> And feast more upon thee, than thou on it.
> COWLEY, *1st Nemæan Ode.*

He sometimes extends his author's thoughts without improving them. In the Olympionic an oath is mentioned in a single word, and Cowley spends three lines in swearing by the *Castalian Stream.* We are told of Theron's bounty, with a hint that he had enemies, which Cowley thus enlarges in rhyming prose:

> But in this thankless world the givers
> Are envied even by the receivers;
> 'Tis now the cheap and frugal fashion
> Rather to hide than pay the obligation:
> Nay, 'tis much worse than so;
> It now an artifice does grow
> Wrongs and outrages to do,
> Lest men should think we owe.
> COWLEY, *2nd Olympique Ode.*

It is hard to conceive that a man of the first rank in learning and wit, when he was dealing out such minute morality in such feeble diction, could imagine, either waking or dreaming, that he imitated Pindar.

In the following odes, where Cowley chooses his own subjects, he sometimes rises to dignity truly Pindaric; and, if some deficiencies of language be forgiven, his strains are such as those of the Theban bard were to his contemporaries:

Begin the song, and strike the living lyre:
Lo how the years to come, a numerous and well-fitted quire,
All hand in hand do decently advance,
And to my song with smooth and equal measures dance;
While the dance lasts, how long soe'er it be,
My music's voice shall bear it company;
 Till all gentle notes be drown'd
 In the last trumpet's dreadful sound.
 COWLEY, *The Resurrection.*

After such enthusiasm, who will not lament to find the poet conclude with lines like these?—

 Stop, stop, my Muse . . .
Hold thy Pindaric Pegasus closely in,
Which does to rage begin . . .
—'Tis an unruly and a hard-mouth'd horse . . .
'Twill no unskilful touch endure,
But flings writer and reader too that sits not sure.

The fault of Cowley, and perhaps of all the writers of the metaphysical race, is that of pursuing his thoughts to the last ramifications, by which he loses the grandeur of generality; for of the greatest things the parts are little; what is little can be but pretty, and by claiming dignity becomes ridiculous. Thus all the power of description is destroyed by a scrupulous enumeration, and the force of metaphors is lost, when the mind by the mention of particulars is turned more upon the original than the secondary sense, more upon that from which the illustration is drawn than that to which it is applied.

Of this we have a very eminent example in the ode entitled *The Muse*, who goes to *take the air* in an intellectual chariot, to which he harnesses Fancy and Judgment, Wit and Eloquence, Memory and Invention; how he distinguished Wit from Fancy, or how Memory could properly contribute to Motion, he has not explained: we are, however, content to suppose that he could have justified his own fiction, and wish to see the Muse begin her career; but there is yet more to be done.

> Let the *postilion* Nature mount, and let
> The *coachman* Art be set;
> And let the airy *footman*, running all beside,
> Make a long row of goodly pride;
> Figures, conceits, raptures, and sentences,
> In a well-worded dress,
> And innocent loves, and pleasant truths, and useful lies,
> In all their gaudy *liveries*.

Every mind is now disgusted with this cumber of magnificence; yet I cannot refuse myself the four next lines:

> Mount, glorious queen, thy travelling throne,
>   And bid it to put on;
> For long though cheerful is the way,
> And life, alas! allows but one ill winter's day.

In the same ode, celebrating the power of the Muse, he gives her prescience, or, in poetical language, the foresight of events hatching in futurity; but having once an egg in his mind, he cannot forbear to show us that he knows what an egg contains:

> Thou into the close nests of Time dost peep,
>   And there with piercing eye
> Through the firm shell and the thick white dost spy
>   Years to come a-forming lie,
> Close in their sacred fecundine asleep.

The same thought is more generally, and therefore more poetically, expressed by Casimir, a writer who has many of the beauties and faults of Cowley:

> Omnibus mundi Dominator horis
> Aptat urgendas per inane pennas,
> Pars adhuc nido latet, et futuros
>   Crescit in annos.

Cowley, whatever was his subject, seems to have been carried, by a kind of destiny, to the light and the familiar, or to conceits which require still more ignoble epithets. A slaughter in the Red Sea *new dyes the water's name;* and England, during the Civil War, was *Albion no more, nor to be named from white.* It is surely by some fascination not easily surmounted, that a writer, professing to revive *the noblest and highest writing in verse,* makes this address to the New Year:

Nay, if thou lov'st me, gentle year,
Let not so much as love be there—
Vain, fruitless love I mean; for, gentle year,
　Although I fear
There's of this caution little need,
　Yet, gentle year, take heed
　How thou dost make
　Such a mistake;
Such love I mean alone
As by thy cruel predecessors has been shown;
For, though I have too much cause to doubt it,
I fain would try, for once, if life can live without it.

The reader of this will be inclined to cry out with Prior:

　Ye critics, say,
　How poor to this was Pindar's style!

Even those who cannot perhaps find in the Isthmian or Nemæan songs what antiquity had disposed them to expect, will at least see that they are ill-represented by such puny poetry; and all will determine that, if this be the old Theban strain, it is not worthy of revival.

To the disproportion and incongruity of Cowley's sentiments must be added the uncertainty and looseness of his measures. He takes the liberty of using in any place a verse of any length, from two syllables to twelve. The verses of Pindar have, as he observes, very little harmony to a modern ear; yet by examining the syllables we perceive them to be regular, and have reason enough for supposing that the ancient audiences were delighted with the sound. The imitator ought therefore to have adopted what he found, and to have added what was wanting; to have preserved a constant return of the same numbers, and to have supplied smoothness of transition and continuity of thought.

It is urged by Dr. Sprat, that the *irregularity of numbers is the very thing* which makes *that kind of poesy fit for all manner of subjects*. But he should have remembered, that what is fit for everything can fit nothing well. The great pleasure of verse arises from the known measure of the lines, and uniform structure of the stanzas, by which the voice is regulated, and the memory relieved.

If the Pindaric style be, what Cowley thinks it, *the noblest and highest kind of writing in verse*, it can be adapted only to high and noble subjects; and it will not be easy to reconcile the poet with the critic, or to conceive how that can be the highest kind of writing in verse which, according to Sprat, *is chiefly to be preferred for its near affinity to prose*.

This lax and lawless versification so much concealed the deficiencies of the barren, and flattered the laziness of the idle, that it immediately overspread our books of poetry; all the boys and girls caught the pleasing fashion, and they that could do nothing else could write like Pindar. The rights of antiquity were invaded, and disorder tried to break into the Latin: a poem on the Sheldonian Theatre, in which all kinds of verse are shaken together, is unhappily inserted in the *Musæ Anglicanæ*. Pindarism prevailed about half a century; but at last died gradually away, and other imitations supply its place.

The Pindarique Odes have so long enjoyed the highest degree of poetical reputation, that I am not willing to dismiss them with unabated censure; and surely though the mode of their composition be erroneous, yet many parts deserve at least that admiration which is due to great comprehension of knowledge, and great fertility of fancy. The thoughts are often new, and often striking; but the greatness of one part is disgraced by the littleness of another; the total negligence of language gives the noblest conceptions the appearance of a fabric august in the plan, but mean in the materials. Yet surely those verses are not without a just claim to praise; of which it may be said with truth, that no man but Cowley could have written them.

The *Davideis* now remains to be considered, a poem which the author designed to have extended to twelve books, merely, as he makes no scruple of declaring, because the Æneid had that number; but he had leisure or perseverance only to write the third part. Epic poems have been left unfinished by Virgil, Statius, Spenser, and Cowley. That we have not the whole *Davideis* is, however, not much to be regretted; for in this undertaking Cowley is, tacitly at least, confessed to have miscarried. There are not many examples of so great a work, produced by an author generally read, and generally praised, that has crept through a century with so little regard. Whatever is said of Cowley, is meant of his other works. Of the *Davideis* no mention is made; it never appears in books, nor emerges in conversation. By the *Spectator* it has been once quoted; by Rymer it has once been praised; and by Dryden, in *Mac Flecknoe*, it has once been imitated; nor do I recollect much other notice from its publication till now in the whole succession of English literature.

Of this silence and neglect, if the reason be inquired, it will be found partly in the choice of the subject, and partly in the performance of the work.

Sacred history has been always read with submissive reverence, and an imagination over-awed and controlled. We have been accustomed to acquiesce in the nakedness and simplicity of the authentic narrative, and to repose on its veracity with such humble confidence as suppresses curiosity. We go with the historian as he goes, and stop with him when he stops. All amplification is frivolous and vain; all addition to that which is already sufficient for the purposes of religion, seems not only useless, but in some degree profane.

Such events as were produced by the visible interposition of Divine Power are above the power of human genius to dignify. The miracle of Creation, however it may teem with images, is best described with little diffusion of language: *He spake the word, and they were made.*

We are told that Saul *was troubled with an evil spirit;* from this Cowley takes an opportunity of describing hell, and telling the history of Lucifer, who was, he says:

Once general of a gilded host of sprites,
Like Hesper leading forth the spangled nights;
But down like lightning, which him struck, he came,
And roar'd at his first plunge into the flame.

Book I.

Lucifer makes a speech to the inferior agents of mischief, in which there is something of heathenism, and therefore of impropriety; and, to give efficacy to his words, concludes by lashing *his breast with his long tail*. Envy, after a pause, steps out, and among other declarations of her zeal utters these lines:

Do thou but threat, loud storms shall make reply,
And thunder echo 't to the trembling sky.
Whilst raging seas swell to so bold an height,
As shall the fire's proud element affright.
Th' old drudging Sun, from his long-beaten way,
Shall at thy voice start, and misguide the day.
The jocund orbs shall break their measur'd pace,
And stubborn poles change their allotted place.
Heaven's gilded troops shall flutter here and there,
Leaving their boasting songs tun'd to a sphere.

Book I.

Every reader feels himself weary with this useless talk of an allegorical being.

It is not only when the events are confessedly miraculous that fancy and fiction lose their effect: the whole system of life, while the Theocracy was yet visible, has an appearance so different from all other scenes of human action that the reader of the Sacred Volume habitually considers it as the peculiar mode of existence of a distinct species of mankind, that lived and acted with manners uncommunicable; so that it is difficult even for imagination to place us in the state of them whose story is related, and by consequence their joys and griefs are not easily adopted, nor can the attention be often interested in anything that befalls them.

To the subject thus originally indisposed to the reception of poetical embellishments the writer brought little that could reconcile impatience or attract curiosity. Nothing can be more disgusting than a narrative spangled with conceits; and conceits are all that the *Davideis* supplies.

One of the great sources of poetical delight is description, or the power of presenting pictures to the mind. Cowley gives inferences instead of images, and shows not what may be supposed to have been seen, but what thoughts the sight might have suggested. When Virgil describes the stone which Turnus lifted against Æneas, he fixes the attention on its bulk and weight:

> Saxum circumspicit ingens,
> Saxum antiquum, ingens, campo quod forte jacebat
> Limes agro positus, litem ut discerneret arvis.

Cowley says of the stone with which Cain slew his brother:

> I saw him fling the stone, as if he meant
> At once his murther and his monument.
>
> *Book I.*

Of the sword taken from Goliah, he says:

> A sword so great, that it was only fit
> To take off his great head who came with it.

Other poets describe death by some of its common appearances. Cowley says, with a learned allusion to sepulchral lamps, real or fabulous:

> 'Twixt his right ribs deep pierc'd the furious blade,
> And open'd wide those secret vessels where
> Life's light goes out, when first they let in air.
>
> *Book IV.*

But he has allusions vulgar as well as learned. In a visionary succession of kings:

> Joas at first does bright and glorious show,
> In life's fresh morn his fame did early crow.
>
> *Book II.*

Describing an undisciplined army, after having said with elegance:

> His forces seem'd no army, but a crowd
> Heartless, unarm'd, disorderly, and loud,
> *Book IV.*

he gives them a fit of the ague.

The allusions, however, are not always to vulgar things; he offends by exaggeration as much as by diminution:

> The king was plac'd alone, and o'er his head
> A well-wrought heaven of silk and gold was spread.
> *Book II.*

Whatever he writes is always polluted with some conceit:

> Where the sun's fruitful beams give metals birth,
> Where he the growth of fatal gold does see—
> Gold, which alone more influence has than he.
> *Book I.*

In one passage he starts a sudden question, to the confusion of philosophy:

> Ye learned heads, whom ivy garlands grace,
> Why does that twining plant the oak embrace?
> The oak for courtship most of all unfit,
> And rough as are the winds that fight with it?
> *Book II.*

His expressions have sometimes a degree of meanness that surpasses expectation:

> Nay, gentle guests, he cries, since now you're in,
> The story of your gallant friend begin.

In a simile descriptive of the morning:

> As glimmering stars just at th' approach of day,
> Cashier'd by troops, at last drop all away.
> *Book IV.*

The dress of Gabriel deserves attention:

> He took for skin a cloud most soft and bright,
> That e'er the midday sun pierc'd through with light:

Upon his cheeks a lively blush he spread,
Wash'd from the morning beauties' deepest red;
An harmless flaming meteor shone for hair,
And fell adown his shoulders with loose care;
He cuts out a silk mantle from the skies,
Where the most sprightly azure pleas'd the eyes;
This he with starry vapours spangles all,
Took in their prime ere they grow ripe and fall;
Of a new rainbow ere it fret or fade,
The choicest piece took out, a scarf is made.

Book II.

This is a just specimen of Cowley's imagery: what might in general expressions be great and forcible, he weakens and makes ridiculous by branching it into small parts. That Gabriel was invested with the softest or brightest colours of the sky, we might have been told, and been dismissed to improve the idea in our different proportions of conception; but Cowley could not let us go till he had related where Gabriel got first his skin, and then his mantle, then his lace, and then his scarf, and related it in the terms of the mercer and tailor.

Sometimes he indulges himself in a digression, always conceived with his natural exuberance, and commonly, even where it is not long, continued till it is tedious:

I' th' library a few choice authors stood,
Yet 'twas well stor'd, for that small store was good;
Writing, man's spiritual physic, was not then
Itself, as now, grown a disease of men.
Learning (young virgin) but few suitors knew;
The common prostitute she lately grew,
And with the spurious brood loads now the press;
Laborious effects of idleness.

As the *Davideis* affords only four books, though intended to consist of twelve, there is no opportunity for such criticisms as epic poems commonly supply. The plan of the whole work is very imperfectly shown by the third part. The duration of an unfinished action cannot be known. Of characters, either not yet introduced, or shown but upon few occasions, the full extent and the nice discriminations cannot be ascertained. The fable is plainly implex, formed rather from the Odyssey than the Iliad: and many artifices of diversification are employed with the skill of a man acquainted with the best models. The past is recalled by narration, and the future anticipated by vision; but he has been so lavish of his poetical art that it is difficult to imagine how he could fill eight books more without practising again the same modes of disposing his matter; and perhaps the perception of this growing incumbrance inclined him to stop. By this abruption posterity lost more instruction than delight. If the continuation of the *Davideis* can be missed, it is for the learning that had been diffused over it, and the notes in which it had been explained.

Had not his characters been depraved, like every other part, by improper decorations, they would have deserved uncommon praise. He gives Saul both the body and mind of a hero:

> His way once chose, he forward thrust outright,
> Nor stepp'd aside for dangers or delight.

And the different beauties of the lofty Merab and the gentle Michol are very justly conceived and strongly painted.

Rymer has declared the *Davideis* superior to the *Jerusalem* of Tasso; "which," says he, "the poet, with all his care, has not totally purged from pedantry." If by pedantry is meant that minute knowledge which is derived from particular sciences and studies, in opposition to the general notions supplied by a wide survey of life and nature, Cowley certainly errs by introducing pedantry far more frequently than Tasso. I know not, indeed, why they should be compared; for the resemblance of Cowley's work to Tasso's is only that they both exhibit the agency of celestial and infernal spirits; in which, however, they differ widely, for Cowley supposes them commonly to operate upon the mind by suggestion; Tasso represents them as promoting or obstructing events by external agency.

Of particular passages that can be properly compared, I remember only the description of heaven, in which the different manner of the two writers is sufficiently discernible. Cowley's is scarcely description, unless it be possible to describe by negatives; for he tells us only what there is not in heaven. Tasso endeavours to represent the splendours and pleasures of the regions of happiness. Tasso affords images; and Cowley sentiments. It happens, however, that Tasso's description affords some reason for Rymer's censure. He says of the Supreme Being:

> Hà sotto i piedi e fato e la natura
> Ministri humili, e 'l moto, e ch' il misura.

The second line has in it more of pedantry than perhaps can be found in any other stanza of the poem.

In the perusal of the *Davideis*, as of all Cowley's works, we find wit and learning unprofitably squandered. Attention has no relief; the affections are never moved; we are sometimes surprised, but never delighted, and find much to admire, but little to approve. Still, however, it is the work of Cowley—of a mind capacious by nature, and replenished by study.

In the general review of Cowley's poetry it will be found that he wrote with abundant fertility, but negligent or unskilful selection; with much thought, but with little imagery; that he is never pathetic, and rarely sublime; but always either ingenious or learned, either acute or profound.

It is said by Denham in his elegy:

> To him no author was unknown;
> Yet what he wrote was all his own.

This wide position requires less limitation when it is affirmed of Cowley than perhaps of any other poet: he read much, and yet borrowed little.

His character of writing was indeed not his own: he unhappily adopted that which was predominant. He saw a certain way to present praise; and not sufficiently inquiring by what means the ancients have continued to delight through all the changes of human manners, he contented himself with a deciduous laurel, of which the verdure in its spring was bright and gay, but which time has been continually stealing from his brows.

He was in his own time considered as of unrivalled excellence. Clarendon represents him as having taken "a flight" beyond all that went before him; and Milton is said to have declared that the three greatest English poets were Spenser, Shakespeare, and Cowley.

His manner he had in common with others; but his sentiments were his own. Upon every subject he thought for himself; and such was his copiousness of knowledge that something at once remote and applicable rushed into his mind; yet it is not likely that he always rejected a commodious idea merely because another had used it: his known wealth was so great that he might have borrowed without loss of credit.

In his Elegy on Sir Henry Wotton, the last lines have such resemblance to the noble epigram of Grotius upon the death of Scaliger, that I cannot but think them copied from it, though they are copied by no servile hand.

One passage in his *Mistress* is so apparently borrowed from Donne that he probably would not have written it had it not mingled with his own thoughts, so as that he did not perceive himself taking it from another:

> Although I think thou never found wilt be,
>   Yet I'm resolv'd to search for thee;
>   The search itself rewards the pains.
> So, though the chymic his great secret miss,
> (For neither it in Art nor Nature is,)
>   Yet things well worth his toil he gains:
>   And does his charge and labour pay
> With good unsought experiments by the way.
>   COWLEY, *Maidenhead.*

> Some that have deeper digg'd Love's mine than I,
> Say, where his centric happiness doth lie:
>   I have lov'd, and got, and told;
> But should I love, get, tell, till I were old,
> I should not find that hidden mystery:
>   Oh, 'tis imposture all:
> And as no chymic yet th' elixir got,
>   But glorifies his pregnant pot,

> If by the way to him befal
> Some odoriferous thing, or medicinal,
> So lovers dream a rich and long delight,
> But get a winter-seeming summer's night.
> DONNE, *Love's Alchymy*.

Jonson and Donne, as Dr. Hurd remarks, were then in the highest esteem.

It is related by Clarendon, that Cowley always acknowledges his obligation to the learning and industry of Jonson; but I have found no traces of Jonson in his works: to emulate Donne appears to have been his purpose; and from Donne he may have learned that familiarity with religious images, and that light allusion to sacred things, by which readers far short of sanctity are frequently offended; and which would not be borne in the present age, when devotion, perhaps not more fervent, is more delicate.

Having produced one passage taken by Cowley from Donne, I will recompense him by another which Milton seems to have borrowed from him. He says of Goliah:

> His spear, the trunk was of a lofty tree,
> Which Nature meant some tall ship's mast should be.
> *Davideis, Book III.*

Milton of Satan:

> His spear, to equal which the tallest pine
> Hewn on Norwegian hills, to be the mast
> Of some great ammiral, were but a wand,
> He walked with.

His diction was in his own time censured as negligent. He seems not to have known, or not to have considered, that words being arbitrary must owe their power to association, and have the influence, and that only, which custom has given them. Language is the dress of thought: and as the noblest mien or most graceful action would be degraded and obscured by a garb appropriated to the gross employments of rustics or mechanics, so the most heroic sentiments will lose their efficacy, and the most splendid ideas drop their magnificence, if they are conveyed by words used commonly upon low and trivial occasions, debased by vulgar mouths and contaminated by inelegant applications.

Truth indeed is always truth, and reason is always reason; they have an intrinsic and unalterable value, and constitute that intellectual gold which defies destruction: but gold may be so concealed in baser matter that only a chemist can recover it; sense may be so hidden in unrefined and plebeian words that none but philosophers can distinguish it; and both may be so buried in impurities as not to pay the cost of their extraction.

The diction, being the vehicle of the thoughts, first presents itself to the intellectual eye; and if the first appearance offends, a further knowledge is not often sought. Whatever professes to benefit by pleasing must please at once. The pleasures of the mind imply something sudden and unexpected; that which elevates must always surprise. What is perceived by slow degrees may gratify us with consciousness of improvement, but will never strike with the sense of pleasure.

Of all this Cowley appears to have been without knowledge, or without care. He makes no selection of words, nor seeks any neatness of phrase: he has no elegance, either lucky or elaborate; as his endeavours were rather to impress sentences upon the understanding than images on the fancy, he has few epithets, and those scattered without peculiar propriety of nice adaptation. It seems to follow from the necessity of the subject rather than the care of the writer, that the diction of his heroic poem is less familiar than that of his slightest writings. He has given not the same numbers, but the same diction, to the gentle Anacreon and the tempestuous Pindar.

His versification seems to have had very little of his care; and if what he thinks be true, that his numbers are unmusical only when they are ill read, the art of reading them is at present lost; for they are commonly harsh to modern ears. He has indeed many noble lines, such as the feeble care of Waller never could produce. The bulk of his thoughts sometimes swelled his verse to unexpected and inevitable grandeur; but his excellence of this kind is merely fortuitous: he sinks willingly down to his general carelessness, and avoids with very little care either meanness or asperity.

His contractions are often rugged and harsh:

> One flings a mountain, and its rivers too
> Torn up with 't.
>
> *Davideis, Book III.*

His rhymes are very often made by pronouns, or particles, or the like unimportant words, which disappoint the ear and destroy the energy of the line.

His combinations of different measures are sometimes dissonant and unpleasing; he joins verses together, of which the former does not slide easily into the latter.

The words *do* and *did*, which so much degrade in present estimation the line that admits them, were in the time of Cowley little censured or avoided: how often he used them, and with how bad an effect, at least to our ears, will appear by a passage in which every reader will lament to see just and noble thoughts defrauded of their praise by inelegance of language:

> Where honour or where conscience *does* not bind,
>   No other law shall shackle me;
>   Slave to myself I will not be;
> Nor shall my future actions be confin'd
>   By my own present mind.
> Who by resolves and vows engag'd *does* stand
>   For days, that yet belong to fate,
> *Does* like an unthrift mortgage his estate,
>   Before it falls into his hand,
>   The bondman of the cloister so,
> All that he *does* receive *does* always owe.
> And still as Time comes in, it goes away,
>   Not to enjoy, but debts to pay!
> Unhappy slave, and pupil to a bell!
> Which his hour's work as well as hours *does* tell:
> Unhappy till the last, the kind releasing knell.
>
> COWLEY, *Ode: Of Liberty.*

His heroic lines are often formed of monosyllables; but yet they are sometimes sweet and sonorous.

He says of the Messiah:

Round the whole earth his dreaded name shall sound,
And reach to worlds that must not yet be found.

In another place, of David:

Yet bid him go securely, when he sends;
'Tis Saul that is his foe, and we his friends.
The man who has his God, no aid can lack;
And we who bid him go, will bring him back.

Yet, amidst his negligence, he sometimes attempted an improved and scientific versification, of which it will be best to give his own account subjoined to this line:

Nor can the glory contain itself in th' endless space.
Davideis, Book I.

"I am sorry that it is necessary to admonish the most part of readers that it is not by negligence that this verse is so loose, long, and, as it were, vast; it is to paint in the number the nature of the thing which it describes, which I would have observed in divers other places of this poem, that else will pass for very careless verses: as before:

And over-runs the neighb'ring fields with violent course.

In the second book:

Down a precipice deep, down he casts them all.

And:

And fell a-down his shoulders with loose care.

In the third:

Brass was his helmet, his boots brass, and o'er
His breast a thick plate of strong brass he wore.

In the fourth:

Like some fair pine o'er-looking all th' ignobler wood.

And:

Some from the rocks cast themselves down headlong.

And many more: but it is enough to instance in a few. The thing is, that the disposition of words and numbers should be such as that, out of the order and sound of them, the things themselves may be represented. This the Greeks were not so accurate as to bind themselves to; neither have our English poets observed it, for aught I can find. The Latins (*qui musas colunt severiores*) sometimes did it; and their prince, Virgil, always; in whom the examples are innumerable, and taken notice of by all judicious men, so that it is superfluous to collect them."

I know not whether he has in many of these instances attained the representation or resemblance that he purposes. Verse can imitate only sound and motion. A *boundless* verse, a *headlong* verse, and a verse of *brass* or of *strong brass*, seem to comprise very incongruous and unsociable ideas. What there is peculiar in the sound of the line expressing *loose care* I cannot discover; nor why the *pine* is *taller* in an Alexandrine than in ten syllables.

But, not to defraud him of his due praise, he has given one example of representative versification which perhaps no other English line can equal:

Begin, be bold, and venture to be wise:
He who defers this work from day to day,
Does on a river's bank expecting stay
Till the whole stream which stopp'd him should be gone,
Which runs, and, as it runs, for ever will run on.

Cowley was, I believe, the first poet that mingled Alexandrines at pleasure with the common heroic of ten syllables; and from him Dryden borrowed the practice, whether ornamental or licentious. He considered the verse of twelve syllables as elevated and majestic, and has therefore deviated into that measure when he supposes the voice heard of the Supreme Being.

The author of the *Davideis* is commended by Dryden for having written it in couplets, because he discovered that any staff was too lyrical for an heroic poem; but this seems to have been known before by May and Sandys, the translators of the *Pharsalia* and the *Metamorphoses*.

In the *Davideis* are some hemistichs, or verses left imperfect by the author, in imitation of Virgil, whom he supposes not to have intended to complete them. That this opinion is erroneous may be probably concluded, because this truncation is imitated by no subsequent Roman poet; because Virgil himself filled up one broken line in the heat of recitation; because in one the sense is now unfinished; and because all that can be done by a broken verse, a line intersected by a *cæsura*, and a full stop, will equally effect.

Of triplets in his *Davideis* he makes no use, and perhaps did not at first think them allowable; but he appears afterwards to have changed his mind, for in the verses on the government of Cromwell he inserts them liberally with great happiness.

After so much criticism on his poems, the Essays which accompany them must not be forgotten. What is said by Sprat of his conversation, that no man could draw from it any suspicion of his excellence in poetry, may be applied to these compositions. No author ever kept his verse and his prose at a greater distance from each other. His thoughts are natural, and his style has a smooth and placid equability, which has never yet obtained its due commendation. Nothing is far-sought or hard-laboured; but all is easy without feebleness, and familiar without grossness.

It has been observed by Felton, in his Essay on the Classics, that Cowley was beloved by every Muse that he courted; and that he has rivalled the ancients in every kind of poetry but tragedy.

It may be affirmed, without any encomiastic fervour, that he brought to his poetic labours a mind replete with learning, and that his pages are embellished with all the ornaments which books could supply; that he was the first who imparted to English numbers the enthusiasm of the greater ode, and the gaiety of the less; that he was equally qualified for sprightly sallies and for lofty flights; that he was among those who freed translation from servility, and, instead of following his author at a distance, walked by his side; and that, if he left versification yet improvable, he left likewise, from time to time, such specimens of excellence as enabled succeeding poets to improve it.

COWLEY'S WILL

The will (occupying two sides of a foolscap sheet of paper) is preserved in the Prerogative Will Office of the Court of Canterbury, and was proved by Thomas Cowley, the poet's brother, on the 31st August, 1667, and first printed (by the present Editor) in *The Shakespeare Society's Papers*.

TESTAMENT

In the name of God Almighty, to whom bee for ever all glory, Amen. I, ABRAHAM COWLEY, of Chertsea, in the county of Surrey, beeing at present by God's mercy in perfect health and understanding, and well considering the uncertainty of human life, most especially in these tymes of sicknes and mortality, doe, in attendance of God's blessed pleasure concerning my life or death, make and declare this my last Will and Testament as followeth. I humbly recommend my soule to that greate God from whom I had it, beseeching him to receive it into his bosome for the merits of his sonne, the saviour of sinners, amongst whome I am one of the greatest, and my body to the earth, from whence it came, in hopes of a happy resurrection. O Lord, I believe, help my unbelief; O Lord, I repent, pardon the weakness of my repentance.

All my worldly goods, moneys, and chattels, I bequeath to my brother Thomas Cowley, whome I doe hereby constitute my sole heyr and executor, hee paying out of y^t estate, wch it has pleased God to bestowe upon me, much above my deserts, these ensueing Legacies.

I leave to my neveu —— Cowley (if hee bee yet alive) ten pounds; To my cosen Beniamin Hind, towards his

education in learning, fivety pounds; To my cosen ——
Gauton, of Nutfield, in Surrey, for ye same use of his
eldest sonne, fivety pounds; To my cosen Mary Gauton,
twenty pounds; To Thomas Fotherby, of Canterbury,
Esquire, one hundred pounds, wch [I] beseech him to
accept of as a small remembrance of his ancient kindness
to mee; To Sir Will Davenant, twenty pounds; To Mr.
Mart Clifford, twenty pounds; To Mr. Thomas Sprat,
twenty pounds; To Mr. Thomas Cook, twenty pounds;
To Dr. Charles Scarburgh, twenty pounds; To Dr.
Thomas Croyden, twenty pounds; To my mayd, Mary
(besides what I ow her, and all my wearing linen),
twenty pounds; To my servant, Thomas Waldron, ten
pounds and most of my wearing clothes at my brother's
choise; To Mary, my brother's mayd, five pounds; To the
poore of the town of Chertsea, twenty pounds.

I doe farther leave to the Honourable John Hervey, of
Ickworth, Esquire, my share and interest in his Highnes
the Duke of York's Theater. And to ye Right Honble the
Earl of St Albans, my Lord, and once kind Master, a
Ring of ten pounds, onely in memory of my duty and
affection to him, not being able to give anything worthy
his acceptance, nor hee (God bee praised) in need of any
gifts from such persons as I.

If anything bee due to mee from Trinity College [Cam-
bridge], I leave it to bee bestowed in books upon yt
library; and I leave besides to Doctor Robert Crane, Fel-
lowe of ye said College, a Ring of five pounds valew, as
a small token of or friendship.

I desire my dear friend, Mr Thomas Sprat, to trouble
himselfe wth ye collection and revision of all such writings of mine (whether printed before or not) as hee shall
thinke fit to be published, Beseeching him not to let any
passe which hee shall judge unworthy of the name of his
friend, and most especially nothing (if anything of yt
kind have escaped my pen) wch may give the least offence in point of religion or good manners. And in consideration of this unpleasant task, I desire him to accept
of my Study of Books.

This I declare to bee my last Will and Testament. Lord have mercy upon my soul. Written by my own hand, signed and sealed, at Chertsea, this 28th day of September, 1665.

ABRAHAM COWLEY.

Signed and sealed in
the presence of
Thomas Waldron.
The mark of ‡ *John Symonds,*
Wheelwright, of Chertsey.

SIR JOHN DENHAM

1615–1668

Born at Dublin—Educated at Oxford and Lincoln's Inn—Addicted to Gaming—Becomes unexpectedly a Poet —Sides with Charles I.—Writes *Cooper's Hill*—Employed by Charles I.—Made Knight of the Bath and Surveyor of the Works—His two Wives—Becomes Insane—Death and Burial in Westminster Abbey—Character and Works.

Of Sir John Denham very little is known but what is related of him by Wood, or by himself.

He was born at Dublin in 1615; the only son of Sir John Denham, of Little Horsely in Essex, then chief baron of the Exchequer in Ireland, and of Eleanor, daughter of Sir Garret More, baron of Mellefont.

Two years afterwards, his father, being made [July 1617] one of the barons of the Exchequer in England, brought him away from his native country, and educated him in London.

In 1631 he was sent to [Trinity College] Oxford, where he was considered "as a dreaming young man, given more to cards and dice than study," and therefore gave no prognostics of his future eminence—nor was suspected to conceal, under sluggishness and laxity, a genius born to improve the literature of his country.

When he was, three years afterwards, removed to Lincoln's Inn, he prosecuted the common law with sufficient appearance of application, yet did not lose his propensity to cards and dice; but was very often plundered by gamesters.

Being severely reproved for this folly, he professed, and perhaps believed, himself reclaimed; and, to testify the sincerity of his repentance, wrote and published *An Essay upon Gaming*.

He seems to have divided his studies between law and poetry; for, in 1636, he translated the second book of the Æneid.

Two years after, his father died, and then, notwithstanding his resolutions and professions, he returned again to the vice of gaming, and lost several thousand pounds that had been left him.

In 1642 he published *The Sophy*. This seems to have given him his first hold of the public attention; for Waller remarked, "that he broke out like the Irish rebellion three score thousand strong when nobody was aware, or in the least suspected it"—an observation which could have had no propriety had his poetical abilities been known before.

He was after that picked for sheriff of Surrey, and made [1642] governor of Farnham Castle for the King; but he soon resigned that charge, and retreated to Oxford, where, in 1643, he published *Cooper's Hill*.

This poem had such reputation as to excite the common artifice by which envy degrades excellence. A report was spread that the performance was not his own, but that he had bought it of a vicar for 40*l*. The same attempt was made to rob Addison of his *Cato*, and Pope of his *Essay on Criticism*.

In 1647 the distresses of the royal family required him to engage in more dangerous employments. He was entrusted by the Queen with a message to the King; and, by whatever means, so far softened the ferocity of Hugh Peters, that by his intercession admission was procured. Of the King's condescension he has given an account in the dedication of his works.

He was afterwards employed in carrying on the King's correspondence, and, as he says, discharged this office with great safety to the royalists; and being accidentally discovered by the adverse party's knowledge of Mr. Cowley's hand, he escaped, happily both for himself and his friends.

He was yet engaged in a greater undertaking. In April 1648 he conveyed James the Duke of York from London into France, and delivered him there to the Queen and Prince of Wales. This year he published his translation of Cato Major.

He now resided in France, as one of the followers of the exiled King; and, to divert the melancholy of their condition, was sometimes enjoined by his master to write occasional verses, one of which amusements was probably his ode or song upon the Embassy to Poland, by which he and Lord Crofts procured a contribution of 10,000*l.* from the Scotch that wandered over that kingdom. Poland was at that time very much frequented by itinerant traders, who, in a country of very little commerce and of great extent, where every man resided on his own estate, contributed very much to the accommodation of life, by bringing to every man's house those little necessaries which it was very inconvenient to want, and very troublesome to fetch. I have formerly read, without much reflection, of the multitude of Scotchmen that travelled with their wares in Poland; and that their numbers were not small, the success of this negotiation gives sufficient evidence.

About this time what estate the war and the gamesters had left him was sold by order of the Parliament; and when, in 1652, he returned to England, he was entertained by the Earl of Pembroke.

Of the next years of his life there is no account. At the Restoration he obtained that which many missed, the reward of his loyalty, being made surveyor of the King's buildings, and dignified with the order of the Bath. He seems now to have learned some attention to money; for Wood says that he got by this place 7000*l.*

After the Restoration he wrote the poem on *Prudence and Justice*, and perhaps some of his other pieces; and as he appears, whenever any serious question comes before him, to have been a man of piety, he consecrated his poetical powers to religion, and made a metrical version of the Psalms of David. In this attempt he has failed; but in sacred poetry who has succeeded?

It might be hoped that the favour of his master and esteem of the public would now make him happy. But human felicity is short and uncertain; a second marriage brought upon him so much disquiet as for a time disordered his understanding; and Butler lampooned him for his lunacy. I know not whether the malignant lines were then made public, nor what provocation incited Butler to do that which no provocation can excuse.

His frenzy lasted not long; and he seems to have regained his full force of mind; for he wrote afterwards his excellent poem upon the death of Cowley, whom he was not long to survive; for on the 19th of March, 1668, he was buried by his side.

Denham is deservedly considered as one of the fathers of English poetry. "Denham and Waller," says Prior, "improved our versification, and Dryden perfected it." He has given specimens of various composition, descriptive, ludicrous, didactic, and sublime.

He appears to have had, in common with almost all mankind, the ambition of being upon proper occasions *a merry fellow*, and, in common with most of them, to have been by nature, or by early habits, debarred from it. Nothing is less exhilarating than the ludicrousness of Denham: he does not fail for want of efforts; he is familiar, he is gross, but he is never merry, unless the *Speech against Peace in the close Committee* be excepted. For grave burlesque, however, his imitation of Davenant shows him to have been well qualified.

Of his more elevated occasional poems there is perhaps none that does not deserve commendation. In the verses to Fletcher we have an image that has since been adopted:

> But whither am I stray'd? I need not raise
> Trophies to thee from other men's dispraise;
> Nor is thy fame on lesser ruins built,
> Nor need thy juster title the foul guilt
> Of eastern kings, who, to secure their reign,
> Must have their brothers, sons, and kindred slain.

After Denham, Orrery, in one of his prologues,

> Poets are sultans, if they had their will;
> For every author would his brother kill.

And Pope,

> Should such a man, too fond to rule alone,
> Bear like the Turk no brother near the throne.

But this is not the best of his little pieces; it is excelled by his poem to Fanshaw, and his elegy on Cowley.

His praise of Fanshaw's version of *Guarini* contains a very sprightly and judicious character of a good translator:

> That servile path thou nobly dost decline,
> Of tracing word by word, and line by line.
> Those are the labour'd births of slavish brains,
> Not the effect of poetry, but pains;
> Cheap vulgar arts, whose narrowness affords
> No flight for thoughts, but poorly stick at words.
> A new and nobler way thou dost pursue,
> To make translations and translators too.
> They but preserve the ashes, thou the flame,
> True to his sense, but truer to his fame.

The excellence of these lines is greater, as the truth which they contain was not at that time generally known.

His poem on the death of Cowley was his last, and, among his shorter works, his best performance: the numbers are musical, and the thoughts are just.

Cooper's Hill is the work that confers upon him the rank and dignity of an original author. He seems to have been, at least among us, the author of a species of composition that may be denominated *local poetry*, of which the fundamental subject is some particular landscape, to be poetically described, with the addition of such embellishments as may be supplied by historical retrospection or incidental meditation.

To trace a new scheme of poetry has in itself a very high claim to praise, and its praise is yet more when it is apparently copied by Garth and Pope, after whose names little will be gained by an enumeration of smaller poets, that have left scarcely a corner of the island not dignified either by rhyme or blank verse.

Cooper's Hill, if it be maliciously inspected, will not be found without its faults. The digressions are too long, the morality too frequent, and the sentiments sometimes such as will not bear a rigorous inquiry.

The four verses which, since Dryden has commended them,

almost every writer for a century past has imitated, are generally known:

> O could I flow like thee, and make thy stream
> My great example, as it is my theme!
> Though deep, yet clear; though gentle, yet not dull;
> Strong without rage, without o'er-flowing full.

The lines are in themselves not perfect; for most of the words, thus artfully opposed, are to be understood simply on one side of the comparison, and metaphorically on the other; and if there be any language which does not express intellectual operations by material images, into that language they cannot be translated. But so much meaning is comprised in few words; the particulars of resemblance are so perspicaciously collected, and every mode of excellence separated from its adjacent fault by so nice a line of limitation; the different parts of the sentence are so accurately adjusted, and the flow of the last couplet is so smooth and sweet, that the passage, however celebrated, has not been praised above its merit. It has beauty peculiar to itself, and must be numbered among those felicities which cannot be produced at will by wit and labour, but must arise unexpectedly in some hour propitious to poetry.

He appears to have been one of the first that understood the necessity of emancipating translation from the drudgery of counting lines and interpreting single words. How much this servile practice obscured the clearest and deformed the most beautiful parts of the ancient authors, may be discovered by a perusal of our earlier versions, some of them the works of men well qualified, not only by critical knowledge, but by poetical genius, who yet, by a mistaken ambition of exactness, degraded at once their originals and themselves.

Denham saw the better way, but has not pursued it with great success. His versions of Virgil are not pleasing; but they taught Dryden to please better. His poetical imitation of Tully on *Old Age* has neither the clearness of prose, nor the sprightliness of poetry.

The "strength of Denham," which Pope so emphatically mentions, is to be found in many lines and couplets, which convey much meaning in few words, and exhibit the sentiment with more weight than bulk.

On the Thames

Though with those streams he no resemblance hold,
Whose foam is amber, and their gravel gold;
His genuine and less guilty wealth t' explore,
Search not his bottom, but survey his shore.

On Strafford

His wisdom such, as once it did appear
Three kingdoms' wonder, and three kingdoms' fear.
While single he stood forth, and seem'd, although
Each had an army, as an equal foe,
Such was his force of eloquence, to make
The hearers more concern'd than he that spake:
Each seem'd to act that part he came to see,
And none was more a looker-on than he;
So did he move our passions, some were known
To wish, for the defence, the crime their own.
Now private pity strove with public hate,
Reason with rage, and eloquence with fate.

On Cowley

To him no author was unknown,
Yet what he wrote was all his own;
Horace's wit, and Virgil's state,
He did not steal, but emulate!
And when he would like them appear,
Their garb, but not their clothes, did wear.

As one of Denham's principal claims to the regard of posterity arises from his improvement of our numbers, his versification ought to be considered. It will afford that pleasure which arises from the observation of a man of judgment, naturally right, forsaking bad copies by degrees, and advancing towards a better practice as he gains more confidence in himself.

In his translation of Virgil, written when he was about twenty-one years old, may be still found the old manner of continuing the sense ungracefully from verse to verse.

>   Then all those
> Who in the dark our fury did escape,
> Returning, know our borrow'd arms, and shape,
> And differing dialect: then their numbers swell
> And grow upon us: first Choroebeus fell
> Before Minerva's altar; next did bleed
> Just Ripheus, whom no Trojan did exceed   }
> In virtue, yet the gods his fate decreed.
> Then Hypanis and Dymas, wounded by
> Their friends; nor thee, Pantheus, thy piety,
> Nor consecrated mitre, from the same
> Ill fate could save; my country's funeral flame
> And Troy's cold ashes I attest, and call
> To witness for myself, that in their fall
> No foes, or death, nor danger I declin'd,
> Did and deserv'd no less, my fate to find.

From this kind of concatenated metre he afterwards refrained, and taught his followers the art of concluding their sense in couplets, which has perhaps been with rather too much constancy pursued.

This passage exhibits one of those triplets which are not infrequent in this first essay, but which it is to be supposed his maturer judgment disapproved, since in his latter works he has totally forborne them.

His rhymes are such as seem found without difficulty by following the sense, and are for the most part as exact at least as those of other poets, though now and then the reader is shifted off with what he can get.

>   O how *transform'd!*
> How much unlike that Hector who *return'd*
> Clad in Achilles' spoils!

And again:

> From thence a thousand lesser poets *sprung*
> Like petty princes from the fall of *Rome.*

Sometimes the weight of rhyme is laid upon a word too feeble to sustain it:

Troy confounded falls
From all her glories: if it might have stood
By any power, by this right hand it *shou'd*.
—And though my outward state misfortune *hath*
Deprest thus low, it cannot reach my faith.

—Thus, by his fraud and our own faith o'ercome,
A feigned tear destroys us, against *whom*
Tydides nor Achilles could prevail,
Nor ten years' conflict, nor a thousand sail.

He is not very careful to vary the ends of his verses: in one passage the word *die* rhymes three couplets in six.

Most of these petty faults are in his first productions, when he was less skilful, or at least less dexterous in the use of words; and though they had been more frequent, they could only have lessened the grace, not the strength of his composition. He is one of the writers that improved our taste, and advanced our language, and whom we ought therefore to read with gratitude, though, having done much, he left much to do.

JOHN MILTON

1608–1674

Born in London—Educated at St. Paul's and at Cambridge—Writes *Comus* and *Lycidas*—Visits Italy—Sees Grotius and Galileo—Returns to London—His "School" —Marries—Publishes his Poems—Writes on Divorce—Sides with the Parliament against Charles I.—Made Secretary of the Latin Tongue to the Parliament and Cromwell— Prints a Reply to Salmasius—Becomes Blind—Loses his Secretaryship—Is in Danger at the Restoration—Receives a Pardon—Publishes *Paradise Lost* and *Paradise Regained* —His three Wives—His Children and Nephews—Dies in London, and is buried in St. Giles', Cripplegate—His Works and Character.

The Life of Milton has been already written in so many forms, and with such minute inquiry, that I might perhaps more properly have contented myself with the addition of a few notes to Mr. Fenton's elegant Abridgment, but that a new narrative was thought necessary to the uniformity of this edition.

John Milton was by birth a gentleman, descended from the proprietors of Milton, near Thame, in Oxfordshire, one of whom forfeited his estate in the times of York and Lancaster. Which side he took I know not: his descendant inherited no veneration for the White Rose.

His grandfather, John [Richard?], was keeper of the forest of Shotover, a zealous papist, who disinherited his son because he had forsaken the religion of his ancestors.

His father, John, who was the son disinherited, had recourse

for his support to the profession of a scrivener. He was a man
eminent for his skill in music (many of his compositions being
still to be found), and his reputation in his profession was
such that he grew rich and retired to an estate. He had probably more than common literature, as his son addresses him in
one of his most elaborate Latin poems. He married a gentlewoman of the name of Caston, a Welsh family, by whom he
had two sons, John, the poet, and Christopher, who studied
the law, and adhered, as the law taught him, to the King's
party, for which he was awhile persecuted, but having, by his
brother's interest, obtained permission to live in quiet, he supported himself so honourably by chamber-practice that soon
after the accession of King James he was knighted and made
a judge; but his constitution being too weak for business, he
retired before any disreputable compliances became necessary.

He had likewise a daughter, Anne, whom he married, with
a considerable fortune, to Edward Philips, who came from
Shrewsbury, and rose in the Crown Office to be secondary: by
him she had two sons, John and Edward, who were educated
by the poet, and from whom is derived the only authentic
account of his domestic manners.

John, the poet, was born in his father's house, at the Spread
Eagle in Bread-street, December 9, 1608, between six and
seven in the morning. His father appears to have been very
solicitous about his education; for he was instructed at first
by private tuition under the care of Thomas Young, who was
afterwards chaplain to the English merchants at Hamburg,
and of whom we have reason to think well, since his scholar
considered him as worthy of an epistolary elegy.

He was then sent to St. Paul's School, under the care of
Mr. Gill, and removed, in the beginning of his sixteenth year,
to Christ's College in Cambridge, where he entered a sizar,
February 12, 1624.

He was at this time eminently skilled in the Latin tongue;
and he himself, by annexing the dates to his first compositions
—a boast of which Politian had given him an example—seems
to commend the earliness of his own proficiency to the notice
of posterity. But the products of his vernal fertility have been
surpassed by many, and particularly by his contemporary

Cowley. Of the powers of the mind it is difficult to form an estimate: many have excelled Milton in their first essays who never rose to works like *Paradise Lost*.

At fifteen, a date which he uses till he is sixteen, he translated or versified two Psalms, 114 and 136, which he thought worthy of the public eye; but they raise no great expectations; they would in any numerous school have obtained praise, but not excited wonder.

Many of his elegies appear to have been written in his eighteenth year, by which it appears that he had then read the Roman authors with very nice discernment. I once heard Mr. Hampton, the translator of Polybius, remark, what I think is true, that Milton was the first Englishman who, after the revival of letters, wrote Latin verses with classic elegance. If any exceptions can be made, they are very few. Haddon and Ascham, the pride of Elizabeth's reign, however they have succeeded in prose, no sooner attempt verses than they provoke derision. If we produced anything worthy of notice before the elegies of Milton, it was perhaps Alabaster's *Roxana*.

Of these exercises, which the rules of the University required, some were published by him in his maturer years. They had been undoubtedly applauded; for they were such as few can form: yet there is reason to suspect that he was regarded in his college with no great fondness. That he obtained no fellowship is certain; but the unkindness with which he was treated was not merely negative. I am ashamed to relate what I fear is true, that Milton was one of the last students in either university that suffered the public indignity of corporal correction.

It was, in the violence of controversial hostility, objected to him, that he was expelled: this he steadily denies, and it was apparently not true; but it seems plain from his own verses to Deodati that he had incurred *rustication*—a temporary dismission into the country, with perhaps the loss of a term.

Me tenet urbs refluâ quam Thamesis alluit undâ,
    Meque nec invitum patria dulcis habet.
Jam nec arundiferum mihi cura revisere Camum,
    Nec dudum *vetiti* me *laris* angit amor.—

Nec duri libet usque minas perferre magistri,
 Cæteraque ingenio non subeunda meo.
Si sit hoc *exilium* patrias adiisse penates,
 Et vacuum curis otia grata sequi,
Non ego vel *profugi* nomen sortemve recuso,
 Lætus et *exilii* conditione fruor.

I cannot find any meaning but this, which even kindness
and reverence can give to the term *vetiti laris*, "a habitation
from which he is excluded"; or how *exile* can be otherwise
interpreted. He declares yet more, that he is weary of endur-
ing *the threats of a rigorous master, and something else, which
a temper like his cannot undergo.* What was more than threat
was probably punishment. This poem, which mentions his *exile,* proves likewise that it was not perpetual; for it concludes
with a resolution of returning some time to Cambridge. And
it may be conjectured, from the willingness with which he
has perpetuated the memory of his exile, that its cause was
such as gave him no shame.

He took both the usual degrees; that of Bachelor in 1628,
and that of Master in 1632; but he left the university with no
kindness for its institution, alienated either by the injudicious
severity of his governors or his own captious perverseness. The
cause cannot now be known, but the effect appears in his writings. His scheme of education, inscribed to Hartlib, super-
sedes all academical instruction, being intended to comprise
the whole time which men usually spend in literature, from
their entrance upon grammar, *till they proceed, as it is called,
masters of arts.* And in his Discourse *on the likeliest Way to
remove Hirelings out of the Church,* he ingenuously proposes
that *the profits of the lands forfeited by the act for superstitious uses should be applied to such academies all over the
land where languages and arts may be taught together: so that
youth may be at once brought up to a competency of learning
and an honest trade, by which means such of them as had the
gift, being enabled to support themselves without tithes by
the latter, may, by the help of the former, become worthy
preachers.*

One of his objections to academical education, as it was

then conducted, is, that men designed for orders in the Church were permitted to act plays, *writhing and unboning their clergy limbs to all the antic and dishonest gestures of Trincalos, buffoons and bawds, prostituting the shame of that ministry which they had, or were near having, to the eyes of courtiers and court-ladies, their grooms and mademoiselles.*

This is sufficiently peevish in a man who, when he mentions his exile from the college, relates with great luxuriance the compensation which the pleasures of the theatre afford him. Plays were therefore only criminal when they were acted by academics.

He went to the university with a design of entering into the Church, but in time altered his mind; for he declared that, whoever became a clergyman must "subscribe slave, and take an oath withal, which, unless he took with a conscience that could retch, he must straight perjure himself. He thought it better to prefer a blameless silence before the office of speaking, bought and begun with servitude and forswearing."

These expressions are, I find, applied to the subscription of the Articles; but it seems more probable that they relate to canonical obedience. I know not any of the Articles which seem to thwart his opinions: but the thoughts of obedience, whether canonical or civil, raised his indignation.

His unwillingness to engage in the ministry, perhaps not yet advanced to a settled resolution of declining it, appears in a letter to one of his friends who had reproved his suspended and dilatory life, which he seems to have imputed to an insatiable curiosity and fantastic luxury of various knowledge. To this he writes a cool and plausible answer, in which he endeavours to persuade him that the delay proceeds not from the delights of desultory study, but from the desire of obtaining more fitness for his task; and that he goes on, *not taking thought of being late, so it give advantage to be more fit.*

When he left the university he returned to his father, then residing at Horton, in Buckinghamshire, with whom he lived five years, in which time he is said to have read all the Greek and Latin writers. With what limitations this universality is to be understood, who shall inform us?

It might be supposed that he who read so much should have

done nothing else; but Milton found time to write the masque of *Comus*, which was presented at Ludlow, then the residence of the Lord President of Wales, in 1634; and had the honour of being acted by the Earl of Bridgewater's sons and daughter. The fiction is derived from Homer's *Circe*; but we never can refuse to any modern the liberty of borrowing from Homer:

> —— a quo ceu fonte perenni
> Vatum Pieriis ora rigantur aquis.

His next production was *Lycidas*, an elegy, written in 1637, on the death of Mr. King, the son of Sir John King, Secretary for Ireland in the time of Elizabeth, James, and Charles. King was much a favourite at Cambridge, and many of the wits joined to do honour to his memory. Milton's acquaintance with the Italian writers may be discovered by a mixture of longer and shorter verses, according to the rules of Tuscan poetry, and his malignity to the Church by some lines which are interpreted as threatening its extermination.

He is supposed about this time to have written his *Arcades*; for while he lived at Horton he used sometimes to steal from his studies a few days, which he spent at Harefield [in Middlesex], the house of the Countess Dowager of Derby, where the *Arcades* made part of a dramatic entertainment.

He began now to grow weary of the country; and had some purpose of taking chambers in the Inns of Court, when the death of his mother set him at liberty to travel, for which he obtained his father's consent, and Sir Henry Wotton's directions, with the celebrated precept of prudence,—*I pensieri stretti, ed il viso sciolto*; "thoughts close, and looks loose."

In 1638 he left England, and went first to Paris, where, by the favour of Lord Scudamore, he had the opportunity of visiting Grotius, then residing at the French court as ambassador from Christina of Sweden. From Paris he hasted into Italy, of which he had, with particular diligence, studied the language and literature; and, though he seems to have intended a very quick perambulation of the country, stayed two months at Florence, where he found his way into the academies, and produced his compositions with such applause as appears to have exalted him in his own opinion, and confirmed him in the hope that, "by labour and intense study, which," says he, "I take to be my portion in this life, joined with a strong propensity of nature," he might "leave something so written to aftertimes, as they should not willingly let it die."

It appears, in all his writings, that he had the usual concomitant of great abilities, a lofty and steady confidence in himself, perhaps not without some contempt of others; for scarcely any man ever wrote so much, and praised so few. Of his praise he was very frugal: as he set its value high, and considered his mention of a name as a security against the waste of time, and a certain preservative from oblivion.

At Florence he could not indeed complain that his merit wanted distinction. Carlo Dati presented him with an encomiastic inscription, in the tumid lapidary style; and Francini wrote him an ode, of which the first stanza is only empty noise; the rest are perhaps too diffuse on common topics, but the last is natural and beautiful.

From Florence he went to Sienna, and from Sienna to Rome, where he was again received with kindness by the learned and the great. Holstenius, the keeper of the Vatican Library, who had resided three years at Oxford, introduced him to Cardinal Barberini; and he, at a musical entertainment, waited for him at the door and led him by the hand into the assembly. Here Selvaggi praised him in a distich, and Salsilli in a tetrastic; neither of them of much value. The Italians were gainers by this literary commerce; for the encomiums with which Milton repaid Salsilli, though not secure against a stern grammarian, turn the balance indisputably in Milton's favour.

Of these Italian testimonies, poor as they are, he was proud enough to publish them before his poems; though he says he cannot be suspected but to have known that they were said *non tam de se, quam supra se.*

At Rome, as at Florence, he stayed only two months; a time indeed sufficient, if he desired only to ramble with an explainer of its antiquities, or to view palaces and count pictures, but certainly too short for the contemplation of learning, policy, or manners.

From Rome he passed on to Naples, in company of a hermit, a companion from whom little could be expected; yet to him Milton owed his introduction to Manso, Marquis of Villa, who had been before the patron of Tasso. Manso was enough delighted with his accomplishments to honour him with a sorry distich, in which he commends him for everything but his religion; and Milton, in return, addressed him in a Latin poem, which must have raised a high opinion of English elegance and literature.

His purpose was now to have visited Sicily and Greece; but, hearing of the differences between the King and Parliament, he thought it proper to hasten home, rather than pass his life in foreign amusements while his countrymen were contending for their rights. He therefore came back to Rome, though the merchants informed him of plots laid against him by the Jesuits, for the liberty of his conversations on religion. He had sense enough to judge that there was no danger, and therefore kept on his way, and acted as before, neither obtruding nor shunning controversy. He had perhaps given some offence by visiting Galileo, then a prisoner in the Inquisition for philosophical heresy; and at Naples he was told by Manso, that, by his declarations on religious questions, he had excluded himself from some distinctions which he should otherwise have paid him. But such conduct, though it did not please, was yet sufficiently safe, and Milton stayed two months more at Rome, and went on to Florence without molestation.

From Florence he visited Lucca. He afterwards went to Venice; and, having sent away a collection of music and other books, travelled to Geneva, which he probably considered as the metropolis of orthodoxy.

Here he reposed, as in a congenial element, and became acquainted with John Deodati and Frederick Spanheim, two learned professors of divinity. From Geneva he passed through France; and came home [August 1639], after an absence of a year and three months.

At his return he heard of the death of his friend Charles Deodati; a man whom it is reasonable to suppose of great merit, since he was thought by Milton worthy of a poem, entitled *Epitaphium Damonis*, written with the common but childish imitation of pastoral life.

He now hired a lodging at the house of one Russel, a tailor, in St. Bride's churchyard, and undertook the education of Edward and John Philips, his sister's sons. Finding his rooms too little, he took [1641] a house and garden in Aldersgate-street, which was not then so much out of the world as it is now, and chose his dwelling at the upper end of a passage, that he might avoid the noise of the street. Here he received more boys, to be boarded and instructed.

Let not our veneration for Milton forbid us to look with some degree of merriment on great promises and small performance—on the man who hastens home because his countrymen are contending for their liberty, and, when he reaches the scene of action, vapours away his patriotism in a private boarding-school. This is the period of his life from which all his biographers seem inclined to shrink. They are unwilling that Milton should be degraded to a school-master; but, since it cannot be denied that he taught boys, one finds out that he taught for nothing, and another that his motive was only zeal for the propagation of learning and virtue; and all tell what they do not know to be true, only to excuse an act which no wise man will consider as in itself disgraceful. His father was alive; his allowance was not ample; and he supplied its deficiencies by an honest and useful employment.

It is told, that in the art of education he performed wonders; and a formidable list is given of the authors, Greek and Latin, that were read in Aldersgate-street, by youth between ten and fifteen or sixteen years of age. Those who tell or receive these stories should consider that nobody can be taught faster than he can learn. The speed of the horseman must be limited by the power of his horse. Every man that has ever undertaken to instruct others, can tell what slow advances he has been able to make, and how much patience it requires to recall vagrant inattention, to stimulate sluggish indifference, and to rectify absurd misapprehension.

The purpose of Milton, as it seems, was to teach something more solid than the common literature of schools, by reading those authors that treat of physical subjects; such as the Georgic, and astronomical treatises of the ancients. This was a scheme of improvement which seems to have busied many literary projectors of that age. Cowley, who had more means than Milton of knowing what was wanting to the embellishments of life, formed the same plan of education in his imaginary college.

But the truth is, that the knowledge of external nature, and the sciences which that knowledge requires or includes, are not the great or the frequent business of the human mind. Whether we provide for action or conversation, whether we wish to be useful or pleasing, the first requisite is the religious and moral knowledge of right and wrong; the next is an acquaintance with the history of mankind, and with those examples which may be said to embody truth, and prove by events the reasonableness of opinions. Prudence and justice are virtues and excellences of all times and of all places; we are perpetually moralists, but we are geometricians only by chance. Our intercourse with intellectual nature is necessary; our speculations upon matter are voluntary, and at leisure. Physiological learning is of such rare emergence, that one man may know another half his life without being able to estimate his skill in hydrostatics or astronomy; but his moral and prudential character immediately appears.

Those authors, therefore, are to be read at schools that supply most axioms of prudence, most principles of moral truth, and most materials for conversation; and these purposes are best served by poets, orators, and historians.

Let me not be censured for this digression as pedantic or paradoxical; for, if I have Milton against me, I have Socrates on my side. It was his labour to turn philosophy from the study of nature to speculations upon life; but the innovators whom I oppose are turning off attention from life to nature. They seem to think that we are placed here to watch the growth of plants, or the motions of the stars. Socrates was rather of opinion, that what we had to learn was, how to do good, and avoid evil.

Ὅττι τοι ἐν μεγάροισι κακόν τ᾽ ἀγαθόν τε τέτυκται.

Of institutions we may judge by their effects. From this wonder-working academy I do not know that there ever proceeded any man very eminent for knowledge: its only genuine product, I believe, is a small *History of Poetry*, written in Latin by his nephew, [Edward] Philips, of which perhaps none of my readers has ever heard.

That in his school, as in everything else which he undertook, he laboured with great diligence, there is no reason for doubting. One part of his method deserves general imitation. He was careful to instruct his scholars in religion. Every Sunday was spent upon theology; of which he dictated a short system, gathered from the writers that were then fashionable in Dutch universities.

He set his pupils an example of hard study and spare diet; only now and then he allowed himself to pass a day of festivity and indulgence with some gay gentlemen of Gray's Inn.

He now began to engage in the controversies of the times, and lent his breath to blow the flames of contention. In 1641 he published a treatise of *Reformation*, in two books, against the Established Church; being willing to help the Puritans, who were, he says, *inferior to the prelates in learning*.

Hall, Bishop of Norwich, had published an *Humble Remonstrance* in defence of Episcopacy; to which, in 1641, five ministers, of whose names the first letters made the celebrated word *Smectymnus*, gave their Answer. Of this Answer a Confutation was attempted by the learned Usher; and to the Confutation Milton published [1641] a Reply, entitled *Of Prelatical Episcopacy, and whether it may be deduced from the Apostolical Times, by virtue of those testimonies which are alleged to that purpose in some late treatises, one whereof goes under the name of James Lord Bishop of Armagh*. I have transcribed this title to show, by his contemptuous mention of Usher, that he had now adopted the puritanical savageness of manners.

His next work was *The Reason of Church Government urged against Prelaty, by Mr. John Milton,* 1642. In this book he discovers, not with ostentatious exultation, but with calm confidence, his high opinion of his own powers, and promises to undertake something, he yet knows not what, that may be of use and honour to his country. "This," says he, "is not to be obtained but by devout prayer to that Eternal Spirit that can enrich with all utterance and knowledge, and sends out his

Seraphim with the hallowed fire of his altar, to touch and purify the lips of whom he pleases. To this must be added, industrious and select reading, steady observation, and insight into all seemly and generous arts and affairs; till which in some measure be compast, I refuse not to sustain this expectation." From a promise like this, at once fervid, pious, and rational, might be expected the *Paradise Lost*.

He published the same year two more pamphlets upon the same question. To one of his antagonists, who affirms that he was *vomited out of the university*, he answers, in general terms, "The Fellows of the College wherein I spent some years, at my parting, after I had taken two degrees, as the manner is, signified many times how much better it would content them that I should stay. As for the common approbation or dislike of that place, as now it is, that I should esteem or disesteem myself the more for that, too simple is the answerer, if he think to obtain with me. Of small practice were the physician who could not judge, by what she and her sister have of long time vomited, that the worser stuff she strongly keeps in her stomach, but the better she is ever kecking at, and is queasy; she vomits now out of sickness; but before it will be well with her, she must vomit with strong physic. The university, in the time of her better health, and my younger judgment, I never greatly admired, but now much less."

This is surely the language of a man who thinks that he has been injured. He proceeds to describe the course of his conduct, and the train of his thoughts; and, because he has been suspected of incontinence, gives an account of his own purity: "That if I be justly charged," says he, "with this crime, it may come upon me with tenfold shame."

The style of his piece is rough, and such perhaps was that of his antagonist. This roughness he justifies, by great examples, in a long digression. Sometimes he tries to be humorous: "Lest I should take him for some chaplain in hand, some squire of the body to his prelate, one who serves not at the altar only, but at the Court-cupboard, he will bestow on us a pretty model of himself; and sets me out half a dozen phthisical mottoes, wherever he had them, hopping short in the measure of convulsion fits; in which labour the agony of his wit having scaped

narrowly, instead of well-sized periods, he greets us with a
quantity of thumb-ring posies.—And thus ends this section, or
rather dissection, of himself." Such is the controversial merriment of Milton; his gloomy seriousness is yet more offensive.
Such is his malignity, *that hell grows darker at his frown.*

His father, after Reading was taken by Essex [May 1643],
came to reside in his house; and his school increased. At Whit-
suntide [1643], in his thirty-fifth year, he married Mary, the
daughter of Mr. Powell, a justice of the peace in Oxfordshire.
He brought her to town with him, and expected all the advantages of a conjugal life. The lady, however, seems not much to
have delighted in the pleasures of spare diet and hard study;
for, as Philips relates, "having for a month led a philosophic
life (after having been used at home to a great house, and
much company and joviality), her friends, possibly incited by
her own desire, made earnest suit by letter to have her company the remaining part of the summer, which was granted,
on condition of her return at Michaelmas or thereabout."

Milton was too busy to much miss his wife: he pursued his
studies; and now and then visited the Lady Margaret Ley,
whom he has mentioned in one of his sonnets. At last Michaelmas arrived; but the lady had no inclination to return to the
sullen gloom of her husband's habitation, and therefore very
willingly forgot her promise. He sent her a letter, but had no
answer; he sent more with the same success. It could be alleged that letters miscarry; he therefore despatched a messenger, being by this time too angry to go himself. His messenger
was sent back with some contempt. The family of the lady
were Cavaliers.

In a man whose opinion of his own merit was like Milton's,
less provocation than this might have raised violent resentment. Milton soon determined to repudiate her for disobedience; and, being one of those who could easily find arguments
to justify inclination, published (in 1644) *The Doctrine and
Discipline of Divorce;* which was followed [1644] by *The
Judgment of Martin Bucer concerning Divorce;* and the next
year, his Tetrachordon, *Expositions upon the four chief Places
of Scripture which treat of Marriage.*

This innovation was opposed, as might be expected, by the

clergy, who, then holding their famous assembly at Westminster, procured that the author should be called before the Lords; "but that House," says Wood, "whether approving the doctrine, or not favouring his accusers, did soon dismiss him."

There seems not to have been much written against him, nor anything by any writer of eminence. The antagonist that appeared is styled by him *a serving man turned solicitor*. Howel in his letters mentions the new doctrine with contempt; and it was, I suppose, thought more worthy of derision than of confutation. He complains of this neglect in two sonnets, of which the first is contemptible, and the second not excellent.

From this time it is observed that he became an enemy to the Presbyterians, whom he had favoured before. He that changes his party by his humour is not more virtuous than he that changes it by his interest; he loves himself rather than truth.

His wife and her relations now found that Milton was not an unresisting sufferer of injuries; and perceiving that he had begun to put his doctrine in practice, by courting a young woman of great accomplishments, the daughter of one Doctor Davis, who was however not ready to comply, they resolved to endeavour a reunion. He went sometimes to the house of one Blackborough, his relation, "in the lane of St. Martin's-le-Grand," and at one of his usual visits was surprised to see his wife come from another room, and implore forgiveness on her knees. He resisted her entreaties for a while; "but partly," says Philips, "his own generous nature, more inclinable to reconciliation than to perseverance in anger and revenge, and partly the strong intercession of friends on both sides, soon brought him to an act of oblivion and a firm league of peace." It were injurious to omit, that Milton afterwards received her father and her brothers in his own house when they were distressed, with other Royalists.

He published about the same time his *Areopagitica, a Speech of Mr. John Milton for the Liberty of unlicensed Printing*. The danger of such unbounded liberty, and the danger of bounding it, have produced a problem in the science of government which human understanding seems hitherto unable to solve. If nothing may be published but what civil authority shall have previously approved, power must always be the standard of truth; if every dreamer of innovations may propagate his projects, there can be no settlement; if every murmurer at government may diffuse discontent, there can be no peace; and if every sceptic in theology may teach his follies, there can be no religion. The remedy against these evils is to punish the authors; for it is yet allowed that every society may punish, though not prevent, the publication of opinions which that society shall think pernicious; but this punishment, though it may crush the author, promotes the book; and it seems not more reasonable to leave the right of printing unrestrained because writers may be afterwards censured, than it would be to sleep with doors unbolted because by our laws we can hang a thief.

But whatever were his engagements, civil or domestic, poetry was never long out of his thoughts.

About this time (1645) a collection of his Latin and English poems appeared, in which the *Allegro* and *Penseroso*, with some others, were first published.

He had taken a larger house in Barbican for the reception of scholars; but the numerous relations of his wife, to whom he generously granted refuge for a while, occupied his rooms. In time, however, they went away, "and the house again," says Philips, "now looked like a house of the Muses only, though the accession of scholars was not great. Possibly his proceeding thus far in the education of youth may have been the occasion of some of his adversaries calling him pedagogue and school-master, whereas it is well known he never set up for a public school, to teach all the young fry of a parish, but only was willing to impart his learning and knowledge to relations, and the sons of some gentlemen who were his intimate friends; besides, that neither his converse nor his writings nor his manner of teaching savoured in the least of pedantry."

Thus laboriously does his nephew extenuate what cannot be denied, and what might be confessed without disgrace. Milton was not a man who could become mean by a mean employment. This, however, his warmest friends seem not to have found; they therefore shift and palliate. He did not sell literature to all comers at an open shop; he was a chamber-milliner, and measured his commodities to his friends.

Philips, evidently impatient of viewing him in this state of degradation, tells us that it was not long continued; and, to raise his character again, has a mind to invest him with military splendour: "He is much mistaken," he says, "if there was not about this time a design of making him Adjutant-General in Sir William Waller's army. But the new-modelling of the army proved an obstruction to the design." An event cannot be set at a much greater distance than by having been only *designed, about some time*, if a man *be not much mistaken*. Milton shall be a pedagogue no longer; for, if Philips be not much mistaken, somebody at some time designed him for a soldier.

About the time that the army was new-modelled (1645) he removed to a smaller house in Holborn, which opened backward into Lincoln's-Inn-Fields. He is not known to have published anything afterwards till the King's death, when, finding his murderers condemned by the Presbyterians, he wrote a treatise to justify it, and *to compose the minds of the people*.

He made some *Remarks on the Articles of Peace between Ormond and the Irish Rebels*. While he contented himself to write, he perhaps did only what his conscience dictated; and if he did not very vigilantly watch the influence of his own passions, and the gradual prevalence of opinions, first willingly admitted and then habitually indulged; if objections, by being overlooked, were forgotten, and desire superinduced conviction; he yet shared only the common weakness of mankind, and might be no less sincere than his opponents. But as faction seldom leaves a man honest, however it might find him, Milton is suspected of having interpolated the book called *Icon Basilike*, which the Council of State, to whom he was now made Latin secretary, employed him to censure, by inserting a prayer taken from Sidney's *Arcadia*, and imputing it to the King, whom he charges, in his *Iconoclastes*, with the use of this prayer, as with a heavy crime, in the indecent language with which prosperity had emboldened the advocates for rebellion to insult all that is venerable or great: "Who would have imagined so little fear in him of the true all-seeing Deity, as, immediately before his death, to pop into the hands of the grave bishop that attended him, as a special relique of his saintly exercises, a prayer stolen word for word from the mouth of a heathen woman praying to a heathen god?"

The papers which the King gave to Dr. Juxon on the scaffold the regicides took away, so that they were at least the publishers of this prayer; and Dr. Birch, who had examined the question with great care, was inclined to think them the forgers. The use of it by adaptation was innocent; and they who could so noisily censure it, with a little extension of their malice could contrive what they wanted to accuse.

King Charles II., being now sheltered in Holland, employed Salmasius, professor of polite learning at Leyden, to write a *Defence* of his father and of monarchy; and, to excite his industry, gave him, as was reported, a hundred jacobuses. Salmasius was a man of skill in languages, knowledge of antiquity, and sagacity of emendatory criticism, almost exceeding all hope of human attainment; and having, by excessive praises, been confirmed in great confidence of himself, though he probably had not much considered the principles of society or the rights of government, undertook the employment without distrust of his own qualifications; and, as his expedition in writing was wonderful, in 1649 published *Defensio Regis*.

To this Milton was required to write a sufficient answer, which he performed (1650) in such a manner, that Hobbes declared himself unable to decide whose language was best, or whose arguments were worst. In my opinion, Milton's periods are smoother, neater, and more pointed; but he delights himself with teasing his adversary as much as with confuting him. He makes a foolish allusion of Salmasius, whose doctrine he considers as servile and unmanly, to the stream of *Salmacis*, which whoever entered left half his virility behind him. Salmasius was a Frenchman, and was unhappily married to a scold. *Tu es Gallus*, says Milton, *et, ut aiunt, nimium gallinaceus*. But his supreme pleasure is to tax his adversary, so renowned for criticism, with vicious Latin. He opens his book with telling that he has used *persona*, which, according to Milton, signifies only a *mask*, in a sense not known to the Romans, by applying it as we apply *person*. But as Nemesis is always on the watch, it is memorable that he has enforced the charge of a solecism by an expression in itself grossly solecistical, when for one of those supposed blunders, he says, as Ker, and I think some one before him, has remarked, *propino te grammatistis tuis* vapulandum. From *vapulo*, which has a passive sense, *vapulandus* can never be derived. No man forgets his original trade: the rights of nations, and of kings, sink into questions of grammar, if grammarians discuss them.

Milton, when he undertook this answer, was weak of body and dim of sight; but his will was forwarded, and what was wanting of health was supplied by zeal. He was rewarded with a thousand pounds, and his book was much read—for paradox, recommended by spirit and elegance, easily gains attention; and he who told every man that he was equal to his King, could hardly want an audience.

That the performance of Salmasius was not dispersed with equal rapidity, or read with equal eagerness, is very credible. He taught only the stale doctrine of authority, and the unpleasing duty of submission; and he had been so long not only the monarch but the tyrant of literature, that almost all mankind was delighted to find him defied and insulted by a new name, not yet considered as any one's rival. If Christina, as is said, commended the *Defence of the People*, her purpose must be to torment Salmasius, who was then at her court; for neither her civil station or her natural character could dispose them to favour the doctrine, who was by birth a queen, and by temper despotic.

That Salmasius was, from the appearance of Milton's book, treated with neglect, there is not much proof; but to a man so long accustomed to admiration, a little praise of his antagonist would be sufficiently offensive, and might incline him to leave Sweden, from which however he was dismissed, not with any mark of contempt, but with a train of attendance scarcely less than regal.

He prepared a reply, which, left as it was imperfect, was published by his son in the year of the Restoration. In the beginning, being probably most in pain for his Latinity, he endeavours to defend his use of the word *persona*; but, if I remember right, he misses a better authority than any that he has found, that of Juvenal in his fourth satire:

—Quid agas cum dira et fœdior omni
Crimine *persona* est?

As Salmasius reproached Milton with losing his eyes in the quarrel, Milton delighted himself with the belief that he had shortened Salmasius's life; and both, perhaps, with more malignity than reason. Salmasius died at the Spa, September 3, 1653; and, as controvertists are commonly said to be killed by their last dispute, Milton was flattered with the credit of destroying him.

Cromwell had now dismissed the Parliament by the authority of which he had destroyed monarchy, and commenced monarch himself, under the title of Protector, but with kingly and more than kingly power. That his authority was lawful, never was pretended; he himself founded his right only in necessity: but Milton, having now tasted the honey of public employment, would not return to hunger and philosophy, but, continuing to exercise his office under a manifest usurpation, betrayed to his power that liberty which he had defended. Nothing can be more just than that rebellion should end in slavery; that he who had justified the murder of his king, for some acts which to him seemed unlawful, should now sell his services and his flatteries to a tyrant, of whom it was evident that he could do nothing lawful.

He had now been blind for some years; but his vigour of intellect was such that he was not disabled to discharge his office of Latin secretary, or continue his controversies. His mind was too eager to be diverted, and too strong to be subdued.

About this time [1654] his first wife died in childbed, having left him three daughters. As he probably did not much love her, he did not long continue the appearance of lamenting her; but, after a short time, married Catherine, the daughter of one Captain Woodcock, of Hackney, a woman doubtless educated in opinions like his own. She died, within a year, of childbirth, or some distemper that followed it; and her husband honoured her memory with a poor sonnet.

The first reply to Milton's *Defensio Populi* was published in 1651, called *Apologia pro Rege et Populo Anglicano, contra Johannis Polypragmatici (alias Miltoni Angli) defensionem destructivam Regis et Populi*. Of this the author was not known; but Milton and his nephew [John] Philips—under whose name he published [1652] an answer, so much corrected by him that it might be called his own—imputed it to Bramhall; and, knowing him no friend to regicides, thought themselves at liberty to treat him as if they had known what they only suspected.

Next year appeared *Regii Sanguinis clamor ad Cœlum*. Of this the author was Peter du Moulin, who was afterwards prebendary of Canterbury; but Morus, or More, a French minister, having the care of its publication, was treated as the writer by Milton in his *Defensio Secunda* [1654], and overwhelmed by such violence of invective that he began to shrink under the tempest, and gave his persecutors the means of knowing the true author. Du Moulin was now in great danger; but Milton's pride operated against his malignity, and both he and his friends were more willing that Du Moulin should escape than that he should be convicted of mistake.

In this second Defence he shows that his eloquence is not merely satirical; the rudeness of his invective is equalled by the grossness of his flattery. "Deserimur, Cromuelle, tu solus superes, ad te summa nostrarum rerum rediit, in te solo consistit, insuperabili tuæ virtuti cedimus cuncti, nemine vel obloquente, nisi qui æquales inæqualis ipse honores sibi quærit, aut digniori concessos invidet, aut non intelligit nihil esse in societate hominum magis vel Deo gratum, vel rationi consentaneum, esse in civitate nihil æquius, utilius, quam potiri rerum dignissimum. Eum te agnoscunt omnes, Cromuelle, ea tu civis maximus et gloriosissimus, dux publici consilii, exercitum fortissimorum imperator, pater patriæ gessisti. Sic tu spontanea bonorum omnium et animitus missa voce salutaris."

Cæsar, when he assumed the perpetual dictatorship, had

not more servile or more elegant flattery. A translation may show its servility, but its elegance is less attainable. Having exposed the unskilfulness or selfishness of the former government, "We were left," says Milton, "to ourselves: the whole national interest fell into your hands, and subsists only in your abilities. To your virtue, overpowering and resistless, every man gives way, except some who, without equal qualifications, aspire to equal honours, who envy the distinctions of merit greater than their own, or who have yet to learn that in the coalition of human society nothing is more pleasing to God, or more agreeable to reason, than that the highest mind should have the sovereign power. Such, Sir, are you by general confession; such are the things achieved by you, the greatest and most glorious of our countrymen, the director of our public councils, the leader of unconquered armies, the father of your country; for by that title does every good man hail you with sincere and voluntary praise."

Next year [1655], having defended all that wanted defence, he found leisure to defend himself. He undertook his own vindication against More, whom he declares in his title to be justly called the author of the *Regii Sanguinis clamor*. In this there is no want of vehemence or eloquence, nor does he forget his wonted wit. "Morus es? an Momus? an uterque idem est?" He then remembers that *Morus* is Latin for a mulberry-tree, and hints at the known transformation:

> —— Poma alba ferebat
> Quæ post nigra tulit Morus.

With this piece ended his controversies; and he from this time gave himself up to his private studies and his civil employment.

As secretary to the Protector he is supposed to have written the Declaration of the reasons for a war with Spain. His agency was considered as of great importance; for when a treaty with Sweden was artfully suspended, the delay was publicly imputed to Mr. Milton's indisposition; and the Swedish agent was provoked to express his wonder that only one man in England could write Latin, and that man blind.

Being now forty-seven years old, and seeing himself disencumbered from external interruptions, he seems to have recollected his former purposes, and to have resumed three great works which he had planned for his future employment—an epic poem, the history of his country, and a dictionary of the Latin tongue.

To collect a dictionary seems a work of all others least practicable in a state of blindness, because it depends upon perpetual and minute inspection and collation. Nor would Milton probably have begun it after he had lost his eyes; but having had it always before him, he continued it, says Philips, *almost to his dying-day; but the papers were so discomposed and deficient that they could not be fitted for the press.* The compilers of the Latin dictionary printed at Cambridge had the use of those collections in three folios; but what was their fate afterwards is not known.

To compile a history from various authors, when they can only be consulted by other eyes, is not easy, nor possible, but with more skilful and attentive help than can be commonly obtained; and it was probably the difficulty of consulting and comparing that stopped Milton's narrative at the Conquest; a period at which affairs were not yet very intricate, nor authors very numerous.

For the subject of his epic poem, after much deliberation, *long choosing, and beginning late,* he fixed upon *Paradise Lost;* a design so comprehensive that it could be justified only by success. He had once designed to celebrate King Arthur, as he hints in his verses to Mansus; but *Arthur was reserved,* says Fenton, *to another destiny.*

It appears, by some sketches of poetical projects left in manuscript, and to be seen in a library at Cambridge, that he had digested his thoughts on this subject into one of those wild dramas which were anciently called Mysteries; and Philips had seen what he terms part of a tragedy, beginning with the first ten lines of Satan's address to the Sun. These mysteries consist of allegorical persons; such as Justice, Mercy, Faith. Of the Tragedy or Mystery of *Paradise Lost* there are two plans:

The Persons	*The Persons*
Michael.	Moses.
Chorus of Angels.	Divine Justice, Wisdom,
Heavenly Love.	Heavenly Love.
Lucifer.	The Evening Star, Hesperus.
Adam, ⎫	Chorus of Angels.
Eve, ⎬ with the Serpent.	Lucifer.
Conscience.	Adam.
Death.	Eve.
Labour, ⎫	Conscience.
Sickness, ⎪	Labour, ⎫
Discontent, ⎬ Mutes.	Sickness, ⎪
Ignorance, ⎪	Discontent, ⎬ Mutes.
with other, ⎭	Ignorance, ⎪
Faith.	Fear, ⎭
Hope.	Death,
Charity.	Faith.
	Hope.
	Charity.

PARADISE LOST

The Persons

Moses προλογίζει, recounting how he assumed his true body; that it corrupts not, because it is with God in the mount; declares the like of Enoch and Elijah; besides the purity of the place, that certain pure winds, dews, and clouds preserve it from corruption; whence exhorts to the sight of God; tells they cannot see Adam in the state of innocence, by reason of their sin.

Justice, ⎫
Mercy, ⎬ debating what should become
Wisdom, ⎭ of man, if he fall.

Chorus of Angels singing a hymn of the Creation.

Act II

Heavenly Love.

Evening Star.

Chorus sing the marriage-song, and describe Paradise.

ACT III

Lucifer contriving Adam's ruin.

Chorus fears for Adam, and relates Lucifer's rebellion and fall.

ACT IV

Adam, }
Eve, } fallen.

Conscience cites them to God's examination.

Chorus bewails, and tells the good Adam has lost.

ACT V

Adam and Eve driven out of Paradise.

—————————— presented by an angel with

Labour, Grief, Hatred, Envy, War, Famine, }
  Pestilence, Sickness, Discontent, Ignorance, } Mutes.
  Fear, Death, }

To whom he gives their names. Likewise Winter, Heat, Tempest, etc.

Faith, }
Hope, } comfort him and instruct him.
Charity, }

Chorus briefly concludes.

Such was his first design, which could have produced only an allegory, or mystery. The following sketch seems to have attained more maturity.

ADAM UNPARADISED:

The angel Gabriel, either descending or entering; showing, since this globe was created, his frequency as much on earth as in heaven; describes Paradise. Next, the Chorus, showing the reason of his coming to keep his watch in Paradise, after Lucifer's rebellion, by command from God; and withal expressing his desire to see and know more concerning this excellent new creature, man. The angel Gabriel, as by his name signifying a prince of power, tracing Paradise with a more free office, passes by the station of the Chorus, and, desired by them, relates what he knew of man; as the creation of

Eve, with their love and marriage. After this, Lucifer appears; after his overthrow bemoans himself, seeks revenge on man. The Chorus prepare resistance at his first approach. At last, after discourse of enmity on either side, he departs: whereat the Chorus sings of the battle and victory in heaven, against him and his accomplices: as before, after the first act, was sung a hymn of the Creation. Here again may appear Lucifer, relating and insulting in what he had done to the destruction of man. Man next, and Eve having by this time been seduced by the Serpent, appears confusedly covered with leaves. Conscience, in a shape, accuses him; Justice cites him to the place whither Jehovah called for him. In the meanwhile, the Chorus entertains the stage, and is informed by some angel the manner of the fall. Here the Chorus bewails Adam's fall; Adam then and Eve return; accuse one another; but especially Adam lays the blame to his wife; is stubborn in his offence. Justice appears, reasons with him, convinces him. The Chorus admonishes Adam, and bids him beware Lucifer's example of impenitence. The angel is sent to banish them out of Paradise; but before causes to pass before his eyes, in shapes, a mask of all the evils of this life and world. He is humbled, relents, despairs; at last appears Mercy, comforts him, promises the Messiah; then calls in Faith, Hope and Charity; instructs him; he repents, gives God the glory, submits to his penalty. The Chorus briefly concludes. Compare this with the former draught.

These are very imperfect rudiments of *Paradise Lost*; but it is pleasant to see great works in their seminal state pregnant with latent possibilities of excellence; nor could there be any more delightful entertainment than to trace their gradual growth and expansion, and to observe how they are sometimes suddenly advanced by accidental hints, and sometimes slowly improved by steady meditation.

Invention is almost the only literary labour which blindness cannot obstruct, and therefore he naturally solaced his solitude by the indulgence of his fancy, and the melody of his numbers.

He had done what he knew to be necessary previous to poetical excellence; he had made himself acquainted with *seemly arts and affairs;* his comprehension was extended by various knowledge, and his memory stored with intellectual treasures. He was skilful in many languages, and had by reading and composition attained the full mastery of his own. He would have wanted little help from books, had he retained the power of perusing them.

But while his greater designs were advancing, having now, like many other authors, caught the love of publication, he amused himself, as he could, with little productions. He sent to the press (1658) a manuscript of Raleigh, called the *Cabinet Council;* and next year gratified his malevolence to the clergy by a *Treatise of Civil Power in Ecclesiastical Cases, and the Means of removing Hirelings out of the Church.*

Oliver was now dead; Richard was constrained to resign: the system of extemporary government, which had been held together only by force, naturally fell into fragments when that force was taken away; and Milton saw himself and his cause in equal danger. But he had still hope of doing something. He wrote letters, which Toland has published, to such men as he thought friends to the new commonwealth: and even in the year of the Restoration he *bated no jot of heart or hope,* but was fantastical enough to think that the nation, agitated as it was, might be settled by a pamphlet, called A *ready and easy Way to establish a Free Commonwealth;* which was, however, enough considered to be both seriously and ludicrously answered.

The obstinate enthusiasm of the commonwealth-men was very remarkable. When the King was apparently returning, Harrington, with a few associates as fanatical as himself, used to meet, with all the gravity of political importance, to settle an equal government by rotation; and Milton, kicking when he could strike no longer, was foolish enough to publish, a few weeks before the Restoration, *Notes* upon a sermon preached by one Griffith, entitled *The Fear of God and the King.* To these notes an answer was written by L'Estrange, in a pamphlet petulantly called *No Blind Guides.*

But whatever Milton could write, or men of greater activity

could do, the King was now about to be restored with the irresistible approbation of the people. He was therefore no longer secretary, and was consequently obliged to quit the house which he held by his office; and proportioning his sense of danger to his opinion of the importance of his writings, thought it convenient to seek some shelter, and hid himself for a time in Bartholomew-close, by West Smithfield.

I cannot but remark a kind of respect, perhaps unconsciously, paid to this great man by his biographers: every house in which he resided is historically mentioned, as if it were an injury to neglect naming any place that he honoured by his presence.

The King, with lenity of which the world has had perhaps no other example, declined to be the judge or avenger of his own or his father's wrongs; and promised to admit into the Act of Oblivion all except those whom the parliament should except; and the parliament doomed none to capital punishment but the wretches who had immediately co-operated in the murder of the King. Milton was certainly not one of them; he had only justified what they had done.

This justification was indeed sufficiently offensive; and (June 16) an order was issued to seize Milton's *Defence*, and Goodwin's *Obstructors of Justice*, another book of the same tendency, and burn them by the common hangman. The attorney-general was ordered to prosecute the authors; but Milton was not seized, nor perhaps very diligently pursued.

Not long after (August 19) the flutter of innumerable bosoms was stilled by an act, which the King, that his mercy might want no recommendation of elegance, rather called an Act of Oblivion than of Grace. Goodwin was named, with nineteen more, as incapacitated for any public trust; but of Milton there was no exception.

Of this tenderness shown to Milton, the curiosity of mankind has not forborne to inquire the reason. Burnet thinks he was forgotten; but this is another instance which may confirm Dalrymple's observation, who says, "that whenever Burnet's narrations are examined, he appears to be mistaken."

Forgotten he was not; for his prosecution was ordered: it must be therefore by design that he was included in the general oblivion. He is said to have had friends in the House, such as Marvel, Morrice, and Sir Thomas Clarges; and undoubtedly a man like him must have had influence. A very particular story of his escape is told by Richardson in his *Memoirs*, which he received from Pope, as delivered by Betterton, who might have heard it from Davenant. In the war between the King and Parliament, Davenant was made prisoner and condemned to die; but was spared at the request of Milton. When the turn of success brought Milton into the like danger, Davenant repaid the benefit by appearing in his favour. Here is a reciprocation of generosity and gratitude so pleasing, that the tale makes its own way to credit. But if help were wanted, I know not where to find it. The danger of Davenant is certain from his own relation; but of his escape there is no account. Betterton's narration can be traced no higher; it is not known that he had it from Davenant. We are told that the benefit exchanged was life for life; but it seems not certain that Milton's life ever was in danger. Goodwin, who had committed the same kind of crime, escaped with incapacitation; and as exclusion from public trust is a punishment which the power of government can commonly inflict without the help of a particular law, it required no great interest to exempt Milton from a censure little more than verbal. Something may be reasonably ascribed to veneration and compassion; to veneration of his abilities, and compassion for his distresses, which made it fit to forgive his malice for his learning. He was now poor and blind; and who would pursue with violence an illustrious enemy, depressed by fortune, and disarmed by nature?

The publication of the Act of Oblivion put him in the same condition with his fellow-subjects. He was, however, upon some pretence now not known, in the custody of the serjeant in December; and, when he was released, upon his refusal of the fees demanded, he and the serjeant were called before the House. He was now safe within the shade of oblivion, and knew himself to be as much out of the power of a griping officer as any other man. How this question was determined is not known. Milton would hardly have contended, but that he knew himself to have right on his side.

He then removed to Jewin-street, near Aldersgate-street;

and being blind and by no means wealthy, wanted a domestic companion and attendant; and therefore, by the recommendation of Dr. Paget, married Elizabeth Minshul, of a gentleman's family in Cheshire, probably without a fortune. All his wives were virgins; for he has declared that he thought it gross and indelicate to be a second husband: upon what other principles his choice was made, cannot now be known; but marriage afforded not much of his happiness. The first wife left him in disgust, and was brought back only by terror; the second, indeed, seems to have been more a favourite, but her life was short. The third, as Philips relates, oppressed his children in his lifetime, and cheated them at his death.

Soon after his marriage, according to an obscure story, he was offered the continuance of his employment, and being pressed by his wife to accept it, answered, "You, like other women, want to ride in your coach; my wish is to live and die an honest man." If he considered the Latin secretary as exercising any of the powers of government, he that had shared authority, either with the Parliament or Cromwell, might have forborne to talk very loudly of his honesty; and if he thought the office purely ministerial, he certainly might have honestly retained it under the King. But this tale has too little evidence to deserve a disquisition: large offers and sturdy rejections are among the common topics of falsehood.

He had so much either of prudence or gratitude, that he forbore to disturb the new settlement with any of his political or ecclesiastical opinions, and from this time devoted himself to poetry and literature. Of his zeal for learning in all its parts, he gave proof by publishing, the next year (1661), *Accidence commenced Grammar*—a little book which has nothing remarkable but that its author, who had been lately defending the supreme powers of his country, and was then writing *Paradise Lost*, could descend from his elevation to rescue children from the perplexity of grammatical confusion, and the trouble of lessons unnecessarily repeated.

About this time Ellwood the Quaker, being recommended to him as one who would read Latin to him, for the advantage of his conversation, attended him every afternoon, except on Sundays. Milton, who, in his letter to Hartlib, had declared, that *to read Latin with an English mouth is as ill a hearing as low French*, required that Ellwood should learn and practise the Italian pronunciation, which, he said, was necessary, if he would talk with foreigners. This seems to have been a task troublesome without use. There is little reason for preferring the Italian pronunciation to our own, except that it is more general; and to teach it to an Englishman is only to make him a foreigner at home. He who travels, if he speaks Latin, may so soon learn the sound which every native gives it, that he need make no provision before his journey; and if strangers visit us, it is their business to practise such conformity to our modes as they expect from us in their own countries. Ellwood complied with the directions, and improved himself by his attendance, for he relates that Milton, having a curious ear, knew by his voice when he read what he did not understand, and would stop him, and *open the most difficult passages*.

In a short time he took a house "in the *Artillery Walk*, leading to *Bunhill Fields*," the mention of which concludes the register of Milton's removals and habitations. He lived longer in this place than any other.

He was now busied by *Paradise Lost*. Whence he drew the original design has been variously conjectured by men who cannot bear to think themselves ignorant of that which, at last, neither diligence nor sagacity can discover. Some find the hint in an Italian tragedy. Voltaire tells a wild and unauthorised story of a farce seen by Milton in Italy, which opened thus: *Let the Rainbow be the Fiddlestick of the Fiddle of Heaven*. It has been already shown that the first conception was a tragedy or mystery, not of a narrative, but a dramatic work, which he is supposed to have begun to reduce to its present form about the time (1655) when he finished his dispute with the defenders of the King.

He long had promised to adorn his native country by some great performance, while he had yet perhaps no settled design, and was stimulated only by such expectations as naturally arose from the survey of his attainments, and the consciousness of his powers. What he should undertake, it was difficult to determine. He was *long choosing, and began late*.

While he was obliged to divide his time between his private studies and affairs of state, his poetical labour must have been often interrupted; and perhaps he did little more in that busy time than construct the narrative, adjust the episodes, proportion the parts, accumulate images and sentiments, and treasure in his memory, or preserve in writing, such hints as books or meditation would supply. Nothing particular is known of his intellectual operations while he was a statesman; for, having every help and accommodation at hand, he had no need of uncommon expedients.

Being driven from all public stations, he is yet too great not to be traced by curiosity to his retirement; where he has been found by Mr. Richardson, the fondest of his admirers, sitting *before his door in a grey coat of coarse cloth, in warm sultry weather, to enjoy the fresh air; and so, as in his own room, receiving the visits of people of distinguished parts as well as quality.* His visitors of high quality must now be imagined to be few; but men of parts might reasonably court the conversation of a man so generally illustrious, that foreigners are reported by Wood to have visited the house in Bread-street where he was born.

According to another account, he was seen in a small house, *neatly enough dressed in black clothes, sitting in a room hung with rusty green; pale, but not cadaverous, with chalkstones in his hands. He said that if it were not for the gout, his blindness would be tolerable.*

In the intervals of his pain, being made unable to use the common exercises, he used to swing in a chair, and sometimes played upon an organ.

He was now confessedly and visibly employed upon his poem, of which the progress might be noted by those with whom he was familiar; for he was obliged, when he had composed as many lines as his memory would conveniently retain, to employ some friend in writing them, having, at least for part of the time, no regular attendant. This gave opportunity to observations and reports.

Mr. Philips observes, that there was a very remarkable circumstance in the composure of *Paradise Lost,* "which I have a particular reason," says he, "to remember; for whereas I had the perusal of it from the very beginning, for some years, as I went from time to time to visit him, in parcels of ten, twenty, or thirty verses at a time (which, being written by whatever hand came next, might possibly want correction as to the orthography and pointing), having, as the summer came on, not been showed any for a considerable while, and desiring the reason thereof, was answered that his vein never happily flowed but from the autumnal equinox to the vernal; and that whatever he attempted at other times was never to his satisfaction, though he courted his fancy never so much; so that in all the years he was about this poem, he may be said to have spent but half his time therein."

Upon this relation Toland remarks, that in his opinion Philips has mistaken the time of the year; for Milton, in his *Elegies*, declares, that with the advance of the spring he feels the increase of his poetical force, *redeunt in carmina vires*. To this it is answered, that Philips could hardly mistake time so well marked; and it may be added, that Milton might find different times of the year favourable to different parts of life. Mr. Richardson conceives it impossible that *such a work should be suspended for six months, or for one. It may go on faster or slower, but it must go on.* By what necessity it must continually go on, or why it might not be laid aside and resumed, it is not easy to discover.

This dependence of the soul upon the seasons, those temporary and periodical ebbs and flows of intellect, may, I suppose, justly be derided as the fumes of vain imagination. *Sapiens dominabitur astris.* The author that thinks himself weather-bound will find, with a little help from hellebore, that he is only idle or exhausted. But while this notion has possession of the head, it produces the inability which it supposes. Our powers owe much of their energy to our hopes; *possunt quia posse videntur*. When success seems attainable, diligence is enforced; but when it is admitted that the faculties are suppressed by a cross-wind, or a cloudy sky, the day is given up without resistance; for who can contend with the course of nature?

From such prepossessions Milton seems not to have been free. There prevailed in his time an opinion that the world was in its decay, and that we have had the misfortune to be produced in the decrepitude of Nature. It was suspected that the whole creation languished, that neither trees nor animals had the height or bulk of their predecessors, and that everything was daily sinking by gradual diminution. Milton appears to suspect that souls partake of the general degeneracy, and is not without some fear that his book is to be written in *an age too late* for heroic poesy.

Another opinion wanders about the world, and sometimes finds reception among wise men—an opinion that restrains the operations of the mind to particular regions, and supposes that a luckless mortal may be born in a degree of latitude too high or too low for wisdom or for wit. From this fancy, wild as it is, he had not wholly cleared his head, when he feared lest the *climate* of his country might be *too cold* for flights of imagination.

Into a mind already occupied by such fancies, another not more reasonable might easily find its way. He that could fear lest his genius had fallen upon too old a world, or too chill a climate, might consistently magnify to himself the influence of the seasons, and believe his faculties to be vigorous only half the year.

His submission to the seasons was at least more reasonable than his dread of decaying nature, or a frigid zone; for general causes must operate uniformly in a general abatement of mental power; if less could be performed by the writer, less likewise would content the judges of his work. Among this lagging race of frosty grovellers he might still have risen into eminence by producing something which *they should not willingly let die*. However inferior to the heroes who were born in better ages, he might still be great among his contemporaries, with the hope of growing every day greater in the dwindle of posterity. He might still be a giant among the pigmies, the one-eyed monarch of the blind.

Of his artifices of study, or particular hours of composition, we have little account, and there was perhaps little to be told. Richardson, who seems to have been very diligent in his inquiries, but discovers always a wish to find Milton discriminated from other men, relates, that "he would sometimes lie awake whole nights, but not a verse could he make; and on a sudden his poetical faculty would rush upon him with an *impetus* or *œstrum*, and his daughter was immediately called to secure what came. At other times he would dictate perhaps forty lines in a breath, and then reduce them to half the number."

These bursts of light, and involutions of darkness, these transient and involuntary excursions and retrocessions of invention, having some appearance of deviation from the common train of nature, are eagerly caught by the lovers of a wonder. Yet something of this inequality happens to every man in every mode of exertion, manual or mental. The mechanic cannot handle his hammer and his file at all times with equal dexterity; there are hours, he knows not why, when *his hand is out*. By Mr. Richardson's relation, casually conveyed, much regard cannot be claimed. That, in his intellectual hour, Milton called for his daughter *to secure what came*, may be questioned; for unluckily it happens to be known that his daughters were never taught to write; nor would he have been obliged, as is universally confessed, to have employed any casual visitor in disburthening his memory, if his daughter could have performed the office.

The story of reducing his exuberance has been told of other authors, and, though doubtless true of every fertile and copious mind, seems to have been gratuitously transferred to Milton.

What he has told us, and we cannot now know more, is, that he composed much of his poem in the night and morning, I suppose before his mind was disturbed with common business; and that he poured out with great fluency his *unpremeditated verse*. Versification, free, like his, from the distresses of rhyme, must, by a work so long, be made prompt and habitual; and, when his thoughts were once adjusted, the words would come at his command.

At what particular times of his life the parts of his work were written, cannot often be known. The beginning of the third book shows that he had lost his sight; and the Introduction to the seventh, that the return of the King had clouded him with discountenance; and that he was offended by the licentious festivity of the Restoration. There are no other internal notes of time. Milton, being now cleared from all effects of his disloyalty, had nothing required from him but the common duty of living in quiet, to be rewarded with the common right of protection; but this, which, when he skulked from the approach of his King, was perhaps more than he hoped, seems not to have satisfied him; for no sooner is he safe, than he finds himself in danger, *fallen on evil days and evil tongues, and with darkness and with danger compassed round*. This darkness, had his eyes been better employed, had undoubtedly deserved compassion: but to add the mention of danger was ungrateful and unjust. He was fallen indeed on *evil days*; the time was come in which regicides could no longer boast their wickedness. But of *evil tongues* for Milton to complain, required impudence at least equal to his other powers; Milton, whose warmest advocates must allow that he never spared any asperity of reproach or brutality of insolence.

But the charge itself seems to be false; for it would be hard to recollect any reproach cast upon him, either serious or ludicrous, through the whole remaining part of his life. He pursued his studies or his amusements without persecution, molestation, or insult. Such is the reverence paid to great abilities, however misused: they who contemplated in Milton the scholar and the wit, were contented to forget the reviler of his King.

When the plague (1665) raged in London, Milton took refuge at Chalfont in Bucks; where Ellwood, who had taken the house for him, first saw a complete copy of *Paradise Lost*, and, having perused it, said to him, "Thou hast said much here of Paradise Lost; but what hast thou to say of Paradise Found?"

Next year, when the danger of infection had ceased, he returned to Bunhill-fields, and designed the publication of his poem. A licence was necessary, and he could expect no great kindness from a chaplain of the Archbishop of Canterbury. He seems, however, to have been treated with tenderness; for though objections were made to particular passages, and among them to the simile of the sun eclipsed in the first book, yet the licence was granted; and he sold his copy, April 27, 1667, to Samuel Simmons, for an immediate payment of 5*l.*, with a stipulation to receive 5*l.* more when thirteen hundred

should be sold of the first edition: and again, 5*l.* after the sale
of the same number of the second edition; and another 5*l.*
after the same sale of the third. None of the three editions
were to be extended beyond fifteen hundred copies.

The first edition was ten books, in a small quarto. The titles
were varied from year to year; and an advertisement, and the
arguments of the books, were omitted in some copies, and
inserted in others.

The sale gave him in two years a right to his second payment, for which the receipt was signed April 26, 1669. The
second edition was not given till 1674; it was printed in small
octavo; and the number of books was increased to twelve, by
a division of the seventh and tenth; and some other small improvements were made. The third edition was published in
1678; and the widow, to whom the copy was then to devolve,
sold all her claims to Simmons for 8*l.*, according to her receipt
given Dec. 21, 1680. Simmons had already agreed to transfer
the whole right to Brabazon Aylmer for 25*l.*; and Aylmer sold
to Jacob Tonson half, August 17, 1683,—half, March 24, 1690,
at a price considerably enlarged. In the history of *Paradise
Lost* a deduction thus minute will rather gratify than fatigue.

The slow sale and tardy reputation of this poem have been
always mentioned as evidences of neglected merit, and of the
uncertainty of literary fame; and inquiries have been made,
and conjectures offered, about the causes of its long obscurity
and late reception. But has the case been truly stated? Have
not lamentation and wonder been lavished on an evil that was
never felt?

That in the reigns of Charles and James the *Paradise Lost*
received no public acclamations is readily confessed. Wit and
literature were on the side of the Court: and who that solicited favour or fashion would venture to praise the defender of
the regicides? All that he himself could think his due, from
evil tongues in *evil days*, was that reverential silence which was
generously preserved. But it cannot be inferred that his poem
was not read, or not, however unwillingly, admired.

The sale, if it be considered, will justify the public. Those
who have no power to judge of past times but by their own,
should always doubt their conclusions. The call for books was

not in Milton's age what it is at present. To read was not then a general amusement; neither traders, nor often gentlemen, thought themselves disgraced by ignorance. The women had not then aspired to literature, nor was every house supplied with a closet of knowledge. Those indeed who professed learning were not less learned than at any other time; but of that middle race of students who read for pleasure or accomplishment, and who buy the numerous products of modern typography, the number was then comparatively small. To prove the paucity of readers, it may be sufficient to remark, that the nation had been satisfied from 1623 to 1664, that is, forty-one years, with only two editions of the works of Shakespeare, which probably did not together make one thousand copies.

The sale of thirteen hundred copies in two years, in opposition to so much recent enmity, and to a style of versification new to all and disgusting to many, was an uncommon example of the prevalence of genius. The demand did not immediately increase; for many more readers than were supplied at first the nation did not afford. Only three thousand were sold in eleven years; for it forced its way without assistance; its admirers did not dare to publish their opinion; and the opportunities now given of attracting notice by advertisements were then very few; the means of proclaiming the publications of new books have been produced by that general literature which now pervades the nation through all its ranks.

But the reputation and price of the copy still advanced, till the Revolution put an end to the secrecy of love, and *Paradise Lost* broke into open view with sufficient security of kind reception.

Fancy can hardly forbear to conjecture with what temper Milton surveyed the silent progress of his work, and marked its reputation stealing its way in a kind of subterraneous current through fear and silence. I cannot but conceive him calm and confident, little disappointed, not at all dejected, relying on his own merit with steady consciousness, and waiting, without impatience, the vicissitudes of opinion, and the impartiality of a future generation.

In the mean time he continued his studies, and supplied the

want of sight by a very odd expedient, of which Philips gives
the following account:

Mr. Philips tells us, "that though he had daily about him
one or other to read, some persons of man's estate, who, of
their own accord, greedily catched at the opportunity of being
his readers, that they might as well reap the benefit of what
they read to him, as oblige him by the benefit of their reading; others of younger years were sent by their parents to the
same end: yet excusing only the eldest daughter, by reason of
her bodily infirmity, and difficult utterance of speech (which,
to say truth, I doubt was the principal cause of excusing her),
the other two were condemned to the performance of reading,
and exactly pronouncing of all the languages of whatever book
he should, at one time or other, think fit to peruse, viz. the
Hebrew (and I think the Syriac), the Greek, the Latin, the
Italian, Spanish, and French. All which sorts of books to be
confined to read, without understanding one word, must needs
be a trial of patience almost beyond endurance. Yet it was
endured by both for a long time, though the irksomeness of
this employment could not be always concealed, but broke out
more and more into expressions of uneasiness; so that at
length they were all (even the eldest also) sent out to learn
some curious and ingenious sorts of manufacture, that are
proper for women to learn, particularly embroideries in gold
or silver."

In this scene of misery which this mode of intellectual labour sets before our eyes, it is hard to determine whether the
daughters or the father are most to be lamented. A language
not understood can never be so read as to give pleasure, and
very seldom so as to convey meaning. If few men would have
had resolution to write books with such embarrassments, few
likewise would have wanted ability to find some better expedient.

Three years after his *Paradise Lost* he published [1670] his
History of England, comprising the whole fable of Geoffry of
Monmouth, and continued to the Norman invasion. Why he
should have given the first part, which he seems not to believe,
and which is universally rejected, it is difficult to conjecture.

The style is harsh; but it has something of rough vigour, which perhaps may often strike, though it cannot please.

On this history the licenser again fixed his claws, and before he could transmit it to the press tore out several parts. Some censures of the Saxon monks were taken away, lest they should be applied to the modern clergy; and a character of the Long Parliament, and Assembly of Divines, was excluded; of which the author gave a copy to the Earl of Anglesea, and which being afterwards published, has been since inserted in its proper place.

The same year were printed *Paradise Regained*, and *Samson Agonistes*, a tragedy written in imitation of the ancients, and never designed by the author for the stage. As these poems were published by another bookseller, it has been asked whether Simmons was discouraged from receiving them by the slow sale of the former. Why a writer changed his bookseller a hundred years ago, I am far from hoping to discover. Certainly, he who in two years sells thirteen hundred copies of a volume in quarto, bought for two payments of 5l. each, has no reason to repent his purchase.

When Milton showed *Paradise Regained* to Ellwood, "This," said he, "is owing to you; for you put it into my head by the question you put to me at Chalfont, which before I had not thought of."

His last poetical offspring was his favourite. He could not, as Ellwood relates, endure to hear *Paradise Lost* preferred to *Paradise Regained*. Many causes may vitiate a writer's judgment of his own works. On that which has cost him much labour he sets a high value, because he is unwilling to think that he has been diligent in vain; what has been produced without toilsome efforts is considered with delight, as a proof of vigorous faculties and fertile invention; and the last work, whatever it be, has necessarily most of the grace of novelty. Milton, however it happened, had this prejudice, and had it to himself.

To that multiplicity of attainments, and extent of comprehension, that entitle this great author to our veneration, may be added a kind of humble dignity, which did not disdain the meanest services to literature. The epic poet, the controvertist, the politician, having already descended to accommodate children with a book of rudiments, now, in the last years of his life, composed a book of logic for the initiation of students in philosophy, and published (1672) *Artis Logicæ plenior Institutio ad Petri Rami Methodum concinnata*; that is, A *new Scheme of Logic, according to the Method of Ramus.* I know not whether, even in this book, he did not intend an act of hostility against the universities; for Ramus was one of the first oppugners of the old philosophy, who disturbed with innovations the quiet of the schools.

His polemical disposition again revived. He had now been safe so long, that he forgot his fears, and published [1673] a *Treatise of true Religion, Heresy, Schism, Toleration, and the best Means to prevent the Growth of Popery.*

But this little tract is modestly written, with respectful mention of the Church of England, and an appeal to the Thirty-nine Articles. His principle of toleration is, agreement in the sufficiency of the Scriptures; and he extends it to all who, whatever their opinions are, profess to derive them from the sacred books. The Papists appeal to other testimonies, and are, therefore, in his opinion, not to be permitted the liberty of either public or private worship; for though they plead conscience, *we have no warrant,* he says, *to regard conscience which is not grounded in Scripture.*

Those who are not convinced by his reasons may be perhaps delighted with his wit. The term *Roman Catholic* is, he says, *one of the Pope's bulls; it is particular universal,* or *Catholic schismatic.*

He has, however, something better. As the best preservative against Popery, he recommends the diligent perusal of the Scriptures, a duty from which he warns the busy part of mankind not to think themselves excused.

He now [1673] reprinted his juvenile poems, with some additions.

In the last year of his life he sent to the press, seeming to take delight in publication, a collection of *Familiar Epistles in Latin,* to which, being too few to make a volume, he added some academical exercises, which perhaps he perused with pleasure, as they recalled to his memory the days of youth;

but for which nothing but veneration for his name could now procure a reader.

When he had attained his sixty-sixth year, the gout, with which he had been long tormented, prevailed over the enfeebled powers of nature. He died, by a quiet and silent expiration, about the 10th of November, 1674, at his house in Bunhill-fields, and was buried next his father in the chancel of St. Giles, at Cripplegate. His funeral was very splendidly and numerously attended.

Upon his grave there is supposed to have been no memorial; but in our time [1737] a monument has been erected in Westminster Abbey *To the Author of "Paradise Lost,"* by Mr. Benson, who has in the inscription bestowed more words upon himself than upon Milton.

When the inscription for the monument of Philips, in which he was said to be *soli Miltono secundus,* was exhibited to Dr. Sprat, then dean of Westminster, he refused to admit it; the name of Milton was, in his opinion, too detestable to be read on the wall of a building dedicated to devotion. Atterbury, who succeeded him, being author of the inscription, permitted its reception. "And such has been the change of public opinion," said Dr. Gregory, from whom I heard this account, "that I have seen erected in the church a statue of that man whose name I once knew considered as a pollution of its walls."

Milton has the reputation of having been in his youth eminently beautiful, so as to have been called the Lady of his college. His hair, which was of a light brown, parted at the fore-top, and hung down upon his shoulders, according to the picture which he has given of Adam. He was, however, not of the heroic stature, but rather below the middle size, according to Mr. Richardson, who mentions him as having narrowly escaped from being *short and thick.* He was vigorous and active, and delighted in the exercise of the sword, in which he is related to have been eminently skilful. His weapon was, I believe, not the rapier, but the back-sword, of which he recommends the use in his book on Education.

His eyes are said never to have been bright; but, if he was a dexterous fencer, they must have been once quick.

His domestic habits, so far as they are known, were those of a severe student. He drank little strong drink of any kind, and fed without excess in quantity, and in his earlier years without delicacy of choice. In his youth he studied late at night; but afterwards changed his hours, and rested in bed from nine to four in the summer, and five in the winter. The course of his day was best known after he was blind. When he first rose he heard a chapter in the Hebrew Bible, and then studied till twelve; then took some exercise for an hour; then dined, then played on the organ and sung, or heard another sing; then studied to six; then entertained his visitors till eight; then supped; and, after a pipe of tobacco and a glass of water, went to bed.

So is his life described; but this even tenour appears attainable only in colleges. He that lives in the world will sometimes have the succession of his practice broken and confused. Visitors, of whom Milton is represented to have had great numbers, will come and stay unseasonably; business, of which every man has some, must be done when others will do it.

When he did not care to rise early he had something read to him by his bedside; perhaps at this time his daughters were employed. He composed much in the morning, and dictated in the day, sitting obliquely in an elbow-chair, with his leg thrown over the arm.

Fortune appears not to have had much of his care. In the civil wars he lent his personal estate to the parliament; but when, after the contest was decided, he solicited repayment, he met not only with neglect, but *sharp rebuke*; and, having tired both himself and his friends, was given up to poverty and hopeless indignation, till he showed how able he was to do greater service. He was then made Latin secretary, with 200*l.* a year; and had 1000*l.* for his *Defence of the People*. His widow, who after his death retired to Nantwich, in Cheshire, and died about 1729, is said to have reported that he lost 2000*l.* by entrusting it to a scrivener; and that, in the general depredation upon the Church, he had grasped an estate of about 60*l.* a year belonging to Westminster Abbey, which, like other sharers of the plunder of rebellion, he was afterwards obliged to return. Two thousand pounds, which he had placed in the Excise-Office, were also lost. There is yet no reason to believe that he was ever reduced to indigence. His wants, being few, were competently supplied. He sold his library before his death, and left his family 1500*l.*, on which his widow laid hold, and only gave 100*l.* to each of his daughters.

His literature was unquestionably great. He read all the languages which are considered either as learned or polite: Hebrew, with its two dialects, Greek, Latin, Italian, French, and Spanish. In Latin his skill was such as places him in the first rank of writers and critics; and he appears to have cultivated Italian with uncommon diligence. The books in which his daughter, who used to read to him, represented him as most delighting, after Homer, which he could almost repeat, were Ovid's *Metamorphoses* and Euripides. His Euripides is, by Mr. Cradock's kindness, now in my hands: the margin is sometimes noted; but I have found nothing remarkable.

Of the English poets he set most value upon Spenser, Shakespeare, and Cowley. Spenser was apparently his favourite: Shakespeare he may easily be supposed to like, with every skilful reader; but I should not have expected that Cowley, whose ideas of excellence were different from his own, would have had much of his approbation. His character of Dryden, who sometimes visited him, was, that he was a good rhymist, but no poet.

His theological opinions are said to have been first Calvinistical; and afterwards, perhaps when he began to hate the Presbyterians, to have tended towards Arminianism. In the mixed questions of theology and government he never thinks that he can recede far enough from popery or prelacy; but what Baudius says of Erasmus seems applicable to him— *magis habuit quod fugeret, quam quod sequeretur*. He had determined rather what to condemn, than what to approve. He has not associated himself with any denomination of Protestants: we know rather what he was not than what he was. He was not of the Church of Rome; he was not of the Church of England.

To be of no Church is dangerous. Religion, of which the rewards are distant, and which is animated only by faith and hope, will glide by degrees out of the mind, unless it be invigorated and reimpressed by external ordinances, by stated calls to worship, and the salutary influence of example. Milton, who appears to have had a full conviction of the truth of Christianity, and to have regarded the Holy Scriptures with the profoundest veneration, to have been untainted by any heretical peculiarity of opinion, and to have lived in a confirmed belief of the immediate and occasional agency of Providence, yet grew old without any visible worship. In the distribution of his hours there was no hour of prayer, either solitary or with his household; omitting public prayers, he omitted all.

Of this omission the reason has been sought upon a supposition, which ought never to be made, that men live with their own approbation, and justify their conduct to themselves. Prayer certainly was not thought superfluous by him who represents our first parents as praying acceptably in the state of innocence, and efficaciously after their fall. That he lived without prayer can hardly be affirmed; his studies and meditations were an habitual prayer. The neglect of it in his family was probably a fault for which he condemned himself, and which he intended to correct, but that death, as too often happens, intercepted his reformation.

His political notions were those of an acrimonious and surly republican, for which it is not known that he gave any better reason than that *a popular government was the most frugal; for the trappings of a monarchy would set up an ordinary commonwealth*. It is surely very shallow policy that supposes money to be the chief good; and even this, without considering that the support and expense of a Court is, for the most part, only a particular kind of traffic, for which money is circulated without any national impoverishment.

Milton's republicanism was, I am afraid, founded in an envious hatred of greatness, and a sullen desire of independence; in petulance impatient of control, and pride disdainful of superiority. He hated monarchs in the State, and prelates in the Church; for he hated all whom he was required to obey. It is to be suspected that his predominant desire was to destroy rather than establish, and that he felt not so much the love of liberty as repugnance to authority.

It has been observed that they who most loudly clamour

for liberty do not most liberally grant it. What we know of Milton's character in domestic relations is that he was severe and arbitrary. His family consisted of women; and there appears in his books something like a Turkish contempt of females, as subordinate and inferior beings. That his own daughters might not break the ranks, he suffered them to be depressed by a mean and penurious education. He thought woman made only for obedience, and man only for rebellion.

Of his family some account may be expected. His sister, first married to Mr. Philips, afterwards married Mr. [Thomas] Agar, a friend of her first husband, who succeeded him in the Crown Office. She had by her first husband Edward and John, the two nephews whom Milton educated; and by her second two daughters.

His brother, Sir Christopher, had two daughters, Mary and Catherine, and a son, Thomas, who succeeded Agar in the Crown Office, and left a daughter living in 1749, in Grosvenor-street.

Milton had children only by his first wife; Anne, Mary, and Deborah. Anne, though deformed, married a master-builder, and died of her first child. Mary died single. Deborah married Abraham Clarke, a weaver in Spitalfields, and lived seventy-six years, to August, 1727. This is the daughter of whom public mention has been made. She could repeat the first lines of Homer, the *Metamorphoses*, and some of Euripides, by having often read them. Yet here incredulity is ready to make a stand. Many repetitions are necessary to fix in memory lines not understood; and why should Milton wish or want to hear them so often? These lines were at the beginning of the poems. Of a book written in a language not understood, the beginning raises no more attention than the end; and, as those that understand it know commonly the beginning best, its rehearsal will seldom be necessary. It is not likely that Milton required any passage to be so much repeated as that his daughter could learn it; nor likely that he desired the initial lines to be read at all; nor that the daughter, weary of the drudgery of pronouncing unideal sounds, would voluntarily commit them to memory.

To this gentlewoman Addison made a present, and promised some establishment, but died soon after. Queen Caroline sent her fifty guineas. She had seven sons and three daughters, but none of them had any children, except her son Caleb and her daughter Elizabeth. Caleb went to Fort St. George in the East Indies, and had two sons, of whom nothing is now known. Elizabeth married Thomas Foster, a weaver in Spital-fields, and had seven children, who all died. She kept a petty grocer's or chandler's shop, first at Holloway, and afterwards in Cock-lane, near Shoreditch church. She knew little of her grandfather, and that little was not good. She told of his harsh-ness to his daughters, and his refusal to have them taught to write; and, in opposition to other accounts, represented him as delicate, though temperate in his diet.

In 1750, April 5, *Comus* was played [at Drury Lane] for her benefit. She had so little acquaintance with diversion or gaiety, that she did not know what was intended when a bene-fit was offered her. The profits of the night were only 130*l.*, though Dr. Newton brought a large contribution; and 20*l.* were given by Tonson, a man who is to be praised as often as he is named. Of this sum 100*l.* were placed in the stocks, after some debate between her and her husband in whose name it should be entered; and the rest augmented their little stock, with which they removed to Islington. This was the greatest benefaction that *Paradise Lost* ever procured the au-thor's descendants; and to this he who has now attempted to relate his Life had the honour of contributing a prologue.

In the examination of Milton's poetical works I shall pay so much regard to time as to begin with his juvenile productions. For his early pieces he seems to have had a degree of fond-ness not very laudable; what he has once written he resolves to preserve, and gives to the public an unfinished poem, which he broke off because he was *nothing satisfied with what he had done,* supposing his readers less nice than himself. These preludes to his future labours are in Italian, Latin, and Eng-lish. Of the Italian I cannot pretend to speak as a critic; but I have heard them commended by a man well qualified to decide their merit. The Latin pieces are lusciously elegant; but the delight which they afford is rather by the exquisite imitation of the ancient writers, by the purity of the diction, and the harmony of the numbers, than by any power of invention, or vigour of sentiment. They are not all of equal value; the elegies excel the odes; and some of the exercises on *Gunpowder Treason* might have been spared.

The English poems, though they make no promises of *Paradise Lost*, have this evidence of genius, that they have a cast original and unborrowed. But their peculiarity is not excellence: if they differ from verses of others, they differ for the worse; for they are too often distinguished by repulsive harshness; the combinations of words are new, but they are not pleasing; the rhymes and epithets seem to be laboriously sought, and violently applied.

That in the early parts of his life he wrote with much care appears from his manuscripts, happily preserved at Cambridge, in which many of his smaller works are found as they were first written, with the subsequent corrections. Such relics show how excellence is acquired; what we hope ever to do with ease we must learn first to do with diligence.

Those who admire the beauties of this great poet sometimes force their own judgment into false approbation of his little pieces, and prevail upon themselves to think that admirable which is only singular. All that short compositions can commonly attain is neatness and elegance. Milton never learned the art of doing little things with grace; he overlooked the milder excellence of suavity and softness; he was a *lion* that had no skill *in dandling the kid*.

One of the poems on which much praise has been bestowed is *Lycidas*, of which the diction is harsh, the rhymes uncertain, and the numbers unpleasing. What beauty there is we must therefore seek in the sentiments and images. It is not to be considered as the effusion of real passion; for passion runs not after remote allusions and obscure opinions. Passion plucks no berries from the myrtle and ivy, nor calls upon Arethuse and Mincius, nor tells of rough *satyrs* and *fauns with cloven heel*. Where there is leisure for fiction there is little grief.

In this poem there is no nature, for there is nothing new. Its form is that of a pastoral, easy, vulgar, and therefore disgusting; whatever images it can supply are long ago exhausted, and its inherent improbability always forces dissatisfaction on the mind. When Cowley tells of Hervey, that they studied together, it is easy to suppose how much he must miss the companion of his labours, and the partner of his discoveries; but what image of tenderness can be excited by these lines?—

> We drove a field, and both together heard
> What time the grey fly winds her sultry horn,
> Battening our flocks with the fresh dews of night.

We know that they never drove a field, and that they had no flocks to batten; and though it be allowed that the representation may be allegorical, the true meaning is so uncertain and remote that it is never sought because it cannot be known when it is found.

Among the flocks, and copses, and flowers, appear the heathen deities—Jove and Phœbus, Neptune and Æolus, with a long train of mythological imagery, such as a college easily supplies. Nothing can less display knowledge, or less exercise invention, than to tell how a shepherd has lost his companion, and must now feed his flocks alone, without any judge of his skill in piping; and how one god asks another god what is become of Lycidas, and how neither god can tell. He who thus grieves will excite no sympathy; he who thus praises will confer no honour.

This poem has yet a grosser fault. With these trifling fictions are mingled the most awful and sacred truths, such as ought never to be polluted with such irreverend combinations. The shepherd likewise is now a feeder of sheep, and afterwards an ecclesiastical pastor, a superintendent of a Christian flock. Such equivocations are always unskilful; but here they are indecent, and at least approach to impiety, of which, however, I believe the writer not to have been conscious.

Such is the power of reputation justly acquired, that its blaze drives away the eye from nice examination. Surely no man could have fancied that he read *Lycidas* with pleasure had he not known its author.

Of the two pieces, *L'Allegro* and *Il Penseroso*, I believe opinion is uniform; every man that reads them reads them with pleasure. The author's design is not, what Theobald has remarked, merely to show how objects derive their colours from the mind, by representing the operation of the same things upon the gay and the melancholy temper, or upon the same man as he is differently disposed; but rather how, among the successive variety of appearances, every disposition of mind takes hold on those by which it may be gratified.

The *cheerful* man hears the lark in the morning; the *pensive* man hears the nightingale in the evening. The *cheerful* man sees the cock strut, and hears the horn and hounds echo in the wood; then walks, *not unseen*, to observe the glory of the rising sun, or listen to the singing milkmaid, and view the labours of the ploughman and the mower; then casts his eyes about him over scenes of smiling plenty, and looks up to the distant tower, the residence of some fair inhabitant; thus he pursues rural gaiety through a day of labour or of play, and delights himself at night with the fanciful narratives of superstitious ignorance.

The *pensive* man, at one time, walks *unseen* to muse at midnight; and at another hears the sullen curfew. If the weather drives him home, he sits in a room lighted only by *glowing embers*, or by a lonely lamp outwatches the north star, to discover the habitation of separate souls, and varies the shades of meditation by contemplating the magnificent or pathetic scenes of tragic and epic poetry. When the morning comes, a morning gloomy with rain and wind, he walks into the dark trackless woods, falls asleep by some murmuring water, and with melancholy enthusiasm expects some dream of prognostication, or some music played by aerial performers.

Both Mirth and Melancholy are solitary, silent inhabitants of the breast, that neither receive nor transmit communication; no mention is therefore made of a philosophical friend, or a pleasant companion. The seriousness does not arise from any participation of calamity, nor the gaiety from the pleasures of the bottle.

The man of *cheerfulness*, having exhausted the country, tries what *towered cities* will afford, and mingles with scenes of splendour gay assemblies and nuptial festivities; but he mingles a mere spectator, as, when the learned comedies of

Jonson or the wild dramas of Shakespeare are exhibited, he attends the theatre.

The *pensive* man never loses himself in crowds, but walks the cloister, or frequents the cathedral. Milton probably had not yet forsaken the Church.

Both his characters delight in music; but he seems to think that cheerful notes would have obtained from Pluto a complete dismission of Eurydice, of whom solemn sounds only procured a conditional release.

For the old age of Cheerfulness he makes no provision; but Melancholy he conducts with great dignity to the close of life. His cheerfulness is without levity, and his pensiveness without asperity.

Through these two poems the images are properly selected, and nicely distinguished; but the colours of the diction seem not sufficiently discriminated. I know not whether the characters are kept sufficiently apart. No mirth can indeed be found in his melancholy; but I am afraid that I always meet some melancholy in his mirth. They are two noble efforts of imagination.

The greatest of his juvenile performances is the *Masque of Comus*, in which may very plainly be discovered the dawn or twilight of *Paradise Lost*. Milton appears to have formed very early that system of diction, and mode of verse, which his maturer judgment approved, and from which he never endeavoured nor desired to deviate.

Nor does *Comus* afford only a specimen of his language; it exhibits likewise his power of description and his vigour of sentiment employed in the praise and defence of virtue. A work more truly poetical is rarely found; allusions, images, and descriptive epithets, embellish almost every period with lavish decoration. As a series of lines, therefore, it may be considered as worthy of all the admiration with which the votaries have received it.

As a drama it is deficient. The action is not probable. A masque, in those parts where supernatural intervention is admitted, must indeed be given up to all the freaks of imagination; but, so far as the action is merely human, it ought to be reasonable, which can hardly be said of the conduct of the two brothers, who, when their sister sinks with fatigue in a path-less wilderness, wander both away together in search of berries too far to find their way back, and leave a helpless Lady to all the sadness and danger of solitude. This, however, is a defect overbalanced by its convenience.

What deserves more reprehension is, that the prologue spoken in the wild wood by the attendant Spirit is addressed to the audience; a mode of communication so contrary to the nature of dramatic representation, that no precedents can support it.

The discourse of the Spirit is too long—an objection that may be made to almost all the following speeches; they have not the sprightliness of a dialogue animated by reciprocal contention, but seem rather declamations deliberately composed, and formally repeated, on a moral question. The auditor therefore listens as to a lecture, without passion, without anxiety.

The song of Comus has airiness and jollity; but, what may recommend Milton's morals as well as his poetry, the invitations to pleasure are so general, that they excite no distinct images of corrupt enjoyment, and take no dangerous hold on the fancy.

The following soliloquies of Comus and the Lady are elegant, but tedious. The song must owe much to the voice, if it ever can delight. At last the Brothers enter, with too much tranquillity; and when they have feared lest their sister should be in danger, and hoped that she is not in danger, the Elder makes a speech in praise of chastity, and the Younger finds how fine it is to be a philosopher.

Then descends the Spirit in form of a shepherd, and the Brother, instead of being in haste to ask his help, praises his singing, and inquires his business in that place. It is remarkable, that at this interview the Brother is taken with a short fit of rhyming. The Spirit relates that the Lady is in the power of Comus; the Brother moralises again; and the Spirit makes a long narration, of no use because it is false, and therefore unsuitable to a good being.

In all these parts the language is poetical, and the sentiments are generous; but there is something wanting to allure attention.

The dispute between the Lady and Comus is the most animated and affecting scene of the drama, and wants nothing but a brisker reciprocation of objections and replies to invite attention and detain it.

The songs are vigorous, and full of imagery; but they are harsh in their diction, and not very musical in their numbers.

Throughout the whole the figures are too bold, and the language too luxuriant for dialogue. It is a drama in the epic style, inelegantly splendid, and tediously instructive.

The *Sonnets* were written in different parts of Milton's life, upon different occasions. They deserve not any particular criticism; for of the best it can only be said, that they are not bad; and perhaps only the eighth and twenty-first are truly entitled to this slender commendation. The fabric of a sonnet, however adapted to the Italian language, has never succeeded in ours, which, having greater variety of termination, requires the rhymes to be often changed.

Those little pieces may be despatched without much anxiety; a greater work calls for greater care. I am now to examine *Paradise Lost*; a poem which, considered with respect to design, may claim the first place, and with respect to performance, the second, among the productions of the human mind.

By the general consent of critics the first praise of genius is due to the writer of an epic poem, as it requires an assemblage of all the powers which are singly sufficient for other compositions. Poetry is the art of uniting pleasure with truth, by calling imagination to the help of reason. Epic poetry undertakes to teach the most important truths by the most pleasing precepts, and therefore relates some great event in the most affecting manner. History must supply the writer with the rudiments of narration, which he must improve and exalt by a nobler art, must animate by dramatic energy, and diversify by retrospection and anticipation; morality must teach him the exact bounds, and different shades, of vice and virtue; from policy, and the practice of life, he has to learn the discriminations of character, and the tendency of the passions, either single or combined; and physiology must supply him with illustrations and images. To put these materials to poetical use, is required an imagination capable of painting nature and realising fiction. Nor is he yet a poet till he has attained the whole extension of his language, distinguished all the delicacies of phrase, and all the colours of words, and learned to adjust their different sounds to all the varieties of metrical modulation.

Bossu is of opinion that the poet's first work is to find a *moral*, which his fable is afterwards to illustrate and establish. This seems to have been the process only of Milton; the moral of other poems is incidental and consequent; in Milton's only it is essential and intrinsic. His purpose was the most useful and the most arduous; *to vindicate the ways of God to man*; to show the reasonableness of religion, and the necessity of obedience to the Divine Law.

To convey this moral, there must be a *fable*, a narration artfully constructed, so as to excite curiosity, and surprise expectation. In this part of his work Milton must be confessed to have equalled every other poet. He has involved in his account of the Fall of Man the events which preceded, and those that were to follow it: he has interwoven the whole system of theology with such propriety, that every part appears to be necessary; and scarcely any recital is wished shorter for the sake of quickening the progress of the main action.

The subject of an epic poem is naturally an event of great importance. That of Milton is not the destruction of a city, the conduct of a colony, or the foundation of an empire. His subject is the fate of worlds, the revolutions of heaven and of earth; rebellion against the Supreme King, raised by the highest order of created beings; the overthrow of their host, and the punishment of their crime; the creation of a new race of reasonable creatures; their original happiness and innocence, their forfeiture of immortality, and their restoration to hope and peace.

Great events can be hastened or retarded only by persons of elevated dignity. Before the greatness displayed in Milton's poem, all other greatness shrinks away. The weakest of his agents are the highest and noblest of human beings, the original parents of mankind; with whose actions the elements consented; on whose rectitude, or deviation of will, depended the state of terrestrial nature, and the condition of all the future inhabitants of the globe.

Of the other agents in the poem, the chief are such as it is irreverence to name on slight occasions. The rest were lower powers;

> —— of which the least could wield
> Those elements, and arm him with the force
> Of all their regions;

powers which only the control of Omnipotence restrains from laying creation waste, and filling the vast expanse of space with ruin and confusion. To display the motives and actions of beings thus superior, so far as human reason can examine them, or human imagination represent them, is the task which this mighty poet has undertaken and performed.

In the examination of epic poems much speculation is commonly employed upon the *characters*. The characters in the *Paradise Lost*, which admit of examination, are those of angels and of man; of angels good and evil; of man in his innocent and sinful state.

Among the angels, the virtue of Raphael is mild and placid, of easy condescension and free communication; that of Michael is regal and lofty, and, as may seem, attentive to the dignity of his own nature. Abdiel and Gabriel appear occasionally, and act as every incident requires; the solitary fidelity of Abdiel is very amiably painted.

Of the evil angels the characters are more diversified. To Satan, as Addison observes, such sentiments are given as suit *the most exalted and most depraved being*. Milton has been censured by Clarke for the impiety which sometimes breaks from Satan's mouth. For there are thoughts, as he justly remarks, which no observation of character can justify, because no good man would willingly permit them to pass, however transiently, through his own mind. To make Satan speak as a rebel, without any such expressions as might taint the reader's imagination, was indeed one of the greatest difficulties in Milton's undertaking, and I cannot but think that he has extricated himself with great happiness. There is in Satan's speeches little that can give pain to a pious ear. The language of rebellion cannot be the same with that of obedience. The malignity of Satan foams in haughtiness and obstinacy; but his expressions are commonly general, and no otherwise offensive than as they are wicked.

The other chiefs of the celestial rebellion are very judiciously discriminated in the first and second books; and the ferocious character of Moloch appears, both in the battle and the council, with exact consistency.

To Adam and to Eve are given, during their innocence, such sentiments as innocence can generate and utter. Their love is pure benevolence and mutual veneration; their repasts are without luxury, and their diligence without toil. Their addresses to their Maker have little more than the voice of admiration and gratitude. Fruition left them nothing to ask; and Innocence left them nothing to fear.

But with guilt enter distrust and discord, mutual accusation and stubborn self-defence; they regard each other with alienated minds, and dread their Creator as the avenger of their transgression. At last they seek shelter in his mercy, soften to repentance, and melt in supplication. Both before and after the Fall the superiority of Adam is diligently sustained.

Of the *probable* and the *marvellous*, two parts of a vulgar epic poem which immerge the critic in deep consideration, the *Paradise Lost* requires little to be said. It contains the history of a miracle, of Creation and Redemption; it displays the power and the mercy of the Supreme Being; the probable therefore is marvellous, and the marvellous is probable. The substance of the narrative is truth; and as truth allows no choice, it is, like necessity, superior to rule. To the accidental or adventitious parts, as to everything human, some slight exceptions may be made. But the main fabric is immovably supported.

It is justly remarked by Addison, that this poem has, by the nature of its subject, the advantage above all others, that it is universally and perpetually interesting. All mankind will, through all ages, bear the same relation to Adam and to Eve, and must partake of that good and evil which extend to themselves.

Of the *machinery*, so called from θεὸς ἀπὸ μηχανῆς, by

which is meant the occasional interposition of supernatural power, another fertile topic of critical remarks, here is no room to speak, because everything is done under the immediate and visible direction of Heaven; but the rule is so far observed, that no part of the action could have been accomplished by any other means.

Of *episodes*, I think there are only two, contained in Raphael's relation of the war in heaven, and Michael's prophetic account of the changes to happen in this world. Both are closely connected with the great action; one was necessary to Adam as a warning, the other as a consolation.

To the completeness or *integrity* of the design nothing can be objected; it has distinctly and clearly what Aristotle requires, a beginning, a middle, and an end. There is perhaps no poem, of the same length, from which so little can be taken without apparent mutilation. Here are no funeral games, nor is there any long description of a shield. The short digressions at the beginning of the third, seventh, and ninth books might doubtless be spared; but superfluities so beautiful, who would take away? or who does not wish that the author of the Iliad had gratified succeeding ages with a little knowledge of himself? Perhaps no passages are more frequently or more attentively read than those extrinsic paragraphs; and, since the end of poetry is pleasure, that cannot be unpoetical with which all are pleased.

The questions, whether the action of the poem be strictly *one*, whether the poem can be properly termed *heroic*, and who is the hero, are raised by such readers as draw their principles of judgment rather from books than from reason. Milton, though he entitled *Paradise Lost* only a *poem*, yet calls it himself *heroic song*. Dryden, petulantly and indecently, denies the heroism of Adam, because he was overcome; but there is no reason why the hero should not be unfortunate, except established practice, since success and virtue do not go necessarily together. Cato is the hero of Lucan; but Lucan's authority will not be suffered by Quintilian to decide. However, if success be necessary, Adam's deceiver was at last crushed; Adam was restored to his Maker's favour, and therefore may securely resume his human rank.

After the scheme and fabric of the poem, must be considered its component parts, the sentiments and the diction.

The *sentiments*, as expressive of manners, or appropriated to characters, are for the greater part unexceptionally just.

Splendid passages, containing lessons of morality, or precepts of prudence, occur seldom. Such is the original formation of this poem, that as it admits no human manners till the Fall, it can give little assistance to human conduct. Its end is to raise the thoughts above sublunary cares or pleasures. Yet the praise of that fortitude with which Abdiel maintained his singularity of virtue against the scorn of multitudes, may be accommodated to all times; and Raphael's reproof of Adam's curiosity after the planetary motions, with the answer returned by Adam, may be confidently opposed to any rule of life which any poet has delivered.

The thoughts which are occasionally called forth in the progress are such as could only be produced by an imagination in the highest degree fervid and active, to which materials were supplied by incessant study and unlimited curiosity. The heat of Milton's mind might be said to sublimate his learning, to throw off into his work the spirit of science, unmingled with its grosser parts.

He had considered creation in its whole extent, and his descriptions are therefore learned. He had accustomed his imagination to unrestrained indulgence, and his conceptions therefore were extensive. The characteristic quality of his poem is sublimity. He sometimes descends to the elegant, but his element is the great. He can occasionally invest himself with grace; but his natural port is gigantic loftiness. He can please when pleasure is required; but it is his peculiar power to astonish.

He seems to have been well acquainted with his own genius, and to know what it was that nature had bestowed upon him more bountifully than upon others; the power of displaying the vast, illuminating the splendid, enforcing the awful, darkening the gloomy, and aggravating the dreadful; he therefore chose a subject on which too much could not be said, on which he might tire his fancy without the censure of extravagance.

The appearances of nature, and the occurrences of life, did

not satiate his appetite of greatness. To paint things as they are requires a minute attention, and employs the memory rather than the fancy. Milton's delight was to sport in the wide regions of possibility; reality was a scene too narrow for his mind. He sent his faculties out upon discovery, into worlds where only imagination can travel, and delighted to form new modes of existence, and furnish sentiment and action to superior beings, to trace the counsels of hell, or accompany the choirs of heaven.

But he could not be always in other worlds; he must sometimes revisit earth, and tell of things visible and known. When he cannot raise wonder by the sublimity of his mind, he gives delight by its fertility.

Whatever be his subject, he never fails to fill the imagination. But his images and descriptions of the scenes or operations of nature do not seem to be always copied from original form, nor to have the freshness, raciness, and energy of immediate observation. He saw nature, as Dryden expresses it, *through the spectacles of books*; and on most occasions calls learning to his assistance. The garden of Eden brings to his mind the vale of Enna, where Proserpine was gathering flowers. Satan makes his way through fighting elements, like Argo between the Cyanean rocks, or Ulysses between the two Sicilian whirlpools, when he shunned Charybdis on the *larboard*. The mythological allusions have been justly censured, as not being always used with notice of their vanity; but they contribute variety to the narration, and produce an alternate exercise of the memory and the fancy.

His similes are less numerous and more various than those of his predecessors. But he does not confine himself within the limits of rigorous comparison: his great excellence is amplitude, and he expands the adventitious image beyond the dimensions which the occasion required. Thus, comparing the shield of Satan to the orb of the moon, he crowds the imagination with the discovery of the telescope, and all the wonders which the telescope discovers.

Of his moral sentiments it is hardly praise to affirm that they excel those of all other poets; for this superiority he was indebted to his acquaintance with the sacred writings. The ancient epic poets, wanting the light of revelation, were very unskilful teachers of virtue: their principal characters may be great, but they are not amiable. The reader may rise from their works with a greater degree of active or passive fortitude, and sometimes of prudence; but he will be able to carry away few precepts of justice, and none of mercy.

From the Italian writers it appears that the advantages of even Christian knowledge may be possessed in vain. Ariosto's pravity is generally known; and though the *Deliverance of Jerusalem* may be considered as a sacred subject, the poet has been very sparing of moral instruction.

In Milton every line breathes sanctity of thought and purity of manners, except when the train of the narration requires the introduction of the rebellious spirits; and even they are compelled to acknowledge their subjection to God, in such a manner as excites reverence and confirms piety.

Of human beings there are but two; but those two are the parents of mankind, venerable before their fall for dignity and innocence, and amiable after it for repentance and submission. In their first state their affection is tender without weakness, and their piety sublime without presumption. When they have sinned, they show how discord begins in mutual frailty, and how it ought to cease in mutual forbearance, how confidence of the Divine favour is forfeited by sin, and how hope of pardon may be obtained by penitence and prayer. A state of innocence we can only conceive, if indeed in our present misery it be possible to conceive it; but the sentiments and worship proper to a fallen and offending being we have all to learn, as we have all to practise.

The poet, whatever be done, is always great. Our progenitors in their first state conversed with angels; even when folly and sin had degraded them, they had not in their humiliation *the port of mean suitors*; and they rise again to reverential regard when we find that their prayers were heard.

As human passions did not enter the world before the Fall, there is in the *Paradise Lost* little opportunity for the pathetic; but what little there is has not been lost. That passion which is peculiar to rational nature, the anguish arising from the consciousness of transgression, and the horrors attending the sense of the Divine displeasure, are very justly described and forcibly impressed. But the passions are moved only on one occasion; sublimity is the general and prevailing quality of this poem; sublimity variously modified, sometimes descriptive, sometimes argumentative.

The defects and faults of *Paradise Lost*—for faults and defects every work of man must have—it is the business of impartial criticism to discover. As, in displaying the excellence of Milton, I have not made long quotations, because of selecting beauties there had been no end, I shall in the same general manner mention that which seems to deserve censure; for what Englishman can take delight in transcribing passages which, if they lessen the reputation of Milton, diminish in some degree the honour of our country?

The generality of my scheme does not admit the frequent notice of verbal inaccuracies; which Bentley, perhaps better skilled in grammar than poetry, has often found, though he sometimes made them, and which he imputed to the obtrusions of a reviser, whom the author's blindness obliged him to employ; a supposition rash and groundless if he thought it true, and vile and pernicious if, as is said, he in private allowed it to be false.

The plan of *Paradise Lost* has this inconvenience, that it comprises neither human actions nor human manners. The man and woman who act and suffer are in a state which no other man or woman can ever know. The reader finds no transaction in which he can by any effort of imagination place himself; he has therefore little natural curiosity or sympathy.

We all, indeed, feel the effects of Adam's disobedience; we all sin like Adam, and like him must all bewail our offences: we have restless and insidious enemies in the fallen angels, and in the blessed spirits we have guardians and friends; in the redemption of mankind we hope to be included; in the description of heaven and hell we are surely interested, as we are all to reside hereafter either in the regions of horror or bliss.

But these truths are too important to be new; they have been taught to our infancy; they have mingled with our solitary thoughts and familiar conversation, and are habitually interwoven with the whole texture of life. Being therefore not new, they raise no unaccustomed emotion in the mind; what we knew before, we cannot learn; what is not unexpected, cannot surprise.

Of the idea suggested by these awful scenes, from some we recede with reverence, except when stated hours require their association; and from others we shrink with horror, or admit them only as salutary inflictions, as counterpoises to our interests and passions. Such images rather obstruct the career of fancy than incite it.

Pleasure and terror are indeed the genuine sources of poetry; but poetical pleasure must be such as human imagination can at least conceive, and poetical terrors such as human strength and fortitude may combat. The good and evil of eternity are too ponderous for the wings of wit; the mind sinks under them in passive helplessness, content with calm belief and humble adoration.

Known truths, however, may take a different appearance, and be conveyed to the mind by a new train of intermediate images. This Milton has undertaken, and performed with pregnancy and vigour of mind peculiar to himself. Whoever considers the few radical positions which the Scriptures afforded him, will wonder by what energetic operation he expanded them to such extent, and ramified them to so much variety, restrained as he was by religious reverence from licentiousness of fiction.

Here is a full display of the united force of study and genius; of a great accumulation of materials, with judgment to digest, and fancy to combine them: Milton was able to select from nature, or from story, from an ancient fable, or from modern science, whatever could illustrate or adorn his thoughts. An accumulation of knowledge impregnated his mind, fermented by study, and exalted by imagination.

It has been therefore said, without an indecent hyperbole, by one of his encomiasts, that in reading *Paradise Lost* we read a book of universal knowledge.

But original deficience cannot be supplied. The want of human interest is always felt. *Paradise Lost* is one of the books which the reader admires and lays down, and forgets to take up again. None ever wished it longer than it is. Its perusal is a duty rather than a pleasure. We read Milton for instruction, retire harassed and overburdened, and look elsewhere for recreation; we desert our master and seek for companions.

Another inconvenience of Milton's design is, that it requires the description of what cannot be described, the agency of spirits. He saw that immateriality supplied no images, and that he could not show angels acting but by instruments of action; he therefore invested them with form and matter. This, being necessary, was therefore defensible; and he should have secured the consistency of his system, by keeping immateriality out of sight, and enticing his reader to drop it from his thoughts. But he has unhappily perplexed his poetry with his philosophy. His infernal and celestial powers are sometimes pure spirit, and sometimes animated body. When Satan walks with his lance upon the *burning marle*, he has a body; when, in his passage between hell and the new world, he is in danger of sinking in the vacuity, and is supported by a gust of rising vapours, he has a body; when he animates the toad, he seems to be mere spirit, that can penetrate matter at pleasure; when he *starts up in his own shape*, he has at least a determined form; and when he is brought before Gabriel, he has *a spear and a shield*, which he had the power of hiding in the toad, though the arms of the contending angels are evidently material.

The vulgar inhabitants of Pandæmonium, being *incorporeal spirits*, are *at large, though without number*, in a limited space: yet in the battle, when they were overwhelmed by mountains, their armour hurt them, *crushed in upon their substance, now grown gross by sinning*. This likewise happened to the uncorrupted angels, who were overthrown the *sooner for their arms, for unarmed they might easily as spirits have evaded by contraction or remove*. Even as spirits they are hardly spiritual; for *contraction* and *remove* are images of matter; but if they could have escaped without their armour, they might have escaped from it, and left only the empty cover to be battered. Uriel, when he rides on a sunbeam, is material; Satan is material when he is afraid of the prowess of Adam.

The confusion of spirit and matter which pervades the

whole narration of the war of heaven fills it with incongruity; and the book in which it is related is, I believe, the favourite of children, and gradually neglected as knowledge is increased.

After the operation of immaterial agents, which cannot be explained, may be considered that of allegorical persons, which have no real existence. To exalt causes into agents, to invest abstract ideas with form, and animate them with activity, has always been the right of poetry. But such airy beings are, for the most part, suffered only to do their natural office, and retire. Thus Fame tells a tale, and Victory hovers over a general, or perches on a standard; but Fame and Victory can do more. To give them any real employment, or ascribe to them any material agency, is to make them allegorical no longer, but to shock the mind by ascribing effects to non-entity. In the *Prometheus* of Æschylus we see Violence and Strength, and in the *Alcestis* of Euripides we see Death brought upon the stage, all as active persons of the drama; but no precedents can justify absurdity.

Milton's allegory of Sin and Death is undoubtedly faulty. Sin is indeed the mother of Death, and may be allowed to be the portress of hell; but when they stop the journey of Satan, a journey described as real, and when Death offers him battle, the allegory is broken. That Sin and Death should have shown the way to hell, might have been allowed; but they cannot facilitate the passage by building a bridge, because the difficulty of Satan's passage is described as real and sensible, and the bridge ought to be only figurative. The hell assigned to the rebellious spirits is described as not less local than the residence of man. It is placed in some distant part of space, separated from the regions of harmony and order by a chaotic waste and an unoccupied vacuity; but Sin and Death worked up a *mole* of *aggravated soil*, cemented with *asphaltus*; a work too bulky for ideal architects.

This unskilful allegory appears to me one of the greatest faults of the poem; and to this there was no temptation but the author's opinion of its beauty.

To the conduct of the narrative some objection may be made. Satan is with great expectation brought before Gabriel in Paradise, and is suffered to go away unmolested. The creation of man is represented as the consequence of the vacuity left in heaven by the expulsion of the rebels; yet Satan mentions it as a report *rife in heaven* before his departure.

To find sentiments for the state of innocence was very difficult; and something of anticipation perhaps is now and then discovered. Adam's discourse of dreams seems not to be the speculation of a new-created being. I know not whether his answer to the angel's reproof for curiosity does not want something of propriety; it is the speech of a man acquainted with many other men. Some philosophical notions, especially when the philosophy is false, might have been better omitted. The angel, in a comparison, speaks of *timorous deer* before deer were yet timorous, and before Adam could understand the comparison.

Dryden remarks, that Milton has some flats among his elevations. This is only to say that all the parts are not equal. In every work one part must be for the sake of others; a palace must have passages; a poem must have transitions. It is no more to be required that wit should always be blazing than that the sun should always stand at noon. In a great work there is a vicissitude of luminous and opaque parts, as there is in the world a succession of day and night. Milton, when he has expatiated in the sky, may be allowed sometimes to revisit earth; for what other author ever soared so high, or sustained his flight so long?

Milton, being well versed in the Italian poets, appears to have borrowed often from them; and as every man catches something from his companions, his desire of imitating Ariosto's levity has disgraced his work with the "Paradise of Fools"—a fiction not in itself ill-imagined, but too ludicrous for its place.

His play on words, in which he delights too often; his equivocations, which Bentley endeavours to defend by the example of the ancients; his unnecessary and ungraceful use of terms of art, it is not necessary to mention, because they are easily remarked, and generally censured, and at last bear so little proportion to the whole that they scarcely deserve the attention of a critic.

Such are the faults of that wonderful performance *Paradise*

Lost, which he who can put in balance with its beauties must be considered not as nice but as dull, as less to be censured for want of candour, than pitied for want of sensibility.

Of *Paradise Regained*, the general judgment seems now to be right, that it is in many parts elegant, and everywhere instructive. It was not to be supposed that the writer of *Paradise Lost* could ever write without great effusions of fancy, and exalted precepts of wisdom. The basis of *Paradise Regained* is narrow: a dialogue without action can never please like an union of the narrative and dramatic powers. Had this poem been written not by Milton, but by some imitator, it would have claimed and received universal praise.

If *Paradise Regained* has been too much depreciated, *Samson Agonistes* has in requital been too much admired. It could only be by long prejudice, and the bigotry of learning, that Milton could prefer the ancient tragedies, with their encumbrance of a chorus, to the exhibitions of the French and English stages; and it is only by a blind confidence in the reputation of Milton that a drama can be praised in which the intermediate parts have neither cause nor consequence, neither hasten nor retard the catastrophe.

In this tragedy are however many particular beauties, many just sentiments and striking lines; but it wants that power of attracting the attention which a well-connected plan produces.

Milton would not have excelled in dramatic writing; he knew human nature only in the gross, and had never studied the shades of character, nor the combinations of concurring, or the perplexity of contending, passions. He had read much, and knew what books could teach, but had mingled little in the world, and was deficient in the knowledge which experience must confer.

Through all his greater works there prevails an uniform peculiarity of *diction*, a mode and cast of expression which bears little resemblance to that of any former writer, and which is so far removed from common use that an unlearned reader, when he first opens his book, finds himself surprised by a new language.

This novelty has been, by those who can find nothing wrong in Milton, imputed to his laborious endeavours after words suitable to the grandeur of his ideas. *Our language,* says Addison, *sunk under him.* But the truth is that, both in prose and verse, he had formed his style by a perverse and pedantic principle. He was desirous to use English words with a foreign idiom. This in all his prose is discovered and condemned; for there judgment operates freely, neither softened by the beauty nor awed by the dignity of his thoughts; but such is the power of his poetry, that his call is obeyed without resistance, the reader feels himself in captivity to a higher and nobler mind, and criticism sinks in admiration.

Milton's style was not modified by his subject; what is shown with greater extent in *Paradise Lost* may be found in *Comus.* One source of his peculiarity was his familiarity with the Tuscan poets; the disposition of his words is, I think, frequently Italian, perhaps sometimes combined with other tongues. Of him, at last may be said what Jonson says of Spenser, that *he wrote no language,* but has formed what Butler calls a *Babylonish dialect,* in itself harsh and barbarous, but made, by exalted genius and extensive learning, the vehicle of so much instruction and so much pleasure that, like other lovers, we find grace in its deformity.

Whatever be the faults of his diction, he cannot want the praise of copiousness and variety: he was master of his language in its full extent; and has selected the melodious words with such diligence, that from his book alone the Art of English Poetry might be learned.

After his diction, something must be said of his *versification.* The *measure,* he says, *is the English heroic verse without rhyme.* Of this mode he had many examples among the Italians, and some in his own country. The Earl of Surrey is said to have translated one of Virgil's books without rhyme; and, besides our tragedies, a few short poems had appeared in blank verse, particularly one tending to reconcile the nation to Raleigh's wild attempt upon Guiana, and probably written by Raleigh himself. These petty performances cannot be supposed to have much influenced Milton, who more probably took his hint from Trissino's *Italia Liberata;* and, finding blank verse easier than rhyme, was desirous of persuading himself that it is better.

Rhyme, he says, and says truly, *is no necessary adjunct of true poetry*. But, perhaps, of poetry as a mental operation, metre or music is no necessary adjunct: it is, however, by the music of metre that poetry has been discriminated in all languages; and, in languages melodiously constructed with a due proportion of long and short syllables, metre is sufficient. But one language cannot communicate its rules to another: where metre is scanty and imperfect, some help is necessary. The music of the English heroic line strikes the ear so faintly, that it is easily lost, unless all the syllables of every line co-operate together; this co-operation can be only obtained by the preservation of every verse unmingled with another as a distinct system of sounds; and this distinctness is obtained and preserved by the artifice of rhyme. The variety of pauses, so much boasted by the lovers of blank verse, changes the measures of an English poet to the periods of a declaimer; and there are only a few happy readers of Milton who enable their audience to perceive where the lines end or begin. *Blank verse*, said an ingenious critic, *seems to be verse only to the eye*.

Poetry may subsist without rhyme, but English poetry will not often please; nor can rhyme ever be safely spared but where the subject is able to support itself. Blank verse makes some approach to that which is called the *lapidary style*; has neither the easiness of prose, nor the melody of numbers, and therefore tires by long continuance. Of the Italian writers without rhyme, whom Milton alleges as precedents, not one is popular; what reason could urge in its defence has been confuted by the ear.

But, whatever be the advantage of rhyme, I cannot prevail on myself to wish that Milton had been a rhymer; for I cannot wish his work to be other than it is; yet, like other heroes, he is to be admired rather than imitated. He that thinks himself capable of astonishing may write blank verse; but those that hope only to please must condescend to rhyme.

The highest praise of genius is original invention. Milton cannot be said to have contrived the structure of an epic poem, and therefore owes reverence to that vigour and amplitude of mind to which all generations must be indebted for the art of poetical narration, for the texture of the fable, the variation of incidents, the interposition of dialogue, and all the stratagems that surprise and enchain attention. But, of all the borrowers from Homer, Milton is perhaps the least indebted. He was naturally a thinker for himself, confident of his own abilities, and disdainful of help or hindrance: he did not refuse admission to the thoughts or images of his predecessors, but he did not seek them. From his contemporaries he neither courted nor received support; there is in his writings nothing by which the pride of other authors might be gratified, or favour gained; no exchange of praise, nor solicitation of support. His great works were performed under discountenance, and in blindness, but difficulties vanished at his touch; he was born for whatever is arduous; and his work is not the greatest of heroic poems, only because it is not the first.

SAMUEL BUTLER

1612–1680

Born at Strensham in Worcestershire—Educated either at Oxford or Cambridge—Enters the Service of the Countess of Kent—Employed by Selden, and acquires the Friendship of Cooper the Painter—Made Steward of Ludlow Castle—Marries—Sir Samuel Luke—Publishes *Hudibras* in Three Parts—His Poverty—Death and Burial in St. Paul's, Covent Garden—Monument in Westminster Abbey—Works and Character.

Of the great author of *Hudibras* there is a Life prefixed to the latter editions of his poem, by an unknown writer, and therefore of disputable authority; and some account is incidentally given by Wood, who confesses the uncertainty of his own narrative; more, however, than they knew cannot now be learned, and nothing remains but to compare and copy them.

Samuel Butler was born in the parish of Strensham, in Worcestershire, according to his biographer, in 1612. This account Dr. Nash finds confirmed by the register. He was christened February 14.

His father's condition is variously represented. Wood mentions him as competently wealthy; but Mr. Longueville, the son of Butler's principal friend, says he was an honest farmer with some small estate, who made a shift to educate his son at the grammar school of Worcester, under Mr. Henry Bright, from whose care he removed for a short time to Cambridge; but for want of money was never made a member of any college. Wood leaves us rather doubtful whether he went to Cambridge or Oxford; but at last makes him pass six or seven years at Cambridge, without knowing in what hall or college: yet it can hardly be imagined that he lived so long in either university but as belonging to one house or another; and it is still less likely that he could have so long inhabited a place of learning with so little distinction as to leave his residence uncertain. Dr. Nash has discovered that his father was owner of a house and a little land, worth about 8*l.* a year, still called *Butler's tenement.*

Wood has his information from his brother, whose narrative placed him at Cambridge, in opposition to that of his neighbours, which sent him to Oxford. The brother's seems the best authority, till, by confessing his inability to tell his hall or college, he gives reason to suspect that he was resolved to bestow on him an academical education; but durst not name a college, for fear of a detection.

He was for some time, according to the author of his Life, clerk to Mr. Jefferys, of Earl's Croomb in Worcestershire, an eminent justice of the peace. In his service he had not only leisure for study, but for recreation: his amusements were music and painting; and the reward of his pencil was the friendship of the celebrated Cooper. Some pictures, said to be his, were shown to Dr. Nash, at Earl's Croomb; but, when he inquired for them some years afterwards, he found them destroyed, to stop windows, and owns that they hardly deserved a better fate.

He was afterwards admitted into the family of the Countess of Kent, where he had the use of a library; and so much recommended himself to Selden, that he was often employed by him in literary business. Selden, as is well known, was steward to the Countess, and is supposed to have gained much of his wealth by managing her estate.

In what character Butler was admitted into that lady's service, how long he continued in it, and why he left it, is, like the other incidents of his life, utterly unknown.

The vicissitudes of his condition placed him afterwards in the family of Sir Samuel Luke, one of Cromwell's officers. Here he observed so much of the character of the sectaries, that he is said to have written or begun his poem at this time; and it is likely that such a design would be formed in a place where he saw the principles and practices of the rebels, audacious and undisguised in the confidence of success.

At length the King returned, and the time came in which loyalty hoped for its reward. Butler, however, was only made secretary to the Earl of Carbury, president of the principality of Wales, who conferred on him the stewardship of Ludlow Castle, when the Court of the Marches was revived.

In this part of his life he married Mrs. Herbert, a gentlewoman of a good family, and lived, says Wood, upon her fortune, having studied the common law, but never practised it. A fortune she had, says his biographer, but it was lost by bad securities.

In 1663 was published the first part, containing three cantos, of the poem of *Hudibras*, which, as Prior relates, was made known at Court by the taste and influence of the Earl of Dorset. When it was known, it was necessarily admired: the King quoted, the courtiers studied, and the whole party of the royalists applauded it. Every eye watched for the golden shower which was to fall upon the author, who certainly was not without his part in the general expectation.

In 1664 the second part appeared; the curiosity of the nation was rekindled, and the writer was again praised and elated. But praise was his whole reward. Clarendon, says Wood, gave him reason to hope for "places and employments of value and credit"; but no such advantages did he ever obtain. It is reported that the King once gave him three hundred guineas; but of this temporary bounty I find no proof.

Wood relates that he was secretary to Villiers Duke of Buckingham, when he was Chancellor of Cambridge: this is doubted by the other writer, who yet allows the Duke to have been his frequent benefactor. That both these accounts are false there is reason to suspect, from a story told by Packe, in his account of the *Life of Wycherley*; and from some verses which Mr. Thyer has published in the author's *Remains*.

"Mr. Wycherley," says Packe, "had always laid hold of any opportunity which offered of representing to the Duke of Buckingham how well Mr. Butler had deserved of the royal family by writing his inimitable *Hudibras*; and that it was a reproach to the Court, that a person of his loyalty and wit should suffer in obscurity, and under the wants he did. The Duke seemed always to hearken to him with attention enough; and after some time undertook to recommend his pretensions to his Majesty. Mr. Wycherley, in hopes to keep him steady to his word, obtained of his Grace to name a day when he might introduce that modest and unfortunate poet to his new patron. At last an appointment was made, and the place of meeting was agreed to be the Roebuck. Mr. Butler and his friend attended accordingly: the Duke joined them; but, as the d——l would have it, the door of the room where they sat was open, and his Grace, who had seated himself near it, observing a pimp of his acquaintance (the creature too was a knight) trip by with a brace of ladies, immediately quitted his engagement, to follow another kind of business, at which he was more ready than in doing good offices to men of desert; though no one was better qualified than he was, both in regard to his fortune and understanding, to protect them, and, from that time to the day of his death, poor Butler never found the least effect of his promise!"

Such is the story. The verses are written with a degree of acrimony such as neglect and disappointment might naturally excite; and such as it would be hard to imagine Butler capable of expressing against a man who had any claim to his gratitude.

Notwithstanding this discouragement and neglect he still prosecuted his design; and in 1678 published the third part, which still leaves the poem imperfect and abrupt. How much more he originally intended, or with what events the action was to be concluded, it is vain to conjecture. Nor can it be thought strange that he should stop here, however unexpectedly. To write without reward is sufficiently unpleasing. He had now arrived at an age when he might think it proper to be in jest no longer, and perhaps his health might now begin to fail.

He died in 1680; and Mr. Longueville, having unsuccessfully solicited a subscription for his interment in Westminster Abbey, buried him at his own cost in the churchyard of Covent Garden. Dr. Simon Patrick read the service.

Granger was informed by Dr. Pearce, who named for his authority Mr. Lowndes of the Treasury, that Butler had a yearly pension of 100*l*. This is contradicted by all tradition, by the complaints of Oldham, and by the reproaches of Dryden, and, I am afraid, will never be confirmed.

About sixty years afterwards, Mr. Barber, a printer, mayor of London, and a friend to Butler's principles, bestowed on him a monument in Westminster Abbey, thus inscribed:

M. S.
Samuelis Butleri,
Qui *Strenshamiæ* in agro *Vigorn.* nat. 1612,
obiit *Lond.* 1680.
Vir doctus imprimis, acer, integer;
Operibus Ingenii, non item præmiis, fœlix:
Satyrici apud nos Carminis Artifex egregius;
Quo simulatæ Religionis Larvam detraxit,
Et Perduellium scelera liberrime exagitavit;
Scriptorum in suo genere, Primus & Postremus.
Ne, cui vivo deerant ferè omnia,
Deesset etiam mortuo Tumulus,
Hoc tandem posito marmore, curavit
Johannes Barber, Civis *Londinensis*, 1721.

After his death were published three small volumes of his posthumous works, I know not by whom collected, or by what authority ascertained; and, lately [1759], two volumes more have been printed by Mr. Thyer of Manchester, indubitably genuine. From none of these pieces can his life be traced, or his character discovered. Some verses, in the last collection, show him to have been among those who ridiculed the institution of the Royal Society, of which the enemies were for some time very numerous and very acrimonious, for what reason it is hard to conceive, since the philosophers professed not to advance doctrines, but to produce facts; and the most zealous enemy of innovation must admit the gradual progress of experience, however he may oppose hypothetical temerity.

In this mist of obscurity passed the life of Butler, a man whose name can only perish with his language. The mode and place of his education are unknown; the events of his life are variously related; and all that can be told with certainty is, that he was poor.

The poem of *Hudibras* is one of those compositions of which a nation may justly boast, as the images which it exhibits are domestic, the sentiments unborrowed and unexpected, and the strain of diction original and peculiar. We must not, however, suffer the pride which we assume as the countrymen of Butler to make any encroachment upon justice, nor appropriate those honours which others have a right to share. The poem of *Hudibras* is not wholly English; the original idea is to be found in the history of *Don Quixote*—a book to which a mind of the greatest powers may be indebted without disgrace.

Cervantes shows a man who, having by the incessant perusal of incredible tales subjected his understanding to his imagination, and familiarised his mind by pertinacious meditations to trains of incredible events and scenes of impossible existence, goes out in the pride of knighthood to redress wrongs and defend virgins, to rescue captive princesses, and tumble usurpers from their thrones, attended by a squire, whose cunning, too low for the suspicion of a generous mind, enables him often to cheat his master.

The hero of Butler is a Presbyterian justice, who, in the confidence of legal authority and the rage of zealous ignorance, ranges the country to repress superstition and correct abuses, accompanied by an Independent clerk, disputatious and obstinate, with whom he often debates, but never conquers him.

Cervantes had so much kindness for Don Quixote, that, however he embarrasses him with absurd distresses, he gives him so much sense and virtue as may preserve our esteem; wherever he is, or whatever he does, he is made by matchless dexterity commonly ridiculous, but never contemptible.

But for poor Hudibras, his poet had no tenderness; he chooses not that any pity should be shown or respect paid him; he gives him up at once to laughter and contempt, without any quality that can dignify or protect him.

In forming the character of Hudibras, and describing his person and habiliments, the author seems to labour with a tumultuous confusion of dissimilar ideas. He had read the history of the mock knights-errant; he knew the notions and manners of a Presbyterian magistrate, and tried to unite the absurdities of both, however distant, in one personage. Thus he gives him that pedantic ostentation of knowledge which has no relation to chivalry, and loads him with martial encumbrances that can add nothing to his civil dignity. He sends him out a *colonelling*, and yet never brings him within sight of war.

If Hudibras be considered as the representative of the Presbyterians, it is not easy to say why his weapons should be represented as ridiculous or useless; for, whatever judgment might be passed upon their knowledge or their arguments, experience had sufficiently shown that their swords were not to be despised.

The hero, thus compounded of swaggerer and pedant, of knight and justice, is led forth to action, with his squire Ralpho, an Independent enthusiast.

Of the contexture of events planned by the author, which is called the action of the poem, since it is left imperfect, no judgment can be made. It is probable that the hero was to be led through many luckless adventures, which would give occasion, like his attack upon the *bear and fiddle*, to expose the ridiculous rigour of the sectaries; like his encounter with Sidrophel and Whacum, to make superstition and credulity contemptible; or, like his recourse to the low retailer of the law, discover the fraudulent practices of different professions.

What series of events he would have formed, or in what manner he would have rewarded or punished his hero, it is now vain to conjecture. His work must have had, as it seems, the defect which Dryden imputes to Spenser; the action could not have been one; there could only have been a succession of incidents, each of which might have happened without the rest, and which could not at all co-operate to any single conclusion.

The discontinuity of the action might, however, have been easily forgiven, if there had been action enough; but I believe every reader regrets the paucity of events, and complains that in the poem of *Hudibras*, as in the history of Thucydides, there is more said than done. The scenes are too seldom changed, and the attention is tired with long conversation.

It is, indeed, much more easy to form dialogues than to contrive adventures. Every position makes way for an argument, and every objection dictates an answer. When two disputants are engaged upon a complicated and extensive question, the difficulty is not to continue, but to end the controversy. But whether it be that we comprehend but few of the possibilities of life, or that life itself affords little variety, every man who has tried knows how much labour it will cost to form such a combination of circumstances as shall have at once the grace of novelty and credibility, and delight fancy without violence to reason.

Perhaps the Dialogue of this poem is not perfect. Some power of engaging the attention might have been added to it by quicker reciprocation, by seasonable interruptions, by sudden questions, and by a nearer approach to dramatic sprightliness; without which fictitious speeches will always tire, however sparkling with sentences, and however variegated with allusions.

The great source of pleasure is variety. Uniformity must tire at last, though it be uniformity of excellence. We love to expect; and when expectation is disappointed or gratified, we want to be again expecting. For this impatience of the present, whoever would please must make provision. The skilful writer *irritat, mulcet,* makes a due distribution of the still and animated parts. It is for want of this artful intertexture, and those necessary changes, that the whole of a book may be tedious, though all the parts are praised.

If inexhaustible wit could give perpetual pleasure, no eye would ever leave half-read the work of Butler; for what poet has ever brought so many remote images so happily together? It is scarcely possible to peruse a page without finding some association of images that was never found before. By the first paragraph the reader is amused, by the next he is delighted, and by a few more strained to astonishment; but astonishment is a toilsome pleasure; he is soon weary of wondering, and longs to be diverted.

> Omnia vult belle Matho dicere, dic aliquando
> Et bene, dic neutrum, dic aliquando male.

Imagination is useless without knowledge: nature gives in vain the power of combination, unless study and observation supply materials to be combined. Butler's treasures of knowledge appear proportioned to his expense: whatever topic employs his mind, he shows himself qualified to expand and illustrate it with all the accessaries that books can furnish; he is found not only to have travelled the beaten road, but the byepaths of literature; not only to have taken general surveys, but to have examined particulars with minute inspection.

If the French boast the learning of Rabelais, we need not be afraid of confronting them with Butler.

But the most violent parts of his performance are those which retired study and native wit cannot supply. He that merely makes a book from books may be useful, but can scarcely be great. Butler had not suffered life to glide beside him unseen or unobserved. He had watched with great diligence the operations of human nature, and traced the effects of opinion, humour, interest, and passion. From such remarks proceeded that great number of sententious distichs which have passed into conversation, and are added as proverbial axioms to the general stock of practical knowledge.

When any work has been viewed and admired, the first question of intelligent curiosity is, how was it performed? *Hudibras* was not a hasty effusion; it was not produced by a sudden tumult of imagination, or a short paroxysm of violent labour. To accumulate such a mass of sentiments at the call of accidental desire, or of sudden necessity, is beyond the reach and power of the most active and comprehensive mind. I am informed by Mr. Thyer of Manchester, the excellent editor of this author's reliques, that he could show something like *Hudibras* in prose. He has in his possession the commonplace book in which Butler reposited, not such events or precepts as are gathered by reading, but such remarks, similitudes, allusions, assemblages, or inferences, as occasion prompted, or meditation produced, those thoughts that were generated in his own mind, and might be usefully applied to some future purpose. Such is the labour of those who write for immortality.

But human works are not easily found without a perishable part. Of the ancient poets every reader feels the mythology tedious and oppressive. Of *Hudibras*, the manners, being founded on opinions, are temporary and local, and therefore become every day less intelligible and less striking. What Cicero says of philosophy is true likewise of wit and humour, that "time effaces the fictions of opinion, and confirms the determinations of Nature." Such manners as depend upon standing relations and general passions are co-extended with the race of man; but those modifications of life and peculiarities of practice, which are the progeny of error and perverseness, or at best of some accidental influence or transient persuasion, must perish with their parents.

Much, therefore, of that humour which transported the last century with merriment is lost to us, who do not know the sour solemnity, the sullen superstition, the gloomy moroseness, and the stubborn scruples of the ancient Puritans; or, if we knew them, derive our information only from books, or from tradition, have never had them before our eyes, and cannot, but by recollection and study, understand the lines in which they are satirised. Our grandfathers knew the picture from the life; we judge of the life by contemplating the picture.

It is scarcely possible, in the regularity and composure of the present time, to image the tumult of absurdity and clamour of contradiction which perplexed doctrine, disordered practice, and disturbed both public and private quiet, in that age when subordination was broken, and awe was hissed away; when any unsettled innovator who could hatch a half-formed notion produced it to the public; when every man might become a preacher, and almost every preacher could collect a congregation.

The wisdom of the nation is very reasonably supposed to reside in the parliament. What can be concluded of the lower classes of the people, when, in one of the parliaments summoned by Cromwell, it was seriously proposed that all the records in the Tower should be burnt, that all memory of things past should be effaced, and that the whole system of life should commence anew?

We have never been witnesses of animosities excited by the use of mince-pies and plum-porridge; nor seen with what abhorrence those who could eat them at all other times of the year would shrink from them in December. An old Puritan, who was alive in my childhood, being, at one of the feasts of the church, invited by a neighbour to partake his cheer, told him that if he would treat him at an alehouse with beer, brewed for all times and seasons, he should accept his kindness, but would have none of his superstitious meats and drinks.

One of the puritanical tenets was the illegality of all games of chance; and he that reads Gataker upon *Lots* may see how much learning and reason one of the first scholars of his age thought necessary to prove that it was no crime to throw a die, or play at cards, or to hide a shilling for the reckoning.

Astrology, however, against which so much of the satire is directed, was not more the folly of the Puritans than of others. It had in that time a very extensive dominion. Its predictions raised hopes and fears in minds which ought to have rejected it with contempt. In hazardous undertakings care was taken to begin under the influence of a propitious planet; and when the king was prisoner in Carisbrook Castle, an astrologer was consulted what hour would be found most favourable to an escape.

What effect this poem had upon the public—whether it shamed imposture, or reclaimed credulity, is not easily determined. Cheats can seldom stand long against laughter. It is certain that the credit of planetary intelligence wore fast away, though some men of knowledge, and Dryden among them, continued to believe that conjunctions and oppositions had a great part in the distribution of good or evil, and in the government of sublunary things.

Poetical action ought to be probable upon certain suppositions, and such probability as burlesque requires is here violated only by one incident. Nothing can show more plainly the necessity of doing something, and the difficulty of finding something to do, than that Butler was reduced to transfer to his hero the flagellation of Sancho, not the most agreeable fiction of Cervantes; very suitable indeed to the manners of that age and nation, which ascribed wonderful efficacy to voluntary penances, but so remote from the practice and opinions of the

Hudibrastic time, that judgment and imagination are alike offended.

The diction of this poem is grossly familiar, and the numbers purposely neglected, except in a few places where the
thoughts, by their native excellence, secure themselves from
violation, being such as mean language cannot express. The
mode of versification has been blamed by Dryden, who regrets
that the heroic measure was not rather chosen. To the critical
sentence of Dryden the highest reverence would be due were
not his decisions often precipitate, and his opinions immature.
When he wished to change the measure, he probably would
have been willing to change more. If he intended that, when
the numbers were heroic, the diction should still remain vulgar, he planned a very heterogeneous and unnatural composition. If he preferred a general stateliness both of sound and
words, he can be only understood to wish Butler had undertaken a different work.

The measure is quick, sprightly, and colloquial, suitable to
the vulgarity of the words and the levity of the sentiments.
But such numbers and such diction can gain regard only when
they are used by a writer whose vigour of fancy and copiousness of knowledge entitle him to contempt of ornaments, and
who, in confidence of the novelty and justness of his conceptions, can afford to throw metaphors and epithets away. To
another that conveys common thoughts in careless versification, it will only be said, "Pauper videri Cinna vult, et est
pauper." The meaning and diction will be worthy of each
other, and criticism may justly doom them to perish together.

Nor even though another Butler should arise, would another
Hudibras obtain the same regard. Burlesque consists in a disproportion between the style and the sentiments, or between
the adventitious sentiments and the fundamental subject. It
therefore, like all bodies compounded of heterogeneous parts,
contains in it a principle of corruption. All disproportion is
unnatural; and from what is unnatural we can derive only the
pleasure which novelty produces. We admire it awhile as a
strange thing; but when it is no longer strange, we perceive
its deformity. It is a kind of artifice which, by frequent repe-

tition, detects itself; and the reader, learning in time what he is to expect, lays down his book, as the spectator turns away from a second exhibition of those tricks of which the only use is to show that they can be played.

EARL OF ROCHESTER

1647–1680

Born at Ditchley, in Oxfordshire—Educated at Oxford
—Becomes a Favourite with Charles II.—Early and con-
tinued Dissipation—His Quarrel with Lord Mulgrave—
Burnet's Account of his last Illness—Death and Burial at
Spilsbury, in Oxfordshire—His Character as a Poet.

John Wilmot, afterwards Earl of Rochester, the son of
Henry, Earl of Rochester, better known by the title of Lord
Wilmot, so often mentioned in Clarendon's *History*, was born
April 10, 1647, at Ditchley in Oxfordshire. After a grammatical education at the school of Burford, he entered a nobleman
into Wadham College in 1659, only twelve years old; and in
1661, at fourteen, was, with some other persons of high rank,
made Master of Arts by Lord Clarendon in person.

He travelled afterwards into France and Italy; and, at his
return, devoted himself to the Court. In 1665 he went to sea
with Sandwich, and distinguished himself at Bergen by uncommon intrepidity; and the next summer served again on
board Sir Edward Spragge, who, in the heat of the engagement,
having a message of reproof to send to one of his captains,
could find no man ready to carry it but Wilmot, who, in an
open boat, went and returned amidst the storm of shot.

But his reputation for bravery was not lasting; he was reproached with slinking away in street quarrels, and leaving his
companions to shift as they could without him; and Sheffield,
Duke of Buckingham, has left a story of his refusal to fight
him.

He had very early an inclination to intemperance, which he

totally subdued in his travels; but, when he became a courtier, he unhappily addicted himself to dissolute and vicious company, by which his principles were corrupted, and his manners depraved. He lost all sense of religious restraint; and, finding it not convenient to admit the authority of laws which he was resolved not to obey, sheltered his wickedness behind infidelity.

As he excelled in that noisy and licentious merriment which wine incites, his companions eagerly encouraged him in excess, and he willingly indulged it; till, as he confessed to Dr. Burnet, he was for five years together continually drunk, or so much inflamed by frequent ebriety as in no interval to be master of himself.

In this state he played many frolics, which it is not for his honour that we should remember, and which are not now distinctly known. He often pursued low amours in mean disguises, and always acted with great exactness and dexterity the characters which he assumed.

He once erected a stage on Tower-hill, and harangued the populace as a mountebank; and, having made physic part of his study, is said to have practised it successfully.

He was so much in favour with King Charles that he was made one of the gentlemen of the bedchamber, and ranger of Woodstock Park.

Having an active and inquisitive mind, he never, except in his paroxysms of intemperance, was wholly negligent of study: he read what is considered as polite learning so much, that he is mentioned by Wood as the greatest scholar of all the nobility. Sometimes he retired into the country, and amused himself with writing libels, in which he did not pretend to confine himself to truth.

His favourite author in French was Boileau, and in English Cowley.

Thus in a course of drunken gaiety and gross sensuality, with intervals of study perhaps yet more criminal, with an avowed contempt of all decency and order, a total disregard to every moral, and a resolute denial of every religious obligation, he lived worthless and useless, and blazed out his youth and his health in lavish voluptuousness; till, at the age of one-and-thirty, he had exhausted the fund of life, and reduced himself to a state of weakness and decay.

At this time he was led to an acquaintance with Dr. Burnet, to whom he laid open with great freedom the tenor of his opinions, and the course of his life, and from whom he received such conviction of the reasonableness of moral duty, and the truth of Christianity, as produced a total change both of his manners and opinions. The account of these salutary conferences is given by Burnet in a book entitled *Some Passages of the Life and Death of John, Earl of Rochester*, which the critic ought to read for its elegance, the philosopher for its arguments, and the saint for its piety. It were an injury to the reader to offer him an abridgment.

He died July 26, 1680, before he had completed his thirty-fourth year; and was so worn away by a long illness that life went out without a struggle.

Lord Rochester was eminent for the vigour of his colloquial wit, and remarkable for many wild pranks and sallies of extravagance. The glare of his general character diffused itself upon his writings; the compositions of a man whose name was heard so often were certain of attention, and from many readers certain of applause. This blaze of reputation is not yet quite extinguished; and his poetry still retains some splendour beyond that which genius has bestowed.

Wood and Burnet give us reason to believe that much was imputed to him which he did not write. I know not by whom the original collection was made, or by what authority its genuineness was ascertained. The first edition was published in the year of his death, with an air of concealment, professing in the title-page to be printed at "Antwerp."

Of some of the pieces, however, there is no doubt. The *Imitation of Horace's Satire*, the *Verses to Lord Mulgrave*, the *Satire against Man*, the *Verses upon Nothing*, and perhaps some others, are, I believe, genuine, and perhaps most of those which this collection exhibits.

As he cannot be supposed to have found leisure for any course of continued study, his pieces are commonly short, such as one fit of resolution would produce.

His songs have no particular character; they tell, like other songs, in smooth and easy language, of scorn and kindness, dismission and desertion, absence and inconstancy, with the commonplaces of artificial courtship. They are commonly smooth and easy; but have little nature, and little sentiment.

His imitation of Horace on Lucilius is not inelegant or unhappy. In the reign of Charles the Second began that adaptation, which has since been very frequent, of ancient poetry to present times; and perhaps few will be found where the parallelism is better preserved than in this. The versification is indeed sometimes careless, but it is sometimes vigorous and weighty.

The strongest effort of his muse is his poem upon *Nothing*. He is not the first who has chosen this barren topic for the boast of his fertility. There is a poem called *Nihil* in Latin by Passerat, a poet and critic of the sixteenth century in France, who, in his own epitaph, expresses his zeal for good poetry thus:

> —— Molliter ossa quiescent
> Sint modo carminibus non onerata malis.

His works are not common, and therefore I shall subjoin his verses.

In examining this performance, *Nothing* must be considered as having not only a negative but a kind of positive signification; as I need not fear thieves, I have *nothing*, and *nothing* is a very powerful protector. In the first part of the sentence it is taken negatively; in the second it is taken positively, as an agent. In one of Boileau's lines it was a question, whether he should use *à rien faire*, or *à ne rien faire*; and the first was preferred because it gave *rien* a sense in some sort positive. *Nothing* can be a subject only in its positive sense, and such a sense is given it in the first line:

> *Nothing*, thou elder brother ev'n to Shade.

In this line, I know not whether he does not allude to a curious book *De Umbra*, by Wowerus, which, having told the qualities of Shade, concludes with a poem, in which are these lines:

Jam primum terram validis circumspice claustris
Suspensam totam, decus admirabile mundi
Terrasque tractusque maris, camposque liquentes
Aeris et vasti laqueata palatia cœli——
Omnibus UMBRA prior.

The positive sense is generally preserved, with great skill, through the whole poem; though sometimes in a subordinate sense, the negative *nothing* is injudiciously mingled. Passerat confounds the two senses.

Another of his most vigorous pieces is his lampoon on Sir Car Scroop, who, in a poem called *The Praise of Satire*, had some lines like these:

He who can push into a midnight fray
His brave companion, and then run away,
Leaving him to be murder'd in the street,
Then put it off with some buffoon conceit:
Him, thus dishonour'd, for a wit you own,
And court him as top fiddler of the town.

This was meant of Rochester, whose *buffoon conceit* was, I suppose, a saying often mentioned, that *every man would be a coward if he durst*; and drew from him those furious verses, to which Scroop made in reply an epigram, ending with these lines:

Thou canst hurt no man's fame with thy ill word;
Thy pen is full as harmless as thy sword.

Of the satire against Man, Rochester can only claim what remains when all Boileau's part is taken away.

In all his works there is sprightliness and vigour, and everywhere may be found tokens of a mind which study might have carried to excellence. What more can be expected from a life spent in ostentatious contempt of regularity, and ended before the abilities of many other men began to be displayed?

Poema CI. V. JOANNIS PASSERATII,

Regii in Academia Parisiensi Professoris,

Ad ornatissimum virum ERRICUM MEMMIUM

Janus adest, festæ poscunt sua dona Kalendæ,
Munus abest festis quod possim offerre Kalendis.
Siccine Castalius nobis exaruit humor?
Usque adeò ingenii nostri est exhausta facultas,
Immunem ut videat redeuntis janitor anni?
Quod nusquam est, potius nova per vestigia quæram.

Ecce autem partes dum sese versat in omnes
Invenit mea Musa NIHIL, ne despice munus.
Nam NIHIL est gemmis, NIHIL est pretiosius auro.
Huc animum, huc igitur vultus adverte benignos;
Res nova narratur quæ nulli audita priorum,
Ausonii et Graii dixerunt cætera vates,
Ausoniæ indictum NIHIL est Græcæque Camœnæ.

E cœlo quacunque Ceres sua prospicit arva,
Aut genitor liquidis orbem complectitur ulnis
Oceanus, NIHIL interitus et originis expers.
Immortale NIHIL, NIHIL omni parte beatum.
Quòd si hinc majestas et vis divina probatur,
Num quid honore deûm, num quid dignabimur aris?
Conspectu lucis NIHIL est jucundius almæ,
Vere NIHIL, NIHIL irriguo formosius horto,
Floridius pratis, Zephyri clementius aura;
In bello sanctum NIHIL est, Martisque tumultu:
Justum in pace NIHIL, NIHIL est in fœdere tutum.
Felix cui NIHIL est, (fuerant hæc vota Tibullo)
Non timet insidias; fures, incendia temnit:
Sollicitas sequitur nullo sub judice lites.
Ille ipse invictis qui subjicit omnia fatis
Zenonis sapiens, NIHIL admiratur et optat.
Socraticique gregis fuit ista scientia quondam,
Scire NIHIL, studio cui nunc incumbitur uni.
Nec quicquam in ludo mavult didicisse juventus,
Ad magnas quia ducit opes, et culmen honorum.
Nosce NIHIL, nosces fertur quod Pythagoreæ
Grano hærere fabæ, cui vox adjuncta negantis.

Multi Mercurio freti duce viscera terræ
Pura liquefaciunt simul, et patrimonia miscent,
Arcano instantes operi, et carbonibus atris,
Qui tandem exhausti damnis, fractique labore,
Inveniunt atque inventum NIHIL usque requirunt,
Hoc dimetiri non ulla decempeda possit:
Nec numeret Libycæ numerum qui callet arenæ:
Et Phœbo ignotum NIHIL est, NIHIL altius astris,
Túque, tibi licet eximium sit mentis acumen,
Omnem in naturam penetrans, et in abdita rerum,
Pace tua, Memmi, NIHIL ignorare vidêris.
Sole tamen NIHIL est, et puro clarius igne.
Tange NIHIL, dicesque NIHIL sine corpore tangi.
Cerne NIHIL, cerni dices NIHIL absque colore.
Surdum audit loquitúrque NIHIL sine voce, volatque
Absque ope pennarum, et graditur sine cruribus ullis.
Absque loco motuque NIHIL per inane vagatur.
Humano generi utilius NIHIL arte medendi.
Ne rhombos igitur, neu Thessala murmura tentet
Idalia vacuum trajectus arundine pectus,
Neu legat Idæo Dictæum in vetrice gramen.
Vulneribus sævi NIHIL auxiliatur amoris.
Vexerit et quemvis trans mœstas portitor undas,
Ad superos imo NIHIL hunc revocabit ab orco.
Inferni NIHIL inflectit præcordia regis,
Parcarûmque colos, et inexorabile pensum.
Obruta Phlegræis campis Titania pubes
Fulmineo sensit NIHIL esse potentius ictu:
Porrigitur magni NIHIL extra mœnia mundi:
Diique NIHIL metuunt. Quid longo carmine plura
Commemorem? virtute NIHIL præstantius ipsa,
Splendidius NIHIL est; NIHIL est Jove denique majus.
Sed tempus finem argutis imponere nugis:
Ne tibi si multa laudem mea carmina charta,
De NIHILO NIHILI pariant fastidia versus.

EARL OF ROSCOMMON
1634?–1684

Born in Ireland—Educated at Caen—Preternatural Intelligence of his Father's Death—Returns to England at the Restoration—His Love of Play—Endeavours to refine the English Language—Death and Burial in Westminster Abbey—Purity and Excellence of his Writings.

Wentworth Dillon, Earl of Roscommon, was the son of James Dillon and Elizabeth Wentworth, sister to the Earl of Strafford. He was born in Ireland during the lieutenancy of Strafford, who, being both his uncle and his godfather, gave him his own surname. His father, the third Earl of Roscommon, had been converted by Usher to the Protestant religion; and when the Popish rebellion broke out, Strafford, thinking the family in great danger from the fury of the Irish, sent for his godson, and placed him at his own seat in Yorkshire, where he was instructed in Latin, which he learned so as to write it with purity and elegance, though he was never able to retain the rules of grammar.

Such is the account given by Mr. Fenton, from whose notes on Waller most of this account must be borrowed, though I know not whether all that he relates is certain. The instructor whom he assigns to Roscommon is one Dr. Hall, by whom he cannot mean the famous Hall, then an old man and a bishop.

When the storm broke out upon Strafford, his house was a shelter no longer; and Dillon, by the advice of Usher, was sent to Caen, where the Protestants had then an university, and continued his studies under Bochart.

Young Dillon, who was sent to study under Bochart, and

who is represented as having already made great proficiency in
literature, could not be more than nine years old. Strafford
went to govern Ireland in 1633, and was put to death eight
years afterwards. That he was sent to Caen is certain: that he
was a great scholar may be doubted.

At Caen he is said to have had some preternatural intelligence of his father's death.

"The Lord Roscommon, being a boy of ten years of age, at
Caen in Normandy, one day was, as it were, madly extravagant
in playing, leaping, getting over the table-boards, etc. 'He was
wont to be sober enough,' they said, 'God grant this bodes no
ill-luck to him!' In the heat of this extravagant fit, he cries
out, '*My father is dead.*' A fortnight after, news came from
Ireland that his father was dead. This account I had from Mr.
Knolles, who was his governor, and then with him,—since secretary to the Earl of Strafford; and I have heard his Lordship's
relations confirm the same."—AUBREY's *Miscellany*, ed. 1696,
p. 89.

The present age is very little inclined to favour any accounts
of this kind, nor will the name of Aubrey much recommend it
to credit: it ought not, however, to be omitted, because better
evidence of a fact cannot easily be found than is here offered,
and it must be by preserving such relations that we may at
last judge how much they are to be regarded. If we stay to
examine this account, we shall see difficulties on both sides:
here is the relation of a fact given by a man who had no interest to deceive, and who could not be deceived himself; and
here is, on the other hand, a miracle which produces no effect;
the order of nature is interrupted to discover not a future but
only a distant event, the knowledge of which is of no use to
him to whom it is revealed. Between these difficulties what
way shall be found? Is reason or testimony to be rejected? I
believe what Osborne says of an appearance of sanctity may be
applied to such impulses or anticipations as this: *Do not
wholly slight them, because they may be true; but do not
easily trust them, because they may be false.*

The state both of England and Ireland was at this time such,
that he who was absent from either country had very little
temptation to return: and therefore Roscommon, when he left

Caen, travelled into Italy, and amused himself with its antiquities, and particularly with medals, in which he acquired uncommon skill.

At the Restoration, with the other friends of monarchy, he came to England, was made captain of the band of pensioners, and learned so much of the dissoluteness of the Court that he addicted himself immoderately to gaming, by which he was engaged in frequent quarrels, and which undoubtedly brought upon him its usual concomitants, extravagance and distress.

After some time a dispute about part of his estate forced him into Ireland, where he was made, by the Duke of Ormond, captain of the guards, and met with an adventure, thus related by Fenton:

"He was at Dublin as much as ever distempered with the same fatal affection for play, which engaged him in one adventure that well deserves to be related. As he returned to his lodgings from a gaming-table he was attacked in the dark by three ruffians, who were employed to assassinate him. The Earl defended himself with so much resolution that he despatched one of the aggressors; whilst a gentleman, accidentally passing that way, interposed and disarmed another; the third secured himself by flight. This generous assistant was a disbanded officer, of a good family and fair reputation, who, by what we call the partiality of fortune, to avoid censuring the iniquities of the times, wanted even a plain suit of clothes to make a decent appearance at the castle. But his Lordship on this occasion presenting him to the Duke of Ormond, with great importunity prevailed with his Grace that he might resign his post of captain of the guards to his friend; which for about three years the gentleman enjoyed, and upon his death the Duke returned the commission to his generous benefactor."

When he had finished his business he returned to London; was made Master of the Horse to the Duchess of York; and married the Lady Frances, daughter of the Earl of Burlington, and widow of Colonel Courteney.

He now busied his mind with literary projects, and formed the plan of a society for refining our language and fixing its standard; *in imitation*, says Fenton, *of those learned and po-*

lite societies with which he had been acquainted abroad. In this design his friend Dryden is said to have assisted him.

The same design, it is well known, was revived by Dr. Swift in the ministry of Oxford; but it has never since been publicly mentioned, though at that time great expectations were formed by some of its establishment and its effects. Such a society might, perhaps, without much difficulty be collected; but that it would produce what is expected from it may be doubted.

The Italian Academy seems to have obtained its end. The language was refined, and so fixed that it has changed but little. The French Academy thought that they refined their language, and doubtless thought rightly; but the event has not shown that they fixed it, for the French of the present time is very different from that of the last century.

In this country an academy could be expected to do but little. If an academician's place were profitable, it would be given by interest; if attendance were gratuitous, it would be rarely paid, and no man would endure the least disgust. Unanimity is impossible; and debate would separate the assembly.

But suppose the philological decree made and promulgated, what would be its authority? In absolute governments there is sometimes a general reverence paid to all that has the sanction of power and the countenance of greatness. How little this is the state of our country needs not to be told. We live in an age in which it is a kind of public sport to refuse all respect that cannot be enforced. The edicts of an English academy would probably be read by many, only that they might be sure to disobey them.

That our language is in perpetual danger of corruption cannot be denied; but what prevention can be found? The present manners of the nation would deride authority, and therefore nothing is left but that every writer should criticise himself.

All hopes of new literary institutions were quickly suppressed by the contentious turbulence of King James's reign; and Roscommon, foreseeing that some violent concussion of the State was at hand, purposed to retire to Rome, alleging that *it was best to sit near the chimney when the chamber smoked;* a sentence of which the application seems not very clear.

His departure was delayed by the gout; and he was so impatient either of hindrance or of pain that he submitted himself to a French empiric, who is said to have repelled the disease into his bowels.

At the moment in which he expired he uttered, with an energy of voice that expressed the most fervent devotion, two lines of his own version of *Dies Iræ:*

> My God, my Father, and my Friend,
> Do not forsake me in my end.

He died in 1684, and was buried [21st January, 1684–5] with great pomp in Westminster Abbey.

His poetical character is given by Mr. Fenton:

"In his writings," says Fenton, "we view the image of a mind which was naturally serious and solid—richly furnished and adorned with all the ornaments of learning, and those ornaments unaffectedly disposed in the most regular and elegant order. His imagination might have probably been more fruitful and sprightly if his judgment had been less severe. But that severity (delivered in a masculine, clear, succinct style) contributed to make him so eminent in the didactical manner, that no man, with justice, can affirm he was ever equalled by any of our nation, without confessing at the same time that he is inferior to none. In some other kinds of writing his genius seems to have wanted fire to attain the point of perfection; but who can attain it?"

From this account of the riches of his mind, who would not imagine that they had been displayed in large volumes and numerous performances? Who would not, after the perusal of this character, be surprised to find that all the proofs of this genius, and knowledge, and judgment, are not sufficient to form a single book, or to appear otherwise than in conjunction with the works of some other writer of the same petty size? But thus it is that characters are written: we know somewhat, and we imagine the rest. The observation, that his imagination would probably have been more fruitful and sprightly if his judgment had been less severe, may be answered by a re-marker somewhat inclined to cavil, by a contrary supposition, that his judgment would probably have been less severe if his imagination had been more fruitful. It is ridiculous to oppose judgment to imagination; for it does not appear that men have necessarily less of one as they have more of the other.

We must allow of Roscommon, what Fenton has not mentioned so distinctly as he ought, and what is yet very much to his honour, that he is perhaps the only correct writer in verse before Addison; and that, if there are not so many or so great beauties in his compositions as in those of some contemporaries, there are at least fewer faults. Nor is this his highest praise, for Mr. Pope has celebrated him as the only moral writer of King Charles's reign:

> Unhappy Dryden! in all Charles's days
> Roscommon only boasts unspotted lays.

His great work is his *Essay on Translated Verse*, of which Dryden writes thus in the preface to his *Miscellanies*:

"It was my Lord Roscommon's *Essay on Translated Verse*," says Dryden, "which made me uneasy, till I tried whether or no I was capable of following his rules, and of reducing the speculation into practice. For many a fair precept in poetry is like a seeming demonstration in the mathematics, very specious in the diagram, but failing in the mechanic operation. I think I have generally observed his instructions; I am sure my reason is sufficiently convinced both of their truth and usefulness; which, in other words, is to confess no less a vanity than to pretend that I have, at least in some places, made examples to his rules."

This declaration of Dryden will, I am afraid, be found little more than one of those cursory civilities which one author pays to another; for when the sum of Lord Roscommon's precepts is collected, it will not be easy to discover how they can qualify their reader for a better performance of translation than might have been attained by his own reflections.

He that can abstract his mind from the elegance of the poetry, and confine it to the sense of the precepts, will find no other direction than that the author should be suitable to the translator's genius; that he should be such as may deserve a translation; that he who intends to translate him should endeavour to understand him; that perspicuity should be studied, and unusual and uncouth names sparingly inserted; and that the style of the original should be copied in its elevation and depression. These are the rules that are celebrated as so definite and important, and for the delivery of which to mankind so much honour has been paid. Roscommon has indeed deserved his praises had they been given with discernment, and bestowed not on the rules themselves, but the art with which they are introduced, and the decorations with which they are adorned.

The *Essay*, though generally excellent, is not without its faults. The story of the Quack, borrowed from Boileau, was not worth the importation: he has confounded the British and Saxon mythology:

> I grant that from some mossy idol oak,
> In double rhymes, our *Thor* and *Woden* spoke.

The oak, as I think Gildon has observed, belonged to the British druids, and Thor and Woden were Saxon deities. Of the *double rhymes*, which he so liberally supposes, he certainly had no knowledge.

His interposition of a long paragraph of blank verses is unwarrantably licentious. Latin poets might as well have introduced a series of iambics among their heroics.

His next work is the translation of the *Art of Poetry*, which has received, in my opinion, not less praise than it deserves. Blank verse, left merely to its numbers, has little operation either on the ear or mind: it can hardly support itself without bold figures and striking images. A poem frigidly didactic, without rhyme, is so near to prose that the reader only scorns it for pretending to be verse.

Having disentangled himself from the difficulties of rhyme, he may justly be expected to give the sense of Horace with great exactness, and to suppress no subtlety of sentiment for the difficulty of expressing it. This demand, however, his translation will not satisfy; what he found obscure, I do not know that he has ever cleared.

Among his smaller works, the *Eclogue* of Virgil and the

Dies Iræ are well translated; though the best line in the *Dies Iræ* is borrowed from Dryden. In return, succeeding poets have borrowed from Roscommon.

In the *Verses on the Lap Dog* the pronouns *thou* and *you* are offensively confounded; and the turn at the end is from Waller.

His versions of the two Odes of Horace are made with great liberty, which is not recompensed by much elegance or vigour.

His political verses are sprightly; and when they were written must have been very popular.

Of the scene of Guarini, and the prologue of *Pompey*, Mrs. Philips, in her letters to Sir Charles Cotterel, has given the history.

"My Lord Roscommon," says she, "is a very ingenious person, of excellent natural parts, and certainly the most hopeful young nobleman in Ireland. He has paraphrased a Psalm admirably well, and the scene of 'Care selve beate,' in *Pastor Fido*, very finely; in many places much better than Sir Richard Fanshaw. He begins it thus:

> Dear happy groves, and you the dark retreat
> Of silent Horror, Rest's eternal seat! etc.

This last he undertook purely out of compliment to me, having heard me say 'twas the best scene in the Italian, and the worst in the English. He was but two hours about it, having certainly as easy and fluent a vein as ever I observed or heard of, and which 'tis great pity he does not improve by practice."

From these lines, which are since somewhat mended, it appears that he did not think a work of two hours fit to endure the eye of criticism without revisal.

When Mrs. Philips was in Ireland, some ladies that had seen her translation of *Pompey* resolved to bring it on the stage at Dublin; and, to promote their design, Lord Roscommon gave them a prologue, and Sir Edward Dering an epilogue; "which," says she, "are the best performances of those kinds I ever saw." If this is not criticism, it is at least gratitude. The thought of bringing Cæsar and Pompey into Ireland, the only country over which Cæsar never had any power, is lucky.

Of Roscommon's works, the judgment of the public seems to be right. He is elegant, but not great; he never labours after exquisite beauties, and he seldom falls into gross faults. His versification is smooth, but rarely vigorous, and his rhymes are remarkably exact. He improved taste, if he did not enlarge knowledge, and may be numbered among the benefactors to English literature.

....

THOMAS OTWAY

1651–1685

Born at Trotton, in Sussex—Educated at Winchester and Oxford—Fails as an Actor—Great Success as a Dramatist—Serves as a Cornet in the English Army in Flanders —His Poverty and tragic End—Buried in St. Clement's Danes—His Works and Character.

Of Thomas Otway, one of the first names in the English drama, little is known; nor is there any part of that little which his biographer can take pleasure in relating.

He was born at Trotton, in Sussex, March 3, 1651–2, the son of Mr. Humphrey Otway, rector of Woolbeding. From Winchester-school, where he was educated, he was entered, in 1669, a commoner of Christ Church [Oxford]; but left the university without a degree, whether for want of money, or from impatience of academical restraint, or mere eagerness to mingle with the world, is not known.

It seems likely that he was in hope of being busy and conspicuous; for he went to London, and commenced player, but found himself unable to gain any reputation on the stage.

This kind of inability he shared with Shakespeare and Jonson, as he shared likewise some of their excellences. It seems reasonable to expect that a great dramatic poet should without difficulty become a great actor; that he who can feel, could express; that he who can excite passion, should exhibit with great readiness its external modes: but, since experience has fully proved that of those powers, whatever be their affinity, one may be possessed in a great degree by him who has very little of the other, it must be allowed that they depend upon different faculties, or on different use of the same faculty; that the actor must have a pliancy of mien, a flexibility of countenance, and a variety of tones, which the poet may be easily supposed to want; or that the attention of the poet and the player have been differently employed; the one has been considering thought, and the other action—one has watched the heart, and the other contemplated the face.

Though he could not gain much notice as a player, he felt in himself such powers as might qualify for a dramatic author; and in 1675, his twenty-fifth year, produced *Alcibiades*, a tragedy; whether from the *Alcibiade* of Palaprat, I have not means to inquire. Langbaine, the great detector of plagiarism, is silent.

In 1677 he published *Titus and Berenice* [a tragedy], translated from Rapin, with the *Cheats of Scapin* [a farce], from Molière; and in 1678 *Friendship in Fashion*, a comedy, which, whatever might be its first reception, was, upon its revival at Drury Lane in 1749, hissed off the stage for immorality and obscenity.

Want of morals or of decency did not in those days exclude any man from the company of the wealthy and the gay, if he brought with him any powers of entertainment; and Otway is said to have been at this time a favourite companion of the dissolute wits. But as he who desires no virtue in his companion has no virtue in himself, those whom Otway frequented had no purpose of doing more for him than to pay his reckoning. They desired only to drink and laugh; their fondness was without benevolence, and their familiarity without friendship. Men of wit, says one of Otway's biographers, received at that time no favour from the great but to share their riots, *from which they were dismissed again to their own narrow circumstances. Thus they languished in poverty without the support of innocence.*

Some exception, however, must be made. The Earl of Plymouth, one of King Charles's natural sons, procured for him a cornet's commission in some troops then sent into Flanders. But Otway did not prosper in his military character, for he soon left his commission behind him, whatever was the reason, and came back to London in extreme indigence, which Rochester mentions with merciless insolence in the *Session of the Poets*:

Tom Otway came next, Tom Shadwell's dear zany,
And swears for heroics he writes best of any;
Don Carlos his pockets so amply had fill'd,
That his mange was quite cured, and his lice were all kill'd.
But Apollo had seen his face on the stage,
And prudently did not think fit to engage
The scum of a play-house, for the prop of an age.

Don Carlos, from which he is represented as having received so much benefit, was played in 1676. It appears by the lampoon to have had great success, and is said to have been played thirty nights together. This, however, it is reasonable to doubt, as so long a continuance of one play upon the stage is a very wide deviation from the practice of that time, when the ardour for theatrical entertainments was not yet diffused through the whole people, and the audience, consisting nearly of the same persons, could be drawn together only by variety.

The *Orphan* was exhibited in 1680. This is one of the few plays that keep possession of the stage, and has pleased for almost a century, through all the vicissitudes of dramatic fashion. Of this play nothing new can easily be said. It is a domestic tragedy drawn from middle life. Its whole power is upon the affections; for it is not written with much comprehension of thought or elegance of expression. But, if the heart is interested, many other beauties may be wanting, yet not be missed.

The same year [1680] produced the *History and Fall of Caius Marius;* much of which is borrowed from the *Romeo and Juliet* of Shakespeare.

In 1683 [1681] was published the first, and next year [1684] the second, parts of *The Soldier's Fortune*, two comedies now forgotten; and in 1685 [Feb. 1680–1] his last and greatest dramatic work, *Venice Preserved*, a tragedy which still continues to be one of the favourites of the public, notwithstanding the want of morality in the original design, and the despicable scenes of vile comedy with which he has diversified his tragic action. By comparing this with his *Orphan*, it will appear that his images were by time become stronger, and his language more energetic. The striking passages are in every mouth; and the public seems to judge rightly of the faults and excellences of this play—that it is the work of a man not attentive to decency, nor zealous for virtue, but of one who conceived forcibly, and drew originally, by consulting nature in his own breast.

Together with those plays he wrote the poems which are in the present collection, and translated from the French the *History of the Triumvirate*.

All this was performed before he was thirty-four years old; for he died April 14, 1685, in a manner which I am unwilling to mention. Having been compelled by his necessities to contract debts, and hunted, as is supposed, by the terriers of the law, he retired to a public-house on Tower-hill, where he is said to have died of want; or, as it is related by one of his biographers, by swallowing, after a long fast, a piece of bread which charity had supplied. He went out, as is reported, almost naked in the rage of hunger, and, finding a gentleman in a neighbouring coffee-house, asked him for a shilling: the gentleman gave him a guinea; and Otway going away bought a roll, and was choked with the first mouthful. All this I hope is not true; and there is this ground of better hope, that Pope, who lived near enough to be well informed, relates in *Spence's Memorials* that he died of a fever caught by violent pursuit of a thief that had robbed one of his friends. But that indigence, and its concomitants, sorrow and despondency, pressed hard upon him, has never been denied, whatever immediate cause might bring him to the grave.

Of the poems which the present collection admits, the longest is the *Poet's Complaint of his Muse*, part of which I do not understand; and in that which is less obscure I find little to commend. The language is often gross, and the numbers are harsh. Otway had not much cultivated versification, nor much replenished his mind with general knowledge. His principal power was in moving the passions; to which Dryden in his latter years left an illustrious testimony. He appears, by some of his verses, to have been a zealous royalist, and had what was in those times the common reward of loyalty—he lived and died neglected.

EDMUND WALLER

1605–1687

Born at Coleshill, in Hertfordshire—Educated at Eton and Cambridge—Returned to Parliament—His first Poetry—Marries a rich Heiress—Sacharissa—His second Marriage—Is a Member of the Long Parliament—Cromwell and Hampden—Publishes his Poems—His Plot in favour of Charles I.—His Life in danger—Escapes with a heavy Fine—Lives in France—Is allowed to return—His Panegyric on Cromwell—His Poem on Charles II.—His Life at the Restoration—Death and Burial at Beaconsfield, in Buckinghamshire—Works and Character.

Edmund Waller was born on the 3rd of March, 1605, at Coleshill, in Hertfordshire. His father was Robert Waller, Esq., of Agmondesham, in Buckinghamshire, whose family was originally a branch of the Kentish Wallers; and his mother was the daughter of John Hampden, of Hampden, in the same county, and sister to Hampden the zealot of rebellion.

His father died while he was yet an infant, but left him a yearly income of three thousand five hundred pounds; which, rating together the value of money and the customs of life, we may reckon more than equivalent to ten thousand at the present time.

He was educated, by the care of his mother, at Eton, and removed afterwards to King's College in Cambridge. He was sent to parliament in his eighteenth, if not in his sixteenth year, and frequented the Court of James I., where he heard a very remarkable conversation, which the writer of the Life prefixed to his Works, who seems to have been well informed of facts, though he may sometimes err in chronology, has delivered as indubitably certain:

"He found Dr. Andrews, Bishop of Winchester, and Dr. Neale, Bishop of Durham, standing behind his Majesty's chair; and there happened something extraordinary," continues this writer, "in the conversation those prelates had with the King, on which Mr. Waller did often reflect. His Majesty asked the bishops, 'My lords, cannot I take my subjects' money when I want it, without all this formality of parliament?' The Bishop of Durham readily answered, 'God forbid, Sir, but you should: you are the breath of our nostrils.' Whereupon the King turned and said to the Bishop of Winchester, 'Well, my lord, what say you?' 'Sir,' replied the bishop, 'I have no skill to judge of parliamentary cases.' The King answered, 'No put-offs, my lord; answer me presently.' 'Then, Sir,' said he, 'I think it is lawful for you to take my brother Neale's money, for he offers it.' Mr. Waller said the company was pleased with his answer, and the wit of it seemed to affect the King; for, a certain lord coming in soon after, his Majesty cried out, 'Oh, my lord, they say you lig with my lady.' 'No, Sir,' says his lordship, in confusion; 'but I like her company because she has so much wit.' 'Why then,' says the King, 'do you not lig with my Lord of Winchester there?'"

Waller's political and poetical life began nearly together. In his eighteenth year he wrote the poem that appears in his works, on *The Prince's Escape at St. Andero*—a piece which justifies the observation made by one of his editors, that he attained, by a felicity like instinct, a style which perhaps will never be obsolete; and that, "were we to judge only by the wording, we could not know what was wrote at twenty, and what at fourscore." His versification was, in his first essay, such as it appears in his last performance. By the perusal of Fairfax's translation of Tasso, to which, as Dryden relates, he confessed himself indebted for the smoothness of his numbers, and by his own nicety of observation, he had already formed such a system of metrical harmony as he never afterwards much needed, or much endeavoured, to improve. Denham corrected his numbers by experience, and gained ground gradually upon the ruggedness of his age; but what was acquired by Denham was inherited by Waller.

The next poem, of which the subject seems to fix the time, is supposed by Mr. Fenton to be the *Address to the Queen*, which he considers as congratulating her arrival, in Waller's twentieth year. He is apparently mistaken; for the mention of the nation's obligations to her frequent pregnancy proves that it was written when she had brought many children. We have, therefore, no date of any other poetical production before that which the murder [Aug. 1628] of the Duke of Buckingham occasioned; the steadiness with which the King received the news in the chapel deserved indeed to be rescued from oblivion.

Neither of these pieces that seem to carry their own dates could have been the sudden effusion of fancy. In the verses on the Prince's escape, the prediction of his marriage with the princess of France must have been written after the event; in the other, the promises of the King's kindness to the descendants of Buckingham, which could not be properly praised till it had appeared by its effects, show that time was taken for revision and improvement. It is not known that they were published till they appeared long afterwards with other poems.

Waller was not one of those idolaters of praise who cultivate their minds at the expense of their fortunes. Rich as he was by inheritance, he took care early to grow richer, by marrying Mrs. Banks, a great heiress in the city, whom the interest of the Court was employed to obtain for Mr. Crofts. Having brought him a son, who died young, and a daughter, who was afterwards married to Mr. Dormer of Oxfordshire, she died in childbed, and left him a widower of about five-and-twenty, gay and wealthy, to please himself with another marriage.

Being too young to resist beauty, and probably too vain to think himself resistible, he fixed his heart, perhaps half fondly and half ambitiously, upon the Lady Dorothy Sidney, eldest daughter of the Earl of Leicester, whom he courted by all the poetry in which Sacharissa is celebrated; the name is derived from the Latin appellation of *sugar*, and implies, if it means anything, a spiritless mildness and dull good-nature, such as excites rather tenderness and esteem, and such as, though always treated with kindness, is never honoured or admired.

Yet he describes Sacharissa as a sublime, predominating beauty, of lofty charms and imperious influence, on whom he looks with amazement rather than fondness, whose chains he wishes, though in vain, to break, and whose presence is *wine* that *inflames to madness*.

His acquaintance with this high-born dame gave wit no opportunity of boasting its influence; she was not to be subdued by the powers of verse, but rejected his addresses, it is said with disdain, and drove him away to solace his disappointment with Amoret or Phillis. She married in 1639 the Earl of Sunderland, who died [Sept. 1643] at Newbury in the King's cause; and, in her old age, meeting somewhere with Waller, asked him when he would again write such verses upon her: "When you are as young, Madam," said he, "and as handsome as you were then."

In this part of his life it was that he was known to Clarendon, among the rest of the men who were eminent in that age for genius and literature; but known so little to his advantage, that they who read his character will not much condemn Sacharissa, that she did not descend from her rank to his embraces, nor think every excellence comprised in wit.

The lady was indeed inexorable; but his uncommon qualifications, though they had no power upon her, recommended him to the scholars and statesmen; and undoubtedly many beauties of that time, however they might receive his love, were proud of his praises. Who they were, whom he dignifies with poetical names, cannot now be known. Amoret, according to Mr. Fenton, was the Lady Sophia Murray. Perhaps by traditions preserved in families more may be discovered.

From the verses written at Penshurst, it has been collected that he diverted his disappointment by a voyage; and his biographers, from his poem on the Whales, think it not improbable that he visited the Bermudas; but it seems much more likely that he should amuse himself with forming an imaginary scene, than that so important an incident as a visit to America should have been left floating in conjectural probability.

From his twenty-eighth to his thirty-fifth year, he wrote his pieces on the Reduction of Sallee; on the Reparation of St. Paul's; to the King on his Navy; the panegyric on the Queen Mother; the two poems to the Earl of Northumberland; and perhaps others, of which the time cannot be discovered.

When he had lost all hopes of Sacharissa, he looked round him for an easier conquest, and gained a lady of the family of Bresse, or Breaux. The time of his marriage is not exactly known. It has not been discovered that his wife was won by his poetry; nor is anything told of her but that she brought him many children. He doubtless praised some whom he would have been afraid to marry, and perhaps married one whom he would have been ashamed to praise. Many qualities contribute to domestic happiness, upon which poetry has no colours to bestow; and many airs and sallies may delight imagination, which he who flatters them never can approve. There are charms made only for distant admiration. No spectacle is nobler than a blaze.

Of this wife, his biographers have recorded that she gave him five sons and eight daughters.

During the long interval of Parliament, he is represented as living among those with whom it was most honourable to converse, and enjoying an exuberant fortune with that independence and liberty of speech and conduct which wealth ought always to produce. He was however considered as the kinsman of Hampden, and was therefore supposed by the courtiers not to favour them.

When the Parliament was called in 1640, it appeared that Waller's political character had not been mistaken. The King's demand of a supply produced one of those noisy speeches which disaffection and discontent regularly dictate; a speech filled with hyperbolical complaints of imaginary grievances. "They," says he, "who think themselves already undone, can never apprehend themselves in danger; and they who have nothing left can never give freely." Political truth is equally in danger from the praises of courtiers, and the exclamations of patriots.

He then proceeds to rail at the clergy, being sure at that time of a favourable audience. His topic is such as will always serve its purpose; an accusation of acting and preaching only for preferment: and he exhorts the Commons *carefully* to *provide* for their *protection against pulpit law.*

It always gratifies curiosity to trace a sentiment. Waller has in his speech quoted Hooker in one passage; and in another has copied him, without quoting. "Religion," says Waller, "ought to be the first thing in our purposes and desires; but that which is first in dignity is not always to precede in order of time; for well-being supposes a being; and the first impediment which men naturally endeavour to remove, is the want of those things without which they cannot subsist. God first assigned unto Adam maintenance of life, and gave him a title to the rest of the creatures before he appointed a law to observe."

"God first assigned Adam," says Hooker, "maintenance of life, and then appointed him a law to observe.—True it is that the kingdom of God must be the first thing in our purpose and desires; but, inasmuch as a righteous life presupposeth life—inasmuch as to live virtuously it is impossible, except we live,—therefore the first impediment which naturally we endeavour to remove is penury, and want of things without which we cannot live."

The speech is vehement; but the great position—that grievances ought to be redressed before supplies are granted—is agreeable enough to law and reason: nor was Waller, if his biographer may be credited, such an enemy to the King as not to wish his distresses lightened; for he relates, "that the King sent particularly to Waller to second his demand of some subsidies to pay off the army; and Sir Henry Vane objecting against first voting a supply, because the King would not accept unless it came up to his proportion, Mr. Waller spoke earnestly to Sir Thomas Jermyn, comptroller of the household, to save his master from the effects of so bold a falsity; 'for,' he said, 'I am but a country gentleman, and cannot pretend to know the King's mind': but Sir Thomas durst not contradict the secretary; and his son, the Earl of St. Alban's, afterwards told Mr. Waller, that his father's cowardice ruined the King."

In the Long Parliament, which, unhappily for the nation, met November 3, 1640, Waller represented Agmondesham the third time, and was considered by the discontented party as a man sufficiently trusty and acrimonious to be employed in managing the prosecution of Judge Crawley for his opinion in favour of ship-money; and his speech shows that he did not disappoint their expectations. He was probably the more ardent, as his uncle Hampden had been particularly engaged in the dispute, and, by a sentence which seems generally to be thought unconstitutional, particularly injured.

He was not, however, a bigot to his party, nor adopted all their opinions. When the great question, whether Episcopacy ought to be abolished, was debated, he spoke against the innovation so coolly, so reasonably, and so firmly, that it is not without great injury to his name that his speech, which was as follows, has been hitherto omitted in his Works:

"There is no doubt but the sense of what this nation had suffered from the present bishops hath produced these complaints; and the apprehensions men have of suffering the like in time to come, make so many desire the taking away of Episcopacy: but I conceive it is possible that we may not now take a right measure of the minds of the people by their petitions; for, when they subscribed them, the bishops were armed with a dangerous commission of making new canons, imposing new oaths, and the like; but now we have disarmed them of that power. These petitioners lately did look upon Episcopacy as a beast armed with horns and claws; but now that we have cut and pared them (and may, if we see cause, yet reduce it into narrower bounds), it may, perhaps, be more agreeable. Howsoever, if they be still in passion, it becomes us soberly to consider the right use and antiquity thereof; and not to comply further with a general desire than may stand with a general good.

"We have already showed that Episcopacy and the evils thereof are mingled like water and oil: we have also, in part, severed them; but I believe you will find that our laws and the present government of the Church are mingled like wine and water; so inseparable, that the abrogation of at least a hundred of our laws is desired in these petitions. I have often heard a noble answer of the Lords, commended in this House, to a proposition of like nature, but of less consequence: they gave no other reason of their refusal but this, *Nolumus mutare Leges Angliæ*: it was the bishops who so answered them: and it would become the dignity and wisdom of this House to answer the people now with a *Nolumus mutare*.

"I see some are moved with a number of hands against the bishops, which, I confess, rather inclines me to their defence; for I look upon Episcopacy as a counterscarp, or outwork, which, if it be taken by this assault of the people, and withal this mystery once revealed, *That we must deny them nothing when they ask it thus in troops*, we may, in the next place, have as hard a task to defend our property as we have lately had to recover it from the Prerogative. If, by multiplying hands and petitions, they prevail for an equality in things ecclesiastical, the next demand perhaps may be *Lex Agraria*, the like equality in things temporal.

"The Roman story tells us that when the people began to flock about the senate, and were more curious to direct and know what was done than to obey, that commonwealth soon came to ruin: their *Legem rogare* grew quickly to be a *Legem ferre*: and after, when their legions had found that they could make a dictator, they never suffered the senate to have a voice any more in such election.

"If these great innovations proceed, I shall expect a flat and level in learning too, as well as in church preferments: *Honos alit Artes*. And though it be true that grave and pious men do study for learning' sake, and embrace virtue for itself, yet it is true, that youth, which is the season when learning is gotten, is not without ambition: nor will ever take pains to excel in anything, when there is not some hope of excelling others in reward and dignity.

"There are two reasons chiefly alleged against our Church government:

"First, Scripture, which, as some men think, points out another form.

"Second, The abuses of the present superiors.

"For Scripture, I will not dispute it in this place; but I am confident that whenever an equal division of lands and goods shall be desired, there will be as many places in Scripture found out which seem to favour that as there are now alleged against the prelacy or preferment of the Church. And as for abuses, when you are now in the Remonstrance told what this and that poor man hath suffered by the bishops, you may be presented with a thousand instances of poor men that have received hard measure from their landlords; and of worldly goods abused, to the injury of others, and disadvantage of the owners.

"And therefore, Mr. Speaker, my humble motion is, that we may settle men's minds herein; and by a question declare our resolution *to reform*, that is, *not to abolish Episcopacy*."

It cannot but be wished that he who could speak in this manner had been able to act with spirit and uniformity.

When the Commons began to set the royal authority at open defiance, Waller is said to have withdrawn from the House, and to have returned with the King's permission; and when the King set up his standard, he sent him a thousand broad pieces. He continued, however, to sit in the rebellious conventicle; but "spoke," says Clarendon, "with great sharpness and freedom, which (now there were so few there that used it, and there was no danger of being over-voted) was not restrained; and therefore used as an argument against those who were gone upon pretence that they were not suffered to declare their opinion freely in the House, which could not be believed, when all men knew what liberty Mr. Waller took, and spoke every day with impunity against the sense and proceedings of the House."

Waller, as he continued to sit, was one of the commissioners nominated by the Parliament to treat with the King at Oxford; and when they were presented, the King said to him, "Though you are the last, you are not the lowest nor the least in my favour." Whitelock, who, being another of the commissioners, was witness of this kindness, imputes it to the King's knowledge of the plot in which Waller appeared afterwards to have been engaged against the Parliament. Fenton, with equal probability, believes that this attempt to promote the royal cause arose from his sensibility of the King's tenderness. Whitelock says nothing of his behaviour at Oxford: he was sent with several others to add pomp to the commission, but was not one of those to whom the trust of treating was imparted.

The engagement, known by the name of Waller's Plot, was soon afterwards discovered. Waller had a brother-in-law, Tomkyns, who was clerk of the Queen's Council, and at the same time had a very numerous acquaintance and great influence in the city. Waller and he, conversing with great confidence, told both their own secrets and those of their friends; and, surveying the wide extent of their conversation, imagined that they found in the majority of all ranks great disapprobation of the violence of the Commons, and unwillingness to continue the war. They knew that many favoured the King, whose fear concealed their loyalty; and many desired peace, though they durst not oppose the clamour for war; and they imagined that if those who had these good intentions could be informed of their own strength, and enabled by intelligence to act together, they might overpower the fury of sedition by refusing to comply with the ordinance for the twentieth part, and the other taxes levied for the support of the rebel army, and by uniting great numbers in a petition for peace. They proceeded with great caution. Three only met in one place, and no man was allowed to impart the plot to more than two others; so that, if any should be suspected or seized, more than three could not be endangered.

Lord Conway joined in the design, and, Clarendon imagines, incidentally mingled, as he was a soldier, some martial hopes or projects, which however were only mentioned, the main design being to bring the loyal inhabitants to the knowledge of each other; for which purpose there was to be appointed one in every district, to distinguish the friends of the King, the adherents to the Parliament, and the neutrals. How far they proceeded does not appear; the result of their inquiry, as Pym declared, was, that within the walls, for one that was for the royalists, there were three against them; but that without the walls, for one that was against them, there were five for them. Whether this was said from knowledge or guess, was perhaps never inquired.

It is the opinion of Clarendon, that in Waller's plan no violence or sanguinary resistance was comprised; that he intended only to abate the confidence of the rebels by public declarations, and to weaken their powers by an opposition to new supplies. This, in calmer times, and more than this, is done without fear; but such was the acrimony of the Commons, that no method of obstructing them was safe.

About this time another design was formed by Sir Nicholas Crispe, a man of loyalty that deserves perpetual remembrance: when he was a merchant in the City, he gave and procured the King, in his exigences, a hundred thousand pounds; and, when he was driven from the Exchange, raised a regiment, and commanded it.

Sir Nicholas flattered himself with an opinion, that some provocation would so much exasperate, or some opportunity so much encourage, the King's friends in the City, that they would break out in open resistance, and then would want only a lawful standard and an authorised commander; and extorted from the King, whose judgment too frequently yielded to importunity, a commission of array, directed to such as he thought proper to nominate, which was sent to London by the Lady Aubigny. She knew not what she carried, but was to deliver it on the communication of a certain token which Sir Nicholas imparted.

This commission could be only intended to lie ready till the time should require it. To have attempted to raise any forces would have been certain destruction; it could be of use only when the forces should appear. This was, however, an act preparatory to martial hostility. Crispe would undoubtedly have put an end to the session of Parliament, had his strength been equal to his zeal; and out of the design of Crispe, which involved very little danger, and that of Waller, which was an act purely civil, they compounded a horrid and dreadful plot.

The discovery of Waller's design is variously related. In Clarendon's *History* it is told that a servant of Tomkyns, lurking behind the hangings when his master was in conference with Waller, heard enough to qualify him for an informer, and carried his intelligence to Pym. A manuscript, quoted in the *Life of Waller*, relates that "he was betrayed by his sister Price and her Presbyterian chaplain Mr. Goode, who stole some of his papers; and if he had not strangely dreamed the night before that his sister had betrayed him, and thereupon burnt the rest of his papers by the fire left in his chimney, he had certainly lost his life by it." The question cannot be decided. It is not unreasonable to believe that the men in power, receiving intelligence from the sister, would employ the servant of Tomkyns to listen at the conference, that they might avoid an act so offensive as that of destroying the brother by the sister's testimony.

The plot was published in the most terrific manner.

On the 31st of May, 1643, at a solemn fast, when they were listening to the sermon, a messenger entered the church, and communicated his errand to Pym, who whispered it to others that were placed near him, and then went with them out of the church, leaving the rest in solicitude and amazement. They immediately sent guards to proper places, and that night apprehended Tomkyns and Waller, having yet traced nothing but that letters had been intercepted, from which it appeared that the Parliament and the city were soon to be delivered into the hands of the Cavaliers.

They perhaps yet knew little themselves, beyond some general and indistinct notices. "But Waller," says Clarendon, "was so confounded with fear, that he confessed whatever he had said, heard, thought, or seen; all that he knew of himself, and all that he suspected of others, without concealing any person, of what degree or quality soever, or any discourse that he had ever upon any occasion entertained with them; what such and such ladies of great honour, to whom, upon the credit of his great wit and very good reputation, he had been admitted, had spoke to him in their chambers upon the proceedings in the Houses, and how they had encouraged him to oppose them: what correspondence and intercourse they had with some ministers of State at Oxford, and how they derived all intelligence thither." He accused the Earl of Portland and Lord Conway as co-operating in the transaction, and testified that the Earl of Northumberland had declared himself disposed in favour of any attempt that might check the violence of the Parliament and reconcile them to the King.

He undoubtedly confessed much which they could never have discovered, and perhaps somewhat which they would wish to have been suppressed; for it is inconvenient, in the conflict of factions, to have that disaffection known which cannot safely be punished.

Tomkyns was seized on the same night with Waller, and appears likewise to have partaken of his cowardice; for he gave notice of Crispe's commission of array, of which Clarendon never knew how it was discovered. Tomkyns had been sent with the token appointed, to demand it from Lady Aubigny, and had buried it in his garden, where, by his direction, it was dug up; and thus the rebels obtained, what Clarendon confesses them to have had, the original copy.

It can raise no wonder that they formed one plot out of these two designs, however remote from each other, when they saw the same agent employed in both, and found the commission of array in the hands of him who was employed in collecting the opinions and affections of the people.

Of the plot, thus combined, they took care to make the most. They sent Pym among the citizens to tell them of their imminent danger and happy escape, and inform them that the design was "to seize the Lord Mayor and all the Committee of Militia, and would not spare one of them." They drew up a vow and covenant, to be taken by every member of either House, by which he declared his detestation of all conspiracies against the Parliament, and his resolution to detect and oppose them. They then appointed a day of thanksgiving for this wonderful delivery, which shut out, says Clarendon, all doubts whether there had been such a deliverance, and whether the plot was real or fictitious.

On June 11 the Earl of Portland and Lord Conway were committed, one to the custody of the mayor, and the other of the sheriff; but their lands and goods were not seized.

Waller was still to immerse himself deeper in ignominy. The Earl of Portland and Lord Conway denied the charge; and there was no evidence against them but the confession of Waller, of which undoubtedly many would be inclined to question the veracity. With these doubts he was so much terrified that he endeavoured to persuade Portland to a declaration like his own, by a letter extant in Fenton's edition. "But for me," says he, "you had never known anything of this business, which was by them prepared for another; and, therefore, I cannot imagine why you should wed it so far as to contract your own ruin by concealing it, and persisting unreasonably to hide that truth, which, without you, already is, and will every day be made more manifest. Can you imagine yourself obliged in honour to keep that secret which is already revealed by another? or possible it should still be a secret, which is known to one of the other sex? . . . If you persist to be cruel to yourself for others' sakes that deserve it not, it will nevertheless be made appear ere long, I fear, to your ruin. Surely, if I had the happiness to wait on you, I could move you to compassionate both yourself and me, who, desperate as my case is, am desirous to die with the honour of being known to have declared the truth. . . . You have no reason to contend to hide what is already revealed—inconsiderately to throw away yourself for the interest of others, to whom you are less obliged than you are aware of."

This persuasion seems to have had little effect. Portland sent (June 29) a letter to the Lords, to tell them that he "is in custody, as he conceives, without any charge; and that by what Mr. Waller hath threatened him with since he was imprisoned, he doth apprehend a very cruel, long, and ruinous restraint:—He therefore prays that he may not find the effects of Mr. Waller's threats by a long and close imprisonment, but may be speedily brought to a legal trial, and then he is confident the vanity and falsehood of those informations which have been given against him will appear."

In consequence of this letter, the Lords ordered Portland and Waller to be confronted; when the one repeated his charge and the other his denial. The examination of the plot being continued (July 1), Thinn, usher of the House of Lords, deposed that Mr. Waller having had a conference with the Lord Portland in an upper room, Lord Portland said, when he came down, "Do me the favour to tell my Lord Northumberland that Mr. Waller has extremely pressed me to save my own life and his, by throwing the blame upon the Lord Conway and the Earl of Northumberland."

Waller, in his letter to Portland, tells him of the reasons which he could urge with resistless efficacy in a personal conference; but he over-rated his own oratory: his vehemence, whether of persuasion or entreaty, was returned with contempt.

One of his arguments with Portland is, that the plot is already known to a woman. This woman was doubtless Lady Aubigny, who, upon this occasion, was committed to custody; but who in reality, when she delivered the commission, knew not what it was.

The Parliament then proceeded against the conspirators, and committed their trial to a council of war. Tomkyns and Chaloner were hanged near their own doors. Tomkyns, when he came to die, said it was a *foolish business*; and indeed there seems to have been no hope that it should escape discovery; for though never more than three met at a time, yet a design so extensive must, by necessity, be communicated to many, who could not be expected to be all faithful, and all prudent. Chaloner was attended at his execution by Hugh Peters. His crime was, that he had commission to raise money for the King; but it appears not that the money was to be expended upon the advancement of either Crispe or Waller's plot.

The Earl of Northumberland, being too great for prosecution, was only once examined before the Lords. The Earl of Portland and Lord Conway persisting to deny the charge, and no testimony but Waller's yet appearing against them, were, after a long imprisonment, admitted to bail. Hassel, the King's messenger, who carried the letters to Oxford, died the night before his trial. Hampden escaped death, perhaps by the interest of his family, but was kept in prison to the end of his life. They whose names were inserted in the commission of array were not capitally punished, as it could not be proved that they had consented to their own nomination; but they were considered as malignants, and their estates were seized.

"Waller, though confessedly," says Clarendon, "the most guilty, with incredible dissimulation acted such a remorse of conscience, that his trial was put off, out of Christian compassion, till he might recover his understanding." What use he made of this interval, with what liberality and success he distributed flattery and money, and how, when he was brought

(July 4, 1643) before the House, he confessed and lamented, and submitted and implored, may be read in the *History of the Rebellion* (B. vii.). The speech, to which Clarendon ascribes the preservation of his *dear-bought life*, is inserted in his Works. The great historian, however, seems to have been mistaken in relating that *he prevailed* in the principal part of his supplication, *not to be tried by a council of war*; for, according to Whitelock, he was, by expulsion from the House, abandoned to the tribunal which he so much dreaded, and, being tried and condemned, was reprieved by Essex; but after a year's imprisonment, in which time resentment grew less acrimonious, paying a fine of ten thousand pounds, he was permitted to *recollect himself in another country*.

Of his behaviour in this part of his life, it is not necessary to direct the reader's opinion. "Let us not," says his last ingenious biographer, "condemn him with untempered severity, because he was not a prodigy which the world hath seldom seen, because his character included not the poet, the orator, and the hero."

For the place of his exile he chose France, and stayed some time at Rouen, where his daughter Margaret was born, who was afterwards his favourite, and his amanuensis. He then removed to Paris, where he lived with great splendour and hospitality; and from time to time amused himself with poetry, in which he sometimes speaks of the rebels, and their usurpation, in the natural language of an honest man.

At last it became necessary, for his support, to sell his wife's jewels; and being reduced, as he said, at last *to the rump-jewel*, he solicited from Cromwell permission to return, and obtained it by the interest of Colonel Scroop, to whom his sister was married. Upon the remains of a fortune which the danger of his life had very much diminished, he lived at Hall Barn, a house built by himself, very near to Beaconsfield, where his mother resided. His mother, though related to Cromwell and Hampden, was zealous for the royal cause, and, when Cromwell visited her, used to reproach him: he in return would throw a napkin at her, and say he would not dispute with his aunt [cousin?]; but finding in time that she acted for the King, as well as talked, he made her a prisoner to her own daughter, in her own house. If he would do anything, he could not do less.

Cromwell, now Protector, received Waller, as his kinsman, to a familiar conversation. Waller, as he used to relate, found him sufficiently versed in ancient history; and when any of his enthusiastic friends came to advise or consult him, could sometimes overhear him discoursing in the cant of the times; but when he returned, he would say, "Cousin Waller, I must talk to these men in their own way"; and resumed the common style of conversation.

He repaid the Protector for his favours (1655) by the famous *Panegyric*, which has been always considered as the first of his poetical productions. His choice of encomiastic topics is very judicious; for he considers Cromwell in his exaltation, without inquiring how he attained it; there is consequently no mention of the rebel or the regicide. All the former part of his hero's life is veiled with shades; and nothing is brought to view but the chief, the governor, the defender of England's honour, and the enlarger of her dominion. The act of violence by which he obtained the supreme power is lightly treated, and decently justified. It was certainly to be desired that the detestable band should be dissolved which had destroyed the Church, murdered the King, and filled the nation with tumult and oppression; yet Cromwell had not the right of dissolving them, for all that he had before done could be justified only by supposing them invested with lawful authority. But combinations of wickedness would overwhelm the world by the advantage which licentious principles afford, did not those who have long practised perfidy grow faithless to each other.

In the poem on the war with Spain are some passages at least equal to the best parts of the *Panegyric*; and in the conclusion the poet ventures yet a higher flight of flattery, by recommending royalty to Cromwell and the nation. Cromwell was very desirous, as appears from his conversation, related by Whitelock, of adding the title to the power of monarchy, and is supposed to have been withheld from it partly by fear of the army, and partly by fear of the laws, which, when he should govern by the name of King, would have restrained his authority. When therefore a deputation was solemnly sent

to invite him to the Crown, he, after a long conference, refused it, but is said to have fainted in his coach when he
parted from them.

The poem on the death of the Protector seems to have been
dictated by real veneration for his memory. Dryden and Sprat
wrote on the same occasion; but they were young men, struggling into notice, and hoping for some favour from the ruling
party. Waller had little to expect: he had received nothing
but his pardon from Cromwell, and was not likely to ask anything from those who should succeed him.

Soon afterwards the Restoration supplied him with another
subject; and he exerted his imagination, his elegance, and his
melody, with equal alacrity, for Charles the Second. It is not
possible to read, without some contempt and indignation,
poems of the same author, ascribing the highest degree of
power and piety to Charles the First, then transferring the
same *power and piety* to Oliver Cromwell, now inviting Oliver
to take the Crown, and then congratulating Charles the Second
on his recovered right. Neither Cromwell nor Charles could
value his testimony as the effect of conviction, or receive his
praises as effusions of reverence; they could consider them but
as the labour of invention, the tribute of dependence.

Poets, indeed, profess fiction; but the legitimate end of
fiction is the conveyance of truth; and he that has flattery
ready for all whom the vicissitudes of the world happen to
exalt, must be scorned as a prostituted mind, that may retain
the glitter of wit, but has lost the dignity of virtue.

The *Congratulation* was considered as inferior in poetical
merit to the *Panegyric*; and it is reported that when the King
told Waller of the disparity, he answered, "Poets, Sir, succeed
better in fiction than in truth."

The *Congratulation* is indeed not inferior to the *Panegyric*,
either by decay of genius or for want of diligence; but, because Cromwell had done much, and Charles had done little,
Cromwell wanted nothing to raise him to heroic excellence but
virtue, and virtue his poet thought himself at liberty to supply.
Charles had yet only the merit of struggling without success,
and suffering without despair. A life of escapes and indigence
could supply poetry with no splendid images.

In the first parliament summoned by Charles the Second (May 8, 1661), Waller sat for Hastings in Sussex, and served for different places in all the parliaments of that reign. In a time when fancy and gaiety were the most powerful recommendations to regard, it is not likely that Waller was forgotten. He passed his time in the company that was highest, both in rank and wit, from which even his obstinate sobriety did not exclude him. Though he drank water, he was enabled by his fertility of mind to heighten the mirth of bacchanalian assemblies; and Mr. Saville said, that "no man in England should keep him company without drinking but Ned Waller."

The praise given him by St. Evremond is a proof of his reputation; for it was only by his reputation that he could be known, as a writer, to a man who, though he lived a great part of a long life upon an English pension, never condescended to understand the language of the nation that maintained him.

In the parliament, "he was," says Burnet, "the delight of the House, and, though old, said the liveliest things of any among them." This, however, is said in his account of the year '75, when Waller was only seventy. His name as a speaker occurs often in Grey's *Collections*; but I have found no extracts that can be more quoted as exhibiting sallies of gaiety than cogency of argument.

He was of such consideration, that his remarks were circulated and recorded. When the Duke of York's influence was high, both in Scotland and England, it drew, says Burnet, a lively reflection from Waller the celebrated wit. "He said, the House of Commons had resolved that the Duke should not reign after the King's death; but the King, in opposition to them, had resolved that he should reign even in his life." If there appear no extraordinary *liveliness* in this *remark*, yet its reception proves the speaker to have been a *celebrated wit*, to have had a name which men of wit were proud of mentioning.

He did not suffer his reputation to die gradually away, which may easily happen in a long life, but renewed his claim to poetical distinction from time to time, as occasions were offered, either by public events or private incidents; and, contenting himself with the influence of his muse, or loving quiet better than influence, he never accepted any office of magistracy.

He was not, however, without some attention to his fortune; for he asked from the King (in 1665) the provostship of Eton College, and obtained it; but Clarendon refused to put the seal to the grant, alleging that it could be held only by a clergyman. It is known that Sir Henry Wotton qualified himself for it by deacon's orders.

To this opposition the *Biographia* imputes the violence and acrimony with which Waller joined Buckingham's faction in the prosecution of Clarendon. The motive was illiberal and dishonest, and showed that more than sixty years had not been able to teach him morality. His accusation is such as conscience can hardly be supposed to dictate without the help of malice. "We were to be governed by janizaries instead of parliaments, and are in danger from a worse plot than that of the 5th of November: then, if the Lords and Commons had been destroyed, there had been a succession; but here both had been destroyed for ever." This is the language of a man who is glad of an opportunity to rail, and ready to sacrifice truth to interest at one time and to anger at another.

A year after the Chancellor's banishment, another vacancy gave him encouragement for another petition, which the King referred to the council, who, after hearing the question argued by lawyers for three days, determined that the office could be held only by a clergyman, according to the Act of Uniformity, since the provosts had always received institution, as for a parsonage, from the bishops of Lincoln. The King then said he could not break the law which he had made; and Dr. Zachary Cradock, famous for a single sermon—at most for two sermons —was chosen by the fellows.

That he asked anything more is not known: it is certain that he obtained nothing, though he continued obsequious to the Court through the rest of Charles's reign.

At the accession of King James, in 1685, he was chosen for Parliament, being then fourscore, at Saltash, in Cornwall; and wrote a *Presage of the Downfall of the Turkish Empire*, which he presented to the King on his birthday. It is remarked by his commentator Fenton, that in reading Tasso he had early imbibed a veneration for the heroes of the Holy War, and a zealous enmity to the Turks, which never left him. James, however, having soon after begun what he thought a Holy War at home, made haste to put all molestation of the Turks out of his power.

James treated him with kindness and familiarity, of which instances are given by the writer of his life. One day, taking him into the closet, the King asked him how he liked one of the pictures: "My eyes," said Waller, "are dim, and I do not know it." The King said it was the Princess of Orange. "She is," said Waller, "like the greatest woman in the world." The King asked who was that; and was answered, "Queen Elizabeth." "I wonder," said the King, "you should think so; but I must confess she had a wise council." "And, Sir," said Waller, "did you ever know a fool choose a wise one?" Such is the story, which I once heard of some other man. Pointed axioms and acute replies fly loose about the world, and are assigned successively to those whom it may be the fashion to celebrate.

When the King knew that he was about to marry his daughter to Dr. Birch, a clergyman, he ordered a French gentleman to tell him that "the King wondered he could think of marrying his daughter to a falling Church." "The King," says Waller, "does me great honour in taking notice of my domestic affairs; but I have lived long enough to observe that this falling Church has got a trick of rising again."

He took notice to his friends of the King's conduct, and said that "he would be left like a whale upon the strand." Whether he was privy to any of the transactions which ended in the Revolution, is not known. His heir joined the Prince of Orange.

Having now attained an age beyond which the laws of nature seldom suffer life to be extended, otherwise than by a future state, he seems to have turned his mind upon preparation for the decisive hour, and therefore consecrated his poetry to devotion. It is pleasing to discover that his piety was without weakness; that his intellectual powers continued vigorous; and that the lines which he composed when *he, for age, could neither read nor write,* are not inferior to the effusions of his youth.

Towards the decline of life he bought a small house with a little land at Coleshill, and said "he should be glad to die, like the stag, where he was roused." This, however, did not happen. When he was at Beaconsfield, he found his legs grow tumid: he went to Windsor, where Sir Charles Scarborough then attended the King, and requested him, as both a friend and physician, to tell him *what that swelling meant.* "Sir," answered Scarborough, "your blood will run no longer." Waller repeated some lines of Virgil, and went home to die.

As the disease increased upon him, he composed himself for his departure; and calling upon Dr. Birch to give him the holy sacrament, he desired his children to take it with him, and made an earnest declaration of his faith in Christianity. It now appeared what part of his conversation with the great could be remembered with delight. He related, that being present when the Duke of Buckingham talked profanely before King Charles, he said to him, "My Lord, I am a great deal older than your Grace, and have, I believe, heard more arguments for atheism than ever your Grace did; but I have lived long enough to see there is nothing in them, and so, I hope, your Grace will."

He died October 21, 1687, and was buried at Beaconsfield, with a monument erected by his son's executors, for which Rymer wrote the inscription, and which I hope is now rescued from dilapidation.

He left several children by his second wife; of whom his daughter [Mary] was married to Dr. [Peter] Birch. Benjamin, the eldest son, was disinherited, and sent to New Jersey, as wanting common understanding. Edmund, the second son, inherited the estate, and represented Agmondesham in parliament, but at last turned Quaker. William, the third son, was a merchant in London. Stephen, the fourth, was an eminent doctor of laws, and one of the commissioners for the Union. There is said to have been a fifth, of whom no account has descended.

The character of Waller, both moral and intellectual, has been drawn by Clarendon, to whom he was familiarly known, with nicety, which certainly none to whom he was not known can presume to emulate. It is therefore inserted here, with such remarks as others have supplied, after which nothing remains but a critical examination of his poetry.

"Edmund Waller," says Clarendon, "was born to a very fair estate, by the parsimony, or frugality, of a wise father and mother; and he thought it so commendable an advantage, that he resolved to improve it with his utmost care, upon which in his nature he was too much intent; and, in order to that, he was so much reserved and retired, that he was scarce ever heard of, till by his address and dexterity he had gotten a very rich wife in the city, against all the recommendation and countenance and authority of the Court, which was thoroughly engaged on the behalf of Mr. Crofts, and which used to be successful, in that age, against any opposition. He had the good fortune to have an alliance and friendship with Dr. Morley, who had assisted and instructed him in the reading many good books, to which his natural parts and promptitude inclined him, especially the poets; and at the age when other men used to give over writing verses (for he was near thirty years of age when he first engaged himself in that exercise, at least that he was known to do so), he surprised the town with two or three pieces of that kind, as if a tenth muse had been newly born to cherish drooping poetry. The Doctor at that time brought him into that company which was most celebrated for good conversation, where he was received and esteemed with great applause and respect. He was a very pleasant discourser in earnest and in jest, and therefore very grateful to all kind of company, where he was not the less esteemed for being very rich.

"He had been even nursed in parliaments, where he sat when he was very young; and so, when they were resumed again (after a long intermission), he appeared in those assemblies with great advantage, having a graceful way of speaking, and by thinking much upon several arguments (which his temper and complexion, that had much of melancholic, inclined him to), he seemed often to speak upon the sudden, when the occasion had only administered the opportunity of saying what he had thoroughly considered, which gave a great

lustre to all he said; which yet was rather of delight than
weight. There needs no more be said to extol the excellence
and power of his wit, and pleasantness of his conversation,
than that it was of magnitude enough to cover a world of
very great faults; that is, so to cover them, that they were not
taken notice of to his reproach; viz. a narrowness in his nature
to the lowest degree; an abjectness and want of courage to
support him in any virtuous undertaking; an insinuation and
servile flattery to the height the vainest and most imperious
nature could be contented with; that it preserved and won his
life from those who were most resolved to take it, and in an
occasion in which he ought to have been ambitious to have
lost it; and then preserved him again from the reproach and
contempt that was due to him for so preserving it, and for
vindicating it at such a price that it had power to reconcile
him to those whom he had most offended and provoked; and
continued to his age with that rare felicity, that his company
was acceptable where his spirit was odious; and he was at least
pitied where he was most detested."

Such is the account of Clarendon; on which it may not be
improper to make some remarks.

"He was very little known till he had obtained a rich wife
in the city."

He obtained a rich wife about the age of three-and-twenty;
an age before which few men are conspicuous much to their
advantage. He was known, however, in parliament and at
court; and, if he spent part of his time in privacy, it is not
unreasonable to suppose that he endeavoured the improvement of his mind as well as of his fortune.

That Clarendon might misjudge the motive of his retirement is the more probable, because he has evidently mistaken
the commencement of his poetry, which he supposes him not
to have attempted before thirty. As his first pieces were perhaps not printed, the succession of his compositions was not
known; and Clarendon, who cannot be imagined to have been
very studious of poetry, did not rectify his first opinion by
consulting Waller's book.

Clarendon observes, that he was introduced to the wits of
the age by Dr. Morley; but the writer of his life relates that he

was already among them, when, hearing a noise in the street, and inquiring the cause, they found *a son* of Ben Jonson under an arrest. This was Morley, whom Waller set free at the expense of one hundred pounds, took him into the country as director of his studies, and then procured him admission into the company of the friends of literature. Of this fact Clarendon had a nearer knowledge than the biographer, and is therefore more to be credited.

The account of Waller's parliamentary eloquence is seconded by Burnet, who, though he calls him "the delight of the House," adds, that "he was only concerned to say that which should make him be applauded; he never laid the business of the House to heart, being a vain and empty though a witty man."

Of his insinuation and flattery it is not unreasonable to believe that the truth is told. Ascham, in his elegant description of those whom in modern language we term Wits, says, that they are *open flatterers, and privy mockers*. Waller showed a little of both, when, upon sight of the Duchess of Newcastle's verses on the *Death of a Stag*, he declared that he would give all his own compositions to have written them; and being charged with the exorbitance of his adulation, answered, that "nothing was too much to be given, that a lady might be saved from the disgrace of such a vile performance." This, however, was no very mischievous or very unusual deviation from truth: had his hypocrisy been confined to such transactions, he might have been forgiven, though not praised; for who forbears to flatter an author or a lady?

Of the laxity of his political principles, and the weakness of his resolution, he experienced the natural effect, by losing the esteem of every party. From Cromwell he had only his recall; and from Charles the Second, who delighted in his company, he obtained only the pardon of his relation Hampden, and the safety of Hampden's son.

As far as conjecture can be made from the whole of his writing, and his conduct, he was habitually and deliberately a friend to monarchy. His deviation towards democracy proceeded from his connection with Hampden, for whose sake he prosecuted Crawley with great bitterness; and the invective which he pronounced on that occasion was so popular, that twenty thousand copies are said by his biographer to have been sold in one day.

It is confessed that his faults still left him many friends, at least many companions. His convivial power of pleasing is universally acknowledged; but those who conversed with him intimately, found him not only passionate, especially in his old age, but resentful; so that the interposition of friends was sometimes necessary.

His wit and his poetry naturally connected him with the polite writers of his time: he was joined with Lord Buckhurst in the translation of Corneille's *Pompey*; and is said to have added his help to that of Cowley in the original draught of the *Rehearsal*.

The care of his fortune, which Clarendon imputes to him in a degree little less than criminal, was either not constant or not successful; for, having inherited a patrimony of three thousand five hundred pounds a year in the time of James the First, and augmented at least by one wealthy marriage, he left, about the time of the Revolution, an income of not more than twelve or thirteen hundred, which, when the different value of money is reckoned, will be found perhaps not more than a fourth part of what he once possessed.

Of this diminution, part was the consequence of the gifts which he was forced to scatter, and the fine which he was condemned to pay, at the detection of his plot; and if his estate, as is related in his Life, was sequestered, he had probably contracted debts when he lived in exile; for we are told, that at Paris he lived in splendour, and was the only Englishman, except the Lord St. Alban's, that kept a table.

His unlucky plot compelled him to sell a thousand a year; of the waste of the rest there is no account, except that he is confessed by his biographer to have been a bad economist. He seems to have deviated from the common practice; to have been a hoarder in his first years, and a squanderer in his last.

Of his course of studies, or choice of books, nothing is known more than that he professed himself unable to read Chapman's translation of Homer without rapture. His opinion concerning the duty of a poet is contained in his declaration, that "he would blot from his works any line that did not contain some motive to virtue."

The characters by which Waller intended to distinguish his writing, are sprightliness and dignity; in his smaller pieces, he endeavours to be gay; in the larger, to be great. Of his airy and light productions, the chief source is gallantry, that attentive reverence of female excellence which has descended to us from the Gothic ages. As his poems are commonly occasional, and his addresses personal, he was not so liberally supplied with grand as with soft images; for beauty is more easily found than magnanimity.

The delicacy which he cultivated restrains him to a certain nicety and caution, even when he writes upon the slightest matter. He has, therefore, in his whole volume nothing burlesque, and seldom anything ludicrous or familiar. He seems always to do his best; though his subjects are often unworthy of his care. It is not easy to think without some contempt on an author who is growing illustrious in his own opinion by verses, at one time, *To a Lady who can do anything, but sleep, when she pleases*; at another, *To a Lady who can sleep when she pleases*; now, *To a Lady, on her passing through a crowd of people*; then, *On a braid of divers colours woven by four Ladies*; *On a Tree cut in paper*; or, *To a Lady, from whom he received the copy of verses on the paper-tree, which, for many years, had been missing*.

Genius now and then produces a lucky trifle. We still read the *Dove* of Anacreon, and *Sparrow* of Catullus; and a writer naturally pleases himself with a performance which owes nothing to the subject. But compositions merely pretty have the fate of other pretty things, and are quitted in time for something useful; they are flowers fragrant and fair, but of short duration; or they are blossoms to be valued only as they foretell fruits.

Among Waller's little poems are some which their excellency ought to secure from oblivion; as, *To Amoret*, comparing the different modes of regard with which he looks on her and Sacharissa; and the verses *On Love*, that begin—"Anger in hasty words or blows."

In others he is not equally successful; sometimes his thoughts are deficient, and sometimes his expression.

The numbers are not always musical; as,

> Fair Venus, in thy soft arms
>   The god of rage confine;
> For thy whispers are the charms
>   Which only can divert his fierce design.
> What though he frown, and to tumult do incline?
>   Thou the flame
>   Kindled in his breast canst tame
> With that snow which unmelted lies on thine.

He seldom indeed fetches an amorous sentiment from the depths of science; his thoughts are for the most part easily understood, and his images such as the superficies of nature readily supplies; he has a just claim to popularity, because he writes to common degrees of knowledge; and is free at least from philosophical pedantry, unless perhaps the end of a song *To the Sun* may be excepted, in which he is too much a Copernican. To which may be added the simile of the Palm in the verses *On her passing through a crowd*; and a line in a more serious poem on the Restoration, about vipers and treacle, which can only be understood by those who happen to know the composition of the *Theriaca*.

His thoughts are sometimes hyperbolical, and his images unnatural:

> —— The plants admire,
> No less than those of old did Orpheus' lyre;
> If she sit down, with tops all tow'rds her bow'd;
> They round about her into arbours crowd:
> Or if she walks, in even ranks they stand,
> Like some well-marshall'd and obsequious band.

In another place:

> While in the park I sing, the listening deer
> Attend my passion, and forget to fear:
> When to the beeches I report my flame,
> They bow their heads, as if they felt the same.

To gods appealing, when I reach their bowers,
With loud complaints they answer me in showers.
To thee a wild and cruel soul is given,
More deaf than trees, and prouder than the heaven!

On the head of a stag:

> O fertile head! which every year
> Could such a crop of wonder bear!
> The teeming earth did never bring
> So soon, so hard, so huge a thing:
> Which might it never have been cast,
> Each year's growth added to the last,
> These lofty branches had supplied
> The Earth's bold sons prodigious pride;
> Heaven with these engines had been scal'd
> When mountains heap'd on mountains fail'd.

Sometimes, having succeeded in the first part, he makes a feeble conclusion. In the song of *Sacharissa's and Amoret's Friendship*, the two last stanzas ought to have been omitted.

His images of gallantry are not always in the highest degree delicate:

> Then shall my love this doubt displace,
>   And gain such trust that I may come
> And banquet sometimes on thy face,
>   But make my constant meals at home.

Some applications may be thought too remote and unconsequential, as in the verses on the *Lady Dancing*:

> The sun in figures such as these
>   Joys with the moon to play:
> To the sweet strains they advance,
> Which do result from their own spheres;
>   As this nymph's dance
> Moves with the numbers which she hears.

Sometimes a thought, which might perhaps fill a distich, is expanded and attenuated till it grows weak and almost evanescent:

Chloris! since first our calm of peace
  Was frighted hence, this good we find,
Your favours with your fears increase,
  And growing mischiefs make you kind.
So the fair tree, which still preserves
  Her fruit and state while no wind blows,
In storms from that uprightness swerves;
  And the glad earth about her strows
  With treasure from her yielding boughs.

His images are not always distinct; as, in the following passage, he confounds *Love* as a person with *love* as a passion:

Some other nymphs, with colours faint,
And pencil slow, may Cupid paint,
And a weak heart in time destroy;
She has a stamp and prints the Boy:
Can, with a single look, inflame
The coldest breast, the rudest tame.

His sallies of casual flattery are sometimes elegant and happy, as that *In return for the Silver Pen*; and sometimes empty and trifling, as that *Upon the Card torn by the Queen*. There are a few lines *Written in the Duchess's Tasso*, which he is said by Fenton to have kept a summer under correction. It happened to Waller, as to others, that his success was not always in proportion to his labour.

Of these petty compositions, neither the beauties nor the faults deserve much attention. The amorous verses have this to recommend them, that they are less hyperbolical than those of some other poets. Waller is not always at the last gasp; he does not die of a frown, nor live upon a smile. There is, however, too much love, and too many trifles. Little things are made too important; and the Empire of Beauty is represented as exerting its influence further than can be allowed by the multiplicity of human passions, and the variety of human wants. Such books, therefore, may be considered as showing the world under a false appearance, and, so far as they obtain credit from the young and unexperienced, as misleading expectation, and misguiding practice.

Of his nobler and more weighty performances, the greater part is panegyrical; for of praise he was very lavish, as is observed by his imitator, Lord Lansdowne:

> No satyr stalks within the hallow'd ground,
> But queens and heroines, kings and gods abound;
> Glory and arms and love are all the sound.

In the first poem, on the danger of the Prince on the coast of Spain, there is a puerile and ridiculous mention of Arion at the beginning; and the last paragraph, on the Cable, is in part ridiculously mean, and in part ridiculously tumid. The poem, however, is such as may be justly praised, without much allowance for the state of our poetry and language at that time.

The two next poems are upon *The King's behaviour at the death of Buckingham*, and upon his *Navy*.

He has, in the first, used the Pagan deities with great propriety:

> 'Twas want of such a precedent as this
> Made the old Heathen frame their gods amiss.

In the poem on *The Navy*, those lines are very noble which suppose the King's power secure against a second deluge; so noble, that it were almost criminal to remark the mistake of *centre* for *surface*, or to say that the empire of the sea would be worth little if it were not that the waters terminate in land.

The poem upon *Sallee* has forcible sentiments; but the conclusion is feeble. That on the *Repair of St. Paul's* has something vulgar and obvious; such as the mention of Amphion; and something violent and harsh, as:

> So all our minds with his conspire to grace
> The Gentiles' great apostle, and deface
> Those state-obscuring sheds, that like a chain
> Seem'd to confine, and fetter him again:
> Which the glad saint shakes off at his command,
> As once the viper from his sacred hand.
> So joys the aged oak when we divide
> The creeping ivy from his injur'd side.

Of the two last couplets, the first is extravagant, and the second mean.

His praise of the Queen is too much exaggerated; and the thought, that she "saves lovers by cutting off hope, as gangrenes are cured by lopping the limb," presents nothing to the mind but disgust and horror.

Of the *Battle of the Summer Islands*, it seems not easy to say whether it is intended to raise terror or merriment. The beginning is too splendid for jest, and the conclusion too light for seriousness. The versification is studied, the scenes are diligently displayed, and the images artfully amplified; but as it ends neither in joy nor sorrow, it will scarcely be read a second time.

The *Panegyric* upon Cromwell has obtained from the public a very liberal dividend of praise, which however cannot be said to have been unjustly lavished; for such a series of verses had rarely appeared before in the English language. Of the lines, some are grand, some are graceful, and all are musical. There is now and then a feeble verse, or a trifling thought; but its great fault is the choice of its hero.

The poem of *The War with Spain* begins with lines more vigorous and striking than Waller is accustomed to produce. The succeeding parts are variegated with better passages and worse. There is something too far-fetched in the comparison of the Spaniards drawing the English on, by saluting St. Lucar with cannon, *to lambs awakening the lion by bleating*. The fate of the Marquis and his Lady, who were burnt in their ship, would have moved more had the poet not made him die like the phœnix, because he had spices about him, nor expressed their affection and their end by a conceit at once false and vulgar:

> Alive, in flames of equal love they burn'd,
> And now together are to ashes turn'd.

The verses to Charles on his return were doubtless intended to counterbalance the panegyric on Cromwell. If it has been thought inferior to that with which it is naturally compared, the cause of its deficience has been already remarked.

The remaining pieces it is not necessary to examine singly.

They must be supposed to have faults and beauties of the same kind with the rest. The Sacred Poems, however, deserve particular regard; they were the work of Waller's declining life—of those hours in which he looked upon the fame and the folly of the time past with the sentiments which his great predecessor Petrarch bequeathed to posterity upon his review of that love and poetry which have given him immortality.

That natural jealousy which makes every man unwilling to allow much excellence in another always produces a disposition to believe that the mind grows old with the body, and that he whom we are now forced to confess superior is hastening daily to a level with ourselves. By delighting to think this of the living we learn to think it of the dead; and Fenton, with all his kindness for Waller, has the luck to mark the exact time when his genius passed the zenith, which he places at his fifty-fifth year. This is to allot the mind but a small portion. Intellectual decay is doubtless not uncommon; but it seems not to be universal. Newton was, in his eighty-fifth year, improving his *Chronology* a few days before his death; and Waller appears not, in my opinion, to have lost at eighty-two any part of his poetical power.

His Sacred Poems do not please like some of his other works; but before the fatal fifty-five, had he written on the same subjects, his success would hardly have been better.

It has been the frequent lamentation of good men that verse has been too little applied to the purposes of worship, and many attempts have been made to animate devotion by pious poetry: that they have very seldom attained their end is sufficiently known; and it may not be improper to inquire why they have miscarried.

Let no pious ear be offended if I advance, in opposition to many authorities, that poetical devotion cannot often please. The doctrines of religion may indeed be defended in a didactic poem; and he who has the happy power of arguing in verse will not lose it because his subject is sacred. A poet may describe the beauty and the grandeur of Nature, the flowers of the spring and the harvests of autumn, the vicissitudes of the tide and the revolutions of the sky, and praise the Maker for his works, in lines which no reader shall lay aside. The subject of the disputation is not piety, but the motives to piety; that of the description is not God, but the works of God.

Contemplative piety, or the intercourse between God and the human soul, cannot be poetical. Man, admitted to implore the mercy of his Creator, and plead the merits of his Redeemer, is already in a higher state than poetry can confer.

The essence of poetry is invention; such invention as, by producing something unexpected, surprises and delights. The topics of devotion are few, and being few are universally known; but, few as there are, they can be made no more; they can receive no grace from novelty of sentiment, and very little from novelty of expression.

Poetry pleases by exhibiting an idea more grateful to the mind than things themselves afford. This effect proceeds from the display of those parts of nature which attract, and the concealment of those which repel, the imagination: but religion must be shown as it is; suppression and addition equally corrupt it; and, such as it is, it is known already.

From poetry the reader justly expects, and from good poetry always obtains, the enlargement of his comprehension and elevation of his fancy; but this is rarely to be hoped by Christians from metrical devotion. Whatever is great, desirable, or tremendous, is comprised in the name of the Supreme Being. Omnipotence cannot be exalted; Infinity cannot be amplified; Perfection cannot be improved.

The employments of pious meditation are faith, thanksgiving, repentance, and supplication. Faith, invariably uniform, cannot be invested by fancy with decorations. Thanksgiving, the most joyful of all holy effusions, yet addressed to a Being without passions, is confined to a few modes, and is to be felt rather than expressed. Repentance, trembling in the presence of the judge, is not at leisure for cadences and epithets. Supplication of man to man may diffuse itself through many topics of persuasion; but supplication to God can only cry for mercy.

Of sentiments purely religious, it will be found that the most simple expression is the most sublime. Poetry loses its lustre and its power because it is applied to the decoration of something more excellent than itself. All that pious verse can do is to help the memory and delight the ear, and for these purposes it may be very useful; but it supplies nothing to the mind. The ideas of Christian theology are too simple for eloquence, too sacred for fiction, and too majestic for ornament: to recommend them by tropes and figures is to magnify by a concave mirror the sidereal hemisphere.

As much of Waller's reputation was owing to the softness and smoothness of his numbers, it is proper to consider those minute particulars to which a versifier must attend.

He certainly very much excelled in smoothness most of the writers who were living when his poetry commenced. The poets of Elizabeth had attained an art of modulation, which was afterwards neglected or forgotten. Fairfax was acknowledged by him as his model; and he might have studied with advantage the poem of Davies, which, though merely philosophical, yet seldom leaves the ear ungratified.

But he was rather smooth than strong; of *the full rescunding line,* which Pope attributes to Dryden, he has given very few examples. The critical decision has given the praise of strength to Denham, and of sweetness to Waller.

His excellence of versification has some abatements. He uses the expletive *do* very frequently; and, though he lived to see it almost universally ejected, was not more careful to avoid it in his last compositions than in his first. Praise had given him confidence; and, finding the world satisfied, he satisfied himself.

His rhymes are sometimes weak words: *so* is found to make the rhyme twice in ten lines, and occurs often as a rhyme through his book.

His double rhymes in heroic verse have been censured by Mrs. Philips, who was his rival in the translation of Corneille's *Pompey;* and more faults might be found, were not the inquiry below attention.

He sometimes uses the obsolete termination of verbs, as *waxeth, affecteth;* and sometimes retains the final syllable of the preterite, as *amazed, supposed,* of which I know not whether it is not to the detriment of our language that we have totally rejected them.

Of triplets he is sparing; but he did not wholly forbear them: of an Alexandrine he has given no example.

The general character of his poetry is elegance and gaiety. He is never pathetic, and very rarely sublime. He seems neither to have had a mind much elevated by nature nor amplified by learning. His thoughts are such as a liberal conversation and large acquaintance with life would easily supply. They had however then, perhaps, that grace of novelty which they are now often supposed to want by those who, having already found them in later books, do not know or inquire who produced them first. This treatment is unjust. Let not the original author lose by his imitators.

Praise, however, should be due before it is given. The author of Waller's Life ascribes to him the first practice of what Erythræus and some late critics call *alliteration*—of using in the same verse many words beginning with the same letter. But this knack, whatever be its value, was so frequent among early writers, that Gascoigne, a writer of the sixteenth century, warns the young poet against affecting it; Shakespeare, in the *Midsummer Night's Dream,* is supposed to ridicule it; and in another play the sonnet of Holofernes fully displays it.

He borrows too many of his sentiments and illustrations from the old Mythology, for which it is vain to plead the example of ancient poets: the deities which they introduced so frequently were considered as realities, so far as to be received by the imagination, whatever sober reason might even then determine. But of these images time has tarnished the splendour. A fiction, not only detected but despised, can never afford a solid basis to any position, though sometimes it may furnish a transient allusion, or slight illustration. No modern monarch can be much exalted by hearing that, as Hercules had his *club,* he has his *navy.*

But of the praise of Waller, though much may be taken away, much will remain; for it cannot be denied that he added something to our elegance of diction, and something to our propriety of thought; and to him may be applied what Tasso said, with equal spirit and justice, of himself and Guarini, when, having perused the *Pastor Fido*, he cried out, "If he had not read *Aminta*, he had not excelled it."

As Waller professed himself to have learned the art of versification from Fairfax, it has been thought proper to subjoin a specimen of his work, which, after Mr. Hoole's translation, will perhaps not be soon reprinted. By knowing the state in which Waller found our poetry, the reader may judge how much he improved it.

I

Erminia's steed (this while) his mistresse bore
Through forrests thicke among the shadie treene,
Her feeble hand the bridle reines forlore,
Halfe in a swoune she was for feare I weene;
But her flit courser spared nere the more,
To beare her through the desart woods vnseene
 Of her strong foes, that chas'd her through the plaine,
 And still pursu'd, but still pursu'd in vaine.

II

Like as the wearie hounds at last retire,
Windlesse, displeased, from the fruitlesse chace,
When the slie beast Tapisht in bush and brire,
No art nor paines can rowse out of his place:
The Christian knights so full of shame and ire
Returned backe, with faint and wearie pace:
 Yet still the fearfull Dame fled, swift as winde,
 Nor euer staid, nor ever lookt behinde.

III

Through thicke and thinne, all night, all day, she driued,
Withouten comfort, companie, or guide,
Her plaints and teares with euery thought reuiued,
She heard and saw her greefes, but nought beside.
But when the sunne his burning chariot diued
In Thetis' waue, and wearie teame vntide,
 On Iordans sandie banks her course she staid,
 At last, there downe she light, and downe she laid.

IV

Her teares, her drinke; her food, her sorrowings,
This was her diet that vnhappie night:
But sleepe (that sweet repose and quiet brings)
To ease the greefes of discontented wight,
Spred foorth his tender, soft, and nimble wings,
In his dull armes foulding the virgin bright:
    And Loue, his mother, and the Graces kept
    Strong watch and warde, while this faire Ladie slept.

V

The birds awakte her with their morning song,
Their warbling musicke pearst her tender eare,
The murmuring brookes and whistling windes among
The ratling boughes, and leaues, their parts did beare;
Her eies vnclos'd beheld the groues along
Of swaines and shepherd groomes, that dwellings weare;
    And that sweet noise birds, winds, and waters sent,
    Prouokte again the virgin to lament.

VI

Her plaints were interrupted with a sound
That seem'd from thickest bushes to proceed,
Some iolly shepherd sung a lustie round,
And to his voice had tun'd his oaten reed;
Thither she went, an old man there she found,
(At whose right hand his little flocke did feed,)
    Sat making baskets his three sonnes among,
    That learn'd their father's art, and learn'd his song.

VII

Beholding one in shining armes appeare,
The seelie man and his were sore dismaid;
But sweet Erminia comforted their feare,
Her ventall vp, her visage open laid,
You happie folke, of heau'n beloued deare,
Worke on (quoth she) upon your harmlesse traid,
    These dreadfull armes I beare no warfare bring
    To your sweet toile, nor those sweet tunes you sing.

VIII

But, father, since this land, these townes and towres,
Destroied are with sword, with fire and spoile,
How may it be vnhurt that you and yours
In safetie thus applie your harmelesse toile?
My sonne (quoth he) this poore estate of ours
Is euer safe from storm of warlike broile;
    This wildernesse doth vs in safetie keepe,
    No thundring drum, no trumpet breakes our sleepe.

IX

Haply iust heau'n's defence and shield of right
Doth loue the innocence of simple swains,
The thunderbolts on highest mountaines light,
And seld or neuer strike the lower plaines:
So kings haue cause to feare *Bellonaes* might,
Not they whose sweat and toile their dinner gaines,
    Nor euer greedie soldier was entised
    By pouertie, neglected and despised.

X

O pouertie, chefe of the heau'nly brood,
Dearer to me than wealth or kingly crowne!
No wish for honour, thirst of others' good,
Can moue my hart, contented with mine owne:
We quench our thirst with water of this flood,
Nor fear we poison should therein be throwne:
    These little flocks of sheepe and tender goates
    Giue milke for food, and wooll to make vs coates.

XI

We little wish, we need but little wealth,
From cold and hunger vs to cloath and feed;
These are my sonnes, their care preserues from stealth
Their father's flocks, nor servants moe I need:
Amid these groues I walke oft for my health,
And to the fishes, birds, and beastes giue heed,
    How they are fed, in forrest, spring, and lake,
    And their contentment for ensample take.

XII

Time was (for each one hath his doting time,
These siluer locks were golden tresses than)
That countrie life I hated as a crime,
And from the forrest's sweet contentment ran.
To Memphis' stately pallace would I clime,
And there became the mightie Caliphes man,
　　And though I but a simple gardner weare,
　　Yet could I marke abuses, see and heare.

XIII

Entised on with hope of future gaine,
I suffred long what did my soule displease;
But when my youth was spent my hope was vaine,
I felt my native strength at last decrease;
I gan my losse of lustie yeeres complaine,
And wisht I had enjoy'd the countries peace!
　　I bod the court farewell, and with content
　　My later age here haue I quiet spent.

XIV

While thus he spake, Erminia husht and still
His wise discourses heard, with great attention;
His speeches graue those idle fancies kill,
Which in her troubled soule bred such dissention;
After much thought reformed was her will,
Within those woods to dwell was her intention,
　　Till fortune should occasion new afford,
　　To turne her home to her desired Lord.

XV

She said therefore, O shepherd fortunate!
That troubles some didst whilom feele and proue,
Yet liust now in this contented state,
Let my mishap thy thoughts to pitie moue,
To entertaine me as a willing mate
In shepherd's life, which I admire and loue;
　　Within these pleasant groues perchance my hart,
　　Of her discomforts, may vnload some part.

XVI

If gold or wealth of most esteemed deare,
If iewels rich, thou diddest hold in prise,
Such store thereof, such plentie haue I heare,
As to a greedie minde might well suffice:
With that downe trickled many a siluer teare,
Two christall streames fell from her watrie eies;
   Part of her sad misfortunes than she told,
   And wept, and with her wept that shepherd old.

XVII

With speeches kinde, he gan the virgin deare
Towards his cottage gently home to guide;
His aged wife there made her homely cheare,
Yet welcomde her, and plast her by her side.
The Princesse cond a poore pastoraes geare,
A kerchiefe course vpon her head she tide;
   But yet her gestures and her lookes (I gesse)
   Were such as ill beseem'd a shepherdesse.

XVIII

Not those rude garments could obscure, and hide
The heau'nly beautie of her angels face,
Nor was her princely ofspring damnifide,
Or ought disparag'de, by those labours bace;
Her little flocks to pasture would she guide,
And milke her goates, and in their folds them place,
   Both cheese and butter could she make, and frame
   Her selfe to please the shepherd and his dame.

JOHN DRYDEN

1631–1700

Born at Aldwinkle, in Northamptonshire—Educated at Westminster and Cambridge—His late appearance as a Poet—His first Verses—His Panegyric on Cromwell—His Poem on the Restoration—His first Play—Revival of the Drama—Heroic Plays with Rhyme—Becomes a constant Writer for the Stage—Made Poet Laureate—His Controversy with Settle and Shadwell—Is ridiculed by the Duke of Buckingham in *The Rehearsal*—Is beaten by Bullies hired by the Earl of Rochester—His Political and Religious Satires—Publishes *Absalom and Achitophel—The Medal—Mac Flecknoe*—Is converted to the Church of Rome—Publishes *The Hind and the Panther*—Loses his Office of Poet Laureate—His Translations from Juvenal, Ovid, and Persius—His Translation of Virgil—*Ode on St. Cecilia's Day*, and *Fables*—Death and Burial in Westminster Abbey—Works and Character.

Of the great poet whose life I am about to delineate, the curiosity which his reputation must excite will require a display more ample than can now be given. His contemporaries, however they reverenced his genius, left his life unwritten; and nothing therefore can be known beyond what casual mention and uncertain tradition have supplied.

John Dryden was born August 9, 1631, at Aldwinkle, near Oundle, the son of Erasmus Dryden of Tichmarsh, who was the third son of Sir Erasmus Dryden, Baronet, of Canons Ashby. All these places are in Northamptonshire; but the original stock of the family was in the county of Huntingdon.

He is reported by his last biographer, Derrick, to have inherited from his father an estate of two hundred a year, and to have been bred, as was said, an Anabaptist. For either of these particulars no authority is given. Such a fortune ought to have secured him from that poverty which seems always to have oppressed him; or, if he had wasted it, to have made him ashamed of publishing his necessities. But though he had many enemies, who undoubtedly examined his life with a scrutiny sufficiently malicious, I do not remember that he is ever charged with waste of his patrimony. He was, indeed, sometimes reproached for his first religion. I am therefore inclined to believe that Derrick's intelligence was partly true, and partly erroneous.

From Westminster School, where he was instructed as one of the King's scholars by Dr. Busby, whom he long after continued to reverence, he was in 1650 [11th May] elected to one of the Westminster scholarships at Cambridge.

Of his school performances has appeared only a poem on the death of Lord Hastings, composed with great ambition of such conceits as, notwithstanding the reformation begun by Waller and Denham, the example of Cowley still kept in reputation. Lord Hastings died of the smallpox; and his poet has made of the pustules first rosebuds, and then gems; at last exalts them into stars, and says:

> No comet need foretell his change drew on,
> Whose corpse might seem a constellation.

At the university he does not appear to have been eager of poetical distinction, or to have lavished his early wit either on fictitious subjects or public occasions. He probably considered that he who proposed to be an author ought first to be a student. He obtained, whatever was the reason, no fellowship in the college. Why he was excluded cannot now be known, and it is vain to guess: had he thought himself injured, he knew how to complain. In the *Life of Plutarch* he mentions his education in the college with gratitude; but in a prologue at Oxford he has these lines:

Oxford to him a dearer name shall be
Than his own mother-university;
Thebes did his green, unknowing youth engage;
He chooses Athens in his riper age.

It was not till the death of Cromwell, in 1658 [Sept. 3], that he became a public candidate for fame, by publishing [1659] *Heroic Stanzas on the late Lord Protector*, which, compared with the verses of Sprat and Waller on the same occasion, were sufficient to raise great expectations of the rising poet.

When the King was restored, Dryden, like the other panegyrists of usurpation, changed his opinion or his profession, and published [1660] *Astræa Redux; a Poem on the happy Restoration and Return of his sacred Majesty King Charles the Second*.

The reproach of inconstancy was on this occasion shared with such numbers, that it produced neither hatred nor disgrace! If he changed, he changed with the nation. It was, however, not totally forgotten when his reputation raised him enemies.

The same year he praised the new King in a second poem on his restoration. In the *Astræa* was the line:

An horrid *stillness* first *invades* the *ear*,
And in that silence we the tempest fear—

for which he was persecuted with perpetual ridicule, perhaps with more than was deserved. *Silence* is indeed mere privation; and, so considered, cannot *invade*; but privation likewise certainly is *darkness*, and probably *cold*; yet poetry has never been refused the right of ascribing effects or agency to them as to positive powers. No man scruples to say that *darkness* hinders him from his work, or that *cold* has killed the plants. Death is also privation; yet who has made any difficulty of assigning to Death a dart and the power of striking?

In settling the order of his works there is some difficulty; for even when they are important enough to be formally offered to a patron, he does not commonly date his dedication; the time of writing and publishing is not always the same; nor can the first editions be easily found, if even from them could be obtained the necessary information.

The time at which his first play was exhibited is not certainly known, because it was not printed till it was some years afterwards altered and revived; but since the plays are said to be printed in the order in which they were written, from the dates of some those of others may be inferred; and thus it may be collected, that in 1663, in the thirty-second year of his life, he commenced a writer for the stage; compelled undoubtedly by necessity, for he appears never to have loved that exercise of his genius, or to have much pleased himself with his own dramas.

Of the stage, when he had once invaded it, he kept possession for many years; not, indeed, without the competition of rivals, who sometimes prevailed, or the censure of critics, which was often poignant and often just; but with such a degree of reputation as made him at least secure of being heard, whatever might be the final determination of the public.

His first piece was a comedy called the *Wild Gallant*. He began with no happy auguries; for his performance was so much disapproved that he was compelled to recall it, and change it from its imperfect state to the form in which it now appears, and which is yet sufficiently defective to vindicate the critics.

I wish that there were no necessity of following the progress of his theatrical fame, or tracing the meanders of his mind through the whole series of his dramatic performances; it will be fit, however, to enumerate them, and to take especial notice of those that are distinguished by any peculiarity, intrinsic or concomitant; for the composition and fate of eight-and-twenty dramas include too much of a poetical life to be omitted.

In 1664 he published the *Rival Ladies*, which he dedicated to the Earl of Orrery, a man of high reputation both as a writer and a statesman. In this play he made his essay of dramatic rhyme, which he defends in his dedication with sufficient certainty of a favourable hearing; for Orrery was himself a writer of rhyming tragedies.

He then joined with Sir Robert Howard in the *Indian*

Queen, a tragedy in rhyme. The parts which either of them wrote are not distinguished.

The *Indian Emperor* was published in 1667. It is a tragedy in rhyme, intended for a sequel to Howard's *Indian Queen*. Of this connection notice was given to the audience by printed bills, distributed at the door; an expedient supposed to be ridiculed in the *Rehearsal*, when Bayes tells how many reams he has printed, to instil into the audience some conception of his plot.

In this play is the description of Night, which Rymer has made famous by preferring it to those of all other poets.

The practice of making tragedies in rhyme was introduced soon after the Restoration, as it seems by the Earl of Orrery, in compliance with the opinion of Charles the Second, who had formed his taste by the French theatre; and Dryden, who wrote, and made no difficulty of declaring that he wrote only to please, and who perhaps knew that by his dexterity of versification he was more likely to excel others in rhyme than without it, very readily adopted his master's preference. He therefore made rhyming tragedies, till, by the prevalence of manifest propriety, he seems to have grown ashamed of making them any longer.

To this play is prefixed a very vehement defence of dramatic rhyme, in confutation of the preface to the *Duke of Lerma*, in which Sir Robert Howard had censured it.

In 1667 he published *Annus Mirabilis, the Year of Wonders*, which may be esteemed one of his most elaborate works.

It is addressed to Sir Robert Howard by a letter, which is not properly a dedication; and, writing to a poet, he has interspersed many critical observations, of which some are common, and some perhaps ventured without much consideration. He began, even now, to exercise the domination of conscious genius, by recommending his own performance: "I am satisfied that as the Prince and General [Rupert and Monk] are incomparably the best subjects I ever had, so what I have written on them is much better than what I have performed on any other. As I have endeavoured to adorn my poem with noble thoughts, so much more to express those thoughts with elocution."

It is written in quatrains, or heroic stanzas of four lines; a measure which he had learned from the *Gondibert* of Davenant, and which he then thought the most majestic that the English language affords. Of this stanza he mentions the incumbrances, increased as they were by the exactness which the age required. It was, throughout his life, very much his custom to recommend his works, by representation of the difficulties that he had encountered, without appearing to have sufficiently considered that where there is no difficulty there is no praise.

There seems to be, in the conduct of Sir Robert Howard and Dryden towards each other, something that is not now easily to be explained. Dryden, in his dedication to the Earl of Orrery [1664], had defended dramatic rhyme; and Howard, in the preface to a collection of plays, had [1665] censured his opinion. Dryden vindicated himself [1667] in his *Dialogue on Dramatic Poetry*; Howard, in his preface to the *Duke of Lerma*, animadverted [1668] on the Vindication; and Dryden, in a preface to the *Indian Emperor*, replied [1668] to the Animadversions with great asperity, and almost with contumely. The dedication to this play is dated the year in which the *Annus Mirabilis* was published. Here appears a strange inconsistency; but Langbaine affords some help, by relating that the answer to Howard was not published in the first edition of the play [1667], but was added [1668] when it was afterwards reprinted; and as the *Duke of Lerma* did not appear till 1668, the same year in which the dialogue was published, there was time enough for enmity to grow up between authors, who, writing both for the theatre, were naturally rivals.

He was now so much distinguished, that in 1668 he succeeded Sir William Davenant as poet laureate. The salary of the laureate had been raised in favour of Jonson, by Charles the First, from a hundred marks to one hundred pounds a year and a tierce of wine; a revenue in those days not inadequate to the conveniences of life.

The same year he published his *Essay on Dramatic Poetry*, an elegant and instructive dialogue, in which we are told by Prior, that the principal character is meant to represent the

Earl of Dorset. This work seems to have given Addison a model for his *Dialogues upon Medals*.

Secret Love, or the Maiden Queen (1668), is a tragicomedy. In the preface he discusses a curious question, whether a poet can judge well of his own productions? and determines very justly, that, of the plan and disposition, and all that can be reduced to principles of science, the author may depend upon his own opinion; but that, in those parts where fancy predominates, self-love may easily deceive. He might have observed, that what is good only because it pleases, cannot be pronounced good till it has been found to please.

Sir Martin Marr-all (1668) is a comedy, published without preface or dedication, and at first without the name of the author. Langbaine charges it, like most of the rest, with plagiarism; and observes, that the song is translated from Voiture, allowing however that both the sense and measure are exactly observed.

The Tempest (1670) is an alteration of Shakespeare's play, made by Dryden in conjunction with Davenant, "whom," says he, "I found of so quick a fancy, that nothing was proposed to him in which he could not suddenly produce a thought extremely pleasant and surprising; and those first thoughts of his, contrary to the Latin proverb, were not always the least happy, and as his fancy was quick, so likewise were the products of it remote and new. He borrowed not of any other, and his imaginations were such as could not easily enter into any other man."

The effect produced by the conjunction of these two powerful minds was, that to Shakespeare's monster Caliban is added a sister-monster Sycorax; and a woman who in the original play had never seen a man, is in this brought acquainted with a man that had never seen a woman.

An Evening's Love, or the Mock Astrologer, a comedy (1671), is dedicated to the illustrious Duke of Newcastle, whom he courts by adding to his praises those of his lady, not only as a lover but a partner of his studies. It is unpleasing to think how many names, once celebrated, are since forgotten. Of Newcastle's works nothing is now known but his *Treatise on Horsemanship*.

The preface seems very elaborately written, and contains
many just remarks on the fathers of the English drama. Shakespeare's plots, he says, are in the hundred novels of Cinthio,
those of Beaumont and Fletcher in Spanish stories; Jonson
only made them for himself. His criticisms upon tragedy,
comedy, and farce are judicious and profound. He endeavours
to defend the immorality of some of his comedies by the example of former writers; which is only to say, that he was not
the first nor perhaps the greatest offender. Against those that
accused him of plagiarism he alleges a favourable expression
of the King: "He only desired that they who accuse me of
thefts would steal him plays like mine"; and then relates how
much labour he spends in fitting for the English stage what
he borrows from others.

Tyrannic Love, or the Royal Martyr (1672), was another
tragedy in rhyme, conspicuous for many passages of strength
and elegance, and many of empty noise and ridiculous turbulence. The rants of Maximin have been always the sport of
criticism; and were at length [1681], if his own confession
may be trusted, the shame of the writer.

Of this play he takes care to let the reader know that it was
"contrived and written" in seven weeks. Want of time was
often his excuse, or perhaps shortness of time was his private
boast in the form of an apology.

It was written before the *Conquest of Granada*, but published after it. The design is to recommend piety. "I considered that pleasure was not the only end of poesy, and that
even the instructions of morality were not so wholly the business of a poet, as that precepts and examples of piety were to
be omitted. For to leave that employment altogether to the
clergy were to forget that religion was first taught in verse,
which the laziness or dullness of succeeding priesthood turned
afterwards into prose." Thus foolishly could Dryden write
rather than not show his malice to the parsons.

About this time, in 1673, Dryden seems to have had his
quiet much disturbed by the success of the *Empress of Morocco*, a tragedy written in rhyme by Elkanah Settle; which
was so much applauded, as to make him think his supremacy

of reputation in some danger. Settle had not only been prosperous on the stage, but, in the confidence of success, had
published his play, "with sculptures" and a preface of defiance. Here was one offence added to another; and for the last
blast of inflammation, it was acted at Whitehall by the court
ladies.

Dryden could not now repress these emotions, which he
called indignation, and others jealousy; but wrote upon the
play and the dedication such criticism as malignant impatience could pour out in haste.

Of Settle he gives this character: "He is an animal of a
most deplored understanding, without conversation. His being
is in a twilight of sense, and some glimmering of thought,
which he can never fashion either into wit or English. His
style is boisterous and rough-hewn; his rhyme incorrigibly
lewd, and his numbers perpetually harsh and ill-sounding.
That little talent which he has is fancy. He sometimes labours
with a thought; but with the pudder he makes to bring it
into the world it is commonly still-born; so that for want of
learning and elocution he will never be able to express anything either naturally or justly!"

This is not very decent; yet this is one of the pages in which
criticism prevails over brutal fury. He proceeds: "He has a
heavy hand at fools, and a great felicity in writing nonsense
for them. Fools they will be in spite of him. His King, his two
Empresses, his villain, and his sub-villain, nay his hero, have
all a certain natural cast of the father. One turn of the countenance goes through all his children: their folly was born and
bred in them, and something of the Elkanah will be visible."

This is Dryden's general declamation: I will not withhold
from the reader a particular remark. Having gone through the
first act, he says, "To conclude this act with the most rumbling
piece of nonsense spoken yet,

'To flattering lightning our feign'd smiles conform,
Which back'd with thunder do but gild a storm.'

"*Conform a smile to lightning*, make a *smile* imitate *lightning*,
and *flattering lightning*: lightning sure is a threatening thing.

And this lightning must *gild a storm*. Now if I must conform by smiles to lightning, then my smiles must gild a storm too: to *gild* with *smiles* is a new invention of gilding. And gild a storm by being *backed with thunder*. Thunder is part of the storm; so one part of the storm must help to *gild* another part, and help by *backing*; as if a man would gild a thing the better for being backed, or having a load upon his back. So that here is *gilding* by *conforming, smiling, lightning, backing*, and *thundering*. The whole is as if I should say thus: I will make my counterfeit smiles look like a flattering stone-horse, which, being backed with a trooper, does but gild the battle. I am mistaken if nonsense is not here pretty thick sown. Sure the poet writ these two lines aboard some smack in a storm, and, being seasick, spewed up a good lump of clotted nonsense at once."

Here is, perhaps, a sufficient specimen; but as the pamphlet, though Dryden's, has never been thought worthy a republication, and is not easily to be found, it may gratify curiosity to quote it more largely.

> " 'Whene'er she bleeds,
> He no severer a damnation needs,
> That dares pronounce the sentence of her death,
> Than the infection that attends that breath.'

"*That attends that breath*. The poet is at *breath* again; *breath* can never 'scape him; and here he brings in a *breath* that must be *infectious* with *pronouncing* a sentence; and this sentence is not to be pronounced till the condemned party *bleeds*; that is, she must be executed first, and sentenced after; and the *pronouncing* of this *sentence* will be infectious; that is, others will catch the disease of that sentence, and this infecting of others will torment a man's self. The whole is thus: *when she bleeds, thou needest no greater hell or torment to thyself than infecting of others by pronouncing a sentence upon her*. What hodgepodge does he make here! Never was Dutch grout such clogging, thick, indigestible stuff. But this is but a taste to stay the stomach: we shall have a more plentiful mess presently.

"Now to dish up the poet's broth that I promised:

'For when we're dead, and our freed souls enlarg'd,
  Of nature's grosser burden we're discharg'd,
  Then gently, as a happy lover's sigh,
  Like wand'ring meteors through the air we'll fly,
  And in our airy walk, as subtle guests,
  We'll steal into our cruel fathers' breasts,
  There read their souls, and track each passion's sphere:
  See how Revenge moves there, Ambition here;
  And in their orbs view the dark characters
  Of sieges, ruins, murders, blood, and wars.
  We'll blot out all those hideous draughts, and write
  Pure and white forms; then with a radiant light
  Their breasts encircle, till their passions be
  Gentle as nature in its infancy;
  Till soften'd by our charms their furies cease,
  And their revenge resolves into a peace.
  Thus by our death their quarrel ends,
  Whom living we made foes, dead we'll make friends.'

"If this be not a very liberal mess, I will refer myself to the stomach of any moderate guest. And a rare mess it is, far excelling any Westminster white-broth. It is a kind of giblet porridge, made of the giblets of a couple of young geese, stodged full of *meteors, orbs, spheres, track, hideous draughts, dark characters, white forms,* and *radiant lights,* designed not only to please appetite, and indulge luxury, but it is also physical, being an approved medicine to purge choler; for it is propounded by Morena, as a receipt to cure their fathers of their choleric humours; and were it written in characters as barbarous as the words, might very well pass for a doctor's bill. To conclude, it is porridge, 'tis a receipt, 'tis a pig with a pudding in the belly, 'tis I know not what; for certainly never any one that pretended to write sense had the impudence before to put such stuff as this into the mouths of those that were to speak it before an audience whom he did not take to be all fools; and after that to print it too, and expose it to the examination of the world. But let us see what we can make of this stuff:

'For when we're dead, and our freed souls enlarg'd'——

"Here he tells us what it is to be *dead*; it is to have *our freed souls set free*. Now if to have a soul set free is to be dead, then to have a *freed soul* set free is to have a dead man die.

'Then gentle, as a happy lover's sigh'—

"They two like one *sigh*, and that one *sigh*, like two wandering meteors,

——'Shall fly through the air'—

"That is, they shall mount above like falling stars, or else they shall skip like two jacks-with-lanterns, or will-with-a-wisp, and madge-with-a-candle.

"*And in their airy walk steal into their cruel fathers' breasts like subtle guests*. So that their *fathers' breasts* must be in an *airy walk*, an airy *walk* of a *flier*. *And there they will read their souls, and track the spheres of their passions*. That is, these walking fliers, jack-with-a-lantern, etc., will put on his spectacles and fall a *reading souls*, and put on his pumps and fall a *tracking of spheres*; so that he will read and run, walk and fly, at the same time! Oh! Nimble Jack! *Then he will see how revenge here, how ambition there*—the birds will hop about. *And then view the dark characters of sieges, ruins, murders, blood, and wars, in their orbs: Track the characters* to their forms! Oh! rare sport for Jack! Never was place so full of game as these breasts! You cannot stir, but flush a sphere, start a character, or unkennel an orb!"

Settle's is said to have been the first play embellished with sculptures; those ornaments seem to have given poor Dryden great disturbance. He tries, however, to ease his pain by venting his malice in a parody.

"The poet has not only been so imprudent to expose all this stuff, but so arrogant to defend it with an epistle—like a saucy booth-keeper that, when he had put a cheat upon the people, would wrangle and fight with any that would not like it, or would offer to discover it; for which arrogance our poet receives this correction; and, to jerk him a little the sharper,

I will not transpose his verse, but by the help of his own words trans-nonsense sense, that, by my stuff, people may judge the better what his is:

Great Boy, thy tragedy and sculptures done
From press, and plates in fleets do homeward come:
And in ridiculous and humble pride,
Their course in ballad-singers' baskets guide,
Whose greasy twigs do all new beauties take,
From the gay shows thy dainty sculptures make.
Thy lines a mess of rhyming nonsense yield,
A senseless tale, with flattering fustian fill'd.
No grain of sense does in our line appear,
Thy words big bulks of boisterous bombast bear.
With noise they move, and from players' mouths rebound,
When their tongues dance to thy words' empty sound.
By thee inspir'd the rumbling verses roll,
As if that rhyme and bombast lent a soul:
And with that soul they seem taught duty too,
To huffing words does humble nonsense bow,
As if it would thy worthless worth enhance,
To th' lowest rank of fops thy praise advance;
To whom, by instinct, all thy stuff is dear;
Their loud claps echo to the theatre.
From breaths of fools thy commendation spreads,
Fame sings thy praise with mouths of loggerheads.
With noise and laughing each thy fustian greets,
'Tis clapt by quires of empty-headed cits,
Who have their tribute sent, and homage given,
As men in whispers send loud noise to heaven.

"Thus I have daubed him with his own puddle: and now we are come from aboard his dancing, masking, rebounding, breathing fleet; and, as if we had landed at Gotham, we meet nothing but fools and nonsense."

Such was the criticism to which the genius of Dryden could be reduced between rage and terror—rage with little provocation, and terror with little danger. To see the highest minds thus levelled with the meanest may produce some solace to the consciousness of weakness, and some mortification to the pride of wisdom. But let it be remembered, that minds are not levelled in their powers but when they are first levelled in their desires. Dryden and Settle had both placed their happiness in the claps of multitudes.

The two parts of the *Conquest of Granada* (1672) are written with a seeming determination to glut the public with dramatic wonders, to exhibit in its highest elevation a theatrical meteor of incredible love and impossible valour, and to leave no room for a wilder flight to the extravagance of posterity. All the rays of romantic heat, whether amorous or warlike, glow in Almanzor by a kind of concentration. He is above all laws; he is exempt from all restraints; he ranges the world at will, and governs wherever he appears. He fights without inquiring the cause, and loves in spite of the obligations of justice, of rejection by his mistress, and of prohibition from the dead. Yet the scenes are, for the most part, delightful; they exhibit a kind of illustrious depravity, and majestic madness, such as, if it is sometimes despised, is often reverenced, and in which the ridiculous is mingled with the astonishing.

In the epilogue to the second part of the *Conquest of Granada,* Dryden indulges his favourite pleasure of discrediting his predecessors; and this epilogue he has defended by a long postscript. He had promised a second dialogue, in which he should more fully treat of the virtues and faults of the English poets who have written in the dramatic, epic, or lyric way. This promise was never formally performed; but, with respect to the dramatic writers, he has given us in his prefaces, and in this postscript, something equivalent; but his purpose being to exalt himself by the comparison, he shows faults distinctly, and only praises excellence in general terms.

A play thus written, in professed defiance of probability, naturally drew upon itself the vultures of the theatre. One of the critics that attacked it was Martin Clifford, to whom Sprat addressed the *Life of Cowley,* with such veneration of his critical powers as might naturally excite great expectations of instruction from his remarks. But let honest credulity beware of receiving characters from contemporary writers. Clifford's remarks, by the favour of Dr. Percy, were at last obtained;

and, that no man may ever want them more, I will extract enough to satisfy all reasonable desire.

In the first letter his observation is only general: "You do live," says he, "in as much ignorance and darkness as you did in the womb: your writings are like a Jack-of-all-trades' shop; they have a variety, but nothing of value; and if thou art not the dullest plant-animal that ever the earth produced, all that I have conversed with are strangely mistaken in thee."

In the second he tells him that Almanzor is not more copied from Achilles than from Ancient Pistol. "But I am," says he, "strangely mistaken if I have not seen this very Almanzor of yours in some disguise about this town, and passing under another name. Pr'ythee tell me true, was not this Huffcap once the Indian Emperor? and at another time did he not call himself Maximin? Was not Lyndaraxa once called Almeria? I mean under Montezuma the Indian Emperor. I protest and vow they are either the same, or so alike that I cannot, for my heart, distinguish one from the other. You are therefore a strange unconscionable thief, that art not content to steal from others, but dost rob thy poor wretched self too."

Now was Settle's time to take his revenge. He wrote a vindication of his own lines; and, if he is forced to yield anything, makes his reprisals upon his enemy. To say that his answer is equal to the censure, is no high commendation. To expose Dryden's method of analysing his expressions, he tries the same experiment upon the same description of the ships in the *Indian Emperor*, of which however he does not deny the excellence; but intends to show, that by studied misconstruction everything may be equally represented as ridiculous. After so much of Dryden's elegant animadversions, justice requires that something of Settle's should be exhibited. The following observations are therefore extracted from a quarto pamphlet of ninety-five pages:

> " 'Fate after him below with pain did move,
>   And Victory could scarce keep pace above.'

"These two lines, if he can show me any sense or thought in, or anything but bombast and noise, he shall make me believe every word in his observations on Morocco sense."

In the *Empress of Morocco* were these lines:

> I'll travel then to some remoter sphere,
> Till I find out new worlds, and crown you there.

On which Dryden made this remark:

"I believe our learned author takes a sphere for a country; the sphere of Morocco, as if Morocco were the globe of earth and water; but a globe is no sphere neither, by his leave," etc. [To which Settle rejoins:] "So *sphere* must not be sense, unless it relate to a circular motion about a globe, in which sense the astronomers use it. I would desire him to expound these lines in *Granada*:

> 'I'll to the turrets of the palace go,
> And add new fire to those that fight below.
> Thence, Hero-like, with torches by my side,
> (Far be the omen tho') my Love I'll guide.
> No, like his better fortune I'll appear,
> With open arms, loose veil, and flowing hair,
> Just flying forward from my rowling sphere.'

"I wonder, if he be so strict, how he dares make so bold with *sphere* himself, and be so critical in other men's writings. Fortune is fancied standing on a globe, not on a *sphere*, as he told us in the first act.

"Because *Elkanah's similes are the most unlike things to what they are compared in the world*, I'll venture to start a simile in his *Annus Mirabilis*: he gives this poetical description of the ship called the London:

> 'The goodly London in her gallant trim,
> The Phœnix-daughter of the vanquisht old,
> Like a rich bride does to the ocean swim,
> And on her shadow rides in floating gold.
> Her flag aloft spread ruffling in the wind,
> And sanguine streamers seem'd the flood to fire:
> The weaver, charm'd with what his loom design'd,
> Goes on to sea, and knows not to retire.

With roomy decks her guns of mighty strength,
Whose low-laid mouths each mounting billow laves,
Deep in her draught, and warlike in her length,
She seems a sea-wasp flying on the waves.'

"What a wonderful pudder is here, to make all these poetical beautifications of a ship! that is, a *phœnix* in the first stanza, and but a *wasp* in the last: nay, to make his humble comparison of a *wasp* more ridiculous, he does not say it flew upon the waves as nimbly as a wasp, or the like, but it seemed a *wasp*. But our author at the writing of this was not in his altitudes, to compare ships to floating palaces; a comparison to the purpose was a perfection he did not arrive to till his *Indian Emperor's* days. But perhaps his similitude has more in it than we imagine; this ship had a great many guns in her, and they, put all together, made the sting in the wasp's tail: for this is all the reason I can guess why it seem'd a *wasp*. But, because we will allow him all we can to help out, let it be a *phœnix sea-wasp*, and the rarity of such an animal may do much towards heightening the fancy.

.   .   .   .

"It had been much more to his purpose, if he had designed to render the author's play little, to have searched for some such pedantry as this:

'Two ifs scarce make one possibility.

.   .   .   .   .

If Justice will take all, and nothing give,
Justice, methinks, is not distributive.
To die or kill you is the alternative;
Rather than take your life, I will not live.'

"Observe how prettily our author chops logic in heroic verse. Three such fustian, canting words as *distributive, alternative*, and *two ifs*, no man but himself would have come within the noise of. But he's a man of general learning, and all comes into his plays.

" 'Twould have done well, too, if he could have met with a rant or two worth the observation: such as,

'Move swiftly, Sun, and fly a lover's pace,
  Leave months and weeks behind thee in thy race.'

"But surely the Sun, whether he flies a lover's or not a lover's pace, leaves weeks and months, nay, years too, behind him in his race.

"Poor Robin, or any other of the philomathematics, would have given him satisfaction in the point.

'If I would kill thee now, thy fate's so low,
  That I must stoop ere I can give the blow.
  But mine is fixt so far above thy crown,
  That all thy men,
  Piled on thy back, can never pull it down.'

"Now where that is, Almanzor's fate is fixed, I cannot guess; but, wherever it is, I believe Almanzor, and think that all Abdalla's subjects, piled upon one another, might not pull down his fate so well as without piling: besides, I think Abdalla so wise a man, that if Almanzor had told him piling his men upon his back might do the feat, he would scarce bear such a weight, for the pleasure of the exploit; but 'tis a huff, and let Abdalla do it if he dare.

   .   .   .   .   .

'The people like a headlong torrent go,
  And every dam they break or overflow.
  But, unoppos'd, they either lose their force,
  Or wind in volumes to their former course.'

"A very pretty allusion, contrary to all sense or reason. Torrents, I take it, let 'em wind never so much, can never return to their former course, unless he can suppose that fountains can go upwards, which is impossible: nay, more, in the foregoing pages he tells us so too. A trick of a very unfaithful memory.

'But can no more than fountains upward flow';

which of a *torrent*, which signifies a rapid stream, is much more impossible. Besides, if he goes to quibble, and say that 'tis possible, by art, water may be made return, and the same

water run twice in one and the same channel, then he quite
confutes what he says; for 'tis by being opposed that it runs
into its former course; for all engines that make water so return do it by compulsion and opposition. Or, if he means a
headlong torrent for a tide, which would be ridiculous, yet
tides do not wind in volumes, but come foreright back (if their
current lies straight) to their former course, and that by opposition of the sea-water that drives them back again.

.   .   .   .

"And for fancy, when he lights of any thing like it, 'tis a
wonder if it be not borrowed. As here, for example of, I find
this fanciful thought in his *Annus Mirabilis*:

> 'Old father Thames raised up his reverend head,
> But fear'd the fate of Simois would return;
> Deep in his ooze he sought his sedgy bed,
> And shrunk his waters back into his urn.'

"This is stolen from Cowley's *Davideis*, p. 9:

> 'Swift Jordan started, and straight backward fled,
> Hiding amongst thick reeds his aged head.

> .   .   .   .   .   .

> And when the Spaniards their assault begin,
> At once beat those without and those within.'

"This Almanzor speaks of himself; and sure for one man
to conquer an army within the city and another without the
city at once is something difficult; but this flight is pardonable
to some we meet with in *Granada*. Osmin, speaking of
Almanzor,

> 'Who, like a tempest that outrides the wind,
> Made a just battle, ere the bodies join'd.'

"Pray what does this honourable person mean by a *tempest
that outrides the wind*? A tempest that outrides itself. To
suppose a tempest without wind is as bad as supposing a man
to walk without feet; for if he supposes the tempest to be
something distinct from the wind, yet, as being the effect of
wind only, to come before the cause is a little preposterous:

so that if he takes it one way, or if he takes it the other, those two *ifs* will scarcely make one *possibility*." Enough of Settle.

Marriage-à-la-Mode (1673) is a comedy dedicated to the Earl of Rochester, whom he acknowledges not only as the defender of his poetry, but the promoter of his fortune. Langbaine places this play in 1673. The Earl of Rochester, therefore, was the famous Wilmot, whom yet tradition always represents as an enemy to Dryden, and who is mentioned by him with some disrespect in the preface to Juvenal.

The Assignation, or Love in a Nunnery, a comedy (1673), was driven off the stage, *against the opinion*, as the author says, *of the best judges*. It is dedicated, in a very elegant address, to Sir Charles Sedley, in which he finds an opportunity for his usual complaint of hard treatment and unreasonable censure.

Amboyna (1673) is a tissue of mingled dialogue in verse and prose, and was perhaps written in less time than *The Royal Martyr*; though the author thought not fit, either ostentatiously or mournfully, to tell how little labour it cost him, or at how short a warning he produced it. It was a temporary performance, written in the time of the Dutch war to inflame the nation against their enemies; to whom he hopes, as he declares in his epilogue, to make his poetry not less destructive than that by which Tyrtæus of old animated the Spartans. This play was written in the second Dutch war in 1673.

The State of Innocence and Fall of Man (1674) is termed by him an opera: it is rather a tragedy in heroic rhyme, but of which the personages are such as cannot decently be exhibited on the stage. Some such production was foreseen by Marvel, who writes thus to Milton:—

> Or if a work so infinite be spann'd,
> Jealous I was, that some less skilful hand
> (Such as disquiet always what is well,
> And by ill imitating would excel)
> Might hence presume the whole creation's day,
> To change in scenes, and show it in a play.

It is another of his hasty productions; for the heat of his imagination raised it in a month.

This composition is addressed to the Princess of Modena, then Duchess of York, in a strain of flattery which disgraces genius, and which it was wonderful that any man that knew the meaning of his own words could use without self-detestation. It is an attempt to mingle earth and heaven, by praising human excellence in the language of religion.

The preface contains an apology for heroic verse and poetic licence; by which is meant not any liberty taken in contracting or extending words, but the use of bold fictions and ambitious figures.

The reason which he gives for printing what was never acted cannot be overpassed:—"I was induced to it in my own defence, many hundred copies of it being dispersed abroad without my knowledge or consent; so that every one gathering new faults, it became at length a libel against me." These copies, as they gathered faults, were apparently manuscript; and he lived in an age very unlike ours, if many hundred copies of fourteen hundred lines were likely to be transcribed. An author has a right to print his own works, and need not seek an apology in falsehood; but he that could bear to write the dedication felt no pain in writing the preface.

Aureng Zebe (1676) is a tragedy founded on the actions of a great prince then reigning, but over nations not likely to employ their critics upon the transactions of the English stage. If he had known and disliked his own character, our trade was not in those times secure from his resentment. His country is at such a distance, that the manners might be safely falsified, and the incidents feigned; for the remoteness of place is remarked by Racine to afford the same conveniences to a poet as length of time.

This play is written in rhyme, and has the appearance of being the most elaborate of all the dramas. The personages are imperial; but the dialogue is often domestic, and therefore susceptible of sentiments accommodated to familiar incidents. The complaint of life is celebrated, and there are many other passages that may be read with pleasure.

This play is addressed to the Earl of Mulgrave, afterwards

Duke of Buckingham, himself, if not a poet, yet a writer of verses, and a critic. In this address Dryden gave the first hints of his intention to write an epic poem. He mentions his design in terms so obscure, that he seems afraid lest his plan should be purloined, as, he says, happened to him when he told it more plainly in his preface to Juvenal. "The subject," says he, "you know is great, the story English, and neither too far distant from the present age, nor too near approaching it."

All for Love, or the World well lost (1678), a tragedy founded upon the story of Antony and Cleopatra, he tells us, "is the only play which he wrote for himself"; the rest were given to the people. It is by universal consent accounted the work in which he has admitted the fewest improprieties of style or character; but it has one fault equal to many, though rather moral than critical, that, by admitting the romantic omnipotence of love, he has recommended, as laudable and worthy of imitation, that conduct which, through all ages, the good have censured as vicious, and the bad despised as foolish.

Of this play the prologue and the epilogue, though written upon the common topics of malicious and ignorant criticism, and without any particular relation to the characters or incidents of the drama, are deservedly celebrated for their elegance and sprightliness.

The Kind Keeper, or Mr. Limberham (1678), is a comedy, which, after the third night, was prohibited as too indecent for the stage. What gave offence was in the printing, as the author says, altered or omitted. Dryden confesses that its indecency was objected to; but Langbaine, who yet seldom favours him, imputes its expulsion to resentment, because it "so much exposed the keeping part of the town."

Œdipus (1679) is a tragedy formed by Dryden and Lee, in conjunction, from the works of Sophocles, Seneca, and Corneille. Dryden planned the scenes, and composed the first and third acts.

Troilus and Cressida (1679) is a play altered from Shakespeare; but so altered that, even in Langbaine's opinion, "the last scene in the third act is a masterpiece." It is introduced by a discourse on "The Grounds of Criticism in Tragedy," to which I suspect that Rymer's book had given occasion.

The *Spanish Friar* (1681) is a tragi-comedy, eminent for the happy coincidence and coalition of the two plots. As it was written against the Papists, it would naturally at that time have friends and enemies; and partly by the popularity which it obtained at first, and partly by the real power both of the serious and risible part, it continued long a favourite of the public.

It was Dryden's opinion, at least for some time, and he maintains it in the dedication of this play, that the drama required an alternative of comic and tragic scenes, and that it is necessary to mitigate by alleviations of merriment the pressure of ponderous events, and the fatigue of toilsome passions. "Whoever," says he, "cannot perform both parts, *is but half a poet for the stage.*"

The *Duke of Guise*, a tragedy (1683), written in conjunction with Lee, as *Œdipus* had been before, seems to deserve notice only for the offence which it gave to the remnant of the Covenanters, and in general to the enemies of the court, who attacked him with great violence, and were answered by him; though at last he seems to withdraw from the conflict, by transferring the greater part of the blame or merit to his partner. It happened that a contract had been made between them, by which they were to join in writing a play; and "he happened," says Dryden, "to claim the performance of that promise just upon the finishing of a poem, when I would have been glad of a little respite before the undertaking of a second task. Two-thirds of it belonged to him; and to me only the first scene of the play, the whole fourth act, and the first half, or somewhat more, of the fifth."

This was a play written professedly for the party of the Duke of York, whose succession was then opposed. A parallel is intended between the Leaguers of France and the Covenanters of England; and this intention produced the controversy.

Albion and Albanius (1685) is a musical drama or opera, written, like the *Duke of Guise*, against the Republicans. With what success it was performed, I have not found.

Don Sebastian (1690) is commonly esteemed either the first or second of his dramatic performances. It is too long to be all acted, and has many characters and many incidents; and though it is not without sallies of frantic dignity, and more noise than meaning, yet as it makes approaches to the possibilities of real life, and has some sentiments which leave a strong impression, it continued long to attract attention. Amidst the distresses of princes, and the vicissitudes of empire, are inserted several scenes which the writer intended for comic; but which, I suppose, that age did not much commend, and this would not endure. There are, however, passages of excellence universally acknowledged; the dispute and the reconciliation of Dorax and Sebastian has always been admired.

This play was first acted in 1690, after Dryden had for some years discontinued dramatic poetry.

Amphitryon is a comedy derived from Plautus and Molière. The dedication is dated Oct. 1690. This play seems to have succeeded at its first appearance, and was, I think, long considered as a very diverting entertainment.

King Arthur (1691) is another opera. It was the last work that Dryden performed for King Charles, who did not live to see it exhibited. In the dedication to the Marquis of Halifax, there is a very elegant character of Charles, and a pleasing account of his latter life. When this was first brought upon the stage, news that the Duke of Monmouth had landed was told in the theatre; upon which the company departed, and *Arthur* was exhibited no more.

Cleomenes (April 1692) is a tragedy, only remarkable as it occasioned an incident related in *The Guardian* [No. 45], and allusively mentioned by Dryden in his preface. As he came out from the representation, he was accosted thus by some airy stripling: "Had I been left alone with a young beauty, I would not have spent my time like your Spartan." "That, Sir," said Dryden, "perhaps is true; but give me leave to tell you that you are no hero."

His last drama was *Love Triumphant*, a tragi-comedy. In his dedication to the Earl of Salisbury he mentions "the lowness of fortune to which he has so voluntarily reduced himself, and of which he has no reason to be ashamed."

This play appeared in 1694. It is said to have been unsuccessful. The catastrophe, proceeding merely from a change of mind, is confessed by the author to be defective. Thus he began and ended his dramatic labours with ill-success.

From such a number of theatrical pieces it will be supposed, by most readers, that he must have improved his fortune; at least, that such diligence with such abilities must have set penury at defiance. But in Dryden's time the drama was very far from that universal approbation which it has now obtained. The playhouse was abhorred by the Puritans, and avoided by those who desired the character of seriousness or decency. A grave lawyer would have debased his dignity, and a young trader would have impaired his credit, by appearing in those mansions of dissolute licentiousness. The profits of the theatre, when so many classes of the people were deducted from the audience, were not great; and the poet had for a long time but a single night. The first that had two nights was Southerne; and the first that had three was Rowe. There were, however, in those days, arts of improving a poet's profit, which Dryden forbore to practise; and a play therefore seldom produced him more than a hundred pounds, by the accumulated gain of the third night, the dedication, and the copy.

Almost every piece had a dedication, written with such elegance and luxuriance of praise, as neither haughtiness nor avarice could be imagined able to resist. But he seems to have made flattery too cheap. That praise is worth nothing of which the price is known.

To increase the value of his copies, he often accompanied his work with a preface of criticism; a kind of learning then almost new in the English language, and which he who had considered with great accuracy the principles of writing was able to distribute copiously, as occasions arose. By these dissertations the public judgment must have been much improved; and Swift, who conversed with Dryden, relates that he regretted the success of his own instructions, and found his readers made suddenly too skilful to be easily satisfied.

His prologues had such reputation, that for some time a play was considered as less likely to be well received, if some of his verses did not introduce it. The price of a prologue was two guineas, till, being asked to write one for Mr. Southerne, he demanded three: "Not," said he, "young man, out of disrespect to you, but the players have had my goods too cheap."

Though he declares, that in his own opinion his genius was not dramatic, he had great confidence in his own fertility; for he is said to have engaged, by contract, to furnish four plays a year.

It is certain that in one year, 1678, he published *All for Love, Assignation*, two parts of the *Conquest of Granada, Sir Martin Marr-all* and the *State of Innocence*, six complete plays; with a celerity of performance, which, though all Langbaine's charges of plagiarism should be allowed, shows such facility of composition, such readiness of language, and such copiousness of sentiment, as since the name of Lopez de Vega perhaps no other author has ever possessed.

He did not enjoy his reputation, however great, nor his profits, however small, without molestation. He had critics to endure, and rivals to oppose. The two most distinguished wits of the nobility, the Duke of Buckingham and Earl of Rochester, declared themselves his enemies.

Buckingham characterised him, in 1671, by the name of Bayes, in the *Rehearsal*; a farce which he is said to have written with the assistance of Butler, the author of *Hudibras*, Martin Clifford of the Charter House, and Dr. Sprat, the friend of Cowley, then his chaplain. Dryden and his friends laughed at the length of time and the number of hands employed upon this performance; in which, though by some artifice of action it yet keeps possession of the stage, it is not possible now to find anything that might not have been written without so long delay, or a confederacy so numerous.

To adjust the minute events of literary history is tedious and troublesome: it requires, indeed, no great force of understanding, but often depends upon inquiries which there is no opportunity of making, or is to be fetched from books and pamphlets not always at hand.

The *Rehearsal* was played in [December] 1671, and yet is represented as ridiculing passages in the *Conquest of Granada* and *Assignation*, which were not published till 1678, in *Marriage-à-la-Mode*, published in 1673, and in *Tyrannic Love*, in 1677. These contradictions show how rashly satire is applied.

It is said that this farce was originally intended against

Davenant, who in the first draught was characterised by the name of Bilboa. Davenant had been a soldier and an adventurer.

There is one passage in the *Rehearsal* still remaining which seems to have related originally to Davenant. Bayes hurts his nose, and comes in with brown paper applied to the bruise: how this affected Dryden does not appear. Davenant's nose had suffered such diminution by mishaps among the women that a patch upon that part evidently denoted him.

It is said likewise that Sir Robert Howard was once meant. The design was probably to ridicule the reigning poet, whoever he might be.

Much of the personal satire, to which it might owe its first reception, is now lost or obscured. Bayes probably imitated the dress and mimicked the manner of Dryden: the cant words which are so often in his mouth may be supposed to have been Dryden's habitual phrases or customary exclamations. Bayes, when he is to write, is blooded and purged: this, as Lamotte relates himself to have heard, was the real practice of the poet.

There were other strokes in the *Rehearsal* by which malice was gratified; the debate between Love and Honour, which keeps Prince Volscius in a single boot, is said to have alluded to the misconduct of the Duke of Ormond, who lost Dublin to the rebels while he was toying with a mistress.

The Earl of Rochester, to suppress the reputation of Dryden, took Settle into his protection, and endeavoured to persuade the public that its approbation had been to that time misplaced. Settle was a while in high reputation: his *Empress of Morocco*, having [1673] first delighted the town, was carried in triumph to Whitehall, and played by the ladies of the court. Now was the poetical meteor at the highest; the next moment began its fall. Rochester withdrew his patronage; seeming resolved, says one of his biographers, "to have a judgment contrary to that of the town"; perhaps being unable to endure any reputation beyond a certain height, even when he had himself contributed to raise it.

Neither critics nor rivals did Dryden much mischief, unless they gained from his own temper the power of vexing him, which his frequent bursts of resentment give reason to suspect.

He is always angry at some past or afraid of some future censure; but he lessens the smart of his wounds by the balm of his own approbation, and endeavours to repel the shafts of criticism by opposing a shield of adamantine confidence.

The perpetual accusation produced against him was that of plagiarism, against which he never attempted any vigorous defence; for though he was perhaps sometimes injuriously censured, he would, by denying part of the charge, have confessed the rest; and, as his adversaries had the proof in their own hands, he, who knew that wit had little power against facts, wisely left, in that perplexity which it generally produces, a question which it was his interest to suppress, and which, unless provoked by vindication, few were likely to examine.

Though the life of a writer, from about thirty-five to sixty-three, may be supposed to have been sufficiently busied by the composition of eight-and-twenty pieces for the stage, Dryden found room in the same space for many other undertakings.

But, how much soever he wrote, he was at least once suspected of writing more; for, in 1679, a paper of verses, called *An Essay on Satire*, was shown about in manuscript, by which the Earl of Rochester, the Duchess of Portsmouth, and others, were so much provoked that, as was supposed (for the actors were never discovered), they procured Dryden, whom they suspected as the author, to be [18th Dec., 1679] waylaid and beaten. This incident is mentioned by the Duke of Buckinghamshire, the true writer, in his *Essay on Poetry*, where he says of Dryden:

> Though prais'd and punish'd for another's rhymes,
> His own deserve as great applause sometimes.

His reputation in time was such that his name was thought necessary to the success of every poetical or literary performance, and therefore he was engaged to contribute something, whatever it might be, to many publications. He prefixed the *Life of Polybius* to the translation of Sir Henry Shere, and those of Lucian and Plutarch to versions of their works by different hands. Of the English *Tacitus* he translated the first book; and, if Gordon be credited, translated it from the French. Such a charge can hardly be mentioned without some degree of indignation; but it is not, I suppose, so much to be inferred that Dryden wanted the literature necessary to the perusal of Tacitus, as that, considering himself as hidden in a crowd, he had no awe of the public, and, writing merely for money, was contented to get it by the nearest way.

In 1680, the *Epistles of Ovid* being translated by the poets of the time, among which one was the work of Dryden, and another of Dryden and Lord Mulgrave, it was necessary to introduce them by a preface; and Dryden, who on such occasions was regularly summoned, prefixed a discourse upon translation, which was then struggling for the liberty that it now enjoys. Why it should find any difficulty in breaking the shackles of verbal interpretation, which must for ever debar it from elegance, it would be difficult to conjecture, were not the power of prejudice every day observed. The authority of Jonson, Sandys, and Holyday had fixed the judgment of the nation; and it was not easily believed that a better way could be found than they had taken, though Fanshaw, Denham, Waller, and Cowley had tried to give examples of a different practice.

In [November] 1681 Dryden became yet more conspicuous by uniting politics with poetry in the memorable satire called *Absalom and Achitophel*, written against the faction which, by Lord Salisbury's incitement, set the Duke of Monmouth at its head.

Of this poem, in which personal satire was applied to the support of public principles, and in which therefore every mind was interested, the reception was eager, and the sale so large, that my father, an old bookseller, told me he had not known it equalled but by Sacheverell's trial.

The reason of this general perusal Addison has attempted to derive from the delight which the mind feels in the investigation of secrets; and thinks that curiosity to decipher the names procured readers to the poem. There is no need to inquire why those verses were read, which, to all the attractions of wit, elegance, and harmony, added the co-operation of all the factious passions, and filled every mind with triumph or resentment.

It could not be supposed that all the provocation given by

Dryden would be endured without resistance or reply. Both his person and his party were exposed in their turns to the shafts of satire, which, though neither so well pointed nor perhaps so well aimed, undoubtedly drew blood.

One of these poems is called *Dryden's Satire to his Muse*, ascribed, though, as Pope says, falsely, to Somers, who was afterwards chancellor. The poem, whosesoever it was, has much virulence, and some sprightliness. The writer tells all the ill that he can collect both of Dryden and his friends.

The poem of *Absalom and Achitophel* had two answers, now both forgotten—one called *Azaria and Hushai*, the other *Absalom Senior* [or *Achitophel transposed*], a poem. Of these hostile compositions, Dryden apparently imputes *Absalom Senior* to Settle, by quoting in his verses against him the second line. *Azaria and Hushai* was, as Wood says, imputed to him, though it is somewhat unlikely that he should write twice on the same occasion. This is a difficulty which I cannot remove, for want of a minuter knowledge of poetical transactions.

The same year [in March 1681-2] he published *The Medal*, of which the subject is a medal struck on Lord Shaftesbury's escape from a prosecution by the *ignoramus* of a grand jury of Londoners.

In both poems he maintains the same principles, and saw them both attacked by the same antagonist. Elkanah Settle, who had answered *Absalom*, appeared with equal courage in opposition to *The Medal*, and published an answer called *The Medal Reversed*, with so much success in both encounters, that he left the palm doubtful, and divided the suffrages of the nation. Such are the revolutions of fame, or such is the prevalence of fashion, that the man whose works have not yet been thought to deserve the care of collecting them, who died forgotten in an hospital, and whose latter years were spent in contriving shows for fairs, and carrying an elegy or epithalamium, of which the beginning and end were occasionally varied, but the intermediate parts were always the same, to every house where there was a funeral or a wedding, might with truth have had inscribed upon his stone:

Here lies the Rival and Antagonist of Dryden.

Settle was, for his rebellion, severely chastised by Dryden under the name of Doeg, in the second part of *Absalom and Achitophel*, and was perhaps for his factious audacity made the city poet, whose annual office was to describe the glories of the Mayor's day. Of these bards he was the last, and seems not much to have deserved even this degree of regard if it was paid to his political opinions; for he afterwards wrote a panegyric on the virtues of Judge Jefferies; and what more could have been done by the meanest zealot for prerogative?

Of translated fragments, or occasional poems, to enumerate the titles, or settle the dates, would be tedious, with little use. It may be observed, that, as Dryden's genius was commonly excited by some personal regard, he rarely writes upon a general topic.

Soon after the accession of King James, when the design of reconciling the nation to the Church of Rome became apparent, and the religion of the court gave the only efficacious title to its favours, Dryden declared himself a convert to popery. This at any other time might have passed with little censure. Sir Kenelm Digby embraced popery; the two Reynolds reciprocally converted one another; and Chillingworth himself was a while so entangled in the wilds of controversy, as to retire for quiet to an infallible church. If men of argument and study can find such difficulties or such motives, as may either unite them to the Church of Rome, or detain them in uncertainty, there can be no wonder that a man, who perhaps never inquired why he was a Protestant, should by an artful and experienced disputant be made a Papist, overborne by the sudden violence of new and unexpected arguments, or deceived by a representation which shows only the doubts on one part, and only the evidence on the other.

That conversion will always be suspected that apparently concurs with interest. He that never finds his error till it hinders his progress towards wealth or honour, will not be thought to love Truth only for herself. Yet it may easily happen that information may come at a commodious time; and as truth and interest are not by any fatal necessity at variance, that one may by accident introduce the other. When opinions are struggling into popularity, the arguments by which they are opposed or defended become more known; and he that changes his profession would perhaps have changed it before, with the like opportunities of instruction. This was the then state of popery; every artifice was used to show it in its fairest form; and it must be owned to be a religion of external appearance sufficiently attractive.

It is natural to hope that a comprehensive is likewise an elevated soul, and that whoever is wise is also honest. I am willing to believe that Dryden, having employed his mind, active as it was, upon different studies, and filled it, capacious as it was, with other materials, came unprovided to the controversy, and wanted rather skill to discover the right, than virtue to maintain it. But inquiries into the heart are not for man; we must now leave him to his Judge.

The priests, having strengthened their cause by so powerful an adherent, were not long before they brought him into action. They engaged him (1686) to defend the controversial papers found in the strong-box of Charles the Second, and what yet was harder, to defend them against Stillingfleet.

With hopes of promoting popery, he was employed to translate Maimbourg's *History of the League*, which he published [1684] with a large introduction. His name is likewise prefixed [1688] to the English *Life of Francis Xavier*; but I know not that he ever owned himself the translator. Perhaps the use of his name was a pious fraud, which, however, seems not to have had much effect; for neither of the books, I believe, was ever popular.

The version of *Xavier's Life* is commended by Brown, in a pamphlet not written to flatter; and the occasion of it is said to have been, that the Queen, when she solicited a son, made vows to him as her tutelary saint.

He was supposed to have undertaken to translate Varillas's *History of Heresies*; and, when Burnet published remarks upon it, to have written an *Answer*; upon which Burnet makes the following observation:

"I have been informed from England, that a gentleman who is known both for poetry and other things had spent three

months in translating M. Varillas's *History*; but that as soon
as my *Reflections* appeared he discontinued his labour, finding
the credit of his author was gone. Now, if he thinks it is recovered by his *Answer*, he [Dryden] will perhaps go on with
his translation; and this may be, for aught I know, as good an
entertainment for him as the conversation that he had set on
between the Hinds and Panthers, and all the rest of animals,
for whom M. Varillas may serve well enough for an author:
and this history and that poem are such extraordinary things
of their kind, that it will be but suitable to see the author of
the worst poem become likewise the translator of the worst
history that the age has produced. If his grace and his wit
improve both proportionably, he will hardly find that he has
gained much by the change he has made, from having no religion, to choose one of the worst. It is true, he had something
to sink from in matter of wit; but as for his morals, it is scarce
possible for him to grow a worse man than he was. He has
lately wreaked his malice on me for spoiling his three months'
labour; but in it he has done me all the honour that any man
can receive from him, which is to be railed at by him. If I had
ill-nature enough to prompt me to wish a very bad wish for
him, it should be, that he would go on and finish his translation. By that it will appear whether the English nation, which
is the most competent judge in this matter, has, upon the seeing our debate, pronounced in M. Varillas's favour or in mine.
It is true, Mr. D. will suffer a little by it; but at least it will
serve to keep him in from other extravagances; and if he gains
little honour by this work, yet he cannot lose so much by it
as he has done by his last employment."

Having probably felt his own inferiority in theological controversy, he was desirous of trying whether, by bringing poetry
to aid his arguments, he might become a more efficacious defender of his new profession. To reason in verse was, indeed,
one of his powers; but subtilty and harmony united are still
feeble, when opposed to truth.

Actuated, therefore, by zeal for Rome, or hope of fame, he
published [April, 1687] the *Hind and the Panther*, a poem, in
which the Church of Rome, figured by the *milk-white Hind*,

defends her tenets against the Church of England, represented by the *Panther*, a beast beautiful, but spotted.

A fable which exhibits two beasts talking theology appears at once full of absurdity; and it was accordingly ridiculed in the *Country Mouse and the City Mouse*, a parody, written by Montague, afterwards Earl of Halifax, and Prior, who then gave the first specimen of his abilities.

The conversion of such a man at such a time was not likely to pass uncensured. Three dialogues were published by the facetious Thomas Brown, of which the two first were called *Reasons of Mr. Bayes's changing his Religion*; and the third, *The Reasons of Mr. Haynes the Player's Conversion and Reconversion*. The first was printed in 1688, the second not till 1690, the third in 1691. The clamour seems to have been long continued, and the subject to have strongly fixed the public attention.

In the two first dialogues Bayes is brought into the company of Crites and Eugenius, with whom he had formerly debated on dramatic poetry. The two talkers in the third are Mr. Bayes and Mr. Haynes.

Brown was a man not deficient in literature, nor destitute of fancy; but he seems to have thought it the pinnacle of excellence to be a *merry fellow*, and therefore laid out his powers upon small jests or gross buffoonery, so that his performances have little intrinsic value, and were read only while they were recommended by the novelty of the event that occasioned them.

These dialogues are like his other works: what sense or knowledge they contain is disgraced by the garb in which it is exhibited. One great source of pleasure is to call Dryden *little* Bayes. Ajax, who happens to be mentioned, is "he that wore as many cowhides upon his shield as would have furnished half the King's army with shoe-leather."

Being asked whether he had seen the *Hind and the Panther*, Crites answers: "Seen it! Mr. Bayes, why, I can stir nowhere but it pursues me; it haunts me worse than a pewter-buttoned serjeant does a decayed cit. Sometimes I meet it in a bandbox, when my laundress brings home my linen; sometimes, whether I will or no, it lights my pipe at a coffee-house; sometimes it surprises me in a trunk-maker's shop; and sometimes it refreshes my memory for me on the backside of a Chancery-lane parcel. For your comfort, Mr. Bayes, I have not only seen it, as you may perceive, but have read it too, and can quote it as freely upon occasion as a frugal tradesman can quote that noble treatise *The Worth of a Penny* to his extravagant 'prentice, that revels in cock-ale, stewed apples, and penny custards."

The whole animation of these compositions arises from a profusion of ludicrous and affected comparisons. "To secure one's chastity," says Bayes, "little more is necessary than to leave off a correspondence with the other sex, which, to a wise man, is no greater a punishment than it would be to a fanatic parson to be forbid seeing *The Cheats* and *The Committee*, or for my Lord Mayor and aldermen to be interdicted the sight of *The London Cuckolds*." This is the general strain, and therefore I shall be easily excused the labour of more transcription.

Brown does not wholly forget past transactions: "You began," says Crites to Bayes, "a very indifferent religion, and have not mended the matter in your last choice. It was but reason that your Muse, which appeared first in a tyrant's quarrel, should employ her last efforts to justify the usurpation of the Hind."

Next year the nation was summoned to celebrate the birth of the Prince. Now was the time for Dryden to rouse his imagination, and strain his voice. Happy days were at hand, and he was willing to enjoy and diffuse the anticipated blessings. He published a poem filled with predictions of greatness and prosperity—predictions of which it is not necessary to tell how they have been verified.

A few months passed after these joyful notes, and every blossom of popish hope was blasted for ever by the Revolution. A Papist now could be no longer laureate. The revenue, which he had enjoyed with so much pride and praise, was transferred to Shadwell, an old enemy, whom he had formerly stigmatised by the name of *Og*. Dryden could not decently complain that he was deposed, but seemed very angry that Shadwell succeeded him, and has therefore celebrated the intruder's inauguration in a poem exquisitely satirical, called *Mac Flecknoe*—of which the *Dunciad*, as Pope himself declares, is an imitation, though more extended in its plan, and more diversified in its incidents.

It is related by Prior, that Lord Dorset, when as chamberlain he was constrained to eject Dryden from his office, gave him from his own purse an allowance equal to the salary. This is no romantic or incredible act of generosity; a hundred a year is often enough given to claims less cogent by men less famed for liberality. Yet Dryden always represented himself as suffering under a public infliction; and once particularly demands respect for the patience with which he endured the loss of his little fortune. His patron might, indeed, enjoin him to suppress his bounty; but, if he suffered nothing, he should not have complained.

During the short reign of King James, he had written nothing for the stage, being, in his opinion, more profitably employed in controversy and flattery. Of praise he might perhaps have been less lavish without inconvenience, for James was never said to have much regard for poetry: he was to be flattered only by adopting his religion.

Times were now changed: Dryden was no longer the court-poet, and was to look back for support to his former trade; and having waited about two years, either considering himself as discountenanced by the public, or perhaps expecting a second Revolution, he produced *Don Sebastian* in 1690; and in the next four years four dramas more.

In 1693 appeared a new version of Juvenal and Persius. Of Juvenal he translated the first, third, sixth, tenth, and sixteenth satires; and of Persius the whole work. On this occasion he introduced his two sons to the public, as nurselings of the Muses. The fourteenth of Juvenal was the work of John, and the seventh of Charles Dryden. He prefixed a very ample preface in the form of a dedication to Lord Dorset; and there gives an account of the design which he had once formed to write an epic poem on the actions either of Arthur or the Black Prince. He considered the epic as necessarily including some kind of supernatural agency, and had imagined a new kind of contest between the guardian angels of kingdoms, of whom he conceived that each might be represented zealous for his charge, without any intended opposition to the purposes of the Supreme Being, of which all created minds must in part be ignorant.

This is the most reasonable scheme of celestial interposition that ever was formed. The surprises and terrors of enchantments, which have succeeded to the intrigues and oppositions of Pagan deities, afford very striking scenes, and open a vast extent to the imagination; but, as Boileau observes, and Boileau will be seldom found mistaken, with this incurable defect, that in a contest between heaven and hell we know at the beginning which is to prevail; for this reason we follow Rinaldo to the enchanted wood with more curiosity than terror.

In the scheme of Dryden there is one great difficulty, which yet he would perhaps have had address enough to surmount. In a war, justice can be but on one side; and, to entitle the hero to the protection of angels, he must fight in defence of indubitable right. Yet some of the celestial beings, thus opposed to each other, must have been represented as defending guilt.

That this poem was never written, is reasonably to be lamented. It would doubtless have improved our numbers, and enlarged our language; and might perhaps have contributed by pleasing instructions to rectify our opinions, and purify our manners.

What he required as the indispensable condition of such an undertaking, a public stipend, was not likely in these times to be obtained. Riches were not become familiar to us, nor had the nation yet learned to be liberal.

This plan he charged Blackmore with stealing; only, says he, "The guardian angels of kingdoms were machines too ponderous for him to manage."

In 1694 he began the most laborious and difficult of all his works, the translation of Virgil; from which he borrowed two months, that he might turn Fresnoy's *Art of Painting* into English prose. The preface, which he boasts to have written in twelve mornings, exhibits a parallel of poetry and painting, with a miscellaneous collection of critical remarks, such as cost a mind stored like his no labour to produce them.

In July [1697] he published his version of the works of Virgil; and, that no opportunity of profit might be lost, dedicated the Pastorals to the Lord Clifford, the Georgics to the Earl of Chesterfield, and the Æneid to the Earl of Mulgrave. This economy of flattery, at once lavish and discreet, did not pass without observation.

This translation was censured [1698] by Milbourne, a clergyman, styled, by Pope, "The Fairest of Critics," because he exhibited his own version to be compared with that which he condemned.

His last work was his *Fables* [fol. 1700], published in consequence, as is supposed, of a contract now in the hands of Mr. Tonson; by which he obliged himself, in consideration of 300*l.*, to finish for the press 10,000 verses.

In this volume is comprised the well-known *Ode on St. Cecilia's Day*, which, as appeared by a letter communicated to Dr. Birch, he spent a fortnight "in composing and correcting." But what is this to the patience and diligence of Boileau, whose *Equivoque*, a poem of only 346 lines, took from his life eleven months to write it, and three years to revise it?

Part of this book of *Fables* is the first Iliad in English, intended as a specimen of a version of the whole. Considering into what hands Homer was to fall, the reader cannot but rejoice that this project went no further.

The time was now at hand which was to put an end to all his schemes and labours. On the 1st of May, 1700, having been some time, as he tells us, a cripple in his limbs, he died in Gerard-street, of a mortification in his leg.

There is extant a wild story relating to some vexatious events that happened at his funeral, which, at the end of Congreve's Life, by a writer of I know not what credit, are thus related, as I find the account transferred to a biographical dictionary:

"On the Wednesday morning following, being May-day, 1700, under the most excruciating dolours, he [Mr. Dryden] died. Dr. Sprat, then bishop of Rochester, sent the next day to Lady Elizabeth, that he would make a present of the ground, which was 40*l*., with all the other Abbey fees, etc., to his deceased friend. Lord Halifax sent also to my Lady and Mr. Charles, that, if they would give him leave to bury Mr. Dryden, he would inter him with a gentleman's private funeral, and afterwards bestow 500*l*. on a monument in the Abbey; which, as they had no reason to refuse, they accepted. On the Saturday following the company came; the corpse was put into a velvet hearse, and eighteen mourning-coaches filled with company attended; when, just before they began to move, Lord Jefferies, with some of his rakish companions, coming by, in wine, asked whose funeral? and being told, 'What,' cries he, 'shall Dryden, the greatest honour and ornament of the nation, be buried after this private manner? No, gentlemen, let all that loved Mr. Dryden, and honour his memory, alight and join with me in gaining my Lady's consent to let me have the honour of his interment, which shall be after another manner than this; and I will bestow 1000*l*. on a monument in the Abbey for him.' The gentlemen in the coaches, not knowing of the Bishop of Rochester's favour, nor of the Lord Halifax's generous design (these two noble spirits having, out of respect to the family, enjoined Lady Elizabeth and her son to keep their favour concealed to the world, and let it pass for her own expense, etc.), readily came out of the coaches, and attended Lord Jefferies up to the lady's bedside, who was then sick: he repeated the purport of what he had before said; but she absolutely refusing, he fell on his knees, vowing never to rise till his request was granted. The rest of the company, by his desire, kneeled also; she, being naturally of a timorous disposition, and then under a sudden surprise, fainted away. As soon as she recovered her speech she cried, *No, no!* 'Enough, gentlemen,' replied he (rising briskly), 'my Lady is very good, she says, *Go, go!*' She repeated her former words with all her strength; but, alas, in vain! her feeble voice was lost in their acclamations of joy; and Lord Jefferies ordered the hearsemen to carry the corpse to Russell's, an undertaker in Cheapside, and leave it there till he sent orders for the embalmment, which, he added, should be after the royal manner. His directions were obeyed, the company dispersed, and Lady Elizabeth and Mr. Charles remained inconsolable. Next

morning Mr. Charles waited on Lord Halifax, etc., to excuse
his mother and himself, by relating the real truth. But neither
his Lordship nor the Bishop would admit of any plea; especially the latter, who had the Abbey lighted, the ground
opened, the choir attending, an anthem ready set, and himself waiting for some hours without any corpse to bury. Russell, after three days' expectance of orders for embalmment
without receiving any, waits on Lord Jefferies; who, pretending ignorance of the matter, turned it off with an ill-natured
jest, saying, those who observed the orders of a drunken frolic
deserved no better; that he remembered nothing at all of it;
and that he might do what he pleased with the corpse. On
this, Mr. Russell waits on the Lady Elizabeth and Mr. Dryden; but alas! it was not in their power to answer. The season
was very hot, the deceased had lived high and fast, and, being
corpulent and abounding with gross humours, grew very offensive. The undertaker, in short, threatened to bring the corpse
home and set it before their door. It cannot be easily imagined what grief, shame and confusion seized this unhappy
family. They begged a day's respite, which was granted. Mr.
Charles wrote a very handsome letter to Lord Jefferies, who
returned it with this cool answer:—'He knew nothing of the
matter, and would be troubled no more about it.' He then
addressed the Lord Halifax and Bishop of Rochester, who were
both too justly, though unhappily, incensed to do anything in
it. In this distress, Dr. Garth, a man who entirely loved Mr.
Dryden, and was withal a man of generosity and great humanity, sent for the corpse to the College of Physicians, in
Warwick Lane, and proposed a funeral by subscription, to
which himself set a most noble example: Mr. Wycherley, and
several others, among whom must not be forgotten Henry
Cromwell, Esq., Captain Gibbons, and Mr. Christopher Met-
calfe (Mr. Dryden's apothecary and intimate friend, since a
collegiate physician), who with many others contributed most
largely to the subscription; and at last a day, about three
weeks after his decease, was appointed for the interment at the
Abbey. Dr. Garth pronounced a fine Latin oration over the
corpse at the college; but the audience being numerous and
the room large, it was requisite the orator should be elevated

that he might be heard; but, as it unluckily happened, there was nothing at hand but an old beer-barrel, which the Doctor with much good-nature mounted; and, in the midst of his oration, beating time to the accent with his foot, the head broke in and his feet sunk to the bottom, which occasioned the malicious report of his enemies that he was turned Tub-Preacher: however, he finished the oration with a superior grace, to the loud acclamations of mirth which inspired the mixed, or rather *mob*, auditors. The procession began to move —a numerous train of coaches attended the hearse—but, good God! in what disorder can only be expressed by a sixpenny pamphlet soon after published, entitled *Dryden's Funeral*. At last the corpse arrived at the Abbey, which was all unlighted. No organ played, no anthem sung; only two of the singing boys preceded the corpse, who sung an ode of Horace, with each a small candle in their hand. The butchers and other mob broke in like a deluge, so that only about eight or ten gentlemen could get admission, and those forced to cut the way with their drawn swords. The coffin, in this disorder, was let down into Chaucer's grave, with as much confusion and as little ceremony as was possible, every one glad to save themselves from the gentlemen's swords or the clubs of the mob. When the funeral was over, Mr. Charles sent a challenge to Lord Jefferies, who refusing to answer it, he sent several others, and went often himself, but could neither get a letter delivered, nor admittance to speak to him, which so justly incensed him, that he resolved, since his lordship refused to answer him like a gentleman, that he would watch an opportunity to meet him, and fight off hand, though with all the rules of honour; which his lordship hearing, left the town; and Mr. Charles could never have the satisfaction to meet him, though he sought it till his death with the utmost application."

This story I once intended to omit, as it appears with no great evidence; nor have I met with any confirmation, but in a letter of Farquhar; and he only relates that the funeral of Dryden was tumultuary and confused.

Supposing the story true, we may remark that the gradual change of manners, though imperceptible in the process, appears great when different times, and those not very distant, are compared. If at this time a young drunken lord should interrupt the pompous regularity of a magnificent funeral, what would be the event, but that he would be justled out of the way, and compelled to be quiet? If he should thrust himself into a house, he would be sent roughly away; and, what is yet more to the honour of the present time, I believe that those who had subscribed to the funeral of a man like Dryden, would not, for such an accident, have withdrawn their contributions.

He was buried among the poets in Westminster Abbey, where, though the Duke of Newcastle had, in a general dedication prefixed by Congreve to his dramatic works, accepted thanks for his intention of erecting him a monument, he lay long without distinction, till the Duke of Buckinghamshire gave him a tablet, inscribed only with the name of DRYDEN.

He married the Lady Elizabeth Howard, daughter of the Earl of Berkshire, with circumstances, according to the satire imputed to Lord Somers, not very honourable to either party. By her he had three sons, Charles, John, and Erasmus-Henry. Charles was usher of the palace to Pope Clement XI.; and, visiting England in 1704, was drowned in an attempt to swim across the Thames at Windsor.

John was author of a comedy called *The Husband his own Cuckold*. He is said to have died at Rome. Henry entered into some religious order. It is some proof of Dryden's sincerity in his second religion, that he taught it to his sons. A man conscious of hypocritical profession in himself, is not likely to convert others; and as his sons were qualified in 1693 to appear among the translators of Juvenal, they must have been taught some religion before their father's change.

Of the person of Dryden I know not any account; of his mind, the portrait which has been left by Congreve, who knew him with great familiarity, is such as adds our love of his manners to our admiration of his genius. "He was," we are told, "of a nature exceedingly humane and compassionate, ready to forgive injuries, and capable of a sincere reconciliation with those that had offended him. His friendship, where he professed it, went beyond his professions. He was of a very easy, of very pleasing access; but somewhat slow, and, as it were, diffident in his advances to others; he had that in his nature which abhorred intrusion into any society whatever. He was therefore less known, and consequently his character became more liable to misapprehensions and misrepresentations: he was very modest, and very easily to be discountenanced in his approaches to his equals or superiors. As his reading had been very extensive, so was he very happy in a memory tenacious of everything that he had read. He was not more possessed of knowledge than he was communicative of it; but then his communication was by no means pedantic, or imposed upon the conversation, but just such, and went so far as, by the natural turn of the conversation in which he was engaged, it was necessarily promoted or required. He was extremely ready and gentle in his correction of the errors of any writer who thought fit to consult him, and full as ready and patient to admit the reprehensions of others, in respect of his own oversights or mistakes."

To this account of Congreve nothing can be objected but the fondness of friendship; and to have excited that fondness in such a mind is no small degree of praise. The disposition of Dryden, however, is shown in this character rather as it exhibited itself in cursory conversation, than as it operated on the more important parts of life. His placability and his friendship indeed were solid virtues; but courtesy and good-humour are often found with little real worth. Since Congreve, who knew him well, has told us no more, the rest must be collected as it can from other testimonies, and particularly from those notices which Dryden has very liberally given us of himself.

The modesty which made him so slow to advance, and so easy to be repulsed, was certainly no suspicion of deficient merit, or unconsciousness of his own value; he appears to have known, in its whole extent, the dignity of his own character, and to have set a very high value on his own powers and performances. He probably did not offer his conversation, because he expected it to be solicited; and he retired from a cold reception, not submissive but indignant, with such reference of his own greatness as made him unwilling to expose it to neglect or violation.

His modesty was by no means inconsistent with ostentatiousness; he is diligent enough to remind the world of his merit, and expresses with very little scruple his high opinion of his own powers; but his self-condemnations are read without scorn or indignation; we allow his claims, and love his frankness.

Tradition, however, has not allowed that his confidence in himself exempted him from jealousy of others. He is accused of envy and insidiousness; and is particularly charged with inciting Creech to translate Horace, that he might lose the reputation which Lucretius had given him.

Of this charge we immediately discover that it is merely conjectural; the purpose was such as no man would confess; and a crime that admits no proof, why should we believe?

He has been described as magisterially presiding over the younger writers, and assuming the distribution of poetical fame; but he who excels has a right to teach, and he whose judgment is incontestable may without usurpation examine and decide.

Congreve represents him as ready to advise and instruct; but there is reason to believe that his communication was rather useful than entertaining. He declares of himself that he was saturnine, and not one of those whose sprightly sayings diverted company; and one of his censurers makes him say:

> Nor wine nor love could ever see me gay;
> To writing bred, I knew not what to say.

There are men whose powers operate only at leisure and in retirement, and whose intellectual vigour deserts them in conversation; whom merriment confuses, and objection disconcerts; whose bashfulness restrains their exertion, and suffers them not to speak till the time of speaking is past; or whose attention to their own character makes them unwilling to utter at hazard what has not been considered, and cannot be recalled.

Of Dryden's sluggishness in conversation it is vain to search or to guess the cause. He certainly wanted neither sentiments nor language: his intellectual treasures were great, though they were locked up from his own use. "His thoughts," when he wrote, "flowed in upon him so fast, that his only care was which to choose, and which to reject." Such rapidity of composition naturally promises a flow of talk; yet we must be content to believe what an enemy says of him, when he likewise says it of himself. But whatever was his character as a companion, it appears that he lived in familiarity with the highest persons of his time. It is related by Carte of the Duke of Ormond, that he used often to pass a night with Dryden, and those with whom Dryden consorted: who they were, Carte has not told, but certainly the convivial table at which Ormond sat was not surrounded with a plebeian society. He was indeed reproached with boasting of his familiarity with the great; and Horace will support him in the opinion, that to please superiors is not the lowest kind of merit.

The merit of pleasing must, however, be estimated by the means. Favour is not always gained by good actions or laudable qualities. Caresses and preferments are often bestowed on the auxiliaries of vice, the procurers of pleasure, or the flatterers of vanity. Dryden has never been charged with any personal agency unworthy of a good character: he abetted vice and vanity only with his pen. One of his enemies has accused him of lewdness in his conversation; but, if accusation without proof be credited, who shall be innocent?

His works afford too many examples of dissolute licentiousness and abject adulation; but they were probably, like his merriment, artificial and constrained; the effects of study and meditation, and his trade rather than his pleasure.

Of the mind that can trade in corruption, and can deliberately pollute itself with ideal wickedness for the sake of spreading the contagion in society, I wish not to conceal or excuse the depravity. Such degradation of the dignity of genius, such abuse of superlative abilities, cannot be contemplated but with grief and indignation. What consolation can be had, Dryden has afforded, by living to repent, and to testify his repentance.

Of dramatic immorality he did not want examples among his predecessors, or companions among his contemporaries; but in the meanness and servility of hyperbolical adulation,

I know not whether, since the days in which the Roman emperors were deified, he has been ever equalled, except by Afra Behn in an address to Eleanor Gwyn. When once he has undertaken the task of praise, he no longer retains shame in himself, nor supposes it in his patron. As many odoriferous bodies are observed to diffuse perfumes from year to year, without sensible diminution of bulk or weight, he appears never to have impoverished his mint of flattery by his expenses, however lavish. He had all the forms of excellence, intellectual and moral, combined in his mind, with endless variation; and when he had scattered on the hero of the day the golden shower of wit and virtue, he had ready for him whom he wished to court on the morrow, new wit and virtue with another stamp. Of this kind of meanness he never seems to decline the practice, or lament the necessity: he considers the great as entitled to encomiastic homage, and brings praise rather as a tribute than a gift, more delighted with the fertility of his invention, than mortified by the prostitution of his judgment. It is indeed not certain that on these occasions his judgment much rebelled against his interest. There are minds which easily sink into submission, that look on grandeur with undistinguishing reverence, and discover no defect where there is elevation of rank and affluence of riches.

With his praises of others and of himself is always intermingled a strain of discontent and lamentation, a sullen growl of resentment, or querulous murmur of distress. His works are undervalued, his merit is unrewarded, and "he has few thanks to pay his stars that he was born among Englishmen." To his critics he is sometimes contemptuous, sometimes resentful, and sometimes submissive. The writer who thinks his works formed for duration, mistakes his interest when he mentions his enemies. He degrades his own dignity by showing that he was affected by their censures, and gives lasting importance to names which, left to themselves, would vanish from remembrance. From this principle Dryden did not often depart; his complaints are for the greater part general; he seldom pollutes his page with an adverse name. He condescended indeed to a controversy with Settle, in which he perhaps may be considered rather as assaulting than repelling; and since Settle is sunk into oblivion, his libel remains injurious only to himself.

Among answers to critics, no poetical attacks, or altercations, are to be included; they are like other poems, effusions of genius, produced as much to obtain praise as to obviate censure. These Dryden practised, and in these he excelled.

Of Collier, Blackmore, and Milbourne, he has made mention in the preface of his *Fables*. To the censure of Collier, whose remarks may be rather termed admonitions than criticisms, he makes little reply; being, at the age of sixty-eight, attentive to better things than the claps of a playhouse. He complains of Collier's rudeness, and the "horse-play of his raillery"; and asserts that "in many places he has perverted by his glosses the meaning" of what he censures; but in other things he confesses that he is justly taxed; and says, with great calmness and candour, "I have pleaded guilty to all thoughts or expressions of mine which can be truly argued of obscenity, profaneness, or immorality, and retract them. If he be my enemy, let him triumph; if he be my friend, as I have given him no personal occasion to be otherwise, he will be glad of my repentance." Yet as our best dispositions are imperfect, he left standing in the same book a reflection on Collier of great asperity, and indeed of more asperity than wit.

Blackmore he represents as made his enemy by the poem of *Absalom and Achitophel*, which "he thinks a little hard upon his fanatic patrons"; and charges him with borrowing the plan of his *Arthur* from the preface to Juvenal, "though he had," says he, "the baseness not to acknowledge his benefactor, but instead of it to traduce me in a libel."

The libel in which Blackmore traduced him was a *Satire against Wit* [1700]; in which, having lamented the exuberance of false wit and the deficiency of true, he proposes that all wit should be re-coined before it is current, and appoints masters of assay who shall reject all that is light or debased.

'Tis true, that when the coarse and worthless dross
Is purg'd away, there will be mighty loss;
Ev'n Congreve, Southerne, *Manly* Wycherley,
When thus refin'd, will grievous sufferers be;

> Into the melting pot when Dryden comes,
> What horrid stench will rise, what noisome fumes!
> How will he shrink when all his lewd allay,
> And wicked mixture, shall be purg'd away!

Thus stands the passage in the last edition; but in the original there was an abatement of the censure, beginning thus:

> But what remains will be so pure, 'twill bear
> Th' examination of the most severe.

Blackmore, finding the censure resented, and the civility disregarded, ungenerously omitted the softer part. Such variations discover a writer who consults his passions more than his virtue; and it may be reasonably supposed that Dryden imputes his enmity to its true cause.

Of Milbourne he wrote only in general terms, such as are always ready at the call of anger, whether just or not: a short extract will be sufficient. "He pretends a quarrel to me, that I have fallen foul upon priesthood; if I have, I am only to ask pardon of good priests, and am afraid his share of the reparation will come to little. Let him be satisfied that he shall never be able to force himself upon me for an adversary: I contemn him too much to enter into competition with him.

"As for the rest of those who have written against me, they are such scoundrels that they deserve not the least notice to be taken of them. Blackmore and Milbourne are only distinguished from the crowd by being remembered to their infamy."

Dryden, indeed, discovered in many of his writings an affected and absurd malignity to priests and priesthood, which naturally raised him many enemies, and which was sometimes as unseasonably resented as it was exerted. Trapp is angry that he calls the sacrificer in the Georgics "The Holy Butcher": the translation is not, indeed, ridiculous; but Trapp's anger arises from his zeal, not for the author, but the priest; as if any reproach of the follies of Paganism could be extended to the preachers of truth.

Dryden's dislike of the priesthood is imputed by Langbaine,

and I think by Brown, to a repulse which he suffered when he solicited ordination; but he denies, in the preface to his *Fables*, that he ever designed to enter into the Church; and such a denial he would not have hazarded if he could have been convicted of falsehood.

Malevolence to the clergy is seldom at a great distance from irreverence of religion, and Dryden affords no exception to this observation. His writings exhibit many passages, which, with all the allowance that can be made for characters and occasions, are such as piety would not have admitted, and such as may vitiate light and unprincipled minds. But there is no reason for supposing that he disbelieved the religion which he disobeyed. He forgot his duty rather than disowned it. His tendency to profaneness is the effect of levity, negligence, and loose conversation, with a desire of accommodating himself to the corruption of the times by venturing to be wicked as far as he durst. When he professed himself a convert to popery, he did not pretend to have received any new conviction of the fundamental doctrines of Christianity.

The persecution of critics was not the worst of his vexations; he was much more disturbed by the importunities of want. His complaints of poverty are so frequently repeated, either with the dejection of weakness sinking in helpless misery, or the indignation of merit claiming its tribute from mankind, that it is impossible not to detest the age which could impose on such a man the necessity of such solicitations, or not to despise the man who could submit to such solicitations without necessity.

Whether by the world's neglect, or his own imprudence, I am afraid that the greatest part of his life was passed in exigences. Such outcries were surely never uttered but in severe pain. Of his supplies or his expenses no probable estimate can now be made. Except the salary of the laureate, to which King James added the office of historiographer, perhaps with some additional emoluments, his whole revenue seems to have been casual; and it is well known that he seldom lives frugally who lives by chance. Hope is always liberal; and they that trust her promises make little scruple of revelling to-day on the profits of the morrow.

Of his plays the profit was not great; and of the produce of his other works very little intelligence can be had. By discoursing with the late amiable Mr. Tonson, I could not find that any memorials of the transactions between his predecessor and Dryden had been preserved, except the following papers:—

I do hereby promise to pay John Dryden, Esq., or order, on the 25th of March, 1699, the sum of two hundred and fifty guineas, in consideration of ten thousand verses, which the said John Dryden, Esq., is to deliver to me, Jacob Tonson, when finished, whereof seven thousand five hundred verses, more or less, are already in the said Jacob Tonson's possession. And I do hereby farther promise, and engage myself, to make up the said sum of two hundred and fifty guineas three hundred pounds sterling to the said John Dryden, Esq., his executors, administrators, or assigns, at the beginning of the second impression of the said ten thousand verses.

In witness whereof I have hereunto set my hand and seal, this 20th day of March, 1698–9,

JACOB TONSON.

Sealed and delivered, being first
    stampt, pursuant to the acts of
    parliament for that purpose, in
    the presence of

BENJ. PORTLOCK,
WILL. CONGREVE.

———

March 24th, 1698.

Received then of Mr. Jacob Tonson the sum of two hundred sixty-eight pounds fifteen shillings, in pursuance of an agreement for ten thousand verses to be delivered by me to the said Jacob Tonson, whereof I have already delivered to him about seven thousand five hundred, more or less; he the said Jacob Tonson being obliged to make up the foresaid sum of two hundred sixty-eight pounds fifteen shillings three hundred pounds, at the beginning of the second impression of the foresaid ten thousand verses;

I say, received by me,

JOHN DRYDEN.

Witness, CHARLES DRYDEN.

Two hundred and fifty guineas at 1*l*. 1*s*. 6*d*. is 268*l*. 15*s*. It is manifest, from the dates of this contract, that it relates to the volume of *Fables*, which contains about twelve thousand verses, and for which therefore the payment must have been afterwards enlarged.

I have been told of another letter yet remaining, in which he desires Tonson to bring him money to pay for a watch which he had ordered for his son, and which the maker would not leave without the price.

The inevitable consequence of poverty is dependence. Dryden had probably no recourse in his exigences but to his bookseller.

The particular character of Tonson I do not know; but the general conduct of traders was much less liberal in those times than in our own; their views were narrower, and their manners grosser. To the mercantile ruggedness of that race the delicacy of the poet was sometimes exposed. Lord Bolingbroke, who in his youth had cultivated poetry, related to Dr. King of Oxford, that one day, when he visited Dryden, they heard, as they were conversing, another person entering the house. "This," said Dryden, "is Tonson. You will take care not to depart before he goes away: for I have not completed the sheet which I promised him; and, if you leave me unprotected, I must suffer all the rudeness to which his resentment can prompt his tongue."

What rewards he obtained for his poems, besides the payment of the bookseller, cannot be known: Mr. Derrick, who consulted some of his relations, was informed that his *Fables* obtained 500*l*. from the Duchess of Ormond—a present not unsuitable to the magnificence of that splendid family; and he quotes Moyle, as relating that 40*l*. were paid by a musical society for the use of *Alexander's Feast*.

In those days the economy of government was yet unsettled,

and the payments of the Exchequer were dilatory and uncertain; of this disorder there is reason to believe that the laureate sometimes felt the effects; for in one of his prefaces he complains of those who, being intrusted with the distribution of the prince's bounty, suffer those that depend upon it to languish in penury.

Of his petty habits or slight amusements, tradition has retained little. Of the only two men whom I have found to whom he was personally known, one told me, that at the house which he frequented, called Will's Coffee-house, the appeal upon any literary dispute was made to him; and the other related, that his armed chair, which in the winter had a settled and prescriptive place by the fire, was in the summer placed in the balcony, and that he called the two places his winter and his summer seat. This is all the intelligence which his two survivors afforded me.

One of his opinions will do him no honour in the present age, though in his own time, at least in the beginning of it, he was far from having it confined to himself. He put great confidence in the prognostications of judicial astrology. In the appendix to the *Life of Congreve* is a narrative of some of his predictions wonderfully fulfilled; but I know not the writer's means of information, or character of veracity. That he had the configurations of the horoscope in his mind, and considered them as influencing the affairs of men, he does not forbear to hint.

> The utmost malice of the stars is past.—
> Now frequent *trines* the happier lights among,
> And *high-rais'd Jove*, from his dark prison freed,
> Those weights took off that on his planet hung,
> Will gloriously the new-laid works succeed.

He has elsewhere shown his attention to the planetary powers; and in the preface to his *Fables* has endeavoured obliquely to justify his superstition by attributing the same to some of the ancients. The letter, added to this narrative, leaves no doubt of his notions or practice.

So slight and so scanty is the knowledge which I have been able to collect concerning the private life and domestic manners of a man whom every English generation must mention with reverence as a critic and a poet.

Dryden may be properly considered as the father of English criticism, as the writer who first taught us to determine upon principles the merit of composition. Of our former poets, the greatest dramatist wrote without rules, conducted through life and nature by a genius that rarely misled, and rarely deserted him. Of the rest, those who knew the laws of propriety had neglected to teach them.

Two *Arts of English Poetry* were written in the days of Elizabeth by Webb and Puttenham, from which something might be learned, and a few hints had been given by Jonson and Cowley; but Dryden's *Essay on Dramatic Poetry* was the first regular and valuable treatise on the art of writing.

He who, having formed his opinions in the present age of English literature, turns back to peruse this dialogue, will not perhaps find much increase of knowledge, or much novelty of instruction; but he is to remember that critical principles were then in the hands of a few, who had gathered them partly from the ancients, and partly from the Italians and French. The structure of dramatic poems was then not generally understood. Audiences applauded by instinct; and poets perhaps often pleased by chance.

A writer who obtains his full purpose loses himself in his own lustre. Of an opinion which is no longer doubted, the evidence ceases to be examined. Of an art universally practised, the first teacher is forgotten. Learning once made popular is no longer learning; it has the appearance of something which we have bestowed upon ourselves, as the dew appears to rise from the field which it refreshes.

To judge rightly of an author, we must transport ourselves to his time, and examine what were the wants of his contemporaries, and what were his means of supplying them. That which is easy at one time was difficult at another. Dryden at least imported his science, and gave his country what it wanted before; or, rather, he imported only the materials, and manufactured them by his own skill.

The *Dialogue on the Drama* was one of his first essays of

criticism, written when he was yet a timorous candidate for reputation, and therefore laboured with that diligence which he might allow himself somewhat to remit, when his name gave sanction to his positions, and his awe of the public was abated, partly by custom, and partly by success. It will not be easy to find, in all the opulence of our language, a treatise so artfully variegated with successive representations of opposite probabilities, so enlivened with imagery, so brightened with illustrations. His portraits of the English dramatists are wrought with great spirit and diligence. The account of Shakespeare may stand as a perpetual model of encomiastic criticism; exact without minuteness, and lofty without exaggeration. The praise lavished by Longinus, on the attestation of the heroes of Marathon, by Demosthenes, fades away before it. In a few lines is exhibited a character, so extensive in its comprehension, and so curious in its limitations, that nothing can be added, diminished, or reformed; nor can the editors and admirers of Shakespeare, in all their emulation of reverence, boast of much more than of having diffused and paraphrased this epitome of excellence, of having changed Dryden's gold for baser metal, of lower value though of greater bulk.

In this, and in all his other essays on the same subject, the criticism of Dryden is the criticism of a poet; not a dull collection of theorems, nor a rude detection of faults, which perhaps the censor was not able to have committed; but a gay and vigorous dissertation, where delight is mingled with instruction, and where the author proves his right of judgment by his power of performance.

The different manner and effect with which critical knowledge may be conveyed, was perhaps never more clearly exemplified than in the performances of Rymer and Dryden. It was said of a dispute between two mathematicians, "malim cum Scaligero errare, quam cum Clavio recte sapere"; that "it was more eligible to go wrong with one than right with the other." A tendency of the same kind every mind must feel at the perusal of Dryden's prefaces and Rymer's discourses. With Dryden we are wandering in quest of Truth; whom we find, if we find her at all, dressed in the graces of elegance; and, if we miss her, the labour of the pursuit rewards itself; we are led only through fragrance and flowers. Rymer, without taking a nearer, takes a rougher way; every step is to be made through thorns and brambles; and Truth, if we meet her, appears repulsive by her mien, and ungraceful by her habit. Dryden's criticism has the majesty of a queen; Rymer's has the ferocity of a tyrant.

As he had studied with great diligence the art of poetry, and enlarged or rectified his notions by experience perpetually increasing, he had his mind stored with principles and observations; he poured out his knowledge with little labour; for of labour, notwithstanding the multiplicity of his productions, there is sufficient reason to suspect that he was not a lover. To write *con amore*, with fondness for the employment, with perpetual touches and retouches, with unwillingness to take leave of his own idea, and an unwearied pursuit of unattainable perfection, was, I think, no part of his character.

His criticism may be considered as general or occasional. In his general precepts, which depend upon the nature of things, and the structure of the human mind, he may doubtless be safely recommended to the confidence of the reader; but his occasional and particular positions were sometimes interested, sometimes negligent, and sometimes capricious. It is not without reason that Trapp, speaking of the praises which he bestows on *Palamon and Arcite*, says, "Novimus judicium Drydeni de poemate quodam Chauceri, pulchro sane illo, et admodum laudando, nimirum quod non modo vere epicum sit, sed Iliada etiam atque Æneada æquet, imo superet. Sed novimus eodem tempore viri illius maximi non semper accuratissimas esse censuras, nec ad severissimam critices normam exactas: illo judice id plerumque optimum est, quod nunc præ manibus habet, et in quo nunc occupatur."

He is therefore by no means constant to himself. His defence and desertion of dramatic rhyme is generally known. Spence, in his remarks on Pope's Odyssey, produces what he thinks an unconquerable quotation from Dryden's preface to the Æneid, in favour of translating an epic poem into blank verse; but he forgets that when his author attempted the Iliad, some years afterwards, he departed from his own decision, and translated into rhyme.

When he has any objection to obviate, or any licence to defend, he is not very scrupulous about what he asserts, nor very cautious, if the present purpose be served, not to entangle himself in his own sophistries. But when all arts are exhausted, like other hunted animals, he sometimes stands at bay; when he cannot disown the grossness of one of his plays, he declares that he knows not any law that prescribes morality to a comic poet.

His remarks on ancient or modern writers are not always to be trusted. His parallel of the versification of Ovid with that of Claudian has been very justly censured by Sewel. His comparison of the first line of Virgil with the first of Statius is not happier. Virgil, he says, is soft and gentle, and would have thought Statius mad, if he had heard him thundering out:

Quæ superimposito moles geminata colosso.

Statius perhaps heats himself, as he proceeds, to exaggeration somewhat hyperbolical; but undoubtedly Virgil would have been too hasty, if he had condemned him to straw for one sounding line. Dryden wanted an instance, and the first that occurred was impressed into the service.

What he wishes to say, he says at hazard; he cited *Gorboduc*, which he had never seen; gives a false account of Chapman's versification; and discovers in the preface to his *Fables* that he translated the first book of the Iliad, without knowing what was in the second.

It will be difficult to prove that Dryden never made any great advances in literature. As having distinguished himself at Westminster under the tuition of Busby, who advanced his scholars to a height of knowledge very rarely attained in grammar-schools, he resided afterwards at Cambridge; it is not to be supposed that his skill in the ancient languages was deficient, compared with that of common students, but his scholastic acquisitions seem not proportionate to his opportunities and abilities. He could not, like Milton or Cowley, have made his name illustrious merely by his learning. He mentions but few books, and those such as lie in the beaten track of regular study; from which if ever he departs, he is in danger of losing himself in unknown regions.

In his *Dialogue on the Drama* he pronounces with great confidence that the Latin tragedy of *Medea* is not Ovid's, because it is not sufficiently interesting and pathetic. He might have determined the question upon surer evidence; for it is quoted by Quintilian as the work of Seneca; and the only line which remains of Ovid's play—for one line is left us—is not there to be found. There was therefore no need of the gravity of conjecture, or the discussion of plot or sentiment, to find what was already known upon higher authority than such discussions can ever reach.

His literature, though not always free from ostentation, will be commonly found either obvious, and made his own by the art of dressing it; or superficial, which, by what he gives, shows what he wanted; or erroneous, hastily collected, and negligently scattered.

Yet it cannot be said that his genius is ever unprovided of matter, or that his fancy languishes in penury of ideas. His works abound with knowledge, and sparkle with illustrations. There is scarcely any science or faculty that does not supply him with occasional images and lucky similitudes; every page discovers a mind very widely acquainted both with art and nature, and in full possession of great stores of intellectual wealth. Of him that knows much, it is natural to suppose that he has read with diligence; yet I rather believe that the knowledge of Dryden was gleaned from accidental intelligence and various conversation, by a quick apprehension, a judicious selection, and a happy memory, a keen appetite of knowledge, and a powerful digestion; by vigilance that permitted nothing to pass without notice, and a habit of reflection that suffered nothing useful to be lost. A mind like Dryden's, always curious, always active, to which every understanding was proud to be associated, and of which every one solicited the regard, by an ambitious display of himself, had a more pleasant, perhaps a nearer way to knowledge than by the silent progress of solitary reading. I do not suppose that he despised books, or intentionally neglected them; but that he was carried out by the impetuosity of his genius to more

vivid and speedy instructors; and that his studies were rather
desultory and fortuitous than constant and systematical.

It must be confessed that he scarcely ever appears to want
book-learning but when he mentions books; and to him may
be transferred the praise which he gives his master Charles:

> His conversation, wit, and parts,
> His knowledge in the noblest useful arts,
>   Were such, dead authors could not give,
>   But habitudes of those that live;
> Who lighting him, did greater lights receive;
>   He drain'd from all, and all they knew,
> His apprehensions quick, his judgment true:
>   That the most learn'd with shame confess
> His knowledge more, his reading only less.

Of all this, however, if the proof be demanded, I will not
undertake to give it; the atoms of probability, of which my
opinion has been formed, lie scattered over all his works; and
by him who thinks the question worth his notice, his works
must be perused with very close attention.

Criticism, either didactic or defensive, occupies almost all
his prose, except those pages which he has devoted to his
patrons; but none of his prefaces were ever thought tedious.
They have not the formality of a settled style, in which the
first half of the sentence betrays the other. The clauses are
never balanced, nor the periods modelled: every word seems to
drop by chance, though it falls into its proper place. Nothing
is cold or languid; the whole is airy, animated, and vigorous;
what is little is gay; what is great is splendid. He may be
thought to mention himself too frequently; but while he forces
himself upon our esteem, we cannot refuse him to stand high
in his own. Everything is excused by the play of images and
the sprightliness of expression. Though all is easy, nothing is
feeble; though all seems careless, there is nothing harsh; and
though since his earlier works more than a century has passed,
they have nothing yet uncouth or obsolete.

He who writes much will not easily escape a manner—such
a recurrence of particular modes as may be easily noted. Dryden is always *another and the same*; he does not exhibit a

second time the same elegances in the same form, nor appears to have any art other than that of expressing with clearness what he thinks with vigour. His style could not easily be imitated, either seriously or ludicrously; for, being always equable and always varied, it has no prominent or discriminative characters. The beauty who is totally free from disproportion of parts and features cannot be ridiculed by an overcharged resemblance.

From his prose, however, Dryden derives only his accidental and secondary praise; the veneration with which his name is pronounced by every cultivator of English literature is paid to him as he refined the language, improved the sentiments, and tuned the numbers of English poetry.

After about half a century of forced thoughts, and rugged metre, some advances towards nature and harmony had been already made by Waller and Denham; they had shown that long discourses in rhyme grew more pleasing when they were broken into couplets, and that verse consisted not only in the number but the arrangement of syllables.

But though they did much, who can deny that they left much to do? Their works were not many, nor were their minds of very ample comprehension. More examples of more modes of composition were necessary for the establishment of regularity, and the introduction of propriety in word and thought.

Every language of a learned nation necessarily divides itself into diction scholastic and popular, grave and familiar, elegant and gross; and from a nice distinction of these different parts arises a great part of the beauty of style. But, if we except a few minds, the favourites of nature, to whom their own original rectitude was in the place of rules, this delicacy of selection was little known to our authors; our speech lay before them in a heap of confusion; and every man took for every purpose what chance might offer him.

There was therefore before the time of Dryden no poetical diction, no system of words at once refined from the grossness of domestic use, and free from the harshness of terms appropriated to particular arts. Words too familiar, or too remote, defeat the purpose of a poet. From those sounds which we hear on small or on coarse occasions, we do not easily receive strong impressions, or delightful images; and words to which we are nearly strangers, whenever they occur, draw that attention on themselves which they should transmit to things.

Those happy combinations of words which distinguish poetry from prose had been rarely attempted: we had few elegances or flowers of speech; the roses had not yet been plucked from the bramble, or different colours had not been joined to enliven one another.

It may be doubted whether Waller and Denham could have over-borne the prejudices which had long prevailed, and which even then were sheltered by the protection of Cowley. The new versification, as it was called, may be considered as owing its establishment to Dryden; from whose time it is apparent that English poetry has had no tendency to relapse to its former savageness.

The affluence and comprehension of our language is very illustriously displayed in our poetical translations of Ancient Writers; a work which the French seem to relinquish in despair, and which we were long unable to perform with dexterity. Ben Jonson thought it necessary to copy Horace almost word by word; Feltham, his contemporary and adversary, considers it as indispensably requisite in a translation to give line for line. It is said that Sandys, whom Dryden calls the best versifier of the last age, has struggled hard to comprise every book of the English *Metamorphoses* in the same number of verses with the original. Holyday had nothing in view but to show that he understood his author, with so little regard to the grandeur of his diction, or the volubility of his numbers, that his metres can hardly be called verses; they cannot be read without reluctance, nor will the labour always be rewarded by understanding them. Cowley saw that such copyers were a servile race; he asserted his liberty, and spread his wings so boldly that he left his authors. It was reserved for Dryden to fix the limits of poetical liberty, and give us just rules and examples of translation.

When languages are formed upon different principles, it is impossible that the same modes of expression should always be elegant in both. While they run on together, the closest translation may be considered as the best; but when they divaricate, each must take its natural course. Where correspondence cannot be obtained, it is necessary to be content with something equivalent. "Translation, therefore," says Dryden, "is not so loose as paraphrase, nor so close as metaphrase."

All polished languages have different styles; the concise, the diffuse, the lofty, and the humble. In the proper choice of style consists the resemblance which Dryden principally exacts from the translator. He is to exhibit his author's thoughts in such a dress of diction as the author would have given them, had his language been English: rugged magnificence is not to be softened; hyperbolical ostentation is not to be repressed; nor sententious affectation to have its point blunted. A translator is to be like his author; it is not his business to excel him.

The reasonableness of these rules seems sufficient for their vindication; and the effects produced by observing them were so happy, that I know not whether they were ever opposed but by Sir Edward Sherburne, a man whose learning was greater than his powers of poetry; and who, being better qualified to give the meaning than the spirit of Seneca, has introduced his version of three tragedies by a defence of close translation. The authority of Horace, which the new translators cited in defence of their practice, he has, by a judicious explanation, taken fairly from them; but reason wants not Horace to support it.

It seldom happens that all the necessary causes concur to any great effect: will is wanting to power, or power to will, or both are impeded by external obstructions. The exigences in which Dryden was condemned to pass his life are reasonably supposed to have blasted his genius, to have driven out his works in a state of immaturity, and to have intercepted the full-blown elegance which longer growth would have supplied.

Poverty, like other rigid powers, is sometimes too hastily accused. If the excellence of Dryden's works was lessened by his indigence, their number was increased; and I know not how it will be proved, that if he had written less he would have written better; or that indeed he would have undergone the toil of an author, if he had not been solicited by something more pressing than the love of praise.

But, as is said by his Sebastian,

What had been, is unknown; what is, appears.

We know that Dryden's several productions were so many successive expedients for his support; his plays were therefore often borrowed; and his poems were almost all occasional.

In an occasional performance no height of excellence can be expected from any mind, however fertile in itself, and however stored with acquisitions. He whose work is general and arbitrary has the choice of his matter, and takes that which his inclination and his studies have best qualified him to display and decorate. He is at liberty to delay his publication till he has satisfied his friends and himself, till he has reformed his first thoughts by subsequent examination, and polished away those faults which the precipitance of ardent composition is likely to leave behind it. Virgil is related to have poured out a great number of lines in the morning, and to have passed the day in reducing them to fewer.

The occasional poet is circumscribed by the narrowness of his subject. Whatever can happen to man has happened so often that little remains for fancy or invention. We have been all born; we have most of us been married; and so many have died before us, that our deaths can supply but few materials for a poet. In the fate of princes the public has an interest; and what happens to them of good or evil, the poets have always considered as business for the Muse. But after so many inauguratory gratulations, nuptial hymns, and funeral dirges, he must be highly favoured by nature, or by fortune, who says anything not said before. Even war and conquest, however splendid, suggest no new images; the triumphal chariot of a victorious monarch can be decked only with those ornaments that have graced his predecessors.

Not only matter but time is wanting. The poem must not be delayed till the occasion is forgotten. The lucky moments of animated imagination cannot be attended; elegances and illustrations cannot be multiplied by gradual accumulation; the composition must be despatched while conversation is yet busy, and admiration fresh; and haste is to be made, lest some other event should lay hold upon mankind.

Occasional compositions may however secure to a writer the praise both of learning and facility; for they cannot be the effect of long study, and must be furnished immediately from the treasures of the mind.

The death of Cromwell was the first public event which called forth Dryden's poetical powers. His heroic stanzas have beauties and defects; the thoughts are vigorous, and, though not always proper, show a mind replete with ideas; the numbers are smooth; and the diction, if not altogether correct, is elegant and easy.

Davenant was perhaps at this time his favourite author, though *Gondibert* never appears to have been popular; and from Davenant he learned to please his ear with the stanza of four lines alternately rhymed.

Dryden very early formed his versification: there are in this early production no traces of Donne's or Jonson's ruggedness; but he did not so soon free his mind from the ambition of forced conceits. In his verses on the Restoration, he says of the King's exile:

> He, toss'd by Fate,
> Could taste no sweets of youth's desired age,
> But found his life too true a pilgrimage.

And afterwards, to show how virtue and wisdom are increased by adversity, he makes this remark:

> Well might the ancient poets then confer
> On Night the honour'd name of *counsellor*,
> Since, struck with rays of prosperous fortune blind,
> We light alone in dark afflictions find.

His praise of Monk's dexterity comprises such a cluster of thoughts unallied to one another, as will not elsewhere be easily found:

> 'Twas Monk, whom Providence design'd to loose
> Those real bonds false freedom did impose.
> The blessed saints that watch'd this turning scene
> Did from their stars with joyful wonder lean,
> To see small clues draw vastest weights along,
> Not in their bulk, but in their order strong.

Thus pencils can by one slight touch restore
Smiles to that changed face that wept before.
With ease such fond chimæras we pursue,
As fancy frames for fancy to subdue:
But, when ourselves to action we betake,
It shuns the mint like gold that chymists make.
How hard was then his task, at once to be
What in the body natural we see!
Man's Architect distinctly did ordain
The charge of muscles, nerves, and of the brain,
Through viewless conduits spirits to dispense
The springs of motion from the seat of sense.
'Twas not the hasty product of a day,
But the well-ripen'd fruit of wise delay.
He, like a patient angler, ere he strook,
Would let them play a-while upon the hook.
Our healthful food the stomach labours thus,
At first embracing what it strait doth crush.
Wise leeches will not vain receipts obtrude,
While growing pains pronounce the humours crude;
Deaf to complaints, they wait upon the ill
Till some safe crisis authorise their skill.

He had not yet learned, indeed he never learned well, to forbear the improper use of mythology. After having rewarded the heathen deities for their care—

With Alga who the sacred altar strows?
To all the sea-gods Charles an offering owes;
A bull to thee, Portunus, shall be slain;
A lamb to you, ye Tempests of the Main—

he tells us, in the language of religion:

Prayer storm'd the skies, and ravish'd Charles from thence
As heaven itself is took by violence.

And afterwards mentions one of the most awful passages of Sacred History.

Other conceits there are, too curious to be quite omitted; as:

For by example most we sinn'd before,
And, glass-like, clearness mix'd with frailty bore.

How far he was yet from thinking it necessary to found his sentiments on nature, appears from the extravagance of his fictions and hyperboles:

> The winds, that never moderation knew,
> Afraid to blow too much, too faintly blew:
> Or, out of breath with joy, could not enlarge
> Their straiten'd lungs.—
> It is no longer motion cheats your view;
> As you meet it, the land approacheth you;
> The land returns, and in the white it wears
> The marks of penitence and sorrow bears.

I know not whether this fancy, however little be its value, was not borrowed. A French poet read to Malherbe some verses, in which he represents France as moving out of its place to receive the king. "Though this," said Malherbe, "was in my time, I do not remember it."

His poem on *The Coronation* has a more even tenor of thought. Some lines deserve to be quoted:

> You have already quench'd sedition's brand;
> And zeal, which burnt it, only warms the land;
> The jealous sects that dare not trust their cause
> So far from their own will as to the laws,
> You for their umpire and their synod take,
> And their appeal alone to Cæsar make.

Here may be found one particle of that old versification, of which, I believe, in all his works, there is not another:

> Nor is it duty, or our hopes alone,
> Create that joy, but full *fruition*.

In the verses to the Lord Chancellor Clarendon, two years afterwards, is a conceit so hopeless at the first view, that few would have attempted it; and so successfully laboured, that though at last it gives the reader more perplexity than pleasure, and seems hardly worth the study that it costs, yet it

must be valued as a proof of a mind at once subtle and comprehensive:

> In open prospect nothing bounds our eye,
> Until the earth seems join'd unto the sky:
> So in this hemisphere our utmost view
> Is only bounded by our king and you:
> Our sight is limited where you are join'd,
> And beyond that no farther heaven can find.
> So well your virtues do with his agree,
> That, though your orbs of different greatness be,
> Yet both are for each other's use dispos'd,
> His to enclose, and yours to be enclos'd.
> Nor could another in your room have been,
> Except an emptiness had come between.

The comparison of the Chancellor to the Indies leaves all
resemblance too far behind it:

> And as the Indies were not found before
> Those rich perfumes which from the happy shore
> The winds upon their balmy wings convey'd,
> Whose guilty sweetness first their world betray'd;
> So by your counsels we are brought to view
> A rich and undiscover'd world in you.

There is another comparison, for there is little else in the
poem, of which, though perhaps it cannot be explained into
plain prosaic meaning, the mind perceives enough to be delighted, and readily forgives its obscurity for its magnificence:

> How strangely active are the arts of peace,
> Whose restless motions less than wars do cease!
> Peace is not freed from labour, but from noise;
> And war more force, but not more pains employs.
> Such is the mighty swiftness of your mind,
> That, like the earth's, it leaves our sense behind;
> While you so smoothly turn and rowl our sphere,
> That rapid motion does but rest appear.
> For as in nature's swiftness, with the throng
> Of flying orbs while ours is borne along,

All seems at rest to the deluded eye,
Mov'd by the soul of the same harmony:
So carried on by your unwearied care,
We rest in peace, and yet in motion share.

To this succeed four lines, which perhaps afford Dryden's first attempt at those penetrating remarks on human nature, for which he seems to have been peculiarly formed:

Let envy then those crimes within you see,
From which the happy never must be free;
Envy that does with misery reside,
The joy and the revenge of ruin'd pride.

Into this poem he seems to have collected all his powers; and after this he did not often bring upon his anvil such stubborn and unmalleable thoughts; but as a specimen of his abilities to unite the most unsociable matter, he has concluded with lines, of which I think not myself obliged to tell the meaning:

Yet unimpaired with labours, or with time,
Your age but seems to a new youth to climb.
Thus heavenly bodies do our time beget,
And measure change, but share no part of it:
And still it shall without a weight increase,
Like this new year, whose motions never cease.
For since the glorious course you have begun
Is led by Charles, as that is by the sun,
It must both weightless and immortal prove,
Because the centre of it is above.

In the *Annus Mirabilis* he returned to the quatrain, which from that time he totally quitted, perhaps from this experience of its inconvenience, for he complains of its difficulty. This is one of his greatest attempts. He had subjects equal to his abilities, a great naval war, and the Fire of London. Battles have always been described in heroic poetry; but a sea-fight and artillery had yet something of novelty. New arts are long in the world before poets describe them; for they borrow everything from their predecessors, and commonly de-

rive very little from nature or from life. Boileau was the first
French writer that had ever hazarded in verse the mention of
modern war, or the effects of gunpowder. We, who are less
afraid of novelty, had already possession of those dreadful
images. Waller had described a sea-fight. Milton had not yet
transferred the invention of fire-arms to the rebellious angels.

This poem is written with great diligence, yet does not fully
answer the expectation raised by such subjects and such a
writer. With the stanza of Davenant he has sometimes his vein
of parenthesis and incidental disquisition, and stops his narrative for a wise remark.

The general fault is, that he affords more sentiment than
description, and does not so much impress scenes upon the
fancy, as deduce consequences and make comparisons.

The initial stanzas have rather too much resemblance to the
first lines of Waller's poem on the war with Spain; perhaps
such a beginning is natural, and could not be avoided without
affectation. Both Waller and Dryden might take their hint
from the poem on the civil war of Rome, "Orbem jam totum,"
etc.

Of the King collecting his navy, he says:

> It seems as every ship their sovereign knows,
>   His awful summons they so soon obey;
> So hear the scaly herds when Proteus blows,
>   And so to pasture follow through the sea.

It would not be hard to believe that Dryden had written the
two first lines seriously, and that some wag had added the
two latter in burlesque. Who would expect the lines that immediately follow, which are indeed perhaps indecently hyperbolical, but certainly in a mode totally different?

> To see this fleet upon the ocean move,
>   Angels drew wide the curtains of the skies;
> And heaven, as if there wanted lights above,
>   For tapers made two glaring comets rise.

The description of the attempt at Bergen will afford a very
complete specimen of the descriptions in this poem:

And now approach'd their fleet from India, fraught
  With all the riches of the rising sun:
And precious sand from southern climates brought
  (The fatal regions where the war begun).

Like hunted castors, conscious of their store,
  Their way-laid wealth to Norway's coast they bring:
There first the North's cold bosom spices bore,
  And winter brooded on the eastern spring.

By the rich scent we found our perfum'd prey,
  Which, flank'd with rocks, did close in covert lie;
And round about their murdering cannon lay,
  At once to threaten and invite the eye.

Fiercer than cannon, and than rocks more hard,
  The English undertake th' unequal war:
Seven ships alone, by which the port is barr'd,
  Besiege the Indies, and all Denmark dare.

These fight like husbands, but like lovers those:
  These fain would keep, and those more fain enjoy;
And to such height their frantic passion grows,
  That what both love, both hazard to destroy.

Amidst whole heaps of spices lights a ball,
  And now their odours arm'd against them fly:
Some preciously by shatter'd porcelain fall,
  And some by aromatic splinters die.

And, though by tempests of the prize bereft,
  In heaven's inclemency some ease we find:
Our foes we vanquish'd by our valour left,
  And only yielded to the seas and wind.

In this manner is the sublime too often mingled with the ridiculous. The Dutch seek a shelter for a wealthy fleet: this surely needed no illustration; yet they must fly, not like all the rest of mankind on the same occasion, but "like hunted castors"; and they might with strict propriety be hunted; for we winded them by our noses—their *perfumes* betrayed them. The Husband and the Lover, though of more dignity than the Castor, are images too domestic to mingle properly with the horrors of war. The two quatrains that follow are worthy of the author.

The account of the different sensations with which the two fleets retired, when the night parted them, is one of the fairest flowers of English poetry.

> The night comes on, we eager to pursue
>   The combat still, and they asham'd to leave;
> 'Till the last streaks of dying day withdrew,
>   And doubtful moon-light did our rage deceive.
>
> In th' English fleet each ship resounds with joy,
>   And loud applause of their great leader's fame:
> In fiery dreams the Dutch they still destroy,
>   And, slumbering, smile at the imagin'd flame.
>
> Not so the Holland fleet, who, tir'd and done,
>   Stretch'd on their decks like weary oxen lie;
> Faint sweats all down their mighty members run
>   (Vast bulks, which little souls but ill supply).
>
> In dreams they fearful precipices tread,
>   Or, shipwreck'd, labour to some distant shore:
> Or, in dark churches, walk among the dead;
>   They wake with horror, and dare sleep no more.

It is a general rule in poetry, that all appropriated terms of art should be sunk in general expressions, because poetry is to speak an universal language. This rule is still stronger with regard to arts not liberal, or confined to few, and therefore far removed from common knowledge; and of this kind, certainly, is technical navigation. Yet Dryden was of opinion that a sea-fight ought to be described in the nautical language; "and certainly," says he, "as those who in a logical dispute keep in general terms would hide a fallacy, so those who do it in any poetical description would veil their ignorance."

Let us then appeal to experience; for by experience at last we learn as well what will please as what will profit. In the battle, his terms seem to have been blown away; but he deals them liberally in the dock:

So here, some pick out bullets from the side,
  Some drive old *oakum* through each *seam* and rift:
Their left-hand does the *calking-iron* guide,
  The rattling *mallet* with the right they lift.

With boiling pitch another near at hand
  (From friendly Sweden brought) the *seams instops*;
Which, well paid o'er, the salt-sea waves withstand,
  And shake them from the rising beak in drops.

Some the *gall'd* ropes with dauby *marling* bind,
  Or sear-cloth masts with strong *tarpawling* coats:
To try new *shrouds* one mounts into the wind,
  And one below their ease or stiffness notes.

I suppose there is not one term which every reader does not wish away.

His digression to the original and progress of navigation, with his prospect of the advancement which it shall receive from the Royal Society, then newly instituted, may be considered as an example seldom equalled of seasonable excursion and artful return.

One line, however, leaves me discontented; he says that, by the help of the philosophers,

> Instructed ships shall sail to quick commerce,
> By which remotest regions are allied.—

Which he is constrained to explain in a note "by a more exact measure of longitude." It had better become Dryden's learning and genius to have laboured science into poetry, and have shown, by explaining longitude, that verse did not refuse the ideas of philosophy.

His description of the Fire is painted by resolute meditation, out of a mind better formed to reason than to feel. The conflagration of a city, with all its tumults of concomitant distress, is one of the most dreadful spectacles which this world can offer to human eyes; yet it seems to raise little emotion in the breast of the poet; he watches the flame coolly from street to street, with now a reflection, and now a simile, till at last he meets the King, for whom he makes a speech, rather tedious in a time so busy; and then follows again the progress of the fire.

There are, however, in this part some passages that deserve attention; as in the beginning:

> The diligence of trades, and noiseful gain,
>   And luxury, more late, asleep were laid!
> All was the Night's, and in her silent reign
>   No sound the rest of Nature did invade
> In this deep quiet——

The expression "All was the Night's" is taken from Seneca, who remarks on Virgil's line,

> *Omnia noctis erant, placida composta quiete,*

that he might have concluded better,

> *Omnia noctis erant.*

The following quatrain is vigorous and animated:

> The ghosts of traitors from the Bridge descend
>   With bold fanatic spectres to rejoice;
> About the fire into a dance they bend,
>   And sing their sabbath notes with feeble voice.

His prediction of the improvements which shall be made in the new city is elegant and poetical, and with an event which poets cannot always boast has been happily verified. The poem concludes with a simile that might have better been omitted.

Dryden, when he wrote this poem, seems not yet fully to have formed his versification, or settled his system of propriety.

From this time he addicted himself almost wholly to the stage, "to which," says he, "my genius never much inclined me," merely as the most profitable market for poetry. By writing tragedies in rhyme, he continued to improve his diction and his numbers. According to the opinion of Harte, who had studied his works with great attention, he settled his principles of versification in 1676, when he produced the play of *Aureng Zebe*; and according to his own account of the short time in which he wrote *Tyrannic Love*, and the *State of Innocence*, he soon obtained the full effect of diligence, and added facility to exactness.

Rhyme has been so long banished from the theatre, that we know not its effects upon the passions of an audience; but it has this convenience, that sentences stand more independent on each other, and striking passages are therefore easily selected and retained. Thus the description of Night in the *Indian Emperor*, and the rise and fall of empire in the *Conquest of Granada*, are more frequently repeated than any lines in *All for Love*, or *Don Sebastian*.

To search his plays for vigorous sallies and sententious elegances, or to fix the dates of any little pieces which he wrote by chance or by solicitation, were labour too tedious and minute.

His dramatic labours did not so wholly absorb his thoughts but that he promulgated the laws of translation in a preface to the *English Epistles of Ovid*, one of which he translated himself, and another in conjunction with the Earl of Mulgrave.

Absalom and Achitophel is a work so well known that particular criticism is superfluous. If it be considered as a poem political and controversial, it will be found to comprise all the excellences of which the subject is susceptible—acrimony of censure, elegance of praise, artful delineation of characters, variety and vigour of sentiment, happy turns of language, and pleasing harmony of numbers—and all these raised to such a height as can scarcely be found in any other English composition.

It is not, however, without faults; some lines are inelegant or improper, and too many are irreligiously licentious. The original structure of the poem was defective; allegories drawn to great length will always break; Charles could not run continually parallel with David.

The subject had likewise another inconvenience: it admitted little imagery or description; and a long poem of mere sentiments easily becomes tedious: though all the parts are forcible, and every line kindles new rapture, the reader, if not relieved by the interposition of something that soothes the fancy, grows weary of admiration, and defers the rest.

As an approach to the historical truth was necessary, the action and catastrophe were not in the poet's power; there is, therefore, an unpleasing disproportion between the beginning and the end. We are alarmed by a faction formed of many sects, various in their principles, but agreeing in their purpose of mischief, formidable for their numbers, and strong by their supports; while the King's friends are few and weak. The chiefs on either part are set forth to view; but, when expectation is at the height, the King makes a speech, and

> Henceforth a series of new times began.

Who can forbear to think of an enchanted castle, with a wide moat and lofty battlements, walls of marble and gates of brass, which vanishes at once into air when the destined knight blows his horn before it?

In the second part, written by Tate, there is a long insertion, which, for its poignancy of satire, exceeds any part of the former. Personal resentment, though no laudable motive to satire, can add great force to general principles. Self-love is a busy prompter.

The Medal, written upon the same principles with *Absalom and Achitophel*, but upon a narrower plan, gives less pleasure, though it discovers equal abilities in the writer. The superstructure cannot extend beyond the foundation; a single character or incident cannot furnish as many ideas as a series of events or multiplicity of agents. This poem, therefore, since time has left it to itself, is not much read, nor perhaps generally understood; yet it abounds with touches both of humorous and serious satire. The picture of a man whose propensions to mischief are such that his best actions are but inability of wickedness, is very skilfully delineated and strongly coloured:

> Power was his aim; but, thrown from that pretence,
> The wretch turn'd loyal in his own defence,
> And malice reconcil'd him to his prince.
> Him, in the anguish of his soul, he serv'd;
> Rewarded faster still than he deserv'd:
> Behold him now exalted into trust;
> His counsels oft convenient, seldom just;
> Ev'n in the most sincere advice he gave,
> He had a grudging still to be a knave.
> The frauds he learnt in his fanatic years

Made him uneasy in his lawful gears,
At best as little honest as he could,
And, like white witches, mischievously good.
To his first bias, longingly, he leans;
And rather would be great by wicked means.

The *Threnodia*, which, by a term I am afraid neither authorised nor analogical, he calls *Augustalis*, is not among his happiest productions. Its first and obvious defect is the irregularity of its metre, to which the ears of that age, however, were accustomed. What is worse, it has neither tenderness nor dignity, it is neither magnificent nor pathetic. He seems to look round him for images which he cannot find, and what he has he distorts by endeavouring to enlarge them. "He is," he says, "petrified with grief," but the marble sometimes relents and trickles in a joke.

The sons of art all med'cines tried,
And every noble remedy applied;
   With emulation each essay'd
   His utmost skill; *nay, more, they pray'd:*
Never was losing game with better conduct play'd.

He had been a little inclined to merriment before upon the prayers of a nation for their dying sovereign; nor was he serious enough to keep heathen fables out of his religion:

With him th' innumerable crowd of armed prayers
Knock'd at the gates of heaven, and knock'd aloud;
The first well-meaning rude petitioners
   All for his life assail'd the throne,
All would have brib'd the skies by offering up their own.
So great a throng not heaven itself could bar;
'Twas almost borne by force, *as in the giants' war*.
   The pray'rs, at least, for his reprieve were heard;
His death, like Hezekiah's, was deferr'd.

There is throughout the composition a desire of splendour without wealth. In the conclusion he seems too much pleased with the prospect of the new reign to have lamented his old master with much sincerity.

He did not miscarry in this attempt for want of skill either in lyric or elegiac poetry. His poem on the death of Mrs. Killigrew is undoubtedly the noblest ode that our language ever has produced. The first part flows with a torrent of enthusiasm. "Fervet immensusque ruit." All the stanzas indeed are not equal. An imperial crown cannot be one continued diamond; the gems must be held together by some less valuable matter.

In his first *Ode for Cecilia's Day*, which is lost in the splendour of the second, there are passages which would have dignified any other poet. The first stanza is vigorous and elegant, though the word *diapason* is too technical, and the rhymes are too remote from one another:

> From harmony, from heavenly harmony,
>   This universal frame began:
> When Nature underneath a heap
>   Of jarring atoms lay,
>   And could not heave her head,
> The tuneful voice was heard from high,
>   Arise, ye more than dead.
> Then cold and hot, and moist and dry,
> In order to their stations leap,
>   And Music's power obey.
> From harmony, from heavenly harmony,
>   This universal frame began:
>   From harmony to harmony
> Through all the compass of the notes it ran,
>   The diapason closing full in man.

The conclusion is likewise striking, but it includes an image so awful in itself that it can owe little to poetry; and I could wish the antithesis of *music untuning* had found some other place:

> As from the power of sacred lays
>   The spheres began to move,
> And sung the great Creator's praise
>   To all the bless'd above:
> So when the last and dreadful hour
> This crumbling pageant shall devour,

> The trumpet shall be heard on high, ⎫
> The dead shall live, the living die, ⎬
> And Music shall untune the sky. ⎭

Of his skill in elegy he has given a specimen in his *Eleonora*, of which the following lines discover their author:

> Though all these rare endowments of the mind
> Were in a narrow space of life confin'd,
> The figure was with full perfection crown'd;
> Though not so large an orb, as truly round:
>
> As when in glory, through the public place,
> The spoils of conquer'd nations were to pass,
> And but one day for triumph was allow'd,
> The consul was constrain'd his pomp to crowd;
> And so the swift procession hurried on,
> That all, though not distinctly, might be shown:
> So in the straiten'd bounds of life confin'd,
> She gave but glimpses of her glorious mind:
> And multitudes of virtues pass'd along,
> Each pressing foremost in the mighty throng,
> Ambitious to be seen, and then make room
> For greater multitudes that were to come.
> Yet unemployed no minute slipp'd away;
> Moments were precious in so short a stay.
> The haste of Heaven to have her was so great, ⎫
> That some were single acts, though each complete; ⎬
> And every act stood ready to repeat. ⎭

This piece, however, is not without its faults; there is so much likeness in the initial comparison that there is no illustration. As a king would be lamented, Eleonora was lamented:

> As, when some great and gracious monarch dies,
> Soft whispers, first, and mournful murmurs, rise
> Among the sad attendants; then the sound
> Soon gathers voice, and spreads the news around,
> Through town and country, till the dreadful blast
> Is blown to distant colonies at last,
> Who then, perhaps, were offering vows in vain

> For his long life, and for his happy reign;
> So slowly by degrees unwilling fame ⎫
> Did matchless Eleonora's fate proclaim, ⎬
> Till public as the loss the news became. ⎭

This is little better than to say in praise of a shrub that it is as green as a tree; or of a brook that it waters a garden as a river waters a country.

Dryden confesses that he did not know the lady whom he celebrates; the praise being therefore inevitably general, fixes no impression upon the reader, nor excites any tendency to love, nor much desire of imitation. Knowledge of the subject is to the poet what durable materials are to the architect.

The *Religio Laici*, which borrows its title from the *Religio Medici* of Browne, is almost the only work of Dryden which can be considered as a voluntary effusion; in this, therefore, it might be hoped that the full effulgence of his genius would be found. But unhappily the subject is rather argumentative than poetical: he intended only a specimen of metrical disputation:

> And this unpolish'd, rugged verse I chose,
> As fittest for discourse, and nearest prose.

This, however, is a composition of great excellence in its kind, in which the familiar is very improperly diversified with the solemn, and the grave with the humorous, in which metre has neither weakened the force nor clouded the perspicuity of argument; nor will it be easy to find another example equally happy of this middle kind of writing, which, though prosaic in some parts, rises to high poetry in others, and neither towers to the skies, nor creeps along the ground.

Of the same kind, or not far distant from it, is the *Hind and the Panther*, the longest of all Dryden's original poems—an allegory intended to comprise and to decide the controversy between the Romanists and Protestants. The scheme of the work is injudicious and incommodious; for what can be more absurd than that one beast should counsel another to rest her faith upon a pope and council? He seems well enough skilled in the usual topics of argument, endeavours to show the necessity of an infallible judge, and reproaches the Reformers with want of unity; but is weak enough to ask, why, since we see without knowing how, we may not have an infallible judge without knowing where?

The Hind at one time is afraid to drink at the common brook, because she may be worried; but, walking home with the Panther, talks by the way of the Nicene Fathers, and at last declares herself to be the Catholic Church.

This absurdity was very properly ridiculed in the *Country Mouse and the City Mouse* of Montague and Prior; and in the detection and censure of the incongruity of the fiction chiefly consists the value of their performance, which, whatever reputation it might obtain by the help of temporary passions, seems, to readers almost a century distant, not very forcible or animated.

Pope, whose judgment was perhaps a little bribed by the subject, used to mention this poem as the most correct specimen of Dryden's versification. It was indeed written when he had completely formed his manner, and may be supposed to exhibit, negligence excepted, his deliberate and ultimate scheme of metre.

We may, therefore, reasonably infer that he did not approve the perpetual uniformity which confines the sense to couplets, since he has broken his lines in the initial paragraph.

> A milk-white Hind, immortal and unchang'd,
> Fed on the lawns, and in the forest rang'd:
> Without unspotted, innocent within,
> She fear'd no danger, for she knew no sin.
> Yet had she oft been chas'd with horns and hounds,
> And Scythian shafts, and many winged wounds
> Aim'd at her heart; was often forc'd to fly,
> And doom'd to death, though fated not to die.

These lines are lofty, elegant, and musical, notwithstanding the interruption of the pause, of which the effect is rather increase of pleasure by variety, than offence by ruggedness.

To the first part it was his intention, he says, "to give the majestic turn of heroic poesy"; and perhaps he might have executed his design not unsuccessfully, had an opportunity of satire, which he cannot forbear, fallen sometimes in his way.

The character of a Presbyterian, whose emblem is the wolf, is not very heroically majestic:

> More haughty than the rest, the wolfish race
> Appear with belly gaunt and famish'd face:
> Never was so deform'd a beast of grace.
> His ragged tail betwixt his legs he wears,
> Close clapp'd for shame; but his rough crest he rears,
> And pricks up his predestinating ears.

His general character of the other sorts of beasts that never go to church, though sprightly and keen, has, however, not much of heroic poesy:

> These are the chief: to number o'er the rest,
> And stand, like Adam, naming every beast,
> Were weary work; nor will the Muse describe
> A slimy born and sun-begotten tribe,
> Who, far from steeples and their sacred sound,
> In fields their sullen conventicles found.
> These gross, half-animated lumps I leave;
> Nor can I think what thoughts they can conceive;
> But, if they think at all, 'tis sure no higher
> Than matter, put in motion, may aspire;
> Souls that can scarce ferment their mass of clay;
> So drossy, so divisible are they,
> As would but serve pure bodies for allay;
> Such souls as shards produce, such beetle things
> As only buzz to Heaven with evening wings;
> Strike in the dark, offending but by chance;
> Such are the blindfold blows of ignorance.
> They know not beings, and but hate a name;
> To them the Hind and Panther are the same.

One more instance, and that taken from the narrative part, where style was more in his choice, will show how steadily he kept his resolution of heroic dignity:

> For when the herd, suffic'd, did late repair
> To ferny heaths and to their forest lair,
> She made a mannerly excuse to stay,

Proffering the Hind to wait her half the way:
That, since the sky was clear, an hour of talk
Might help her to beguile the tedious walk.
With much good-will the motion was embrac'd,
To chat a while on their adventures past:
Nor had the grateful Hind so soon forgot
Her friend and fellow-sufferer in the plot.
Yet, wondering how of late she grew estrang'd,
Her forehead cloudy and her count'nance chang'd,
She thought this hour th' occasion would present
To learn her secret cause of discontent,
Which well she hop'd might be with ease redress'd, ⎫
Considering her a well-bred, civil beast,   ⎬
And more a gentlewoman than the rest.   ⎭
After some common talk what rumours ran,
The lady of the spotted muff began.

The second and third parts he professes to have reduced to
diction more familiar and more suitable to dispute and conversation; the difference is not, however, very easily perceived;
the first has familiar, and the two others have sonorous, lines.
The original incongruity runs through the whole; the King is
now Cæsar and now the Lion; and the name Pan is given to
the Supreme Being.

But when this constitutional absurdity is forgiven, the poem
must be confessed to be written with great smoothness of
metre, a wide extent of knowledge, and an abundant multiplicity of images; the controversy is embellished with pointed
sentences, diversified by illustrations, and enlivened by sallies
of invective. Some of the facts to which allusions are made are
now become obscure, and perhaps there may be many satirical
passages little understood.

As it was by its nature a work of defiance, a composition
which would naturally be examined with the utmost acrimony
of criticism, it was probably laboured with uncommon attention, and there are, indeed, few negligences in the subordinate
parts. The original impropriety, and the subsequent unpopu-
larity of the subject, added to the ridiculousness of its first
elements, has sunk it into neglect; but it may be usefully stud-

ied, as an example of poetical ratiocination, in which the argument suffers little from the metre.

In the poem on *The Birth of the Prince of Wales* nothing is very remarkable but the exorbitant adulation, and that insensibility of the precipice on which the King was then standing, which the laureate apparently shared with the rest of the courtiers. A few months cured him of controversy, dismissed him from court, and made him again a playwright and translator.

Of Juvenal there had been a translation by Stapylton, and another by Holyday; neither of them is very poetical. Stapylton is more smooth, and Holyday's is more esteemed for the learning of his notes. A new version was proposed to the poets of that time, and undertaken by them in conjunction. The main design was conducted by Dryden, whose reputation was such that no man was unwilling to serve the Muses under him.

The general character of this translation will be given when it is said to preserve the wit, but to want the dignity, of the original. The peculiarity of Juvenal is a mixture of gaiety and stateliness, of pointed sentences and declamatory grandeur. His points have not been neglected; but his grandeur none of the band seemed to consider as necessary to be imitated, except Creech, who undertook the thirteenth satire. It is therefore, perhaps, possible to give a better representation of that great satirist, even in those parts which Dryden himself has translated, some passages excepted, which will never be excelled.

With Juvenal was published Persius, translated wholly by Dryden. This work, though like all other productions of Dryden it may have shining parts, seems to have been written merely for wages, in an uniform mediocrity, without any eager endeavour after excellence, or laborious effort of the mind.

There wanders an opinion among the readers of poetry, that one of these satires is an exercise of the school. Dryden says that he once translated it at school; but not that he preserved or published the juvenile performance.

Not long afterwards he undertook, perhaps, the most arduous work of its kind, a translation of Virgil, for which he had shown how well he was qualified by his version of the

Pollio, and two episodes, one of *Nisus and Euryalus*, the other of *Mezentius and Lausus*.

In the comparison of Homer and Virgil, the discriminative excellence of Homer is elevation and comprehension of thought, and that of Virgil is grace and splendour of diction. The beauties of Homer are therefore difficult to be lost, and those of Virgil difficult to be retained. The massy trunk of sentiment is safe by its solidity, but the blossoms of elocution easily drop away. The author, having the choice of his own images, selects those which he can best adorn; the translator must, at all hazards, follow his original, and express thoughts which perhaps he would not have chosen. When to this primary difficulty is added the inconvenience of a language so much inferior in harmony to the Latin, it cannot be expected that they who read the Georgics and the Æneid should be much delighted with any version.

All these obstacles Dryden saw, and all these he determined to encounter. The expectation of his work was undoubtedly great; the nation considered its honour as interested in the event. One gave him the different editions of his author, another helped him in the subordinate parts. The arguments of the several books were given him by Addison.

The hopes of the public were not disappointed. He produced, says Pope, "the most noble and spirited translation I know in any language." It certainly excelled whatever had appeared in English, and appears to have satisfied his friends, and, for the most part, to have silenced his enemies. Milbourne, indeed, a clergyman, attacked it; but his outrages seem to be the ebullitions of a mind agitated by stronger resentment than bad poetry can excite, and previously resolved not to be pleased.

His criticism extends only to the Preface, Pastorals, and Georgics; and as he professes to give his antagonist an opportunity of reprisal, he has added his own version of the first and fourth Pastorals, and the first Georgic. The world has forgotten his book; but since his attempt has given him a place in literary history, I will preserve a specimen of his criticism, by inserting his remarks on the invocation before the first Georgic, and of his poetry, by annexing his own version.

" 'What makes a plenteous harvest, when to turn
  The fruitful soil, and when to sow the corn.'—*Ver.* 1.

It's *unlucky*, they say, *to stumble at the threshold*, but what
has a *plenteous harvest* to do here? *Virgil* would not pretend
to prescribe *rules* for *that* which depends not on the *husbandman's* care, but the *disposition of Heaven* altogether. Indeed,
the *plenteous crop* depends somewhat on the *good method of
tillage*, and where the *land's* ill manured, the *corn*, without a
miracle, can be but *indifferent*; but the *harvest* may be *good*,
which is its *properest* epithet, though the *husbandman's skill*
were never so *indifferent*. The next *sentence* is *too literal*, and
when to plough had been *Virgil's* meaning, and intelligible
to everybody; and *when to sow the corn* is a needless *addition*.

'The care of sheep, of oxen, and of kine,
 And when to geld the lambs, and sheer the swine,'—*Ver.* 3.

would as well have fallen under the *cura boum, quis cultus
habendo sit pecori*, as Mr. D.'s *deduction* of particulars.

'The birth and genius of the fruitful bee
 I sing, Mæcenas, and I sing to thee.'—*Ver.* 5.

But where did *experientia* ever signify *birth and genius*? or
what ground was there for such a *figure* in this place? How
much more manly is Mr. Ogilby's version!

'What makes rich grounds, in what celestial signs
 'Tis good to plough, and marry elms with vines;
 What best fits cattle, what with sheep agrees,
 And several arts improving frugal bees;
 I sing, Mæcenas.'

Which four lines, tho' faulty enough, are yet much more to
the purpose than Mr. D.'s six.

'From fields and mountains to my song repair.'—*Ver.* 22.

For *patrium linquens nemus, saltusque Lycæi*——Very well explain'd!

'Inventor, Pallas, of the fattening oil,
 Thou founder of the plough, and plough-man's toil!'
                                          Ver. 23, 24.

Written as if *these* had both been *Pallas's invention. The plough-man's toil's* impertinent.

> '—— The shroud-like cypress'—— —Ver. 25.

Why *shroud-like?* Is a *cypress* pull'd up by the *roots,* which the *sculpture* in the *last Eclogue* fills *Silvanus's* hand with, so very like a *shroud?* Or did not Mr. D. think of that kind of *cypress* us'd often for *scarves and hat-bands* at funerals formerly, or for *widows' vails,* etc.?—if so, 'twas a *deep, good thought.*

> ———— 'That wear
> The rural honours, and increase the year.'—Ver. 26.

What's meant by *increasing the year?* Did the *gods* or *goddesses* add more *months,* or *days,* or *hours* to it? Or how can *arva tueri* signify to *wear rural honours?* Is this to *translate* or *abuse* an *author?* The next *couplet* is borrow'd from Ogilby, I suppose, because *less to the purpose* than ordinary:

> 'The patron of the world, and Rome's peculiar guard.'
> —Ver. 33.

Idle, and none of Virgil's, no more than the sense of the *precedent couplet;* so, again, he *interpolates* Virgil with that and *the round circle of the year to guide powerful of blessings, which thou strew'st around.* A ridiculous *Latinism,* and an *impertinent addition;* indeed the whole *period* is but one piece of *absurdity* and *nonsense,* as those who lay it with the *original* must find.

> 'And Neptune shall resign the fasces of the sea.'

Was he *consul* or *dictator* there?

> 'And watry virgins for thy bed shall strive.'—Ver. 42, 43.

Both absurd *interpolations.*

> 'Where in the void of heaven a place is free.
> Ah! happy, D——n, were that place for thee!'—Ver. 47, 48.

But where is *that void?* Or what does our *translator* mean by it? He knows what Ovid says *God* did to prevent such a *void* in heaven; perhaps this was then forgotten: but Virgil talks more sensibly.

'The scorpion ready to receive thy laws.'—*Ver.* 49.

No, he would not then have *gotten out of his way* so fast.

'Though Proserpine affects her silent seat.'—*Ver.* 56.

What made *her* then so *angry* with Ascalaphus for preventing her return? She was now mus'd to Patience under the *determinations* of Fate, rather than *fond* of her *residence*.

> 'Pity the poet's and the plough-man's cares,
> Interest thy greatness in our mean affairs,
> And use thyself betimes to hear our prayers.'
>   *Ver.* 61, 62, 63.

Which is such a wretched *perversion* of Virgil's *noble thought* as Vicars would have blush'd at; but Mr. Ogilby makes us some amends by his better lines:

> 'O wheresoe'er thou art, from thence incline,
> And grant assistance to my bold design!
> Pity, with me, poor husbandmen's affairs,
> And now, as if translated, hear our prayers.'

This is *sense*, and *to the purpose*: the other poor *mistaken stuff*."

Such were the strictures of Milbourne, who found few abettors, and of whom it may be reasonably imagined that many who favoured his design were ashamed of his insolence.

When admiration had subsided, the translation was more coolly examined, and found, like all others, to be sometimes erroneous, and sometimes licentious. Those who could find faults thought they could avoid them; and Dr. Brady attempted in blank verse a translation of the Æneid, which when dragged into the world did not live long enough to cry. I have never seen it; but that such a version there is, or has been, perhaps some old catalogue informed me.

With not much better success, Trapp, when his Tragedy and his Prelections had given him reputation, attempted [1718] another blank version of the Æneid; to which, notwithstanding the slight regard with which it was treated, he had afterwards perseverance enough to add the Eclogues and

Georgics. His book may continue its existence as long as it is the clandestine refuge of school-boys.

Since the English ear has been accustomed to the mellifluence of Pope's numbers, and the diction of poetry has become more splendid, new attempts have been made to translate Virgil; and all his works have been attempted by men better qualified to contend with Dryden. I will not engage myself in an invidious comparison by opposing one passage to another—a work of which there would be no end, and which might be often offensive without use.

It is not by comparing line with line that the merit of great works is to be estimated, but by their general effects and ultimate results. It is easy to note a weak line, and write one more vigorous in its place; to find a happiness of expression in the original, and transplant it by force into the version: but what is given to the parts may be subducted from the whole, and the reader may be weary, though the critic may commend. Works of imagination excel by their allurement and delight; by their power of attracting and detaining the attention. That book is good in vain which the reader throws away. He only is the master who keeps the mind in pleasing captivity; whose pages are perused with eagerness, and in hope of new pleasure are perused again; and whose conclusion is perceived with an eye of sorrow, such as the traveller casts upon departing day.

By his proportion of this predomination I will consent that Dryden should be tried; of this, which, in opposition to reason, makes Ariosto the darling and the pride of Italy; of this, which, in defiance of criticism, continues Shakespeare the sovereign of the drama.

His last work was his *Fables*, in which he gave us the first example of a mode of writing which the Italians call *rifaccimento*, a renovation of ancient writers by modernising their language. Thus the old poem of Boiardo has been new-dressed by Domenichi and Berni. The works of Chaucer, upon which this kind of rejuvenescence has been bestowed by Dryden, require little criticism. The tale of the Cock seems hardly worth revival; and the story of Palamon and Arcite, containing an action unsuitable to the times in which it is placed, can hardly be suffered to pass without censure of the hyperbolical commendation which Dryden has given it in the general Preface, and in a poetical Dedication, a piece where his original fondness of remote conceits seems to have revived.

Of the three pieces borrowed from Boccace, *Sigismunda* may be defended by the celebrity of the story. *Theodore and Honoria*, though it contains not much moral, yet afforded opportunities of striking description. And *Cymon* was formerly a tale of such reputation, that at the revival of letters it was translated into Latin by one of the Beroalds.

Whatever subjects employed his pen, he was still improving our measures and embellishing our language.

In this volume are interspersed some short original poems, which, with his prologues, epilogues, and songs, may be comprised in Congreve's remark, that even those, if he had written nothing else, would have entitled him to the praise of excellence in his kind.

One composition must however be distinguished. The *Ode for St. Cecilia's Day*, perhaps the last effort of his poetry, has been always considered as exhibiting the highest flight of fancy, and the exactest nicety of art. This is allowed to stand without a rival. If indeed there is any excellence beyond it in some other of Dryden's works, that excellence must be found. Compared with the *Ode on Killigrew*, it may be pronounced perhaps superior in the whole; but without any single part equal to the first stanza of the other.

It is said to have cost Dryden a fortnight's labour; but it does not want its negligences; some of the lines are without correspondent rhymes; a defect which I never detected but after an acquaintance of many years, and which the enthusiasm of the writer might hinder him from perceiving.

His last stanza has less emotion than the former; but it is not less elegant in the diction. The conclusion is vicious; the music of Timotheus, which *raised a mortal to the skies*, had only a metaphorical power; that of Cecilia, which *drew an angel down*, had a real effect: the crown therefore could not reasonably be divided.

In a general survey of Dryden's labours, he appears to have a mind very comprehensive by nature, and much enriched with acquired knowledge. His compositions are the effects of a vigorous genius operating upon large materials.

The power that predominated in his intellectual operations was rather strong reason than quick sensibility. Upon all occasions that were presented, he studied rather than felt, and produced sentiments not such as nature enforces, but meditation supplies. With the simple and elemental passions, as they spring separate in the mind, he seems not much acquainted; and seldom describes them but as they are complicated by the various relations of society, and confused in the tumults and agitations of life.

What he says of love may contribute to the explanation of his character:

> Love various minds does variously inspire;
> It stirs in gentle bosoms gentle fire,
> Like that of incense on the altar laid:
> But raging flames tempestuous souls invade;
> A fire which every windy passion blows,
> With pride it mounts, or with revenge it glows.

Dryden's was not one of the *gentle bosoms:* Love as it subsists in itself, with no tendency but to the person loved, and wishing only for correspondent kindness; such Love as shuts out all other interest, the Love of the Golden Age, was too soft and subtle to put his faculties in motion. He hardly conceived it but in its turbulent effervescence with some other desires; when it was inflamed by rivalry, or obstructed by difficulties; when it invigorated ambition, or exasperated revenge.

He is therefore, with all his variety of excellence, not often pathetic; and had so little sensibility of the power of effusions purely natural, that he did not esteem them in others. Simplicity gave him no pleasure; and for the first part of his life he looked on Otway with contempt, though at last, indeed very late, he confessed that in his play *there* was *Nature, which is the greatest beauty*.

We do not always know our own motives. I am not certain whether it was not rather the difficulty which he found in exhibiting the genuine operations of the heart, than a servile submission to an injudicious audience, that filled his plays with false magnificence. It was necessary to fix attention; and the mind can be captivated only by recollection, or by curiosity; by reviving natural sentiments, or impressing new appearances of things: sentences were readier at his call than images; he could more easily fill the ear with splendid novelty, than awaken those ideas that slumber in the heart.

The favourite exercise of his mind was ratiocination; and, that argument might not be too soon at an end, he delighted to talk of liberty and necessity, destiny and contingence; these he discusses in the language of the school with so much profundity, that the terms which he uses are not always understood. It is indeed learning, but learning out of place.

When once he had engaged himself in disputation, thoughts flowed in on either side: he was now no longer at a loss; he had always objections and solutions at command: "verbaque provisam rem"—give him matter for his verse, and he finds without difficulty verse for his matter.

In comedy, for which he professes himself not naturally qualified, the mirth which he excites will perhaps not be found so much to arise from any original humour, or peculiarity of character nicely distinguished and diligently pursued, as from incidents and circumstances, artifices and surprises; from jests of action rather than of sentiment. What he had of humorous or passionate, he seems to have had not from nature, but from other poets; if not always as a plagiary, at least as an imitator.

Next to argument, his delight was in wild and daring sallies of sentiment, in the irregular and eccentric violence of wit. He delighted to tread upon the brink of meaning, where light and darkness begin to mingle; to approach the precipice of absurdity, and hover over the abyss of unideal vacancy. This inclination sometimes produced nonsense, which he knew; as:

> Move swiftly, Sun, and fly a lover's pace,
> Leave weeks and months behind thee in they race.
>   Amamel flies
> To guard thee from the demons of the air;
> My flaming sword above them to display,
> All keen, and ground upon the edge of day.

And sometimes it issued in absurdities, of which perhaps he was not conscious:

> Then we upon our orb's last verge shall go,
>   And see the ocean leaning on the sky;
> From thence our rolling neighbours we shall know,
>   And on the lunar world securely pry.

These lines have no meaning; but may we not say, in imitation of Cowley on another book,

> 'Tis so like *sense*, 'twill serve the turn as well?

This endeavour after the grand and the new produced many sentiments either great or bulky, and many images either just or splendid:

> I am as free as Nature first made man, ⎫
> Ere the base laws of servitude began, ⎬
> When wild in woods the noble savage ran. ⎭
> —'Tis but because the Living death ne'er knew,
> They fear to prove it as a thing that's new:
> Let me th' experiment before you try,
> I'll show you first how easy 'tis to die.

> —There with a forest of their darts he strove,
> And stood like *Capaneus* defying Jove,
> With his broad sword the boldest beating down,
> While Fate grew pale lest he should win the town,
> And turn'd the iron leaves of his dark book
> To make new dooms, or mend what it mistook.

> —I beg no pity for this mouldering clay;
> For if you give it burial, there it takes
> Possession of your earth;
> If burnt, and scatter'd in the air, the winds
> That strew my dust diffuse my royalty,
> And spread me o'er your clime; for where one atom
> Of mine shall light, know there Sebastian reigns.

Of these quotations the two first may be allowed to be great, the two latter only tumid.

Of such selection there is no end. I will add only a few
more passages; of which the first, though it may perhaps be
quite clear in prose, is not too obscure for poetry, as the meaning that it has is noble:

> No, there is a necessity in Fate,
> Why still the brave bold man is fortunate;
> He keeps his object ever full in sight,
> And that assurance holds him firm and right;
> True, 'tis a narrow way that leads to bliss,
> But right before there is no precipice;
> Fear makes men look aside, and so their footing miss.

Of the images which the two following citations afford, the
first is elegant, the second magnificent; whether either be just,
let the reader judge:

> What precious drops are these,
> Which silently each other's track pursue,
> Bright as young diamonds in their infant dew?

> ————Resign your castle————
> —Enter, brave Sir; for when you speak the word,
> The gates shall open of their own accord;
> The genius of the place its Lord shall meet,
> And bow its towery forehead at your feet.

These bursts of extravagance Dryden calls the "Dalilahs of
the Theatre"; and owns that many noisy lines of Maximin and
Almanzor call out for vengeance upon him; "but I knew,"
says he, "that they were bad enough to please, even when I
writ them." There is surely reason to suspect that he pleased
himself as well as his audience; and that these, like the harlots
of other men, had his love, though not his approbation.

He had sometimes faults of a less generous and splendid
kind. He makes, like almost all other poets, very frequent use
of mythology, and sometimes connects religion and fable too
closely without distinction.

He descends to display his knowledge with pedantic ostentation; as when, in translating Virgil, he says "tack to the
larboard"—and "veer starboard"; and talks, in another work,

of "Virtue spooming before the wind." His vanity now and then betrays his ignorance:

> They Nature's king through Nature's optics view'd:
> Revers'd, they view'd him lessen'd to their eyes.

He had heard of reversing a telescope, and unluckily reverses the object.

He is sometimes unexpectedly mean. When he describes the Supreme Being as moved by prayer to stop the Fire of London, what is his expression?

> A hollow crystal pyramid he takes,
>   In firmamental waters dipt above,
> Of it a broad *extinguisher* he makes,
>   And *hoods* the flames that to their quarry strove.

When he describes the Last Day, and the decisive tribunal, he intermingles this image:

> When rattling bones together fly
> From the four quarters of the sky.

It was indeed never in his power to resist the temptation of a jest. In his Elegy on Cromwell:

> No sooner was the Frenchman's cause embrac'd,
> Than the *light Monsieur* the *grave Don* outweigh'd;
> His fortune turn'd the scale——

He had a vanity, unworthy of his abilities, to show, as may be suspected, the rank of the company with whom he lived, by the use of French words, which had then crept into conversation; such as *fraîcheur* for *coolness*, *fougue* for *turbulence*, and a few more, none of which the language has incorporated or retained. They continue only where they stood first, perpetual warnings to future innovators.

These are his faults of affectation; his faults of negligence are beyond recital. Such is the unevenness of his compositions, that ten lines are seldom found together without something of which the reader is ashamed. Dryden was no rigid judge of his own pages; he seldom struggled after supreme excellence, but snatched in haste what was within his reach; and when he

could content others, was himself contented. He did not keep
present to his mind an idea of pure perfection; nor compare
his works, such as they were, with what they might be made.
He knew to whom he should be opposed. He had more music
than Waller, more vigour than Denham, and more nature
than Cowley; and from his contemporaries he was in no danger. Standing therefore in the highest place, he had no care
to rise by contending with himself; but, while there was no
name above his own, was willing to enjoy fame on the easiest
terms.

He was no lover of labour. What he thought sufficient he
did not stop to make better; and allowed himself to leave
many parts unfinished, in confidence that the good lines would
overbalance the bad. What he had once written, he dismissed
from his thoughts; and I believe there is no example to be
found of any correction or improvement made by him after
publication. The hastiness of his productions might be the effect of necessity; but his subsequent neglect could hardly have
any other cause than impatience of study.

What can be said of his versification will be little more than
a dilatation of the praise given it by Pope:

> Waller was smooth; but Dryden taught to join ⎫
> The varying verse, the full-resounding line, ⎬
> The long majestic march, and energy divine. ⎭

Some improvements had been already made in English
numbers; but the full force of our language was not yet felt;
the verse that was smooth was commonly feeble. If Cowley
had sometimes a finished line, he had it by chance. Dryden
knew how to choose the flowing and the sonorous words, to
vary the pauses and adjust the accents, to diversify the ca-
dence, and yet preserve the smoothness of his metre.

Of triplets and Alexandrines, though he did not introduce
the use, he established it. The triplet has long subsisted among
us. Dryden seems not to have traced it higher than to Chapman's Homer; but it is to be found in Phaer's Virgil, written
in the reign of Mary, and in Hall's *Satires*, published five years
before the death of Elizabeth.

The Alexandrine was, I believe, first used by Spenser, for

the sake of closing his stanza with a fuller sound. We had a longer measure of fourteen syllables, into which the Æneid was translated by Phaer, and other works of the ancients by other writers, of which Chapman's Iliad was, I believe, the last.

The two first lines of Phaer's third Æneid will exemplify this measure:

When Asia's state was overthrown, and Priam's kingdom stout,
All guiltless, by the power of gods above was rooted out.

As these lines had their break, or *cæsura*, always at the eighth syllable, it was thought, in time, commodious to divide them: and quatrains of lines, alternately, consisting of eight and six syllables, make the most soft and pleasing of our lyric measures, as:

> Relentless Time, destroying power,
> Which stone and brass obey,
> Who giv'st to ev'ry flying hour
> To work some new decay.

In the Alexandrine, when its power was once felt, some poems, as Drayton's *Polyolbion*, were wholly written; and sometimes the measures of twelve and fourteen syllables were interchanged with one another. Cowley was the first that inserted the Alexandrine at pleasure among the heroic lines of ten syllables, and from him Dryden professes to have adopted it.

The triplet and Alexandrine are not universally approved. Swift always censured them, and wrote some lines to ridicule them. In examining their propriety, it is to be considered that the essence of verse is regularity, and its ornament is variety. To write verse is to dispose syllables and sounds harmonically by some known and settled rule—a rule, however, lax enough to substitute similitude for identity, to admit change without breach of order, and to relieve the ear without disappointing it. Thus a Latin hexameter is formed from dactyls and spondees differently combined; the English heroic admits of acute or grave syllables variously disposed. The Latin never deviates into seven feet, or exceeds the number of seventeen syllables;

but the English Alexandrine breaks the lawful bounds, and surprises the reader with two syllables more than he expected.

The effect of the triplet is the same; the ear has been accustomed to expect a new rhyme in every couplet, but is on a sudden surprised with three rhymes together, to which the reader could not accommodate his voice, did he not obtain notice of the change from the braces of the margins. Surely there is something unskilful in the necessity of such mechanical direction.

Considering the metrical art simply as a science, and consequently excluding all casualty, we must allow that triplets and Alexandrines, inserted by caprice, are interruptions of that constancy to which science aspires. And though the variety which they produce may very justly be desired, yet, to make our poetry exact, there ought to be some stated mode of admitting them.

But till some such regulation can be formed, I wish them still to be retained in their present state. They are sometimes convenient to the poet. Fenton was of opinion that Dryden was too liberal, and Pope too sparing, in their use.

The rhymes of Dryden are commonly just, and he valued himself for his readiness in finding them; but he is sometimes open to objection.

It is the common practice of our poets to end the second line with a weak or grave syllable:

> Together o'er the Alps methinks we fly,
> Fir'd with ideas of fair *Italy*.
>> POPE, *Epistle to Jervas*.

Dryden sometimes puts the weak rhyme in the first:

> Laugh, all the powers that favour *tyranny*,
> And all the standing army of the sky.

Sometimes he concludes a period or paragraph with the first line of a couplet, which, though the French seem to do it without irregularity, always displeases in English poetry.

The Alexandrine, though much his favourite, is not always very diligently fabricated by him. It invariably requires a break at the sixth syllable; a rule which the modern French poets never violate, but which Dryden sometimes neglected:

And with paternal thunder vindicates his throne.

Of Dryden's works it was said by Pope, that "he could select from them better specimens of every mode of poetry than any other English writer could supply." Perhaps no nation ever produced a writer that enriched his language with such variety of models. To him we owe the improvement, perhaps the completion of our metre, the refinement of our language, and much of the correctness of our sentiments. By him we were taught "sapere et fari," to think naturally and express forcibly. Though Davies has reasoned in rhyme before him, it may be perhaps maintained that he was the first who joined argument with poetry. He showed us the true bounds of a translator's liberty. What was said of Rome, adorned by Augustus, may be applied by an easy metaphor to English poetry embellished by Dryden, "lateritiam invenit, marmoream reliquit." He found it brick, and he left it marble.

The invocation before the Georgics is here inserted from Mr. Milbourne's version, that, according to his own proposal, his verses may be compared with those which he censures.

What makes the richest *tilth*, beneath what signs
To *plough*, and when to match your *elms* and *vines*;
What care with *flocks*, and what with *herds* agrees,
And all the management of frugal *bees*;
I sing, *Mæcenas!* Ye immensely clear,
Vast orbs of light, which guide the rolling year;
Bacchus, and mother *Ceres*, if by you
We fat'ning *corn* for hungry *mast* pursue,
If, taught by you, we first the *cluster* prest,
And *thin cold streams* with *sprightly juice* refresht;
Ye *fawns*, the present *numens* of the field,
Wood-Nymphs and *fawns*, your kind assistance yield;
Your gifts I sing: and thou, at whose fear'd stroke
From rending earth the fiery *courser* broke,
Great *Neptune*, O assist my artful song!

And thou to whom the woods and groves belong,
Whose snowy heifers on her flowry plains
In mighty herds the *Cæan Isle* maintains!
Pan, happy shepherd, if thy cares divine
E'er to improve thy *Mœnalus* incline,
Leave thy *Lycæan wood* and *native grove*,
And with thy lucky smiles our work approve;
Be *Pallas* too, sweet oil's inventor, kind;
And he who first the crooked *plough* design'd!
Sylvanus, god of all the woods, appear,
Whose hands a new-drawn tender *cypress* bear!
Ye *gods* and *goddesses*, who e'er with love
Would guard our pastures, and our fields improve;
You, who new plants from unsown lands supply,
And with condensing clouds obscure the sky,
And drop 'em softly thence in fruitfull showers;
Assist my enterprize, ye gentler powers!

And thou, great *Cæsar!* tho we know not yet
Among what gods thou'lt fix thy lofty seat;
Whether thou'lt be the kind *tutelar god*
Of thy own *Rome*, or with thy awfull nod
Guide the vast world, while thy great hand shall bear ⎫
The fruits and seasons of the turning year, ⎬
And thy bright brows thy mother's myrtles wear; ⎭
Whether thou'lt all the boundless ocean sway,
And sea-men only to thyself shall pray,
Thule, the farthest island, kneel to thee,
And, that thou may'st her son by marriage be,
Tethys will for the happy purchase yield
To make a *dowry* of her watry field:
Whether thou'lt add to heaven a *brighter sign*,
And o'er the *summer months* serenely shine;
Where between *Cancer* and *Erigone*
There yet remains a spacious *room* for thee;
Where the hot *Scorpion* too his arms declines,
And more to thee than half his *arch* resigns;
Whate'er thou'lt be; for sure the realms below
No just pretence to thy command can show;

No such ambition sways thy vast desires,
Tho *Greece* her own *Elysian Fields* admires,
And now, at last, contented *Proserpine*
Can all her mother's earnest prayers decline.
Whate'er thou'lt be, O guide our gentle course,
And with thy smiles our bold attempts enforce;
With me th' unknowing *rustics* wants relieve,
And, tho on earth, our sacred vows receive!

The original of the following letter is preserved in the Library at Lambeth, and was kindly imparted to the public by the Rev. Dr. Vyse.

DRYDEN TO HIS SONS IN ITALY

MS. in Lambeth Library, marked No. 933 [Gibson Papers, vol. i.], p. 56

Sept. the 3rd, our Style [1697].

DEAR SONS,—Being now at Sir William Bowyer's in the country, I cannot write at large, because I find myself somewhat indisposed with a cold, and am thick of hearing, rather worse than I was in town. I am glad to find, by your letter of July 26th, your style, that you are both in health; but wonder you should think me so negligent as to forget to give you an account of the ship in which your parcel is to come. I have written to you two or three letters concerning it, which I have sent by safe hands, as I told you, and doubt not but you have them before this can arrive to you. Being out of town, I have forgotten the ship's name, which your mother will inquire, and put it into her letter, which is joined with mine. But the master's name I remember: he is called Mr. Ralph Thorp; the ship is bound to Leghorn, consigned to Mr. Peter and Mr. Tho. Ball, merchants. I am of your opinion, that by Tonson's means almost all our letters have miscarried for this last year. But, however, he has missed of his design in the Dedication, though he had prepared the book for it; for in every figure of Æneas he has caused him to be drawn like King William, with a hooked nose.

After my return to town, I intend to alter a play of

Sir Robert Howard's, written long since, and lately put into my hands: 'tis called *The Conquest of China by the Tartars*. It will cost me six weeks' study, with the probable benefit of a hundred pounds. In the meantime I am writing a song for St. Cecilia's Feast, who, you know, is the patroness of music. This is troublesome, and no way beneficial; but I could not deny the Stewards of the Feast, who came in a body to me to desire that kindness, one of them being Mr. Bridgeman, whose parents are your mother's friends. I hope to send you thirty guineas between Michaelmas and Christmas, of which I will give you an account when I come to town. I remember the counsel you give me in your letter; but dissembling, though lawful in some cases, is not my talent; yet, for your sake, I will struggle with the plain openness of my nature, and keep in my just resentments against that degenerate order. In the mean time I flatter not myself with any manner of hopes, but do my duty, and suffer for God's sake; being assured, beforehand, never to be rewarded, though the times should alter. Towards the latter end of this month, September, Charles will begin to recover his perfect health, according to his nativity, which, casting it myself, I am sure is true, and all things hitherto have happened accordingly to the very time that I predicted them: I hope at the same time to recover more health, according to my age. Remember me to poor Harry, whose prayers I earnestly desire. My Virgil succeeds in the world beyond its desert or my expectation. You know the profits might have been more; but neither my conscience nor my honour would suffer me to take them: but I never can repent of my constancy, since I am thoroughly persuaded of the justice of the cause for which I suffer. It has pleased God to raise up many friends to me amongst my enemies, though they who ought to have been my friends are negligent of me. I am called to dinner, and cannot go on with this letter, which I desire you to excuse; and am

Your most affectionate father,
JOHN DRYDEN.

JOHN POMFRET

1667–1703

Born at Luton in Bedfordshire—Educated at Cambridge — Rector of Malden in Bedfordshire — Publishes *The Choice*—Marries—Death and Character.

Of Mr. John Pomfret nothing is known but from a slight and confused account prefixed to his poems by a nameless friend, who relates that he was the son of the Rev. Mr. Pomfret, vicar of Luton in Bedfordshire, that he was bred at Cambridge, entered into orders, and was rector of Malden in Bedfordshire, and might have risen in the Church; but that when he applied to Dr. Compton, Bishop of London, for institution to a living of considerable value, to which he had been presented, he found a troublesome obstruction raised by a malicious interpretation of some passage in his *Choice*, from which it was inferred that he considered happiness as more likely to be found in the company of a mistress than of a wife.

This reproach was easily obliterated: for it had happened to Pomfret as to all other men who plan schemes of life, he had departed from his purpose, and was then married.

The malice of his enemies had, however, a very fatal consequence; the delay constrained his attendance in London, where he caught the small-pox, and died in 1703, in the thirty-sixth year of his age.

He published his poems in 1699; and has been always the favourite of that class of readers who, without vanity or criticism, seek only their own amusement.

His *Choice* exhibits a system of life adapted to common

notions, and equal to common expectations; such a state as affords plenty and tranquillity, without exclusion of intellectual pleasures. Perhaps no composition in our language has been oftener perused than Pomfret's *Choice*.

In his other poems there is an easy volubility; the pleasure of smooth metre is afforded to the ear, and the mind is not oppressed with ponderous or entangled with intricate sentiment. He pleases many, and he who pleases many must have some species of merit.

EARL OF DORSET

1637–8 — 1705–6

Birth and Parentage—Educated under a Private Tutor—Represents East Grinstead in the Restoration Parliament—His early Dissipation—His Valour and Gaiety—Writes a famous Ballad at Sea, *To all you ladies now at land*—Created Earl of Middlesex—Succeeds his Father as Earl of Dorset—Sides with the Prince of Orange against James II.—Twice married—His Patronage of Poets—Death at Bath, and Burial at Wythiam in Sussex.

Of the Earl of Dorset the character has been drawn so largely and so elegantly by Prior, to whom he was familiarly known, that nothing can be added by a casual hand; and, as its author is so generally read, it would be useless officiousness to transcribe it.

Charles Sackville was born January 24, 1637–8. Having been educated under a private tutor, he travelled into Italy, and returned a little before the Restoration. He was chosen into the first parliament that was called, for East Grinstead, in Sussex, and soon became a favourite of Charles II., but undertook no public employment, being too eager of the riotous and licentious pleasures which young men of high rank who aspired to be thought wits at that time imagined themselves entitled to indulge.

One of these frolics has, by the industry of Wood, come down to posterity. Sackville, who was then Lord Buckhurst, with Sir Charles Sedley and Sir Thomas Ogle, got drunk at the Cock in Bow-street by Covent-garden, and, going into the balcony, exposed themselves to the populace in very indecent postures. At last, as they grew warmer, Sedley stood forth naked and harangued the populace in such profane language that the public indignation was awakened; the crowd attempted to force the door, and, being repulsed, drove in the performers with stones, and broke the windows of the house.

For this misdemeanour they were indicted, and Sedley was fined 500*l.*; what was the sentence of the others is not known. Sedley employed Killigrew and another to procure a remission from the King; but (mark the friendship of the dissolute!) they begged the fine for themselves, and exacted it to the last groat.

In 1665 Lord Buckhurst attended the Duke of York as a volunteer in the Dutch war, and was in the battle of June 3rd, when eighteen great Dutch ships were taken, fourteen others were destroyed, and Opdam the admiral, who engaged the Duke, was blown up beside him, with all his crew.

On the day before the battle he is said to have composed the celebrated song, *To all you ladies now at land*, with equal tranquillity of mind and promptitude of wit. Seldom any splendid story is wholly true. I have heard from the late Earl of Orrery, who was likely to have good hereditary intelligence, that Lord Buckhurst had been a week employed upon it, and only retouched or finished it on the memorable evening. But even this, whatever it may subtract from his facility, leaves him his courage.

He was soon after made a gentleman of the bedchamber, and sent on short embassies to France.

In 1674, the estate of his uncle, James Cranfield, Earl of Middlesex, came to him by its owner's death, and the title was conferred on him the year after. In 1677 he became, by the death of his father, Earl of Dorset, and inherited the estate of his family.

In 1684, having buried his first wife, of the family of Bagot, who left him no child, he married a daughter of the Earl of Northampton, celebrated both for beauty and understanding.

He received some favourable notice from King James; but soon found it necessary to oppose the violence of his innovations, and with some other Lords appeared in Westminster Hall to countenance the Bishops at their trial.

As enormities grew every day less supportable, he found it necessary to concur in the Revolution. He was one of those Lords who sat every day in council to preserve the public peace after the King's departure; and, what is not the most illustrious action of his life, was employed to conduct the Princess Anne to Nottingham, with a guard, such as might alarm the populace as they passed with false apprehensions of her danger. Whatever end may be designed, there is always something despicable in a trick.

He became, as may be easily supposed, a favourite of King William, who, the day after his accession, made him lord-chamberlain of the household, and gave him afterwards the Garter. He happened to be among those that were tossed, with the King, in an open boat sixteen hours, in very rough and cold weather, on the coast of Holland. His health afterwards declined; and, on January 29, 1705–6, he died at Bath.

He was a man whose elegance and judgment were universally confessed, and whose bounty to the learned and witty was generally known. To the indulgent affection of the public Lord Rochester bore ample testimony in this remark: "*I know not how it is, but Lord Buckhurst may do what he will, yet is never in the wrong.*"

If such a man attempted poetry, we cannot wonder that his works were praised. Dryden, whom, if Prior tells truth, he distinguished by his beneficence, and who lavished his blandishments on those who are not known to have so well deserved them, undertaking to produce authors of our own country superior to those of antiquity, says, "*I would instance your Lordship in satire, and Shakespeare in tragedy.*" Would it be imagined that, of this rival to antiquity, all the satires were little personal invectives, and that his longest composition was a song of eleven stanzas?

The blame, however, of this exaggerated praise falls on the encomiast, not upon the author; whose performances are, what they pretend to be, the effusions of a man of wit—gay, vigorous, and airy. His verses to Howard show great fertility of mind, and his *Dorinda* has been imitated by Pope.

GEORGE STEPNEY

1663–1707

Born at Westminster—Educated at Trinity College,
Cambridge—His Political Employments—Death and Burial in Westminster Abbey—Works and Character.

George Stepney, descended from the Stepneys of Prendergast in Pembrokeshire, was born at Westminster in 1663.
Of his father's condition or fortune we have no account. Having received the first part of his education at Westminster,
where he passed six years in the college, he went at nineteen
to Cambridge, where he continued a friendship begun at
school with Mr. Montague, afterwards Earl of Halifax. They
came to London together, and are said to have been invited
into public life by the Earl of Dorset.

His qualifications recommended him to many foreign employments, so that his time seems to have been spent in ne-
gotiations. In 1692 he was sent envoy to the Elector of
Brandenburgh; in 1693 to the Imperial Court; in 1694 to the
Elector of Saxony; in 1696 to the Electors of Mentz and
Cologne, and the Congress at Frankfort; in 1698 a second
time to Brandenburgh; in 1699 to the King of Poland; in
1701 again to the Emperor; and in 1706 to the States General. In 1697 he was made one of the commissioners of trade.
His life was busy, and not long. He died [at Chelsea] in 1707,
and is buried in Westminster Abbey, with this epitaph, which
Jacob transcribed:

H. S. E.

Georgius Stepneius, Armiger,
Vir
Ob Ingenii acumen,
Literarum Scientiam,
Morum Suavitatem,
Rerum Usum,
Virorum Amplissimorum Consuetudinem
Linguæ, Styli, ac Vitæ Elegantiam,
Præclara Officia cum Britanniæ tum Europæ
præstita,
Sua ætate multum celebratus,
Apud posteros semper celebrandus;
Plurimas Legationes obiit
Ea Fide, Diligentia, ac Felicitate,
Ut Augustissimorum Principum
Gulielmi & Annæ
Spem in illo repositam
Nunquam fefellerit,
Haud raro superaverit.
Post longum honorum Cursum
Brevi Temporis Spatio confectum,
Cum Naturæ parum, Famæ satis vixerat,
Animam ad altiora aspirantem placide efflavit.

On the left hand:

G. S.

Ex Equestri Familia Stepneiorum,
De Prendergast, in Comitatu
Pembrochiensi oriundus,
Westmonasterii natus est, A.D. 1663.
Electus in Collegium
Sancti Petri Westmonast. A. 1676.
Sancti Trinitatis Cantab. 1682.
Consiliariorum quibus Commercii
Cura commissa est 1697.
Chelseiæ mortuus; &, comitante
Magnâ Procerum
Frequentiâ, huc elatus, 1707.

It is reported that the juvenile compositions of Stepney *made grey authors blush*. I know not whether his poems will appear such wonders to the present age. One cannot always easily find the reason for which the world has sometimes conspired to squander praise. It is not very unlikely that he wrote very early as well as he ever wrote; and the performances of youth have many favourers, because the authors yet lay no claim to public honours, and are therefore not considered as rivals by the distributors of fame.

He apparently professed himself a poet, and added his name [1693] to those of the other wits in the version of Juvenal; but he is a very licentious translator, and does not recompense his neglect of the author by beauties of his own. In his original poems, now and then, a happy line may perhaps be found, and now and then a short composition may give pleasure; but there is, in the whole, little either of the grace of wit, or the vigour of nature.

JOHN PHILIPS

1676–1708

Born at Bampton in Oxfordshire—Educated at Winchester and Christ Church, Oxford—Publishes *The Splendid Shilling*, *Blenheim*, and *Cider*—Death and Burial in Hereford Cathedral—Monument in Westminster Abbey —Works and Character.

John Philips was born on the 30th of December, 1676, at Bampton in Oxfordshire, of which place his father, Dr. Stephen Philips, archdeacon of Salop, was minister. The first part of his education was domestic; after which he was sent to Winchester, where, as we are told by Dr. Sewel, his biographer, he was soon distinguished by the superiority of his exercises; and, what is less easily to be credited, so much endeared himself to his schoolfellows by his civility and good nature, that they, without murmur or ill-will, saw him indulged by the master with particular immunities. It is related that, when he was at school, he seldom mingled in play with the other boys, but retired to his chamber, where his sovereign pleasure was to sit, hour after hour, while his hair was combed by somebody whose service he found means to procure.

At school he became acquainted with the poets ancient and modern, and fixed his attention particularly on Milton.

In 1694 he entered himself at Christchurch, a college at that time in the highest reputation, by the transmission of Busby's scholars to the care first of Fell, and afterwards of Aldrich. Here he was distinguished as a genius eminent among the eminent, and for friendship particularly intimate with Mr. Smith, the author of *Phædra and Hippolitus*. The profession which he intended to follow was that of physic; and he took much delight in natural history, of which botany was his favourite part.

His reputation was confined to his friends and to the university, till about 1703 he extended it to a wider circle by *The Splendid Shilling*, which struck the public attention with a mode of writing new and unexpected.

This performance raised him so high, that when Europe resounded with the victory of Blenheim, he was, probably with an occult opposition to Addison, employed to deliver the acclamation of the Tories. It is said that he would willingly have declined the task, but that his friends urged it upon him. It appears that he wrote this poem at the house of Mr. St. John.

Blenheim was published in 1705. The next year produced his greatest work, the poem upon *Cider*, in two books, which was received with loud praises, and continued long to be read, as an imitation of Virgil's Georgic which needed not shun the presence of the original.

He then grew probably more confident of his own abilities, and began to meditate a poem on the *Last Day*—a subject on which no mind can hope to equal expectation.

This work he did not live to finish; his diseases, a slow consumption and an asthma, put a stop to his studies, and on Feb. 15, 1708, at the beginning of his thirty-third year, put an end to his life. He was buried in the Cathedral of Hereford; and Sir Simon Harcourt, afterwards Lord Chancellor, gave him a monument in Westminster Abbey. The inscription at Westminster was written, as I have heard, by Dr. Atterbury, though commonly given to Dr. Freind.

His Epitaph at Hereford
JOHANNES PHILIPS

Obiit 15 die Feb. Anno { Dom. 1708.
{ Ætat. suæ 32.

Cujus
Ossa si requiras, hanc Urnam inspice:
Si ingenium nescias, ipsius Opera consule;
Si Tumulum desideras,

Templum adi *Westmonasteriense:*
Qualis quantusque Vir fuerit,
Dicat elegans illa & preclara,
Quæ cenotaphium ibi decorat,
Inscriptio.
Quàm interim erga Cognatos pius & officiosus,
Testetur hoc saxum
A Maria Philips Matre ipsius pientissimâ,
Dilecti Filii Memoriæ non sine Lacrymis dicatum.

His Epitaph at Westminster

Herefordiæ conduntur Ossa,
Hoc in Delubro statuitur Imago,
Britanniam omnem pervagatur Fama
JOHANNIS PHILIPS:
Qui Viris bonis doctisque juxta charus,
Immortale suum Ingenium,
Eruditione multiplici excultum,
Miro animi candore,
Eximiâ morum simplicitate
Honestavit.
Litterarum Amœniorum sitim,
Quam Wintoniæ Puer sentire cœperat,
Inter Ædis Christi Alumnos jugiter explevit.
In illo Musarum Domicilio
Præclaris Æmulorum studiis excitatus,
Optimis scribendi Magistris semper intentus,
Carmina sermone Patrio composuit
A Græcis Latinisque fontibus feliciter deducta,
Atticis Romanisque auribus omnino digna,
Versuum quippe Harmoniam
Rythmo didicerat.
Antiquo illo, libero multiformi
Ad res ipsas apto prorsus, & attemperato,
Non numeris in eundem ferè orbem redeuntibus,
Non Clausularum similiter cadentium sono
Metiri:
Uni in hoc laudis genere Miltono secundus,
Primoque pœne Par.

Res seu Tenues, seu Grandes, seu Mediocres
Ornandas sumserat,
Nusquam, non quod decuit,
Et videt, & assecutus est,
Egregius, quocunque Stylum verteret,
Fandi author, & Modorum artifex.
Fas sit Huic,
Auso licèt à tuâ Metrorum Lege discedere
O Poesis Anglicanæ Pater, atque Conditor, Chaucere,
Alterum tibi latus claudere,
Vatum certe Cineres, tuos undique stipantium
Non dedecebit Chorum.
SIMON HARCOURT Miles,
Viri benè de se, de Litteris meriti
Quoad viveret Fautor,
Post Obitum piè memor,
Hoc illi Saxum poni voluit.
J. PHILIPS, STEPHANI, S. T. P. Archidiaconi
Salop, Filius, natus est Bamptoniæ
in agro Oxon. Dec. 30, 1676.
Obiit Herefordiæ, Feb. 15, 1708.

Philips has always been praised, without contradiction, as a
man modest, blameless, and pious, who bore narrowness of
fortune without discontent, and tedious and painful maladies
without impatience; beloved by those that knew him, but not
ambitious to be known. He was probably not formed for a
wide circle. His conversation is commended for its innocent
gaiety, which seems to have flowed only among his intimates;
for I have been told that he was in company silent and barren,
and employed only upon the pleasures of his pipe. His ad-
diction to tobacco is mentioned by one of his biographers,
who remarks that in all his writings, except *Blenheim*, he has
found an opportunity of celebrating the fragrant fume. In
common life he was probably one of those who please by not
offending, and whose person was loved because his writings
were admired. He died honoured and lamented before any
part of his reputation had withered, and before his patron
St. John had disgraced him.

His works are few. *The Splendid Shilling* has the uncommon merit of an original design, unless it may be thought precluded by the ancient *Centos*. To degrade the sounding words and stately construction of Milton by an application to the lowest and most trivial things, gratifies the mind with a momentary triumph over that grandeur which hitherto held its captives in admiration; the words and things are presented with a new appearance, and novelty is always grateful where it gives no pain.

But the merit of such performances begins and ends with the first author. He that should again adapt Milton's phrase to the gross incidents of common life, and even adapt it with more art, which would not be difficult, must yet expect but a small part of the praise which Philips has obtained; he can only hope to be considered as the repeater of a jest.

"The parody on Milton," says Gildon, "is the only tolerable production of its author." This is a censure too dogmatical and violent. The poem of *Blenheim* was never denied to be tolerable, even by those who do not allow its supreme excellence. It is indeed the poem of a scholar, *all inexpert of war* —of a man who writes books from books, and studies the world in a college. He seems to have formed his ideas of the field of Blenheim from the battles of the heroic ages, or the tales of chivalry, with very little comprehension of the qualities necessary to the composition of a modern hero, which Addison has displayed with so much propriety. He makes Marlborough behold at a distance the slaughter made by Tallard, then haste to encounter and restrain him, and mow his way through ranks made headless by his sword.

He imitates Milton's numbers indeed, but imitates them very injudiciously. Deformity is easily copied; and whatever there is in Milton which the reader wishes away, all that is obsolete, peculiar, or licentious, is accumulated with great care by Philips. Milton's verse was harmonious, in proportion to the general state of our metre in Milton's age; and if he had written after the improvements made by Dryden, it is reasonable to believe that he would have admitted a more pleasing modulation of numbers into his work: but Philips sits down with a resolution to make no more music than he found—to

want all that his master wanted, though he is very far from
having what his master had. Those asperities, therefore, that
are venerable in the *Paradise Lost* are contemptible in the
Blenheim.

There is a Latin ode written to his patron St. John, in return
for a present of wine and tobacco, which cannot be passed
without notice. It is gay and elegant, and exhibits several artful accommodations of classic expressions to new purposes. It
seems better turned than the odes of Hannes.

To the poem on *Cider*, written in imitation of the Georgics,
may be given this peculiar praise, that it is grounded in truth,
that the precepts which it contains are exact and just, and that
it is, therefore, at once a book of entertainment and of science.
This I was told by [Philip] Miller, the great gardener and
botanist, whose expression was, that *there were many books
written on the same subject in prose, which do not contain so
much truth as that poem.*

In the disposition of his matter, so as to intersperse precepts
relating to the culture of trees with sentiments more generally alluring, and in easy and graceful transitions from one
subject to another, he has very diligently imitated his master;
but he unhappily pleased himself with blank verse, and supposed that the numbers of Milton, which impress the mind
with veneration, combined as they are with subjects of incon-
ceivable grandeur, could be sustained by images which at most
can rise only to elegance. Contending angels may shake the
regions of heaven in blank verse; but the flow of equal measures, and the embellishment of rhyme, must recommend to
our attention the art of engrafting, and decide the merit of
the *redstreak* and *pearmain*.

What study could confer, Philips had obtained; but natural
deficience cannot be supplied. He seems not born to greatness
and elevation. He is never lofty, nor does he often surprise
with unexpected excellence; but perhaps to his last poem may
be applied what Tully said of the work of Lucretius, that *it is
written with much art, though with few blazes of genius.*

WILLIAM WALSH

1663 — 1707–8

Born at Abberley, in Worcestershire—Educated at Oxford—Dryden's high Character of him—His early Encouragement—Buried at Abberley—Works and Character.

William Walsh, the son of Joseph Walsh, Esq., of Abberley, in Worcestershire, was born in 1663, as appears from the account of Wood, who relates that at the age of fifteen he became, in 1678, a gentleman commoner of Wadham College.

He left the university without a degree, and pursued his studies at London and at home. That he studied, in whatever place, is apparent from the effect; for he became, in Mr. Dryden's opinion, *the best critic in the nation.*

He was not, however, merely a critic or a scholar, but a man of fashion, and, as Dennis remarks, ostentatiously splendid in his dress. He was likewise a member of Parliament and a courtier, knight of the shire for his native county in several parliaments; in another the representative of Richmond in Yorkshire; and gentleman of the horse to Queen Anne, under the Duke of Somerset.

Some of his verses show him to have been a zealous friend to the Revolution; but his political ardour did not abate his reverence or kindness for Dryden, to whom he gave a Dissertation on Virgil's Pastorals, in which, however studied, he discovers some ignorance of the laws of French versification.

In 1705 he began to correspond with Mr. Pope, in whom he discovered very early the power of poetry. Their letters are written upon the pastoral comedy of the Italians, and those pastorals which Pope was then preparing to publish.

The kindnesses which are first experienced are seldom forgotten. Pope always retained a grateful memory of Walsh's notice, and mentioned him in one of his latter pieces among those that had encouraged his juvenile studies.

                    Granville the polite,
        And knowing Walsh, would tell me I could write.

In his *Essay on Criticism* he had given him more splendid praise; and, in the opinion of his learned commentator, sacrificed a little of his judgment to his gratitude.

The time of his death I have not learned. It must have happened between 1707, when he wrote to Pope, and 1711, when Pope praised him in his Essay. The epitaph makes him forty-six years old: if Wood's account be right, he died in 1709.

He is known more by his familiarity with greater men, than by anything done or written by himself.

His works are not numerous. In prose he wrote [1691] A *Dialogue concerning Women, being a Defence of the Sex,* which Dryden honoured with a Preface.

Esculapius, or the Hospital of Fools, published after his death.

A *Collection of Letters and Poems, amorous and gallant,* was published in the volumes called Dryden's *Miscellany,* and some other occasional pieces.

To his Poems and Letters is prefixed a very judicious Preface upon Epistolary Composition and Amorous Poetry.

In his *Golden Age Restored* there was something of humour while the facts were recent, but it now strikes no longer. In his imitation of Horace, the first stanzas are happily turned, and in all his writings there are pleasing passages. He has, however, more elegance than vigour, and seldom rises higher than to be pretty.

EDMUND SMITH

1668–1710

Born at Handley, in Worcestershire—Educated at
Westminster and Oxford—His Character by Oldisworth
—Excels in Latin Verse—His loose Life and slovenly
Habits—His Tragedy of *Phædra and Hippolitus*—Buried
at Hartham, in Wiltshire—Works and Character—Gilbert
Walmsley.

Edmund Smith is one of those lucky writers who have,
without much labour, attained high reputation, and who are
mentioned with reverence rather for the possession than the
exertion of uncommon abilities.

Of his life little is known; and that little claims no praise
but what can be given to intellectual excellence, seldom employed to any virtuous purpose. His character, as given by
Mr. Oldisworth, with all the partiality of friendship, which is
said by Dr. Burton to show "what fine things one man of
parts can say to another," and which, however, comprises great
part of what can be known of Mr. Smith, it is better to transcribe at once than to take by pieces. I shall subjoin such little
memorials as accident has enabled me to collect.

A CHARACTER OF THE AUTHOR

Mr. Edmund Smith was the only son of an eminent
merchant, one Mr. Neale, by a daughter of the late Baron
Lechmere. Some misfortunes of his father, which were
soon after followed by his death, were the occasion of
the son's being left very young in the hands of a near
relation (one who married Mr. Neale's sister), whose
name was Smith.

This gentleman and his lady treated him as their own child, and put him to Westminster School under the care of Dr. Busby; whence, after the loss of his faithful and generous guardian (whose name he assumed and retained), he was removed to Christchurch in Oxford, and there by his aunt handsomely maintained till her death; after which he continued a member of that learned and ingenious society till within five years of his own; though, some time before his leaving Christchurch, he was sent for by his mother to Worcester, and owned and acknowledged as her legitimate son; which had not been mentioned but to wipe off the aspersions that were ignorantly cast by some on his birth. It is to be remembered for our author's honour, that, when at the Westminster election he stood a candidate for one of the universities, he so signally distinguished himself by his conspicuous performances, that there arose no small contention between the representative electors of Trinity College in Cambridge and Christchurch in Oxon, which of those two royal societies should adopt him as their own. But the electors of Trinity College having the preference of choice that year, they resolutely elected him; who yet, being invited at the same time to Christchurch, chose to accept of a studentship there.

Mr. Smith's perfections, as well natural as acquired, seem to have been formed upon Horace's plan; who says, in his *Art of Poetry,*

——Ego nec studium sine divite venâ,
Nec rude quid prosit video ingenium: alterius sic
Altera poscit opem res, et conjurat amice.

He was endowed by Nature with all those excellent and necessary qualifications which are previous to the accomplishment of a great man. His memory was large and tenacious, yet by a *curious felicity chiefly* susceptible of the finest impressions it received from the best authors he read, which it always preserved in their primitive strength and amiable order.

He had a quickness of apprehension, and vivacity of

understanding, which easily took in and surmounted the most subtle and knotty parts of mathematics and metaphysics. His wit was prompt and flowing, yet solid and piercing; his taste delicate, his head clear, and his way of expressing his thoughts perspicuous and engaging. I shall say nothing of his person, which yet was so well *turned*, that no neglect of himself in his dress could render it disagreeable: insomuch that the fair sex, who observed and esteemed him, at once commended and reproved him by the name of the *handsome* sloven. An eager but generous and noble emulation grew up with him; which (as it were a rational sort of instinct) pushed him upon striving to excel in every art and science that could make him a credit to his college, and that college the ornament of the most learned and polite university; and it was his happiness to have several contemporaries and fellow-students who exercised and excited this virtue in themselves and others, thereby becoming so deservedly in favour with this age, and so good a proof of its nice discernment. His judgment, naturally good, soon ripened into an exquisite fineness and distinguishing sagacity, which as it was active and busy, so it was vigorous and manly, keeping even paces with a rich and strong imagination, always upon the wing, and never tired with aspiring. Hence it was, that, though he writ as young as Cowley, he had no puerilities; and his earliest productions were so far from having anything in them mean and trifling, that, like the junior compositions of Mr. Stepney, they may make grey authors blush. There are many of his first essays in oratory, in epigram, elegy, and epic, still handed about the university in manuscript, which show a masterly hand; and, though maimed and injured by frequent transcribing, make their way into our most celebrated miscellanies, where they shine with uncommon lustre. Besides those verses in the Oxford books, which he could not help setting his name to, several of his compositions came abroad under other names, which his own singular modesty and faithful silence strove in vain to conceal. The Encœnia and Public Collections of the University upon State subjects were never in such esteem, either for Elegy or Congratulation, as when he contributed most largely to them; and it was natural for those who knew his peculiar way of writing to turn to his share in the work, as by far the most relishing part of the entertainment. As his parts were extraordinary, so he well knew how to improve them; and not only to polish the diamond, but enchase it in the most solid and durable metal.

Though he was an academic the greatest part of his life, yet he contracted no sourness of temper, no spice of pedantry, no itch of disputation, or obstinate contention for the old or new philosophy, no assuming way of dictating to others; which are faults (though excusable) which some are insensibly led into who are constrained to dwell long within the walls of a private college. His conversation was pleasant and instructive; and what Horace said of Plotius, Varius, and Virgil, might justly be applied to him:

Nil ego contulerim jucundo sanus Amico.—*Sat.* v. l. 1.

As correct a writer as he was in his most elaborate pieces, he read the works of others with candour, and reserved his greatest severity for his own compositions; being readier to cherish and advance than damp or depress a rising genius, and as patient of being excelled himself (if any could excel him) as industrious to excel others.

'Twere to be wished he had confined himself to a particular profession, who was capable of surpassing in any; but in this, his want of application was in a great measure owing to his want of due encouragement.

He passed through the exercises of the college and university with unusual applause; and though he often suffered his friends to call him off from his retirements, and to lengthen out those jovial avocations, yet his return to his studies was so much the more passionate, and his intention upon those refined pleasures of reading and thinking so vehement (to which his facetious and unbended intervals bore no proportion), that the habit grew upon him, and the series of meditation and reflection being kept up whole weeks together, he could better sort his ideas, and take in the sundry parts of a science at one view, without interruption or confusion. Some indeed of his acquaintance, who were pleased to distinguish between the wit and the scholar, extolled him altogether on the account of the first of these titles; but others, who knew him better, could not forbear doing him justice as a prodigy in both kinds. He had signalised himself, in the schools, as a philosopher and polemic of extensive knowledge and deep penetration; and went through all the courses with a wise regard to the dignity and importance of each science. I remember him in the Divinity School responding and disputing with a perspicuous energy, a ready exactness, and commanding force of argument, when Dr. Jane worthily presided in the chair; whose condescending and disinterested commendation of him gave him such a reputation as silenced the envious malice of his enemies, who durst not contradict the approbation of so profound a master in theology. None of those self-sufficient creatures, who have either trifled with philosophy by attempting to ridicule it, or have encumbered it with novel terms and burdensome explanations, understood its real weight and purity half so well as Mr. Smith. He was too discerning to allow of the character of unprofitable, rugged, and abstruse, which some superficial sciolists (so very smooth and polite as to admit of no impression), either out of an unthinking indolence or an ill-grounded prejudice, had affixed to this sort of studies. He knew the thorny terms of philosophy served well to fence in the true doctrines of religion, and looked upon school-divinity as upon a rough but well-wrought army, which might at once adorn and defend the Christian hero, and equip him for the combat.

Mr. Smith had a long and perfect intimacy with all the Greek and Latin classics, with whom he had carefully compared whatever was worth perusing in the French, Spanish, and Italian (to which languages he was no stranger), and in all the celebrated writers of his own country. But then, according to the curious observation of the late Earl of Shaftesbury, he kept the poet in awe by regular criticism; and, as it were, married the two arts for their mutual support and improvement. There was not a tract of credit, upon that subject, which he had not diligently examined, from Aristotle down to Hedelin and Bossu; so that, having each rule constantly before him, he could carry the art through every poem, and at once point out the graces and deformities. By this means he seemed to read with a design to correct, as well as imitate.

Being thus prepared, he could not but taste every little delicacy that was set before him; though it was impossible for him at the same time to be fed and nourished with anything but what was substantial and lasting. He considered the ancients and moderns not as parties or rivals for fame, but as architects upon one and the same plan, the Art of Poetry; according to which he judged, approved and blamed, without flattery or detraction. If he did not always commend the compositions of others, it was not ill-nature (which was not in his temper), but strict justice would not let him call a few flowers set in ranks, a glib measure, and so many couplets, by the name of poetry: he was of Ben Jonson's opinion, who could not admire

—— Verses as smooth and soft as cream,
In which there was neither depth nor stream.

And therefore, though his want of complaisance for some men's overbearing vanity made him enemies, yet the better part of mankind were obliged by the freedom of his reflections.

His Bodleian Speech, though taken from a remote and imperfect copy, hath shown the world how great a master he was of the Ciceronian eloquence, mixed with the conciseness and force of Demosthenes, the elegant and moving turns of Pliny, and the acute and wise reflections of Tacitus.

Since Temple and Roscommon, no man understood Horace better, especially as to his happy diction, rolling numbers, beautiful imagery, and alternate mixture of the soft and the sublime. This endeared Dr. Hannes's odes to him, the finest genius for Latin lyric since the Augustan age. His friend Mr. Philips's ode to Mr. St. John (late Lord Bolingbroke), after the manner of Horace's Lusory or Amatorian Odes, is certainly a masterpiece; but Mr. Smith's *Pocockius* is of the sublimer kind, though, like Waller's writings upon Oliver Cromwell, it wants not the most delicate and surprising turns peculiar to the person praised. I do not remember to have seen anything like it in Dr. Bathurst, who had made some attempts this way with applause.

He was an excellent judge of humanity; and so good an historian, that in familiar discourse he would talk over the most memorable facts in antiquity, the lives, actions, and characters of celebrated men, with amazing facility and accuracy. As he had thoroughly read and digested Thuanus's works, so he was able to copy after him; and his talent in this kind was so well known and allowed, that he had been singled out by some great men to write a history, which it was for their interest to have done with the utmost art and dexterity. I shall not mention for what reasons this design was dropped, though they are very much to Mr. Smith's honour. The truth is, and I speak it before living witnesses, whilst an agreeable company could fix him upon a subject of useful literature, nobody shone to greater advantage: he seemed to be that Memmius whom Lucretius speaks of:

— Quem tu, Dea, tempore in omni
Omnibus ornatum voluisti excellere rebus.

His works are not many, and those scattered up and down in Miscellanies and Collections, being wrested from him by his friends with great difficulty and reluctance. All of them together make but a small part of that much greater body which lies dispersed in the possession of numerous acquaintance, and cannot perhaps be made entire without great injustice to him, because few of them had his last hand, and the transcriber was often obliged to take the liberties of a friend. His condolence for the death of Mr. Philips is full of the noblest beauties, and hath done justice to the ashes of that second Milton, whose writings will last as long as the English language, generosity and valour. For him Mr. Smith had contracted a perfect friendship; a passion he was most susceptible of, and whose laws he looked upon as sacred and inviolable.

Every subject that passed under his pen had all the life, proportion, and embellishments bestowed on it which an exquisite skill, a warm imagination, and a cool judgment, possibly could bestow on it. The epic, lyric, elegiac, every sort of poetry he touched upon (and he had touched upon a great variety), was raised to its proper height, and the differences between each of them observed with a judicious accuracy. We saw the old rules and new beauties placed in admirable order by each other; and there was a predominant fancy and spirit of his own infused, superior to what some draw off from the ancients, or from poesies here and there culled out of the moderns, by a painful industry and servile imitation. His contrivances were adroit and magnificent; his images lively and adequate; his sentiments charming and majestic; his expressions natural and bold; his numbers various and sounding; and that enamelled mixture of classical wit, which, without redundance and affectation, sparkled through his writings, and was no less pertinent than agreeable.

His *Phædra* is a consummate tragedy, and the success of it was as great as the most sanguine expectations of his friends could promise or foresee. The number of nights, and the common method of filling the house, are not always the surest marks of judging what encouragement a play meets with: but the generosity of all the persons of a refined taste about town was remarkable on this occasion; and it must not be forgotten how zealously Mr. Addison espoused his interest, with all the elegant judgment and diffusive good-nature for which that accomplished gentleman and author is so justly valued by mankind. But as to *Phædra*, she has certainly made a finer figure under Mr. Smith's conduct, upon the English stage, than either in Rome or Athens; and if she excels the Greek and Latin *Phædra*, I need not say she surpasses the French one, though embellished with whatever regular beauties and moving softness Racine himself could give her.

No man had a juster notion of the difficulty of composing than Mr. Smith, and he sometimes would create greater difficulties than he had reason to apprehend. Writing with ease what (as Mr. Wycherley speaks) may be easily written, moved his indignation. When he was writing upon a subject, he would seriously consider what Demosthenes, Homer, Virgil, or Horace, if alive, would say upon that occasion, which whetted him to exceed himself as well as others. Nevertheless, he could not, or would not, finish several subjects he undertook; which may be imputed either to the briskness of his fancy, still hunting after new matter, or to an occasional indolence, which spleen and lassitude brought upon him, and which, of all his foibles, the world was least inclined to forgive. That this was not owing to conceit and vanity, or a fulness of himself (a frailty which has been imputed to no less men than Shakespeare and Jonson), is clear from hence; because he left his works to the entire disposal of his friends, whose most rigorous censures he even courted and solicited, submitting to their animadversions, and the freedom they took with him, with an unreserved and prudent resignation.

I have seen sketches and rough draughts of some poems he designed, set out analytically, wherein the fable, structure, and connection, the images, incidents, moral, episodes, and a great variety of ornaments, were so finely laid out, so well fitted to the rules of art, and squared so exactly to the precedents of the ancients, that I have often looked on these poetical elements with the same concern with which curious men are affected at the sight of the most entertaining remains and ruins of an antique figure or building. Those fragments of the learned, which some men have been so proud of their pains in collecting, are useless rarities, without form and without life, when compared with these embryos which wanted not spirit enough to preserve them; so that I cannot help thinking that, if some of them were to come abroad, they would be as highly valued by the poets as the sketches of Julio and Titian are by the painters, though there is nothing in them but a few outlines as to the design and proportion.

It must be confessed that Mr. Smith had some defects in his conduct which those are most apt to remember who could imitate him in nothing else. His freedom with himself drew severer acknowledgments from him than all the malice he ever provoked was capable of advancing, and he did not scruple to give even his misfortunes the hard name of faults; but if the world had half his good-nature, all the shady parts would be entirely struck out of his character.

A man who, under poverty, calamities, and disappointments, could make so many friends, and those so truly valuable, must have just and noble ideas of the passion of friendship, in the success of which consisted the greatest, if not the only, happiness of his life. He knew very well what was due to his birth, though Fortune threw him short of it in every other circumstance of life. He avoided making any, though perhaps reasonable, complaints of her dispensations, under which he had honour enough to be easy, without touching the favours she flung in his way when offered to him at the price of a more durable reputation. He took care to have no dealings with mankind in which he could not be just; and he desired to be at no other expense in his pretensions than that of intrinsic merit, which was the only burthen and reproach he ever brought upon his friends. He could say, as Horace did of himself, what I never yet saw translated:

—— Meo sum pauper in ære.

At his coming to town no man was more surrounded

by all those who really had or pretended to wit, or more courted by the great men, who had then a power and opportunity of encouraging arts and sciences, and gave proofs of their fondness for the name of Patron in many instances, which will ever be remembered to their glory. Mr. Smith's character grew upon his friends by intimacy, and outwent the strongest prepossessions which had been conceived in his favour. Whatever quarrel a few sour creatures, whose obscurity is their happiness, may possibly have to the age, yet amidst a studied neglect and total disuse of all those ceremonial attendances, fashionable equipments, and external recommendations, which are thought necessary introductions into the *grande monde*, this gentleman was so happy as still to please; and whilst the rich, the gay, the noble, and honourable, saw how much he excelled in wit and learning, they easily forgave him all other differences. Hence it was that both his acquaintance and retirements were his own free choice. What Mr. Prior observes upon a very great character was true of him, *that most of his faults brought their excuse with them.*

Those who blamed him most understood him least, it being the custom of the vulgar to charge an excess upon the most complaisant, and to form a character by the morals of a few, who have sometimes spoiled an hour or two in good company. Where only fortune is wanting to make a great name, that single exception can never pass upon the best judges and most equitable observers of mankind; and when the time comes for the world to spare their pity, we may justly enlarge our demands upon them for their admiration.

Some few years before his death, he had engaged himself in several considerable undertakings, in all which he prepared the world to expect mighty things from him. I have seen about ten sheets of his *English Pindar*, which exceeded anything of that kind I could ever hope for in our own language. He had drawn out the plan of a tragedy of the *Lady Jane Grey*, and had gone through several scenes of it. But he could not well have bequeathed that work to better hands than where, I hear, it is at present lodged; and the bare mention of two such names may justify the largest expectations, and is sufficient to make the town an agreeable invitation.

His greatest and noblest undertaking was *Longinus*. He had finished an entire translation of the *Sublime*, which he sent to the Rev. Mr. Richard Parker, a friend of his, late of Merton College, an exact critic in the Greek tongue, from whom it came to my hands. The French version of Monsieur Boileau, though truly valuable, was far short of it. He proposed a large addition to this work of notes and observations of his own, with an entire system of the Art of Poetry, in three books, under the titles of *Thought, Diction*, and *Figure*. I saw the last of these perfect, and in a fair copy, in which he showed great judgment and reading; and particularly had reformed the art of rhetoric, by reducing that vast and confused heap of terms with which a long succession of pedants had encumbered the world to a very narrow compass, comprehending all that was useful and ornamental in poetry. Under each head and chapter he intended to make remarks upon all the ancients and moderns, the Greek, Latin, English, French, Spanish, and Italian poets, and to note their several beauties and defects.

What remains of his works is left, as I am informed, in the hands of men of worth and judgment, who loved him. It cannot be supposed they would suppress anything that was his, but out of respect to his memory and for want of proper hands to finish what so great a genius had begun.

Such is the declamation of Oldisworth, written while his admiration was yet fresh, and his kindness warm; and therefore such as, without any criminal purpose of deceiving, shows a strong desire to make the most of all favourable truth. I cannot much commend the performance. The praise is often indistinct, and the sentences are loaded with words of more pomp than use. There is little, however, that can be contradicted, even when a plainer tale comes to be told.

Edmund Neale, known by the name of Smith, was born at Handley, the seat of the Lechmeres, in Worcestershire. The year of his birth is uncertain.

He was educated at Westminster. It is known to have been the practice of Dr. Busby to detain those youth long at school of whom he had formed the highest expectations. Smith took his Master's degree on the 8th of July, 1696: he therefore was probably admitted into the university in 1689, when we may suppose him twenty years old.

His reputation for literature in his college was such as has been told; but the indecency and licentiousness of his behaviour drew upon him, Dec. 24, 1694, while he was yet only Bachelor, a public admonition, entered upon record, in order to his expulsion. Of this reproof the effect is not known. He was probably less notorious. At Oxford, as we all know, much will be forgiven to literary merit; and of that he had exhibited sufficient evidence by his excellent ode on the death of the great Orientalist, Dr. Pocock, who died in 1691, and whose praise must have been written by Smith when he had been but two years in the university.

This ode, which closed the second volume of the *Musæ Anglicanæ*, though perhaps some objections may be made to its Latinity, is by far the best lyric composition in that collection; nor do I know where to find it equalled among the modern writers. It expresses, with great felicity, images not classical in classical diction; its digressions and returns have been deservedly recommended by Trapp as models for imitation.

He had several imitations of Cowley:

> Testitur hinc tot sermo coloribus
> Quot tu, Pococki, dissimilis tui
>   Orator effers, quot vicissim
>   Te memores celebrare gaudent.

I will not commend the figure which makes the orator *pronounce the colours,* or give to *colours memory* and *delight.* I quote it, however, as an imitation of these lines:

Who had so many languages in store,
That only Fame shall speak of him in more.

The simile by which an old man, retaining the fire of his youth, is compared to Etna flaming through the snow, which Smith has used with great pomp, is stolen from Cowley, however little worth the labour of conveyance.

He proceeded to take his degree of Master of Arts, July 8, 1696. Of the exercises which he performed on that occasion, I have not heard anything memorable.

As his years advanced, he advanced in reputation; for he continued to cultivate his mind, though he did not amend his irregularities; by which he gave so much offence, that, April 24, 1700, the Dean and Chapter declared "the place of Mr. Smith void, he having been convicted of riotous behaviour in the house of Mr. Cole, an apothecary; but it was referred to the Dean when and upon what occasion the sentence should be put in execution."

Thus tenderly was he treated; the governors of his college could hardly keep him, and yet wished that he would not force them to drive him away.

Some time afterwards he assumed an appearance of decency; in his own phrase, he *whitened* himself, having a desire to obtain the censorship, an office of honour and some profit in the college; but, when the election came, the preference was given to Mr. Foulkes, his junior: the same, I suppose, that joined with Freind in an addition of part of Demosthenes. The censor is a tutor; and it was not thought proper to trust the superintendence of others to a man who took so little care of himself.

From this time Smith employed his malice and his wit against the Dean, Dr. Aldrich, whom he considered as the opponent of his claim. Of his lampoon upon him, I once heard a single line too gross to be repeated.

But he was still a genius and a scholar, and Oxford was unwilling to lose him: he was endured, with all his pranks and his vices, two years longer; but on Dec. 20, 1705, at the instance of all the canons, the sentence declared five years before was put in execution.

The execution was, I believe, silent and tender; for one of his friends, from whom I learned much of his life, appeared not to know it.

He was now driven to London, where he associated himself with the Whigs, whether because they were in power, or because the Tories had expelled him, or because he was a Whig by principle, may perhaps be doubted. He was, however, caressed by men of great abilities, whatever were their party, and was supported by the liberality of those who delighted in his conversation.

There was once a design, hinted at by Oldisworth, to have made him useful. One evening, as he was sitting with a friend at a tavern, he was called down by the waiter, and, having stayed some time below, came up thoughtful. After a pause, said he to his friend, "He that wanted me below was Addison, whose business was to tell me that a History of the Revolution was intended, and to propose that I should undertake it. I said, 'What shall I do with the character of Lord Sunderland?' and Addison immediately returned, 'When, Rag, were you drunk last?' and went away."

Captain Rag was a name which he got at Oxford by his negligence of dress.

This story I heard from the late Mr. Clark of Lincoln's Inn, to whom it was told by the friend of Smith.

Such scruples might debar him from some profitable employments; but as they could not deprive him of any real esteem, they left him many friends; and no man was ever better introduced to the theatre than he, who, in that violent conflict of parties, had a Prologue and an Epilogue from the first wits on either side.

But learning and nature will now and then take different courses. His play pleased the critics, and the critics only. It was, as Addison has recorded, hardly heard the third night. Smith had indeed trusted entirely to his merit, had insured no band of applauders, nor used any artifice to force success, and found that naked excellence was not sufficient for its own support.

The play, however, was bought by Lintot, who advanced the price from fifty guineas, the current rate, to sixty: and Halifax, the general patron, accepted the dedication. Smith's indolence kept him from writing the dedication, till Lintot, after fruitless importunity, gave notice that he would publish the play without it. Now, therefore, it was written; and Halifax expected the author with his book, and had prepared to reward him with a place of 300*l*. a year. Smith, by pride, or caprice, or indolence, or bashfulness, neglected to attend him, though doubtless warned and pressed by his friends, and at last missed his reward by not going to solicit it.

Addison has, in the *Spectator*, mentioned the neglect of Smith's tragedy as disgraceful to the nation, and imputes it to the fondness for operas then prevailing. The authority of Addison is great; yet the voice of the people, when to please the people is the purpose, deserves regard. In this question I cannot but think the people in the right. The fable is mythological, a story which we are accustomed to reject as false; and the manners are so distant from our own, that we know them not from sympathy, but by study: the ignorant do not understand the action; the learned reject it as a school-boy's tale—*incredulus odi*. What I cannot for a moment believe, I cannot for a moment behold with interest or anxiety. The sentiments thus remote from life are removed yet further by the diction, which is too luxuriant and splendid for dialogue, and envelops the thoughts rather than displays them. It is a scholar's play, such as may please the reader rather than the spectator; the work of a vigorous and elegant mind, accustomed to please itself with its own conceptions, but of little acquaintance with the course of life.

Dennis tells us, in one of his pieces, that he had once a design to have written the tragedy of *Phædra*, but was convinced that the action was too mythological.

In 1708, a year after the exhibition of *Phædra*, died John Philips, the friend and fellow-collegian of Smith, who, on that occasion, wrote a poem, which justice must place among the best elegies which our language can show, an elegant mixture of fondness and admiration, of dignity and softness. There are some passages too ludicrous; but every human performance has its faults.

This elegy it was the mode among his friends to purchase

for a guinea; and, as his acquaintance was numerous, it was a very profitable poem.

Of his *Pindar*, mentioned by Oldisworth, I have never otherwise heard. His *Longinus* he intended to accompany with some illustrations, and had selected his instances of the false *sublime* from the works of Blackmore.

He resolved to try again the fortune of the stage, with the story of Lady Jane Grey. It is not unlikely that his experience of the inefficacy and incredibility of a mythological tale might determine him to choose an action from English history, at no great distance from our own times, which was to end in a real event, produced by the operation of known characters.

A subject will not easily occur that can give more opportunities of informing the understanding, for which Smith was unquestionably qualified, or for moving the passions, in which I suspect him to have had less power.

Having formed his plan and collected materials, he declared that a few months would complete his design; and, that he might pursue his work with less frequent avocations, he was, in June 1710, invited by Mr. George Ducket to his house at Hartham, in Wiltshire. Here he found such opportunities of indulgence as did not much forward his studies, and particularly some strong ale, too delicious to be resisted. He eat and drank till he found himself plethoric; and, then resolving to ease himself by evacuation, he wrote to an apothecary in the neighbourhood a prescription of a purge so forcible, that the apothecary thought it his duty to delay it till he had given notice of its danger. Smith, not pleased with the contradiction of a shopman, and boastful of his own knowledge, treated the notice with rude contempt, and swallowed his own medicine, which in July 1710, brought him to the grave. He was buried at Hartham.

Many years afterwards, Ducket communicated to Oldmixon, the historian, an account pretended to have been received from Smith, that Clarendon's *History* was, in its publication, corrupted by Aldrich, Smalridge, and Atterbury; and that Smith was employed to forge and insert the alterations.

This story was published triumphantly by Oldmixon, and may be supposed to have been eagerly received; but its progress was soon checked; for finding its way into the *Journal* of Trevoux, it fell under the eye of Atterbury, then an exile in France, who immediately denied the charge, with this remarkable particular, that he never in his whole life had once spoken to Smith; his company being, as must be inferred, not accepted by those who attended to their characters.

The charge was afterwards very diligently refuted by Dr. Burton of Eton, a man eminent for literature, and though not of the same party with Aldrich and Atterbury, too studious of truth to leave them burthened with a false charge. The testimonies which he has collected have convinced mankind that either Smith or Ducket was guilty of wilful and malicious falsehood.

This controversy brought into view those parts of Smith's life which, with more honour to his name, might have been concealed.

Of Smith I can yet say a little more. He was a man of such estimation among his companions, that the casual censures or praises which he dropped in conversation were considered, like those of Scaliger, as worthy of preservation.

He had great readiness and exactness of criticism, and by a cursory glance over a new composition would exactly tell all its faults and beauties.

He was remarkable for the power of reading with great rapidity, and of retaining with great fidelity what he so easily collected.

He therefore always knew what the present question required; and, when his friends expressed their wonder at his acquisitions, made in a state of apparent negligence and drunkenness, he never discovered his hours of reading or method of study, but involved himself in affected silence, and fed his own vanity with their admiration.

One practice he had, which was easily observed: if any thought or image was presented to his mind, that he could use or improve, he did not suffer it to be lost, but, amidst the jollity of a tavern, or in the warmth of conversation, very diligently committed it to paper.

Thus it was that he had gathered two quires of hints for his new tragedy; of which Rowe, when they were put into his hands, could make, as he says, very little use, but which the collector considered as a valuable stock of materials.

When he came to London, his way of life connected him with the licentious and dissolute; and he affected the airs and gaiety of a man of pleasure; but his dress was always deficient; scholastic cloudiness still hung about him; and his merriment was sure to produce the scorn of his companions.

With all his carelessness, and all his vices, he was one of the murmurers at Fortune; and wondered why he was suffered to be poor, when Addison was caressed and preferred: nor would a very little have contented him; for he estimated his wants at 600l. a year.

In his course of reading, it was particular that he had diligently perused, and accurately remembered, the old romances of knight-errantry.

He had a high opinion of his own merit, and was something contemptuous in his treatment of those whom he considered as not qualified to oppose or contradict him. He had many frailties; yet it cannot but be supposed that he had great merit, who could obtain to the same play a Prologue from Addison, and an Epilogue from Prior; and who could have at once the patronage of Halifax and the praise of Oldisworth.

For the power of communicating these minute memorials, I am indebted to my conversation with Gilbert Walmsley, late Registrar of the Ecclesiastical Court of Lichfield, who was acquainted both with Smith and Ducket; and declared that, if the tale concerning Clarendon were forged, he should suspect Ducket of the falsehood; "for Rag was a man of great veracity."

Of Gilbert Walmsley, thus presented to my mind, let me indulge myself in the remembrance. I knew him very early; he was one of the first friends that literature procured me, and I hope that at least my gratitude made me worthy of his notice.

He was of an advanced age, and I was only yet a boy; yet he never received my notions with contempt. He was a Whig, with all the virulence and malevolence of his party; yet difference of opinion did not keep us apart. I honoured him, and he endured me.

He had mingled with the gay world without exemption from its vices or its follies, but had never neglected the cultivation of his mind; his belief of revelation was unshaken; his learning preserved his principles; he grew first regular, and then pious.

His studies had been so various, that I am not able to name a man of equal knowledge. His acquaintance with books was great; and what he did not immediately know he could at least tell where to find. Such was his amplitude of learning, and such his copiousness of communication, that it may be doubted whether a day now passes in which I have not some advantage from his friendship.

At this man's table I enjoyed many cheerful and instructive hours, with companions such as are not often found; with one who has lengthened, and one who has gladdened life; with Dr. James, whose skill in physic will be long remembered; and with David Garrick, whom I hoped to have gratified with this character of our common friend: but what are the hopes of man! I am disappointed by that stroke of death, which has eclipsed the gaiety of nations, and impoverished the public stock of harmless pleasure.

In the library at Oxford is the following ludicrous Analysis of Pocockius:

Ex Autographo

[Sent by the Author to Mr. Urry]

Opusculum hoc, Halberdarie amplissime, in lucem proferre hactenus distuli, judicii tui acumen subveritus magis quam bipennis. Tandem aliquando Oden hanc ad te mitto sublimem, teneram, flebilem, suavem, qualem demum divinus (si Musis vacaret) scripsissit Gastrellus: adeo scilicet sublimem ut inter legendum dormire, adeo flebilem ut ridere velis. Cujus elegantiam ut melius inspicias, versuum ordinem et materiam breviter referam. 1^{mus} versus de duobus præliis decantatis. 2^{dus} et 3us de Lotharingio, cuniculis subterraneis, saxis, ponto, hostibus, et Asia. 4^{tus} et 5^{tus} de catenis, subdibus, uncis, draconibus, tigribus et crocodilis. 6us, 7us, 8us, 9us, de Gomorrha, de Babylone, Babele, et quodum domi suæ peregrino. 10us, aliquid de quodam Pocockio. 11us, 12us, de Syriâ, Solymâ. 13us, 14us, de Hoseâ, et quercu, et de juvene quodam valde sene. 15us, 16us, de Ætna, et quomodo Ætnâ Pocockio fit valde similis. 17us, 18us, de tubâ, astro, umbrâ, flammis, rotis, Pocockio non neglecto. Cætera de Christianis, Ottomanis, Babyloniis, Arabibus, et gravissimâ agrorum melancholiâ; de Cæsare *Flacco*, Nestore, et miserando juvenis cujusdam florentissimi fato, anno ætatis suæ centesimo præmaturè abrepto. Quæ omnia cum accuratè expenderis, necesse est ut oden hanc meam admirandâ planè varietati constare fatearis. Subito ad Batavos proficiscor, lauro ab illis donandus. Prius vero Pembrochienses voco ad certamen Poeticum. Vale.

   Illustrissima tua deosculor crura,

         E. Smith.

RICHARD DUKE

1668? — 1710–11

Born at Westminster—Educated at Cambridge—His
Friendship with Otway—Contributes to Dryden's *Ovid*
and *Juvenal*—Enters the Church—Made Vicar of Witney
—Death.

Of Mr. Richard Duke I can find few memorials. He was
bred at Westminster and Cambridge; and Jacob relates that
he was some time tutor to the Duke of Richmond.

He appears from his writings to have been not ill qualified
for poetical compositions; and being conscious of his powers,
when he left the university he enlisted himself among the
wits. He was the familiar friend of Otway; and was engaged,
among other popular names, in the translations of Ovid
[1680] and Juvenal [1693]. In his *Review*, though unfinished,
are some vigorous lines. His poems are not below mediocrity,
nor have I found much in them to be praised.

With the wit he seems to have shared the dissoluteness
of the times; for some of his compositions are such as he must
have reviewed with detestation in his later days, when he published those Sermons which Felton has commended.

Perhaps, like some other foolish young men, he rather
talked than lived viciously, in an age when he that would be
thought a wit was afraid to say his prayers; and whatever
might have been bad in the first part of his life, was surely
condemned and reformed by his better judgment.

In 1683, being then Master of Arts, and Fellow of Trinity
College in Cambridge, he wrote a poem on the marriage of
the Lady Anne with George Prince of Denmark.

He then took orders; and, being made prebendary of Gloucester, became proctor in convocation for that church, and chaplain to Queen Anne.

In 1710 he was presented by the Bishop of Winchester to the wealthy living of Witney in Oxfordshire, which he enjoyed but a few months. On February 10, 1710–11, having returned from an entertainment, he was found dead the next morning. His death is mentioned in Swift's *Journal*.

WILLIAM KING

1663–1712

Born in London—Educated at Westminster and Oxford—Made Gazetteer—Buried in Westminster Abbey—Works and Character.

William King was born in London in 1663, the son of Ezekiel King, a gentleman. He was allied to the family of Clarendon.

From Westminster School, where he was a scholar on the foundation under the care of Dr. Busby, he was at eighteen elected to Christ Church in 1681, where he is said to have prosecuted his studies with so much intenseness and activity, that before he was eight years' standing he had read over, and made remarks upon, twenty-two thousand odd hundred books and manuscripts. The books were certainly not very long, the manuscripts not very difficult, nor the remarks very large; for the calculator will find that he despatched seven a day for every day of his eight years, with a remnant that more than satisfies most other students. He took his degree in the most expensive manner, as a *grand compounder*; whence it is inferred that he inherited a considerable fortune.

In 1688, the same year in which he was made Master of Arts, he published a confutation of Varillas's account of Wicliffe; and, engaging in the study of the civil law, became Doctor in 1692, and was admitted advocate at Doctors' Commons.

He had already made some translations from the French, and written some humorous and satirical pieces, when in 1694 Molesworth published his *Account of Denmark*, in which he treats the Danes and their monarch with great contempt, and takes the opportunity of insinuating those wild principles by which he supposes liberty to be established, and by which his adversaries suspect that all subordination and government is endangered.

This book offended Prince George; and the Danish minister presented a memorial against it. The principles of its author did not please Dr. King; and therefore he undertook to confute part, and laugh at the rest. The controversy is now forgotten; and books of this kind seldom live long when interest and resentment have ceased.

In 1697 he mingled in the controversy between Boyle and Bentley; and was one of those who tried what wit could perform in opposition to learning, on a question which learning only could decide.

In 1699 was published by him *A Journey to London*, after the method of Dr. Martin Lister, who had published *A Journey to Paris*; and in 1700 he satirised the Royal Society, at least Sir Hans Sloane, their president, in two dialogues, intituled *The Transactioneer*.

Though he was a regular advocate in the courts of civil and canon law, he did not love his profession, nor indeed any kind of business which interrupted his voluptuary dreams, or forced him to rouse from that indulgence in which only he could find delight. His reputation as a civilian was yet maintained by his judgments in the Courts of Delegates, and raised very high by the address and knowledge which he discovered in 1700, when he defended the Earl of Anglesea against his lady, afterwards Duchess of Buckinghamshire, who sued for a divorce and obtained it.

The expense of his pleasures and neglect of business had now lessened his revenues; and he was willing to accept of a settlement in Ireland, where, about 1702, he was made judge of the Admiralty, commissioner of the prizes, keeper of the records in Birmingham's Tower, and vicar-general to Dr. Marsh, the primate.

But it is vain to put wealth within the reach of him who will not stretch out his hand to take it. King soon found a friend, as idle and thoughtless as himself, in Upton, one of the judges, who had a pleasant house called Mountown, near Dublin, to which King frequently retired, delighting to neglect his interest, forget his cares, and desert his duty.

Here he wrote *Mully of Mountown*, a poem, by which, though fanciful readers in the pride of sagacity have given it a poetical interpretation, was meant originally no more than it expressed, as it was dictated only by the author's delight in the quiet of Mountown.

In 1708, when Lord Wharton was sent to govern Ireland, King returned to London, with his poverty, his idleness, and his wit, and published some essays called *Useful Transactions*. His *Voyage to the Island of Cajamai* is particularly commended. He then wrote the *Art of Love*, a poem remarkable, notwithstanding its title, for purity of sentiment; and in 1709 imitated Horace in an *Art of Cookery*, which he published, with some letters to Dr. Lister.

In 1710 he appeared as a lover of the Church, on the side of Sacheverell; and was supposed to have concurred at least in the projection of *The Examiner*. His eyes were open to all the operations of Whiggism; and he bestowed some strictures upon Dr. Kennet's adulatory sermon at the funeral of the Duke of Devonshire.

The *History of the Heathen Gods*, a book composed for schools, was written by him in 1711. The work is useful; but might have been produced without the powers of King. The same year he published *Rufinus*, an historical essay, and a poem, intended to dispose the nation to think as he thought of the Duke of Marlborough and his adherents.

In 1711, competence, if not plenty, was again put into his power. He was, without the trouble of attendance, or the mortification of a request, made Gazetteer. Swift, Freind, Prior, and other men of the same party, brought him the key of the Gazetteer's office. He was now again placed in a profitable employment, and again threw the benefit away. An act of insolvency made his business at that time particularly troublesome; and he would not wait till hurry should be at an end, but impatiently resigned it, and returned to his wonted indigence and amusements.

One of his amusements at Lambeth, where he resided, was

to mortify Dr. Tenison, the archbishop, by a public festivity, on the surrender of Dunkirk to Hill—an event with which Tenison's political bigotry did not suffer him to be delighted. King was resolved to counteract his sullenness, and at the expense of a few barrels of ale filled the neighbourhood with honest merriment.

In the autumn of 1712 his health declined; he grew weaker by degrees, and died on Christmas-day. Though his life had not been without irregularity, his principles were pure and orthodox, and his death was pious.

After this relation, it will be naturally supposed that his poems were rather the amusements of idleness than efforts of study—that he endeavoured rather to divert than astonish—that his thought seldom aspired to sublimity—and that, if his verse was easy and his images familiar, he attained what he desired. His purpose is to be merry; but perhaps, to enjoy his mirth, it may be sometimes necessary to think well of his opinions.

THOMAS SPRAT
1636–1713

Born at Tallaton, in Devonshire—Educated at Oxford
—His Poem on Cromwell's Death—Made Chaplain to Vil-
liers, Duke of Buckingham—His Friendship with Cowley
—Made Vicar of St. Margaret's, Westminster, Dean of
Westminster, and Bishop of Rochester—Story of his
Preaching—Burial in Westminster Abbey—Works and
Character.

Thomas Sprat was born in 1636, at Tallaton, in Devonshire, the son of a clergyman; and having been educated, as
he tells of himself, not at Westminster or Eton, but at a little
school by the churchyard side, became a commoner of Wadham College, in Oxford, in 1651; and, being chosen scholar
next year, proceeded through the usual academical course, and
in 1657 [June 11] became Master of Arts. He obtained a
fellowship, and commenced poet.

In 1659 his poem on the death of Oliver was published
with those of Dryden and Waller. In his dedication to Dr.
Wilkins he appears a very willing and liberal encomiast, both
of the living and the dead. He implores his patron's excuse of
his verses, both as falling "so infinitely below the full and
sublime genius of that excellent poet who made this way of
writing free of our nation," and being "so little equal and
proportioned to the renown of a prince on whom they were
written; such great actions and lives deserving to be the subject of the noblest pens and most divine fancies." He proceeds: "Having so long experienced your care and indulgence,
and been formed, as it were, by your own hands, not to entitle

you to anything which my meanness produces would be not only injustice, but sacrilege."

He published the same year a poem on the *Plague of Athens* —a subject of which it is not easy to say what could recommend it. To these he added afterwards a poem on Mr. Cowley's death.

After the Restoration he took orders, and by Cowley's recommendation was made chaplain to the Duke of Buckingham, whom he is said to have helped in writing the *Rehearsal*. He was likewise chaplain to the King.

As he was the favourite of Wilkins, at whose house began those philosophical conferences and inquiries which in time produced the Royal Society, he was consequently engaged in the same studies, and became one of the fellows; and when, after their incorporation, something seemed necessary to reconcile the public to the new institution, he undertook to write its history, which he published in 1667. This is one of the few books which selection of sentiment and elegance of diction have been able to preserve, though written upon a subject flux and transitory. The history of the Royal Society is now read, not with the wish to know what they were then doing, but how their Transactions are exhibited by Sprat.

In the next year he published *Observations on Sorbiere's Voyage into England, in a Letter to Mr. Wren*. This is a work not ill performed; but perhaps rewarded with at least its full proportion of praise.

In 1668 he published Cowley's Latin poems, and prefixed in Latin the Life of the author, which he afterwards amplified, and placed [1669] before Cowley's English works, which were by will committed to his care.

Ecclesiastical benefices now fell fast upon him. In 1668 he became a prebendary of Westminster, and had afterwards the church of St. Margaret, adjoining to the Abbey. He was in 1680 made canon of Windsor, in 1683 [Sept. 21] dean of Westminster, and in 1684 [Nov. 2] Bishop of Rochester.

The Court having thus a claim to his diligence and gratitude, he was required to write the history of the Ryehouse Plot; and in 1685 published *A true Account and Declaration of the horrid Conspiracy against the late King, his present*

Majesty, and the present Government—a performance which he thought convenient, after the Revolution, to extenuate and excuse.

The same year [1685], being Clerk of the Closet to the King [James II.], he was made dean of the chapel-royal; and the year afterwards received the last proof of his master's confidence, by being appointed one of the commissioners for ecclesiastical affairs. On the critical day, when the *Declaration* distinguished the true sons of the Church of England, he stood neuter, and permitted it to be read at Westminster, but pressed none to violate his conscience; and, when the Bishop of London was brought before them, gave his voice in his favour.

Thus far he suffered interest or obedience to carry him, but farther he refused to go. When he found that the powers of the ecclesiastical commission were to be exercised against those who had refused the *Declaration*, he wrote to the lords, and other commissioners, a formal profession of his unwillingness to exercise that authority any longer, and withdrew himself from them. After they had read his letter, they adjourned for six months, and scarcely ever met afterwards.

When King James was frighted away, and a new government was to be settled, Sprat was one of those who considered, in a conference, the great question, whether the crown was vacant, and manfully spoke in favour of his old master.

He complied, however, with the new establishment, and was left unmolested; but in 1692 a strange attack was made upon him by one Robert Young and Stephen Blackhead, both men convicted of infamous crimes, and both, when the scheme was laid, prisoners in Newgate. These men drew up an association, in which they whose names were subscribed declared their resolution to restore King James, to seize the Princess of Orange, dead or alive, and to be ready with 30,-000 men to meet King James when he should land. To this they put the names of Sancroft, Sprat, Marlborough, Salisbury, and others. The copy of Dr. Sprat's name was obtained by a fictitious request, to which an answer *in his own hand* was desired. His hand was copied so well, that he confessed it might have deceived himself. Blackhead, who had carried the letter, being sent again with a plausible message, was very curious to see the house, and particularly importunate to be let in to the study, where, as is supposed, he designed to leave the association. This, however, was denied him; and he dropped it in a flower-pot in the parlour.

Young now laid an information before the Privy Council; and May 7, 1692, the bishop was arrested, and kept at a messenger's under a strict guard eleven days. His house was searched, and directions were given that the flower-pots should be inspected. The messengers, however, missed the room in which the paper was left. Blackhead went, therefore, a third time, and finding his paper where he had left it, brought it away.

The bishop, having been enlarged, was, on June the 10th and 13th, examined again before the Privy Council, and confronted with his accusers. Young persisted, with the most obdurate impudence, against the strongest evidence; but the resolution of Blackhead by degrees gave way. There remained at last no doubt of the bishop's innocence, who, with great prudence and diligence, traced the progress and detected the characters of the two informers, and published an account of his own examination and deliverance, which made such an impression upon him, that he commemorated it through life by a yearly day of thanksgiving.

With what hope, or what interest, the villains had contrived an accusation which they must know themselves utterly unable to prove was never discovered.

After this he passed his days in the quiet exercise of his function. When the cause of Sacheverell put the public in commotion, he honestly appeared among the friends of the Church. He lived to his seventy-ninth year, and died [at Bromley, in Kent] May 20, 1713.

Burnet is not very favourable to his memory; but he and Burnet were old rivals. On some public occasion they both preached before the House of Commons. There prevailed in those days an indecent custom: when the preacher touched any favourite topic in a manner that delighted his audience, their approbation was expressed by a loud *hum*, continued in proportion to their zeal or pleasure. When Burnet preached, part of his congregation *hummed* so loudly and so long that he sat down to enjoy it, and rubbed his face with his handkerchief. When Sprat preached, he likewise was honoured with the like animating *hum*; but he stretched out his hand to the congregation, and cried, "Peace, peace, I pray you peace."

This I was told in my youth by my father, an old man, who had been no careless observer of the passages of those times.

Burnet's sermon, says Salmon, was remarkable for sedition, and Sprat's for loyalty. Burnet had the thanks of the House; Sprat had no thanks, but a good living from the King, which, he said, was of as much value as the thanks of the Commons.

The works of Sprat, besides his few poems, are *The History of the Royal Society, The Life of Cowley, The Answer to Sorbiere, The History of the Ryehouse Plot, The Relation of his own Examination,* and a volume of *Sermons.* I have heard it observed, with great justness, that every book is of a different kind, and that each has its distinct and characteristical excellence.

My business is only with his poems. He considered Cowley as a model; and supposed that, as he was imitated, perfection was approached. Nothing therefore but Pindaric liberty was to be expected. There is in his few productions no want of such conceits as he thought excellent; and of those our judgment may be settled by the first that appears in his praise of Cromwell, where he says that Cromwell's "fame, like man, will grow white as it grows old."

EARL OF HALIFAX

1661–1715

Born at Horton, in Northamptonshire—Educated at Westminster and Cambridge—His Poem on Charles II.'s Death—Joins with Prior in *The Country Mouse and City Mouse*—Introduced to William III.—His several Offices —Made Chancellor of the Exchequer and Earl of Halifax —His Patronage of Poets—Burial in Westminster Abbey.

The Life of the Earl of Halifax was properly that of an artful and active statesman, employed in balancing parties, contriving expedients, and combating opposition, and exposed to the vicissitudes of advancement and degradation; but, in this collection, poetical merit is the claim to attention; and the account which is here to be expected may properly be proportioned not to his influence in the state, but to his rank among the writers of verse.

Charles Montague was born April 16, 1661, at Horton, in Northamptonshire, the son of Mr. George Montague, a younger son of the Earl of Manchester. He was educated first in the country, and then removed to Westminster, where, in 1677, he was chosen a King's scholar, and recommended himself to Busby by his felicity in extemporary epigrams. He contracted a very intimate friendship with Mr. Stepney; and in 1682, when Stepney was elected at Cambridge, the election of Montague being not to proceed till the year following, he was afraid lest by being placed at Oxford he might be separated from his companion, and therefore solicited to be removed to Cambridge, without waiting for the advantages of another year.

It seems indeed time to wish for a removal; for he was already a school-boy of one-and-twenty.

His relation, Dr. Montague, was then master of the college in which he was placed a fellow-commoner, and took him under his particular care. Here he commenced an acquaintance with the great Newton, which continued through his life, and was at last attested by a legacy.

In 1685 his verses on the death of King Charles made such impression on the Earl of Dorset, that he was invited to town, and introduced by that universal patron to the other wits. In 1687 he joined with Prior in the *Country Mouse and the City Mouse*, a burlesque of Dryden's *Hind and Panther*. He signed the invitation to the Prince of Orange, and sat in the Convention. He about the same time married the Countess Dowager of Manchester, and intended to have taken orders; but afterwards altering his purpose, he purchased for 1500*l*. the place of one of the clerks of the council.

After he had written his epistle on the victory of the Boyne, his patron Dorset introduced him to King William with this expression: "Sir, I have brought a *mouse* to wait on your Majesty." To which the King is said to have replied, "You do well to put me in the way of making a *man* of him"; and ordered him a pension of 500*l*. This story, however current, seems to have been made after the event. The King's answer implies a greater acquaintance with our proverbial and familiar diction than King William could possibly have attained.

In 1691, being a member of the House of Commons, he argued warmly in favour of a law to grant the assistance of counsel in trials for high treason; and, in the midst of his speech, falling into some confusion, was for a while silent; but, recovering himself, observed, "how reasonable it was to allow counsel to men called as criminals before a court of justice, when it appeared how much the presence of that assembly could disconcert one of their own body."

After this he rose fast into honours and employments, being made one of the commissioners of the Treasury, and called to the Privy Council. In 1694 he became Chancellor of the Exchequer, and the next year engaged in the great attempt of the re-coinage, which was in two years happily completed. In

1696 he projected the *general fund*, and raised the credit of the Exchequer; and, after inquiry concerning a grant of Irish crown-lands, it was determined by a vote of the Commons, that Charles Montague, Esquire, *had deserved his Majesty's favour*. In 1698, being advanced to the first commission of the Treasury, he was appointed one of the regency in the King's absence: the next year he was made Auditor of the Exchequer, and the year after [4th Dec., 1700] created Baron Halifax. He was however impeached by the Commons; but the articles were dismissed by the Lords.

At the accession of Queen Anne [8th March, 1702] he was dismissed from the council; and in the first parliament of her reign was again attacked by the Commons, and again escaped by the protection of the Lords. In 1704 he wrote an answer to Bromley's speech against occasional conformity. He headed the inquiry into the danger of the Church. In 1706 he proposed and negotiated the Union with Scotland; and when the Elector of Hanover received the Garter, after the act had passed for securing the Protestant Succession, he was appointed to carry the ensigns of the order to the Electoral court. He sat as one of the judges of Sacheverell, but voted for a mild sentence. Being now no longer in favour, he contrived to obtain a writ for summoning the Electoral Prince to parliament as Duke of Cambridge.

At the Queen's death [1st Aug., 1714] he was appointed one of the regents; and at the accession of George the First was made [14th Oct., 1714] Earl of Halifax, Knight of the Garter, and first Commissioner of the Treasury, with a grant to his nephew of the reversion of the auditorship of the Exchequer. More was not to be had, and this he kept but a little while; for on the 19th of May, 1715, he died of an inflammation of his lungs.

Of him, who from a poet became a patron of poets, it will be readily believed that the works could not miss of celebration. Addison began to praise him early, and was followed or accompanied by other poets; perhaps by almost all, except Swift and Pope, who forbore to flatter him in his life, and after his death spoke of him, Swift with slight censure, and Pope in the character Bufo with acrimonious contempt.

He was, as Pope says, "fed with dedications"; for Tickell affirms that no dedication was unrewarded. To charge all unmerited praise with the guilt of flattery, and to suppose that the encomiast always knows and feels the falsehoods of his assertions, is surely to discover great ignorance of human nature and human life. In determinations depending not on rules, but on experience and comparison, judgment is always in some degree subject to affection. Very near to admiration is the wish to admire.

Every man willingly gives value to the praise which he receives, and considers the sentence passed in his favour as the sentence of discernment. We admire in a friend that understanding that selected us for confidence; we admire more, in a patron, that judgment which, instead of scattering bounty indiscriminately, directed it to us; and, if the patron be an author, those performances which gratitude forbids us to blame, affectation will easily dispose us to exalt.

To these prejudices, hardly culpable, interest adds a power always operating, though not always, because not willingly, perceived. The modesty of praise wears gradually away; and perhaps the pride of patronage may be in time so increased, that modest praise will no longer please.

Many a blandishment was practised upon Halifax, which he would never have known, had he no other attractions than those of his poetry, of which a short time has withered the beauties. It would now be esteemed no honour, by a contributor to the monthly bundles of verses, to be told, that, in strains either familiar or solemn, he sings like Montague.

THOMAS PARNELL

1679–1718

Born at Dublin—Educated at Trinity College, Dublin
—Made Archdeacon of Clogher—Marries—Loses his Wife
—Introduced to Swift and Pope.

The Life of Dr. Parnell is a task which I should very
willingly decline, since it has been lately written by Goldsmith, a man of such variety of powers, and such felicity of
performance, that he always seemed to do best that which he
was doing; a man who had the art of being minute without
tediousness, and general without confusion; whose language
was copious without exuberance, exact without constraint, and
easy without weakness.

What such an author has told, who would tell again? I have
made an abstract from his larger narrative; and have this grati-
fication from my attempt, that it gives me an opportunity of
paying due tribute to the memory of Goldsmith.

Τὸ γὰρ γέρας ἔστι θανόντων.

Thomas Parnell was the son of a commonwealth-man of the
same name, who at the Restoration left Congleton in Cheshire, where the family had been established for several cen-
turies, and, settling in Ireland, purchased an estate, which,
with his lands in Cheshire, descended to the poet, who was
born at Dublin in 1679: and, after the usual education at a
grammar-school, was at the age of thirteen admitted into the
college, where, in 1700 [July 9], he became Master of Arts,
and was the same year ordained a deacon, though under the
canonical age, by a dispensation from the Bishop of Derry.

About three years afterwards he was made a priest; and in 1705 [February 9] Dr. Ashe, the Bishop of Clogher, conferred upon him the Archdeaconry of Clogher. About the same time he married Mrs. Anne Minchin, an amiable lady, by whom he had two sons who died young, and a daughter who long survived him.

At the ejection of the Whigs, in the end of Queen Anne's reign, Parnell was persuaded to change his party, not without much censure from those whom he forsook, and was received by the new ministry as a valuable reinforcement. When the Earl of Oxford was told that Dr. Parnell waited among the crowd in the outer room, he went by the persuasion of Swift, with his treasurer's staff in his hand, to inquire for him, and to bid him welcome; and, as may be inferred from Pope's dedication, admitted him as a favourite companion to his convivial hours, but, as it seems often to have happened in those times to the favourites of the great, without attention to his fortune, which, however, was in no great need of improvement.

Parnell, who did not want ambition or vanity, was desirous to make himself conspicuous, and to show how worthy he was of high preferment. As he thought himself qualified to become a popular preacher, he displayed his elocution with great success in the pulpits of London; but the Queen's death putting an end to his expectations, abated his diligence; and Pope represents him as falling from that time into intemperance of wine. That in his latter life he was too much a lover of the bottle, is not denied; but I have heard it imputed to a cause more likely to obtain forgiveness from mankind, the untimely death of a darling son; or, as others tell, the loss of his wife, who died [1711] in the midst of his expectations.

He was now to derive every future addition to his preferments from his personal interest with his private friends, and he was not long unregarded. He was warmly recommended by Swift to Archbishop King, who gave him a prebend in 1713; and in May 1716 presented him to the vicarage of Finglass, in the diocese of Dublin, worth 400l. a year. Such notice from such a man inclines me to believe that the vice of which he has been accused was not gross, or not notorious.

But his prosperity did not last long. His end, whatever was

its cause, was now approaching. He enjoyed his preferment little more than a year, for in July 1717, in his thirty-eighth year, he died at Chester on his way to Ireland.

He seems to have been one of those poets who take delight in writing. He contributed to the papers of that time, and probably published more than he owned. He left many compositions behind him, of which Pope selected those which he thought best, and dedicated them to the Earl of Oxford. Of these Goldsmith has given an opinion, and his criticism it is seldom safe to contradict. He bestows just praise upon the *Rise of Woman*, the *Fairy Tale*, and the *Pervigilium Veneris*; but has very properly remarked, that in the *Battle of Frogs and Mice* the Greek names have not in English their original effect.

He tells us that the *Bookworm* is borrowed from Beza; but he should have added, with modern applications; and when he discovers that *Gay Bacchus* is translated from Augurellus, he ought to have remarked that the latter part is purely Parnell's. Another poem, *When Spring comes on*, is, he says, taken from the French. I would add, that the description of *Barrenness*, in his verses to Pope, was borrowed from Secundus; but lately searching for the passage which I had formerly read, I could not find it. The *Night-Piece on Death* is indirectly preferred by Goldsmith to Gray's *Church-yard*; but, in my opinion, Gray has the advantage in dignity, variety, and originality of sentiment. He observes, that the story of the *Hermit* is in More's *Dialogues* and Howell's *Letters*, and supposes it to have been originally Arabian.

Goldsmith has not taken any notice of the *Elegy to an Old Beauty*, which is perhaps the meanest, nor of the *Allegory on Man*, the happiest of Parnell's performances. The hint of the *Hymn to Contentment* I suspect to have been borrowed from Cleveland.

The general character of Parnell is not great extent of comprehension, or fertility of mind. Of the little that appears, still less is his own. His praise must be derived from the easy sweetness of his diction: in his verses there is more happiness than pains; he is sprightly without effort, and always delights, though he never ravishes; everything is proper, yet everything seems casual. If there is some appearance of elaboration in *The*

Hermit, the narrative, as it is less airy, is less pleasing. Of his other compositions it is impossible to say whether they are the productions of Nature, so excellent as not to want the help of Art, or of Art so refined as to resemble Nature.

This criticism relates only to the pieces published by Pope. Of the large appendages which I find in the last edition, I can only say that I know not whence they came, nor have ever inquired whither they are going. They stand upon the faith of the compilers.

SAMUEL GARTH

1670? — 1718–19

Of a Yorkshire Family—Educated at Cambridge—Admitted a Fellow of the College of Physicians—Publishes *The Dispensary*, a Poem—Sides with the Whigs—His Popularity—Knighted by George I.—His *Ovid*—Burial at Harrow-on-the-Hill.

Samuel Garth was of a good family in Yorkshire, and from some school in his own country became a student at Peter-House, in Cambridge, where he resided till he became Doctor of Physic on July the 7th, 1691. He was examined before the College at London on March the 12th, 1691–2, and admitted Fellow June 26th, 1692. He was soon so much distinguished by his conversation and accomplishments as to obtain very extensive practice; and, if a pamphlet of those times may be credited, had the favour and confidence of one party, as Radcliffe had of the other.

He is always mentioned as a man of benevolence; and it is just to suppose that his desire of helping the helpless disposed him to so much zeal for the *Dispensary*; an undertaking of which some account, however short, is proper to be given.

Whether what Temple says be true, that physicians have had more learning than the other faculties, I will not stay to inquire; but, I believe, every man has found in physicians great liberality and dignity of sentiment, very prompt effusion of beneficence, and willingness to exert a lucrative art where there is no hope of lucre. Agreeably to this character, the College of Physicians, in July 1687, published an edict, requiring all the fellows, candidates, and licentiates to give gratuitous advice to the neighbouring poor.

This edict was sent to the Court of Aldermen; and a question being made to whom the appellation of the *poor* should be extended, the College answered, that it should be sufficient to bring a testimonial from the clergyman officiating in the parish where the patient resided.

After a year's experience, the physicians found their charity frustrated by some malignant opposition, and made to a great degree vain by the high price of physic: they therefore voted, in August 1688, that the laboratory of the College should be accommodated to the preparation of medicines, and another room prepared for their reception; and that the contributors to the expense should manage the charity.

It was now expected that the apothecaries would have undertaken the care of providing medicines; but they took another course. Thinking the whole design pernicious to their interest, they endeavoured to raise a faction against it in the College, and found some physicians mean enough to solicit their patronage, by betraying to them the counsels of the College. The greater part, however, enforced by a new edict, in 1694, the former order of 1687, and sent it to the mayor and aldermen, who appointed a committee to treat with the College, and settle the mode of administering the charity.

It was desired by the aldermen, that the testimonials of churchwardens and overseers should be admitted; and that all hired servants, and all apprentices to handicraftsmen, should be considered as *poor*. This likewise was granted by the College.

It was then considered who should distribute the medicines, and who should settle their prices. The physicians procured some apothecaries to undertake the dispensation, and offered that the Warden and Company of the Apothecaries should adjust the price. This offer was rejected; and the apothecaries who had engaged to assist the charity were considered as traitors to the company, threatened with the imposition of troublesome offices, and deterred from the performance of their engagements. The apothecaries ventured upon public opposition, and presented a kind of remonstrance against the design to the committee of the city, which the physicians con-descended to confute: and at least the traders seem to have prevailed among the sons of trade; for the proposal of the College having been considered, a paper of approbation was drawn up, but postponed and forgotten.

The physicians still persisted; and in 1696 a subscription was raised by themselves, according to an agreement prefixed to the *Dispensary*. The poor were for a time supplied with medicines; for how long a time I know not. The medicinal charity, like others, began with ardour, but soon remitted, and at last died gradually away.

About the time of the subscription begins the action of the *Dispensary*. The poem, as its subject was present and popular, co-operated with passions and prejudices then prevalent, and, with such auxiliaries to its intrinsic merit, was universally and liberally applauded. It was on the side of charity against the intrigues of interest, and of regular learning against licentious usurpation of medical authority, and was therefore naturally favoured by those who read and can judge of poetry.

In 1697 Garth spoke that which is now called the Harveian Oration; which the authors of the *Biographia* mention with more praise than the passage quoted in their notes will fully justify. Garth speaking of the mischiefs done by quacks, has these expressions: "Non autem telis vulnerat ista agyrtarum colluvies, sed theriacâ quædam magis perniciosa, non pyrio, sed pulvere nescio quo exotico certat, non globulis plumbeis, sed pilulis æque lethalibus interficit." This was certainly thought fine by the author, and is still admired by his biog-rapher [Dr. Campbell]. In October 1702 he became one of the censors of the College.

Garth, being an active and zealous Whig, was a member of the Kit-Cat club, and by consequence familiarly known to all the great men of that denomination. In 1710, when the gov-ernment fell into other hands, he wrote to Lord Godolphin, on his dismission, a short poem, which was criticised in *The Examiner*, and so successfully either defended or excused by Mr. Addison, that, for the sake of the vindication, it ought to be preserved.

At the accession [1714] of the present family his merits

were acknowledged and rewarded. He was knighted with the sword of his hero, Marlborough; and was made physician-in-ordinary to the King, and physician-general to the army.

He then undertook an edition of Ovid's *Metamorphoses*, translated by several hands; which he recommended by a Preface, written with more ostentation than ability: his notions are half-formed, and his materials immethodically confused. This was his last work. He died Jan. 18, 1718–19, and was buried at Harrow-on-the-Hill.

His personal character seems to have been social and liberal. He communicated himself through a very wide extent of acquaintance; and though firm in a party, at a time when firmness included virulence, yet he imparted his kindness to those who were not supposed to favour his principles. He was an early encourager of Pope, and was at once the friend of Addison and of Granville. He is accused of voluptuousness and irreligion; and Pope, who says, that "if ever there was a good Christian, without knowing himself to be so, it was Dr. Garth," seems not able to deny what he is angry to hear and loth to confess.

Pope afterwards declared himself convinced that Garth died in the communion of the Church of Rome, having been privately reconciled. It is observed by Louth, that there is less distance than is thought between scepticism and popery; and that a mind, wearied with perpetual doubt, willingly seeks repose in the bosom of an infallible church.

His poetry has been praised at least equally to its merit. In the *Dispensary* there is a strain of smooth and free versification; but few lines are eminently elegant. No passages fall below mediocrity, and few rise much above it. The plan seems formed without just proportion to the subject; the means and end have no necessary connection. Resnel, in his Preface to Pope's *Essay*, remarks that Garth exhibits no discrimination of characters; and that what anyone says might with equal propriety have been said by another. The general design is perhaps open to criticism; but the composition can seldom be charged with inaccuracy or negligence. The author never slumbers in self-indulgence; his full vigour is always exerted; scarcely a line is left unfinished, nor is it easy to find an expression used by constraint, or a thought imperfectly expressed. It was remarked by Pope, that the *Dispensary* had been corrected in every edition, and that every change was an improvement. It appears, however, to want something of poetical ardour, and something of general delectation; and therefore, since it has been no longer supported by accidental and intrinsic popularity, it has been scarcely able to support itself.

NICHOLAS ROWE

1673–1718

Born at Little Barford, in Bedfordshire—Educated at
Westminster—Entered at the Middle Temple—His first
Tragedy, *The Ambitious Stepmother*—His other Tragedies—Made Poet Laureate—Translates Lucan—Buried
in Westminster Abbey—Works and Character.

Nicholas Rowe was born at Little Berkford [or Barford],
in Bedfordshire, in 1673. His family had long possessed a considerable estate, with a good house, at Lamerton, in Devonshire. The ancestor from whom he descended in a direct line
received the arms borne by his descendants for his bravery in
the Holy War. His father, John Rowe, who was the first that
quitted his paternal acres to practise any art of profit, professed the law, and published Benlow's and Dallison's Reports
in the reign of James the Second, when, in opposition to the
notions, then diligently propagated, of dispensing power, he
ventured to remark how low his authors rated the prerogative.
He was made a serjeant, and died April 30, 1692. He was
buried in the Temple Church.

Nicholas was first sent to a private school at Highgate; and,
being afterwards removed to Westminster, was at twelve years
chosen one of the King's scholars. His master was Busby, who
suffered none of his scholars to let their powers lie useless; and
his exercises in several languages are said to have been written
with uncommon degrees of excellence, and yet to have cost
him very little labour.

At sixteen he had, in his father's opinion, made advances in
learning sufficient to qualify him for the study of law, and was

entered a student of the Middle Temple, where for some time he read statutes and reports, with proficiency proportionate to the force of his mind, which was already such that he endeavoured to comprehend law, not as a series of precedents, or collection of positive precepts, but as a system of rational government, and impartial justice.

When he was nineteen, he was by the death of his father left more to his own direction, and probably from that time suffered law gradually to give way to poetry. At twenty-five he produced [1700] *The Ambitious Stepmother*, which was received with so much favour, that he devoted himself from that time wholly to elegant literature.

His next tragedy (1702) was *Tamerlane*, in which, under the name of Tamerlane, he intended to characterise King William, and Lewis the Fourteenth under Bajazet. The virtues of Tamerlane seem to have been arbitrarily assigned him by his poet, for I know not that history gives any other qualities than those which make a conqueror. The fashion, however, of the time was to accumulate upon Lewis all that can raise horror and detestation; and whatever good was withheld from him, that it might not be thrown away, was bestowed upon King William.

This was the tragedy which Rowe valued most, and that which probably, by the help of political auxiliaries, excited most applause; but occasional poetry must often content itself with occasional praise. *Tamerlane* has for a long time been acted only once a year, on the night when King William landed. Our quarrel with Lewis has been long over; and it now gratifies neither zeal nor malice to see him painted with aggravated features, like a Saracen upon a sign.

The Fair Penitent, his next production (1703), is one of the most pleasing tragedies on the stage, where it still keeps its turns of appearing, and probably will long keep them, for there is scarcely any work of any poet at once so interesting by the fable, and so delightful by the language. The story is domestic, and therefore easily received by the imagination, and assimilated to common life; the diction is exquisitely harmonious, and soft or sprightly as occasion requires.

The character of Lothario seems to have been expanded by

Richardson into Lovelace; but he has excelled his original in the moral effect of the fiction. Lothario, with gaiety which cannot be hated, and bravery which cannot be despised, retains too much of the spectator's kindness. It was in the power of Richardson alone to teach us at once esteem and detestation, to make virtuous resentment overpower all the benevolence which wit, elegance, and courage naturally excite; and to lose at last the hero in the villain.

The fifth act is not equal to the former; the events of the drama are exhausted, and little remains but to talk of what is past. It has been observed, that the title of the play does not sufficiently correspond with the behaviour of Calista, who at last shows no evident signs of repentance, but may be reasonably suspected of feeling pain from detection rather than from guilt, and expresses more shame than sorrow, and more rage than shame.

His next (1706) was *Ulysses*; which, with the common fate of mythological stories, is now generally neglected. We have been too early acquainted with the poetical heroes to expect any pleasure from their revival; to show them as they have already been shown, is to disgust by repetition; to give them new qualities, or new adventures, is to offend by violating received notions.

The Royal Convert (1708) seems to have a better claim to longevity. The fable is drawn from an obscure and barbarous age, to which fictions are more easily and properly adapted; for when objects are imperfectly seen, they easily take forms from imagination. The scene lies among our ancestors in our own country, and therefore very easily catches attention. Rodogune is a personage truly tragical, of high spirit and violent passions, great with tempestuous dignity, and wicked with a soul that would have been heroic if it had been virtuous. The motto seems to tell that this play was not successful.

Rowe does not always remember what his characters require. In *Tamerlane* there is some ridiculous mention of the God of Love; and Rodogune, a savage Saxon, talks of Venus, and the eagle that bears the thunder of Jupiter.

This play discovers its own date, by a prediction of the Union, in imitation of Cranmer's prophetic promises to Henry the Eighth. The anticipated blessings of union are not very naturally introduced, nor very happily expressed.

He once (1704) tried to change his hand. He ventured on a comedy, and produced *The Biter*; with which, though it was unfavourably treated by the audience, he was himself delighted, for he is said to have sat in the house laughing with great vehemence whenever he had in his own opinion produced a jest; but finding that he and the public had no sympathy of mirth, he tried at lighter scenes no more.

After *The Royal Convert* appeared (1714) *Jane Shore*, written, as its author professes, *in imitation of Shakespeare's style*. In what he thought himself an imitator of Shakespeare, it is not easy to conceive. The numbers, the diction, the sentiments, and the conduct, everything in which imitation can consist, are remote in the utmost degree from the manner of Shakespeare; whose dramas it resembles only as it is an English story, and as some of the persons have their names in history. This play, consisting chiefly of domestic scenes and private distress, lays hold upon the heart. The wife is forgiven because she repents, and the husband is honoured because he forgives. This, therefore, is one of those pieces which we still welcome on the stage.

His last tragedy (1715) was *Lady Jane Grey*. This subject had been chosen by Mr. Smith, whose papers were put into Rowe's hands such as he describes them in his Preface. This play has likewise sunk into oblivion. From this time he gave nothing more to the stage.

Being by a competent fortune exempted from any necessity of combating his inclination, he never wrote in distress, and therefore does not appear to have ever written in haste. His works were finished to his own approbation, and bear few marks of negligence or hurry. It is remarkable, that his prologues and epilogues are all his own, though he sometimes supplied others; he afforded help, but did not solicit it.

As his studies necessarily made him acquainted with Shakespeare, and acquaintance produced veneration, he undertook (1709) an edition of his works, from which he neither received much praise, nor seems to have expected it; yet, I believe, those who compare it with former copies will find that he has done more than he promised, and that, without the pomp of notes or boasts of criticism, many passages are happily restored. He prefixed a Life of the author, such as tradition, then almost expiring, could supply, and a Preface which cannot be said to discover much profundity or penetration. He at least contributed to the popularity of his author.

He was willing enough to improve his fortune by other arts than poetry. He was under-secretary for three years when the Duke of Queensberry [died 1711] was secretary of state, and afterwards applied to the Earl of Oxford for some public employment. Oxford enjoined him to study Spanish; and when, some time afterwards, he came again and said that he had mastered it, dismissed him with this congratulation, "Then, Sir, I envy you the pleasure of reading *Don Quixote* in the original."

This story is sufficiently attested; but why Oxford, who desired to be thought a favourer of literature, should thus insult a man of acknowledged merit, or how Rowe, who was so keen a Whig that he did not willingly converse with men of the opposite party, could ask preferment from Oxford, it is not now possible to discover. Pope, who told the story, did not say on what occasion the advice was given, and, though he owned Rowe's disappointment, doubted whether any injury was intended him, but thought it rather Lord Oxford's *odd way*.

It is likely that he lived on discontented through the rest of Queen Anne's reign, but the time came at last when he found kinder friends. At the accession of King George [1714] he was made poet-laureate,—I am afraid by the ejection of poor Nahum Tate, who (1715) died in the Mint, where he was forced to seek shelter by extreme poverty. He was made likewise one of the land-surveyors of the Customs of the port of London. The Prince of Wales chose him clerk of his council, and the Lord Chancellor Parker, as soon as he received the seals, appointed him, unasked, Secretary of the Presentations. Such an accumulation of employments undoubtedly produced a very considerable revenue.

Having already translated some parts of Lucan's *Pharsalia*, which had been published in the *Miscellanies* [of Tonson], and doubtless received many praises, he undertook a version of the whole work, which he lived to finish, but not to publish. It seems to have been printed under the care of Dr. Welwood, who prefixed the author's Life, in which is contained the following character:

"As to his person, it was graceful and well-made: his face regular, and of a manly beauty. As his soul was well lodged, so its rational and animal faculties excelled in a high degree. He had a quick and fruitful invention, a deep penetration, and a large compass of thought, with a singular dexterity and easiness in making his thoughts to be understood. He was master of most parts of polite learning, especially the classical authors, both Greek and Latin; understood the French, Italian, and Spanish languages, and spoke the first fluently, and the other two tolerably well.

"He had likewise read most of the Greek and Roman histories in their original languages, and most that are writ in English, French, Italian, and Spanish. He had a good taste in philosophy, and, having a firm impression of religion upon his mind, he took great delight in divinity and ecclesiastical history, in both which he made great advances in the times he retired into the country, which were frequent. He expressed, on all occasions, his full persuasion of the truth of revealed religion, and being a sincere member of the Established Church himself, he pitied, but condemned not, those that dissented from it. He abhorred the principle of persecuting men upon the account of their opinions in religion, and, being strict in his own, he took it not upon him to censure those of another persuasion. His conversation was pleasant, witty, and learned, without the least tincture of affectation or pedantry; and his inimitable manner of diverting and enlivening the company made it impossible for any one to be out of humour when he was in it. Envy and detraction seemed to be entirely foreign to his constitution, and whatever provocations he met with at any time, he passed them over without the least thought of resentment or revenge. As Homer had a Zoilus, so Mr. Rowe had sometimes his; for there were not wanting malevolent people, and pretenders to poetry too, that would now and then bark at his best performances; but he was so much conscious of his own genius, and had so much good-nature, as to forgive them, nor could he ever be tempted to return them an answer.

"The love of learning and poetry made him not the less fit for business, and nobody applied himself closer to it when it required his attendance. The late Duke of Queensberry, when he was Secretary of State, made him his Secretary for Public Affairs; and when that truly great man came to know him well, he was never so pleased as when Mr. Rowe was in his company. After the Duke's death [1711] all avenues were stopped to his preferment, and during the rest of that reign he passed his time with the Muses and his books, and sometimes the conversation of his friends.

"When he had just got to be easy in his fortune, and was in a fair way to make it better, death swept him away, and in him deprived the world of one of the best men, as well as one of the best geniuses, of the age. He died like a Christian and a philosopher, in charity with all mankind, and with an absolute resignation to the will of God. He kept up his good-humour to the last, and took leave of his wife and friends, immediately before his last agony, with the same tranquillity of mind, and the same indifference for life, as though he had been upon taking but a short journey. He was twice married: first to a daughter of Mr. Parsons, one of the auditors of the revenue, and afterwards to [Anne Devenish] a daughter of Mr. Devenish, a good family in Dorsetshire. By the first he had a son, and by the second a daughter, married afterwards to Mr. Fane. He died the 6th of December, 1718, in the forty-fifth year of his age, and was buried the 19th of the same month in Westminster Abbey, in the aisle where many of our English poets are interred, over against Chaucer, his body being attended by a select number of his friends, and the dean and choir officiating at the funeral."

To this character, which is apparently given with the fondness of a friend, may be added the testimony of Pope, who says, in a letter to Blount, "Mr. Rowe accompanied me, and passed a week in the Forest. I need not tell you how much a man of his turn entertained me; but I must acquaint you there is a vivacity and gaiety of disposition, almost peculiar to him, which makes it impossible to part from him without that uneasiness which generally succeeds all our pleasures."

Pope has left behind him another mention of his companion, less advantageous, which is thus reported by Dr. Warburton:

"Rowe, in Mr. Pope's opinion, maintained a decent character, but had no heart. Mr. Addison was justly offended with some behaviour which arose from that want, and estranged himself from him, which Rowe felt very severely. Mr. Pope, their common friend, knowing this, took an opportunity, at some juncture of Mr. Addison's advancement, to tell him how poor Rowe was grieved at his displeasure, and what satisfaction he expressed at Mr. Addison's good fortune, which he expressed so naturally that he (Mr. Pope) could not but think him sincere. Mr. Addison replied, 'I do not suspect that he feigned, but the levity of his heart is such that he is struck with any new adventure, and it would affect him just in the same manner if he heard I was going to be hanged.' Mr. Pope said, he could not deny but Mr. Addison understood Rowe well."

This censure time has not left us the power of confirming or refuting; but observation daily shows that much stress is not to be laid on hyperbolical accusations and pointed sentences, which even he that utters them desires to be applauded rather than credited. Addison can hardly be supposed to have meant all that he said. Few characters can bear the microscopic scrutiny of wit quickened by anger; and perhaps the best advice to authors would be, that they should keep out of the way of one another.

Rowe is chiefly to be considered as a tragic writer and a translator. In his attempt at comedy he failed so ignominiously that his *Biter* is not inserted in his works; and his occasional poems and short compositions are rarely worthy of either praise or censure, for they seem the casual sports of a mind seeking rather to amuse its leisure than to exercise its powers.

In the construction of his dramas there is not much art; he is not a nice observer of the unities. He extends time and varies place as his convenience requires. To vary the place is not, in my opinion, any violation of Nature, if the change be made between the acts; for it is no less easy for the spectator to suppose himself at Athens in the second act, than at Thebes in the first; but to change the scene, as is done by Rowe, in the middle of an act, is to add more acts to the play, since an act is so much of the business as is transacted without interruption. Rowe, by this licence, easily extricates himself from difficulties, as in *Jane Grey*, when we have been terrified with all the dreadful pomp of public execution, and are wondering how the heroine or the poet will proceed, no sooner has Jane pronounced some prophetic rhymes, than—pass and be gone— the scene closes, and Pembroke and Gardiner are turned out upon the stage.

I know not that there can be found in his plays any deep search into nature, any accurate discriminations of kindred qualities or nice display of passion in its progress; all is general and undefined. Nor does he much interest or affect the auditor, except in *Jane Shore*, who is always seen and heard with pity. Alicia is a character of empty noise, with no resemblance to real sorrow or to natural madness.

Whence, then, has Rowe his reputation? From the reasonableness and propriety of some of his scenes, from the elegance of his diction, and the suavity of his verse. He seldom moves either pity or terror, but he often elevates the sentiments; he seldom pierces the breast, but he always delights the ear, and often improves the understanding.

His translation of the *Golden Verses*, and of the first book of Quillet's Poem, have nothing in them remarkable. The *Golden Verses* are tedious.

The version of Lucan is one of the greatest productions of English poetry, for there is perhaps none that so completely exhibits the genius and spirit of the original. Lucan is distinguished by a kind of dictatorial or philosophic dignity, rather, as Quintilian observes, declamatory than poetical; full of ambitious morality and pointed sentences, comprised in vigorous and animated lines. This character Rowe has very diligently and successfully preserved. His versification, which is such as his contemporaries practised, without any attempt at innovation or improvement, seldom wants either melody or force. His author's sense is sometimes a little diluted by additional infusions, and sometimes weakened by too much expansion; but such faults are to be expected in all translations, from the constraint of measures and dissimilitude of languages. The *Pharsalia* of Rowe deserves more notice than it obtains, and as it is more read will be more esteemed.

JOSEPH ADDISON

1672-1719

Born at Milston, in Wiltshire—Educated at the Charter-house and Oxford—Is praised by Dryden—Early Friendship for Steele—Intended for the Church—Encouraged by Somers and Montague—Travels in Italy—Interview with Boileau—Publishes his Travels—Letter in Verse from Italy—Writes *The Campaign*, a Poem—*Rosamond*, an Opera—Made Secretary to Lord Wharton—*The Tatler* —*The Spectator*—*The Whig Examiner*—Origin of Newspapers—*Cato*, a Tragedy—*The Drummer*, a Comedy—Made Secretary to the Regency—*The Freeholder*—Made Secretary of State—Marries the Countess of Warwick—Resigns his Secretaryship—Alleged Quarrel with Steele—Death and Burial in Westminster Abbey—Works and Character.

Joseph Addison was born on the 1st of May, 1672, at Milston, of which his father, Lancelot Addison, was then rector, near Ambrosebury in Wiltshire, and appearing weak and unlikely to live, he was christened the same day. After the usual domestic education, which, from the character of his father, may be reasonably supposed to have given him strong impressions of piety, he was committed to the care of Mr. Naish at Ambrosebury, and afterwards of Mr. Taylor at Salisbury.

Not to name the school or the masters of men illustrious for literature, is a kind of historical fraud, by which honest fame is injuriously diminished; I would therefore trace him through the whole process of his education. In 1683, in the beginning of his twelfth year, his father, being made Dean of Lichfield, naturally carried his family to his new residence, and, I believe, placed him for some time, probably not long, under Mr. Shaw, then master of the school at Lichfield, father of the late Dr. Peter Shaw. Of this interval his biographers have given no account, and I know it only from a story of a *barring-out*, told me, when I was a boy, by Andrew Corbet of Shropshire, who had heard it from Mr. Pigot, his uncle.

The practice of *barring-out* was a savage licence, practised in many schools to the end of the last century, by which the boys, when the periodical vacation drew near, growing petulant at the approach of liberty, some days before the time of regular recess, took possession of the school, of which they barred the doors, and bade their master defiance from the windows. It is not easy to suppose that on such occasions the master would do more than laugh; yet, if tradition may be credited, he often struggled hard to force or surprise the garrison. The master, when Pigot was a school-boy, was *barred-out* at Lichfield; and the whole operation, as he said, was planned and conducted by Addison.

To judge better of the probability of this story, I have inquired when he was sent to the Chartreux; but, as he was not one of those who enjoyed the founder's benefaction, there is no account preserved of his admission. At the school of the Chartreux, to which he was removed either from that of Salisbury or Lichfield, he pursued his juvenile studies under the care of Dr. Ellis, and contracted that intimacy with Sir Richard Steele which their joint labours have so effectually recorded.

Of this memorable friendship the greater praise must be given to Steele. It is not hard to love those from whom nothing can be feared, and Addison never considered Steele as a rival; but Steele lived, as he confesses, under an habitual subjection to the predominating genius of Addison, whom he always mentioned with reverence, and treated with obsequiousness.

Addison, who knew his own dignity, could not always forbear to show it, by playing a little upon his admirer; but he was in no danger of retort: his jests were endured without resistance or resentment.

But the sneer of jocularity was not the worst. Steele, whose imprudence of generosity, or vanity of profusion, kept him always incurably necessitous, upon some pressing exigence, in an evil hour, borrowed 100*l.* of his friend, probably without much purpose of repayment; but Addison, who seems to have had other notions of 100*l.*, grew impatient of delay, and reclaimed his loan by an execution. Steele felt with great sensibility the obduracy of his creditor, but with emotions of sorrow rather than of anger.

In 1687 he was entered into Queen's College in Oxford, where, in 1689, the accidental perusal of some Latin verses gained him the patronage of Dr. Lancaster, afterwards provost of Queen's College; by whose recommendation he was elected into Magdalen College as a Demy, a term by which that society denominates those which are elsewhere called Scholars; young men who partake of the founder's benefaction, and succeed in their order to vacant fellowships.

Here he continued to cultivate poetry and criticism, and grew first eminent by his Latin compositions, which are indeed entitled to particular praise. He has not confined himself to the imitation of any ancient author, but has formed his style from the general language, such as a diligent perusal of the productions of different ages happened to supply.

His Latin compositions seem to have had much of his fondness, for he collected a second volume of the *Musæ Anglicanæ*, perhaps for a convenient receptacle, in which all his Latin pieces are inserted, and where his poem on the Peace has the first place. He afterwards presented the collection to Boileau, who, from that time, "conceived," says Tickell, "an opinion of the English genius for poetry." Nothing is better known of Boileau, than that he had an injudicious and peevish contempt of modern Latin, and therefore his profession of regard was probably the effect of his civility rather than approbation.

Three of his Latin poems are upon subjects on which perhaps he would not have ventured to have written in his own language: *The Battle of the Pigmies and Cranes; The Barom-*

eter; and A *Bowling-green*. When the matter is low or scanty, a dead language in which nothing is mean because nothing is familiar, affords great conveniences; and by the sonorous magnificence of Roman syllables, the writer conceals penury of thought, and want of novelty, often from the reader, and often from himself.

In his twenty-second year he first showed his power of English poetry, by some verses addressed to Dryden; and soon afterwards published a translation of the greater part of the Fourth Georgic upon Bees; after which, says Dryden, "my latter swarm is scarcely worth the hiving."

About the same time he composed the arguments prefixed to the several books of Dryden's Virgil; and produced an essay on the Georgics, juvenile, superficial, and uninstructive, without much either of the scholar's learning or the critic's penetration.

His next paper of verses contained a character of the principal English poets, inscribed to Henry Sacheverell, who was then, if not a poet, a writer of verses; as is shown by his version of a small part of Virgil's Georgics, published in the *Miscellanies*, and a Latin encomium on Queen Mary, in the *Musæ Anglicanæ*. These verses exhibit all the fondness of friendship; but on one side or the other friendship was afterwards too weak for the malignity of faction.

In this poem is a very confident and discriminate character of Spenser, whose work he had then never read. So little sometimes is criticism the effect of judgment. It is necessary to inform the reader, that about this time he was introduced by Congreve to Montague, then Chancellor of the Exchequer. Addison was then learning the trade of a courtier, and subjoined Montague as a poetical name to those of Cowley and of Dryden.

By the influence of Mr. Montague, concurring, according to Tickell, with his natural modesty, he was diverted from his original design of entering into holy orders. Montague alleged the corruption of men who engaged in civil employments without liberal education; and declared, that, though he was represented as an enemy to the Church, he would never do it any injury but by withholding Addison from it.

Soon after (in 1695) he wrote a poem to King William, with a rhyming introduction addressed to Lord Somers. King William had no regard to elegance or literature; his study was only war; yet by a choice of ministers, whose disposition was very different from his own, he procured, without intention, a very liberal patronage to poetry. Addison was caressed both by Somers and Montague.

In 1697 appeared his Latin verses on the peace of Ryswick, which he dedicated to Montague, and which was afterwards called by Smith "the best Latin poem since the Æneid." Praise must not be too rigorously examined; but the performance cannot be denied to be vigorous and elegant.

Having yet no public employment, he obtained (in 1699) a pension of 300*l*. a year, that he might be enabled to travel. He stayed a year at Blois, probably to learn the French language; and then proceeded in his journey to Italy, which he surveyed with the eyes of a poet.

While he was travelling at leisure, he was far from being idle; for he not only collected his observations on the country, but found time to write his *Dialogues on Medals,* and four acts of *Cato.* Such at least is the relation of Tickell. Perhaps he only collected his materials, and formed his plan.

Whatever were his other employments in Italy, he there wrote the *Letter to Lord Halifax,* which is justly considered as the most elegant, if not the most sublime, of his poetical productions. But in about two years he found it necessary to hasten home; being, as Swift informs us, distressed by indigence, and compelled to become the tutor of a travelling squire, because his pension was not remitted.

At his return he published his *Travels,* with a dedication to Lord Somers. As his stay in foreign countries was short, his observations are such as might be supplied by a hasty view, and consist chiefly in comparisons of the present face of the country with the descriptions left us by the Roman poets, from whom he made preparatory collections, though he might have spared the trouble, had he known that such collections had been made twice before by Italian authors.

The most amusing passage of his book is his account of the minute republic of San Marino; of many parts it is not a very severe censure to say, that they might have been written at home. His elegance of language, and variegation of prose and verse, however, gains upon the reader; and the book, though a while neglected, became in time so much the favourite of the public, that before it was reprinted it rose to five times its price.

When he returned to England (in 1703), with a meanness of appearance which gave testimony of the difficulties to which he had been reduced, he found his old patrons out of power, and was therefore, for a time, at full leisure for the cultivation of his mind, and a mind so cultivated gives reason to believe that little time was lost.

But he remained not long neglected or useless. The victory at Blenheim (13th August, 1704) spread triumph and confidence over the nation; and Lord Godolphin, lamenting to Lord Halifax that it had not been celebrated in a manner equal to the subject, desired him to propose it to some better poet. Halifax told him that there was no encouragement for genius; that worthless men were unprofitably enriched with public money, without any care to find or employ those whose appearance might do honour to their country. To this Godolphin replied, that such abuses should in time be rectified; and that if a man could be found capable of the task then proposed, he should not want an ample recompense. Halifax then named Addison, but required that the Treasurer should apply to him in his own person. Godolphin sent the message by Mr. Boyle, afterwards Lord Carlton; and Addison, having undertaken the work, communicated it to the Treasurer while it was yet advanced no further than the simile of the Angel, and was immediately rewarded by succeeding Mr. Locke in the place of Commissioner of Appeals.

In the following year he was at Hanover with Lord Halifax; and the year after he was made Under-Secretary of State, first to Sir Charles Hedges, and in a few months more to the Earl of Sunderland.

About this time the prevalent taste for Italian operas inclined him to try what would be the effect of a musical drama in our own language. He therefore wrote the opera of *Rosamond*, which, when exhibited on the stage, was either hissed or neglected; but, trusting that the readers would do him more justice, he published it, with an inscription to the Duchess of Marlborough, a woman without skill, or pretensions to skill, in poetry or literature. His dedication was therefore an instance of servile absurdity, to be exceeded only by Joshua Barnes's dedication of a Greek Anacreon to the Duke.

His reputation had been somewhat advanced by *The Tender Husband*, a comedy which Steele dedicated to him, with a confession that he owed to him several of the most successful scenes. To this play Addison supplied a Prologue.

When [1709] the Marquis of Wharton was appointed Lord Lieutenant of Ireland, Addison attended him as his secretary; and was made keeper of the records in Birmingham's Tower, with a salary of 300*l*. a year. The office was little more than nominal, and the salary was augmented for his accommodation.

Interest and faction allow little to the operation of particular dispositions, or private opinions. Two men of personal characters more opposite than those of Wharton and Addison could not easily be brought together. Wharton was impious, profligate, and shameless, without regard, or appearance of regard, to right and wrong: whatever is contrary to this may be said of Addison; but as agents of a party they were connected, and how they adjusted their other sentiments we cannot know.

Addison must however not be too hastily condemned. It is not necessary to refuse benefits from a bad man, when the acceptance implies no approbation of his crimes; nor has the subordinate officer any obligation to examine the opinions or conduct of those under whom he acts, except that he may not be made the instrument of wickedness. It is reasonable to suppose that Addison counteracted, as far as he was able, the malignant and blasting influence of the Lieutenant; and that at least by his intervention some good was done, and some mischief prevented.

When he was in office, he made a law to himself, as Swift has recorded, never to remit his regular fees in civility to his friends: "For," said he, "I may have a hundred friends; and if my fee be two guineas, I shall, by relinquishing my right, lose two hundred guineas, and no friend gain more than two; there is therefore no proportion between the good imparted and the evil suffered."

He was in Ireland when Steele, without any communication of his design, began the publication of *The Tatler*: but he was not long concealed: by inserting a remark on Virgil, which Addison had given him, he discovered himself. It is indeed not easy for any man to write upon literature or common life, so as not to make himself known to those with whom he familiarly converses, and who are acquainted with his track of study, his favourite topic, his peculiar notions, and his habitual phrases.

If Steele desired to write in secret, he was not lucky; a single month detected him. His first *Tatler* was published April 12 (1709); and Addison's contribution appeared May 26. Tickell observes, that *The Tatler* began and was concluded without his concurrence. This is doubtless literally true; but the work did not suffer much by his unconsciousness of its commencement, or his absence at its cessation; for he continued his assistance to December 23, and the paper stopped on January 2 [1710–11]. He did not distinguish his pieces by any signature; and I know not whether his name was not kept secret till the papers were collected into volumes.

To *The Tatler*, in about two months, succeeded *The Spectator*; a series of essays of the same kind, but written with less levity, upon a more regular plan, and published daily. Such an undertaking showed the writers not to distrust their own copiousness of materials or facility of composition, and their performance justified their confidence. They found, however, in their progress, many auxiliaries. To attempt a single paper was no terrifying labour; many pieces were offered, and many were received.

Addison had enough of the zeal of party; but Steele had at that time almost nothing else. *The Spectator*, in one of the first papers, showed the political tenets of its authors; but a resolution was soon taken, of courting general approbation by general topics, and subjects on which faction had produced no diversity of sentiments; such as literature, morality, and familiar life. To this practice they adhered with few deviations.

The ardour of Steele once broke out in praise of Marlborough; and when Dr. Fleetwood prefixed to some sermons a Preface, overflowing with Whiggish opinions, that it might be read by the Queen it was reprinted in *The Spectator*.

To teach the minuter decencies and inferior duties, to regulate the practice of daily conversation, to correct those depravities which are rather ridiculous than criminal, and remove those grievances which, if they produce no lasting calamities, impress hourly vexation, was first attempted by Casa in his book of *Manners*, and Castiglione in his *Courtier*; two books yet celebrated in Italy for purity and elegance, and which, if they are now less read, are neglected only because they have effected that reformation which their authors intended, and their precepts now are no longer wanted. Their usefulness to the age in which they were written is sufficiently attested by the translations which almost all the nations of Europe were in haste to obtain.

This species of instruction was continued, and perhaps advanced by the French, among whom La Bruyère's *Manners of the Age*, though, as Boileau remarked, it is written without connection, certainly deserves praise, for liveliness of description and justness of observation.

Before the *Tatler* and *Spectator*, if the writers for the theatre are excepted, England had no masters of common life. No writers had yet undertaken to reform either the savageness of neglect or the impertinence of civility, to show when to speak or to be silent, how to refuse or how to comply. We had many books to teach us our more important duties, and to settle opinions in philosophy or politics; but an *arbiter elegantiarum* —a judge of propriety—was yet wanting, who should survey the track of daily conversation, and free it from thorns and prickles, which tease the passer, though they do not wound him.

For this purpose nothing is so proper as the frequent publication of short papers, which we read not as study, but amusement. If the subject be slight, the treatise is short. The busy may find time, and the idle may find patience.

This mode of conveying cheap and easy knowledge began among us in the Civil War, when it was much the interest of either party to raise and fix the prejudices of the people. At that time appeared *Mercurius Aulicus, Mercurius Rusticus,* and *Mercurius Civicus.* It is said, that when any title grew popular it was stolen by the antagonist, who by this stratagem conveyed his notions to those who would not have received him had he not worn the appearance of a friend. The tumult of those unhappy days left scarcely any man leisure to treasure up occasional compositions; and so much were they neglected, that a complete collection is nowhere to be found.

These *Mercuries* were succeeded [1681] by L'Estrange's *Observator,* and that by Leslie's *Rehearsal,* and perhaps by others; but hitherto nothing had been conveyed to the people, in this commodious manner, but controversy relating to the Church or State, of which they taught many to talk whom they could not teach to judge.

It has been suggested, that the Royal Society was instituted soon after the Restoration to divert the attention of the people from public discontent. The *Tatler* and *Spectator* had the same tendency; they were published at a time when two parties, loud, restless, and violent, each with plausible declarations, and each perhaps without any distinct termination of its views, were agitating the nation; to minds heated with political contest they supplied cooler and more inoffensive reflections; and it is said by Addison, in a subsequent work, that they had a perceptible influence upon the conversation of that time, and taught the frolic and the gay to unite merriment with decency—an effect which they can never wholly lose, while they continue to be among the first books by which both sexes are initiated in the elegances of knowledge.

The *Tatler* and *Spectator* adjusted, like Casa, the unsettled practice of daily intercourse by propriety and politeness; and, like La Bruyère, exhibited the "Characters and Manners of the Age." The personages introduced in these papers were not merely ideal—they were then known, and conspicuous in various stations. Of *The Tatler* this is told by Steele in his last paper; and of *The Spectator* by Budgell, in the Preface to *Theophrastus,* a book which Addison has recommended, and which he was suspected to have revised, if he did not write it. Of those portraits, which may be supposed to be sometimes embellished, and sometimes aggravated, the originals are now partly known, and partly forgotten.

But to say that they united the plans of two or three eminent writers, is to give them but a small part of their due praise; they superadded literature and criticism, and sometimes towered far above their predecessors; and taught, with great justness of argument and dignity of language, the most important duties and sublime truths.

All these topics were happily varied with elegant fictions and refined allegories, and illuminated with different changes of style and felicities of invention.

It is recorded by Budgell, that of the characters feigned or exhibited in *The Spectator*, the favourite of Addison was Sir Roger de Coverley, of whom he had formed a very delicate and discriminate idea, which he would not suffer to be violated; and, therefore, when Steele had shown him innocently picking up a girl in the Temple, and taking her to a tavern, he drew upon himself so much of his friend's indignation, that he was forced to appease him by a promise of forbearing Sir Roger for the time to come.

The reason which induced Cervantes to bring his hero to the grave, *para mi sola nacio Don Quixote, y yo para el*, made Addison declare, with undue vehemence of expression, that he would kill Sir Roger, being of opinion that they were born for one another, and that any other hand would do him wrong.

It may be doubted whether Addison ever filled up his original delineation. He describes his knight as having his imagination somewhat warped; but of this perversion he has made very little use. The irregularities in Sir Roger's conduct seem not so much the effects of a mind deviating from the beaten track of life by the perpetual pressure of some overwhelming idea, as of habitual rusticity, and that negligence which solitary grandeur naturally generates.

The variable weather of the mind, the flying vapours of incipient madness, which from time to time cloud reason, without eclipsing it, it requires so much nicety to exhibit, that Addison seems to have been deterred from prosecuting his own design.

To Sir Roger, who, as a country gentleman, appears to be a

Tory, or, as it is gently expressed, an adherent to the landed interest, is opposed Sir Andrew Freeport, a new man, a wealthy merchant, zealous for the moneyed interest, and a Whig. Of this contrariety of opinions it is probable more consequences were at first intended than could be produced when the resolution was taken to exclude party from the paper. Sir Andrew does but little, and that little seems not to have pleased Addison, who, when he dismissed him from the club, changed his opinions. Steele had made him, in the true spirit of unfeeling commerce, declare that he "would not build an hospital for idle people"; but at last he buys land, settles in the country, and builds, not a manufactory, but an hospital for twelve old husbandmen—for men with whom a merchant has little acquaintance, and whom he commonly considers with little kindness.

Of essays thus elegant, thus instructive, and thus commodiously distributed, it is natural to suppose the approbation general, and the sale numerous. I once heard it observed, that the sale may be calculated by the product of the tax, related in the last number [No. 555] to produce more than 20l. a week, and therefore stated at 21l., or 3l. 10s. a day; this, at a halfpenny a paper, will give 1680 for the daily number.

This sale is not great; yet this, if Swift be credited, was likely to grow less; for he declares that *The Spectator*, whom he ridicules for his endless mention of the *fair sex*, had before his recess wearied his readers.

The next year (1713), in which *Cato* came upon the stage, was the grand climacteric of Addison's reputation. Upon the death of Cato he had, as is said, planned a tragedy in the time of his travels, and had for several years the four first acts finished, which were shown to such as were likely to spread their admiration. They were seen by Pope and by Cibber, who relates that Steele, when he took back the copy, told him, in the despicable cant of literary modesty, that, whatever spirit his friend had shown in the composition, he doubted whether he would have courage sufficient to expose it to the censure of a British audience.

The time, however, was now come when those who affected to think liberty in danger, affected likewise to think that a stage-play might preserve it; and Addison was importuned, in the name of the tutelary deities of Britain, to show his courage and his zeal by finishing his design.

To resume his work he seemed perversely and unaccountably unwilling; and by a request which perhaps he wished to be denied, desired Mr. Hughes to add a fifth act. Hughes supposed him serious; and, undertaking the supplement, brought in a few days some scenes for his examination; but he had in the meantime gone to work himself, and produced half an act, which he afterwards completed, but with brevity irregularly disproportionate to the foregoing parts, like a task performed with reluctance, and hurried to its conclusion.

It may yet be doubted whether *Cato* was made public by any change of the author's purpose; for Dennis charged him with raising prejudices in his own favour by false positions of preparatory criticism, and with *poisoning the town* by contradicting in *The Spectator* the established rule of poetical justice, because his own hero, with all his virtues, was to fall before a tyrant. The fact is certain; the motives we must guess.

Addison was, I believe, sufficiently disposed to bar all avenues against all danger. When Pope brought him the Prologue, which is properly accommodated to the play, there were these words, "Britons, *arise!* be worth like this approved"; meaning nothing more than, Britons, erect and exalt yourselves to the approbation of public virtue. Addison was frighted lest he should be thought a promoter of insurrection, and the line was liquidated to "Britons, attend."

Now, "heavily in clouds came on the day, the great, the important day," when Addison was to stand the hazard of the theatre. That there might, however, be left as little hazard as was possible on the first night [14th April, 1713], Steele, as himself relates, undertook to pack an audience. This, says Pope, had been tried for the first time in favour of *The Distrest Mother*; and was now, with more efficacy, practised for *Cato*.

The danger was soon over. The whole nation was at that time on fire with faction. The Whigs applauded every line in which liberty was mentioned as a satire on the Tories; and the Tories echoed every clap to show that the satire was unfelt.

The story of Bolingbroke is well known. He called Booth to his box, and gave him fifty guineas for defending the cause of liberty so well against a perpetual dictator. The Whigs, says Pope, design a second present, when they can accompany it with as good a sentence.

The play, supported thus by the emulation of factious praise, was acted night after night for a longer time than, I believe, the public had allowed to any drama before; and the author, as Mrs. Porter long afterwards related, wandered through the whole exhibition behind the scenes with restless and unappeasable solicitude.

When it was printed, notice was given that the Queen [Anne] would be pleased if it was dedicated to her; "but, as he had designed that compliment elsewhere, he found himself obliged," says Tickell, "by his duty on the one side, and his honour on the other, to send it into the world without any dedication."

Human happiness has always its abatements; the brightest sunshine of success is not without a cloud. No sooner was *Cato* offered to the reader, than it was attacked by the acute malignity of Dennis, with all the violence of angry criticism. Dennis, though equally zealous, and probably by his temper more furious than Addison, for what they called liberty, and though a flatterer of the Whig ministry, could not sit quiet at a successful play, but was eager to tell friends and enemies that they had misplaced their admirations. The world was too stubborn for instruction; with the fate of the censurer of Corneille's *Cid*, his animadversions showed his anger without effect, and *Cato* continued to be praised.

Pope had now an opportunity of courting the friendship of Addison by vilifying his old enemy, and could give resentment its full play without appearing to revenge himself. He therefore published [1713] *Dr. Norris's Narrative of the Frenzy of Mr. John Dennis*—a performance which left the objections to the play in their full force, and therefore discovered more desire of vexing the critic than of defending the poet.

Addison, who was no stranger to the world, probably saw the selfishness of Pope's friendship, and, resolving that he should have the consequences of his officiousness to himself, informed Dennis by Steele, that he was sorry for the insult; and that, whenever he should think fit to answer his remarks, he would do it in a manner to which nothing could be objected.

The greatest weakness of the play is in the scenes of love, which are said by Pope to have been added to the original plan upon a subsequent review, in compliance with the popular practice of the stage. Such an authority it is hard to reject, yet the love is so intimately mingled with the whole action, that it cannot easily be thought extrinsic and adventitious; for, if it were taken away, what would be left?—or how were the four acts filled in the first draught?

At the publication the wits seemed proud to pay their attendance with encomiastic verses. The best are from an unknown hand, which will perhaps lose somewhat of their praise when the author is known to be Jeffreys.

Cato had yet other honours. It was censured as a party-play by a "Scholar of Oxford," and defended in a favourable examination by Dr. Sewell. It was translated by Salvini into Italian, and acted at Florence; and by the Jesuits of St. Omer's into Latin, and played by their pupils. Of this version a copy was sent to Mr. Addison: it is to be wished that it could be found, for the sake of comparing their version of the soliloquy with that of Bland.

A tragedy was written on the same subject by Des Champs, a French poet, which was translated, with a criticism on the English play. But the translator and the critic are now forgotten.

Dennis lived on unanswered, and therefore little read. Addison knew the policy of literature too well to make his enemy important by drawing the attention of the public upon a criticism which, though sometimes intemperate, was often irrefragable.

While *Cato* was upon the stage, another daily paper, called *The Guardian*, was published by Steele. To this Addison gave great assistance, whether occasionally or by previous engagement is not known.

The character of Guardian was too narrow and too serious: it might properly enough admit both the duties and the decencies of life, but seemed not to include literary speculations, and was in some degree violated by merriment and burlesque. What had the Guardian of the Lizards to do with clubs of tall or of little men, with nests of ants, or with Strada's prolusions?

Of this paper nothing is necessary to be said, but that it found many contributors, and that it was a continuation of *The Spectator*, with the same elegance, and the same variety, till some unlucky sparkle from a Tory paper set Steele's politics on fire, and wit at once blazed into faction. He was soon too hot for neutral topics, and quitted *The Guardian* [1st Sept., 1713] to write [8th Oct., 1713] *The Englishman*.

The papers of Addison are marked in *The Spectator* by one of the letters in the name of Clio, and in *The Guardian* by *a hand*; whether it was, as Tickell pretends to think, that he was unwilling to usurp the praise of others, or as Steele, with far greater likelihood, insinuates, that he could not without discontent impart to others any of his own. I have heard that his avidity did not satisfy itself with the air of renown, but that with great eagerness he laid hold on his proportion of the profits.

Many of these papers were written with powers truly comic, with nice discrimination of characters, and accurate observation of natural or accidental deviations from propriety; but it was not supposed that he had tried a comedy on the stage, till Steele after his death declared him the author of *The Drummer*. This, however, Steele did not know to be true by any direct testimony; for when Addison put the play into his hands, he only told him it was the work of a "gentleman in the company"; and when it was received, as is confessed, with cold disapprobation, he was probably less willing to claim it. Tickell omitted it in his collection; but the testimony of Steele, and the total silence of any other claimant, has determined the public to assign it to Addison, and it is now printed with his other poetry. Steel carried *The Drummer* to the playhouse, and afterwards to the press, and sold the copy for fifty guineas.

To the opinion of Steele may be added the proof supplied by the play itself, of which the characters are such as Addison would have delineated, and the tendency such as Addison would have promoted. That it should have been ill received would raise wonder, did we not daily see the capricious distribution of theatrical praise.

He was not all this time an indifferent spectator of public affairs. He wrote, as different exigencies required (in 1707), *The Present State of the War, and the Necessity of an Augmentation*; which, however judicious, being written on temporary topics, and exhibiting no peculiar powers, laid hold on no attention, and has naturally sunk by its own weight into neglect. This cannot be said of the few papers entitled *The Whig Examiner*, in which is employed all the force of gay malevolence and humorous satire. Of this paper, which just appeared and expired, Swift remarks, with exultation, that "it is now down among the dead men." He might well rejoice at the death of that which he could not have killed. Every reader of every party, since personal malice is past, and the papers which once inflamed the nation are read only as effusions of wit, must wish for more of *The Whig Examiners*; for on no occasion was the genius of Addison more vigorously exerted, and on none did the superiority of his powers more evidently appear. His *Trial of Count Tariff*, written to expose the treaty of commerce with France, lived no longer than the question that produced it.

Not long afterwards [18th June, 1714] an attempt was made to revive *The Spectator*, at a time indeed by no means favourable to literature, when the succession of a new family to the throne filled the nation with anxiety, discord, and confusion; and either the turbulence of the times, or the satiety of the readers, put a stop to the publication, after an experiment of eighty numbers, which were afterwards collected into an eighth volume, perhaps more valuable than any one of those that went before it. Addison produced more than a fourth part; and the other contributors are by no means unworthy of appearing as his associates. The time that had passed during the suspension of *The Spectator*, though it had not lessened his power of humour, seems to have increased his disposition to seriousness: the proportion of his religious to his comic papers is greater than in the former series.

The Spectator, from its recommencement, was published

only three times a week; and no discriminative marks were added to the papers. To Addison, Tickell has ascribed twenty-three.

The Spectator had many contributors; and Steele, whose negligence kept him always in a hurry, when it was his turn to furnish a paper, called loudly for the letters, of which Addison, whose materials were more, made little use, having recourse to sketches and hints, the product of his former studies, which he now reviewed and completed; among these are named by Tickell the *Essays on Wit*, those on the *Pleasures of the Imagination*, and the *Criticism on Milton*.

When [1714] the House of Hanover took possession of the throne, it was reasonable to expect that the zeal of Addison would be suitably rewarded. Before the arrival of King George, he was made Secretary to the Regency, and was required by his office to send notice to Hanover that the Queen was dead, and that the throne was vacant. To do this would not have been difficult to any man but Addison, who was so overwhelmed with the greatness of the event, and so distracted by choice of expression, that the Lords, who could not wait for the niceties of criticism, called Mr. Southwell, a clerk in the House, and ordered him to despatch the message. Southwell readily told what was necessary in the common style of business, and valued himself upon having done what was too hard for Addison.

He was better qualified for *The Freeholder*, a paper which he published twice a week, from Dec. 23, 1715, to the middle of the next year. This was undertaken in defence of the established government, sometimes with argument, sometimes with mirth. In argument he had many equals; but his humour was singular and matchless. Bigotry itself must be delighted with the Tory Fox-hunter.

There are, however, some strokes less elegant and less decent; such as the Pretender's Journal, in which one topic of ridicule is his poverty. This mode of abuse had been employed by Milton against King Charles II.:

—————————————*Jacobæi*
Centum, exulantis viscera marsupii regis.

And Oldmixon delights to tell of some alderman of London, that he had more money than the exiled princes; but that which might be expected from Milton's savageness, or Oldmixon's meanness, was not suitable to the delicacy of Addison.

Steele thought the humour of *The Freeholder* too nice and gentle for such noisy times; and is reported to have said, that the ministry made use of a lute, when they should have called for a trumpet.

This year (August 2, 1716) he married the Countess Dowager of Warwick, whom he had solicited by a very long and anxious courtship, perhaps with behaviour not very unlike that of Sir Roger to his disdainful widow; and who, I am afraid, diverted herself often by playing with his passion. He is said to have first known her by becoming tutor to her son. "He formed," said Tonson, "the design of getting that lady, from the time when he was first recommended into the family." In what part of his life he obtained the recommendation, or how long, and in what manner he lived in the family, I know not. His advances at first were certainly timorous, but grew bolder as his reputation and influence increased; till at last the lady was persuaded to marry him, on terms much like those on which a Turkish princess is espoused, to whom the Sultan is reported to pronounce, "Daughter, I give thee this man for thy slave." The marriage, if uncontradicted report can be credited, made no addition to his happiness; it neither found them nor made them equal. She always remembered her own rank, and thought herself entitled to treat with very little ceremony the tutor of her son. Rowe's ballad of *The Despairing Shepherd* is said to have been written, either before or after marriage, upon this memorable pair; and it is certain that Addison has left behind him no encouragement for ambitious love.

The year after (April 16, 1717) he rose to his highest elevation, being made Secretary of State. For this employment he might be justly supposed qualified by long practice of business, and by his regular ascent through other offices; but expectation is often disappointed; it is universally confessed that he was unequal to the duties of his place. In the House of Commons he could not speak, and therefore was useless to the defence of the government. In the office, says Pope, he could not issue an order without losing his time in quest of fine expressions. What he gained in rank, he lost in credit; and, finding by experience his own inability, was forced to solicit his dismission, with a pension of 1500*l.* a year. His friends palliated this relinquishment, of which both friends and enemies knew the true reason, with an account of declining health, and the necessity of recess and quiet.

He now returned to his vocation, and began to plan literary occupations for his future life. He purposed a tragedy on the death of Socrates; a story of which, as Tickell remarks, the basis is narrow, and to which I know not how love could have been appended. There would, however, have been no want either of virtue in the sentiments, or elegance in the language.

He engaged in a nobler work, a defence of the *Christian Religion*, of which part was published after his death; and he designed to have made a new poetical version of the Psalms.

These pious compositions Pope imputed to a selfish motive, upon the credit, as he owns, of Tonson, who having quarrelled with Addison, and not loving him, said, that when he laid down the Secretary's office, he intended to take orders, and obtain a bishopric; "for," said he, "I always thought him a priest in his heart."

That Pope should have thought this conjecture of Tonson worth remembrance, is a proof, but indeed, so far as I have found, the only proof, that he retained some malignity from their ancient rivalry. Tonson pretended but to guess it; no other mortal ever suspected it; and Pope might have reflected, that a man who had been Secretary of State in the ministry of Sunderland, knew a nearer way to a bishopric than by defending religion, or translating the Psalms.

It is related that he had once a design to make an English Dictionary, and that he considered Dr. Tillotson as the writer of highest authority. There was formerly sent to me by Mr. Locker, clerk of the Leathersellers' Company, who was eminent for curiosity and literature, a collection of examples selected from Tillotson's works, as Locker said, by Addison. It came too late to be of use, so I inspected it but slightly, and remember it indistinctly. I thought the passages too short.

Addison, however, did not conclude his life in peaceful studies; but relapsed, when he was near his end, to a political dispute.

It so happened that (1718–19) a controversy was agitated with great vehemence between those friends of long continuance, Addison and Steele. It may be asked, in the language of Homer, what power or what cause should set them at variance. The subject of their dispute was of great importance. The Earl of Sunderland proposed an Act, called The Peerage Bill, by which the number of Peers should be fixed, and the King restrained from any new creation of nobility unless when an old family should be extinct. To this the Lords would naturally agree; and the King [George I.], who was yet little acquainted with his own prerogative, and, as is now well known, almost indifferent to the possessions of the crown, had been persuaded to consent. The only difficulty was found among the Commons, who were not likely to approve the perpetual exclusion of themselves and their posterity. The bill therefore was eagerly opposed, and among others by Sir Robert Walpole, whose speech was published.

The Lords might think their dignity diminished by improper advancements, and particularly by the introduction of twelve new Peers at once, to produce a majority of Tories in the last reign; an act of authority violent enough, yet certainly legal, and by no means to be compared with that contempt of national right with which, some time afterwards, by the instigation of Whiggism, the Commons, chosen by the people for three years, chose themselves for seven. But, whatever might be the disposition of the Lords, the people had no wish to increase their power. The tendency of the Bill, as Steele observed in a letter to the Earl of Oxford, was to introduce an aristocracy; for a majority in the House of Lords, so limited, would have been despotic and irresistible.

To prevent this subversion of the ancient establishment, Steele, whose pen readily seconded his political passions, endeavoured to alarm the nation by a pamphlet called *The Plebeian*. To this an answer was published [1719] by Addison, under the title of *The Old Whig*, in which it is not discovered that Steele was then known to be the advocate for the Commons. Steele replied by a second *Plebeian;* and, whether by ignorance or by courtesy, confined himself to his question, without any personal notice of his opponent. Nothing hitherto was committed against the laws of friendship, or proprieties of decency; but controvertists cannot long retain their kindness for each other. *The Old Whig* answered *The Plebeian,* and could not forbear some contempt of "Little Dicky, whose trade it was to write pamphlets." Dicky, however, did not lose his settled veneration for his friend; but contented himself with quoting some lines of *Cato,* which were at once detection and reproof. The Bill was laid aside during that session; and Addison died before the next, in which its commitment was rejected by 269 to 177.

Every reader surely must regret that these two illustrious friends, after so many years passed in confidence and endearment, in unity of interest, conformity of opinion, and fellowship of study, should finally part in acrimonious opposition. Such a controversy was "Bellum plusquam *civile,*" as Lucan expresses it. Why could not faction find other advocates? But among the uncertainties of the human state, we are doomed to number the instability of friendship.

Of this dispute I have little knowledge but from the *Biographia Britannica. The Old Whig* is not inserted in Addison's works, nor is it mentioned by Tickell in his Life; why it was omitted, the biographers doubtless give the true reason; the fact was too recent, and those who had been heated in the contention were not yet cool.

The necessity of complying with times, and of sparing persons, is the great impediment of biography. History may be formed from permanent monuments and records; but Lives can only be written from personal knowledge, which is growing every day less, and in a short time is lost for ever. What is known can seldom be immediately told; and when it might be told, it is no longer known. The delicate features of the mind, the nice discriminations of character, and the minute peculiarities of conduct, are soon obliterated; and it is surely better that caprice, obstinacy, frolic, and folly, however they might delight in the description, should be silently forgotten, than that, by wanton merriment and unseasonable detection, a pang should be given to a widow, a daughter, a brother, or a friend. As the process of these narratives is now bringing me among my contemporaries, I begin to feel myself "waking upon ashes under which the fire is not extinguished," and coming to the time of which it will be proper rather to say "nothing that is false, than all that is true."

The end of this useful life was now approaching. Addison had for some time been oppressed by shortness of breath, which was now aggravated by a dropsy; and finding his danger pressing, he prepared to die conformably to his own precepts and professions.

During this lingering decay, he sent, as Pope relates, a message by the Earl of Warwick to Mr. Gay, desiring to see him. Gay, who had not visited him for some time before, obeyed the summons, and found himself received with great kindness. The purpose for which the interview had been solicited was then discovered. Addison told him that he had injured him; but that, if he recovered, he would recompense him. What the injury was he did not explain, nor did Gay ever know; but supposed that some preferment designed for him had, by Addison's intervention, been withheld.

Lord Warwick was a young man, of very irregular life, and perhaps of loose opinions. Addison, for whom he did not want respect, had very diligently endeavoured to reclaim him; but his arguments and expostulations had no effect. One experiment, however, remained to be tried: when he found his life near its end, he directed the young Lord to be called; and when he desired, with great tenderness, to hear his last injunctions, told him, "I have sent for you, that you may see how a Christian can die." What effect this awful scene had on the Earl, I know not; he likewise died himself in a short time.

In Tickell's excellent elegy on his friend are these lines:

> He taught us how to live; and, oh! too high
> The price of knowledge, taught us how to die—

in which he alludes, as he told Dr. Young, to this moving interview.

Having given directions to Mr. Tickell for the publication

of his works, and dedicated them on his death-bed to his friend Mr. Craggs, he died June 17, 1719, at Holland House, leaving no child but a daughter.

Of his virtue it is a sufficient testimony, that the resentment of party has transmitted no charge of any crime. He was not one of those who are praised only after death; for his merit was so generally acknowledged, that Swift, having observed that his election passed without a contest, adds, that, if he proposed himself for king, he would hardly have been refused.

His zeal for his party did not extinguish his kindness for the merit of his opponents: when he was secretary in Ireland, he refused to intermit his acquaintance with Swift.

Of his habits, or external manners, nothing is so often mentioned as that timorous or sullen taciturnity, which his friends called modesty by too mild a name. Steele mentions with great tenderness "that remarkable bashfulness, which is a cloak that hides and muffles merit"; and tells us, that "his abilities were covered only by modesty, which doubles the beauties which are seen, and gives credit and esteem to all that are concealed." Chesterfield affirms, that "Addison was the most timorous and awkward man that he ever saw." And Addison, speaking of his own deficience in conversation, used to say of himself, that, with respect to intellectual wealth, "he could draw bills for a thousand pounds, though he had not a guinea in his pocket."

That he wanted current coin for ready payment, and by that want was often obstructed and distressed; that he was often oppressed by an improper and ungraceful timidity; every testimony concurs to prove: but Chesterfield's representation is doubtless hyperbolical. That man cannot be supposed very unexpert in the arts of conversation and practice of life, who, without fortune or alliance, by his usefulness and dexterity, became Secretary of State; and who died at forty-seven, after having not only stood long in the highest rank of wit and literature, but filled one of the most important offices of State.

The time in which he lived had reason to lament his obstinacy of silence: "for he was," says Steele, "above all men in that talent we call humour, and enjoyed it in such perfection, that I have often reflected, after a night spent with him apart from all the world, that I had had the pleasure of conversing with an intimate acquaintance of Terence and Catullus, who had all their wit and nature, heightened with humour more exquisite and delightful than any other man ever possessed." This is the fondness of a friend; let us hear what is told us by a rival: "Addison's conversation," says Pope, "had something in it more charming than I have found in any other man. But this was only when familiar: before strangers, or perhaps a single stranger, he preserved his dignity by a stiff silence."

This modesty was by no means inconsistent with a very high opinion of his own merit. He demanded to be the first name in modern wit: and, with Steele to echo him, used to depreciate Dryden, whom Pope and Congreve defended against them. There is no reason to doubt that he suffered too much pain from the prevalence of Pope's poetical reputation; nor is it without strong reason suspected that by some disingenuous acts he endeavoured to obstruct it. Pope was not the only man whom he insidiously injured, though the only man of whom he could be afraid.

His own powers were such as might have satisfied him with conscious excellence. Of very extensive learning he has indeed given no proofs. He seems to have had small acquaintance with the sciences, and to have read little except Latin and French; but of the Latin poets his *Dialogues on Medals* show that he had perused the works with great diligence and skill. The abundance of his own mind left him little indeed of adventitious sentiments; his wit always could suggest what the occasion demanded. He had read with critical eyes the important volume of human life, and knew the heart of man from the depths of stratagem to the surface of affectation.

What he knew he could easily communicate. "This," says Steele, "was particular in this writer, that, when he had taken his resolution, or made his plan for what he designed to write, he would walk about the room, and dictate it into language with as much freedom and ease as any one could write it down, and attend to the coherence and grammar of what he dictated."

Pope, who can be less suspected of favouring his memory, declares that he wrote very fluently, but was slow and scrupulous in correcting; that many of his *Spectators* were written very fast, and sent immediately to the press; and that it seemed to be for his advantage not to have time for much revisal.

"He would alter," says Pope, "anything to please his friends, before publication; but would not retouch his pieces afterwards; and I believe not one word in *Cato*, to which I made an objection, was suffered to stand."

The last line of *Cato* is Pope's, having been originally written

And, oh! 'twas this that ended Cato's life.

Pope might have made more objections to the six concluding lines. In the first couplet the words "from hence" are improper; and the second line is taken from Dryden's Virgil. Of the next couplet, the first verse being included in the second, is therefore useless; and in the third Discord is made to produce Strife.

Of the course of Addison's familiar day, before his marriage, Pope has given a detail. He had in the house with him Budgell, and perhaps Philips. His chief companions were Steele, Budgell, [Ambrose] Philips, Carey, Davenant, and Colonel Brett. With one or other of these he always breakfasted. He studied all morning; then dined at a tavern; and went afterwards to Button's.

Button had been a servant in the Countess of Warwick's family, who, under the patronage of Addison, kept a coffee-house on the south side of Russell-street, about two doors from Covent-garden. Here it was that the wits of that time used to assemble. It is said, when Addison had suffered any vexation from the Countess, he withdrew the company from Button's house.

From the coffee-house he went again to a tavern, where he often sat late, and drank too much wine. In the bottle, discontent seeks for comfort, cowardice for courage, and bashfulness for confidence. It is not unlikely that Addison was first seduced to excess by the manumission which he obtained from the servile timidity of his sober hours. He that feels oppression from the presence of those to whom he knows himself superior, will desire to set loose his powers of conversation; and who, that ever asked succours from Bacchus, was able to preserve himself from being enslaved by his auxiliary?

Among those friends it was that Addison displayed the elegance of his colloquial accomplishments, which may easily be supposed such as Pope represents them. The remark of Mandeville, who, when he had passed an evening in his company, declared that he was a parson in a tye-wig, can detract little from his character; he was always reserved to strangers, and was not incited to uncommon freedom by a character like that of Mandeville.

From any minute knowledge of his familiar manners, the intervention of sixty years has now debarred us. Steele once promised Congreve and the public a complete description of his character; but the promises of authors are like the vows of lovers. Steele thought no more on his design, or thought on it with anxiety that at last disgusted him, and left his friend in the hands of Tickell.

One slight lineament of his character Swift has preserved. It was his practice, when he found any man invincibly wrong, to flatter his opinions by acquiescence, and sink him yet deeper in absurdity. This artifice of mischief was admired by Stella; and Swift seems to approve her admiration.

His works will supply some information. It appears from his various pictures of the world, that, with all his bashfulness, he had conversed with many distinct classes of men, had surveyed their ways with very diligent observation, and marked with great acuteness the effects of different modes of life. He was a man in whose presence nothing reprehensible was out of danger; quick in discerning whatever was wrong or ridiculous, and not unwilling to expose it. "There are," says Steele, "in his writings, many oblique strokes upon some of the wittiest men of the age." His delight was more to excite merriment than detestation; and he detects follies rather than crimes.

If any judgment be made, from his books, of his moral character, nothing will be found but purity and excellence. Knowledge of mankind indeed, less extensive than that of Addison, will show, that to write, and to live, are very different. Many who praise virtue, do no more than praise it. Yet it is reasonable to believe that Addison's professions and practice were at no great variance, since, amidst that storm of faction in which most of his life was passed, though his station made him conspicuous, and his activity made him formidable, the character given him by his friends was never contradicted by his enemies: of those with whom interest or opinion united him, he had not only the esteem, but the kindness; and of others, whom the violence of opposition drove against him, though he might lose the love, he retained the reverence.

It is justly observed by Tickell, that he employed wit on the side of virtue and religion. He not only made the proper use of wit himself, but taught it to others; and from his time it has been generally subservient to the cause of reason and of truth. He has dissipated the prejudice that had long connected gaiety with vice, and easiness of manners with laxity of principles. He has restored virtue to its dignity, and taught innocence not to be ashamed. This is an elevation of literary character, "above all Greek, above all Roman fame." No greater felicity can genius attain than that of having purified intellectual pleasure, separated mirth from indecency, and wit from licentiousness; of having taught a succession of writers to bring elegance and gaiety to the aid of goodness; and, if I may use expressions yet more awful, of having "turned many to righteousness."

Addison, in his life, and for some time afterwards, was considered by the greater part of readers as supremely excelling both in poetry and criticism. Part of his reputation may be probably ascribed to the advancement of his fortune; when, as Swift observes, he became a statesman, and saw poets waiting at his levee, it was no wonder that praise was accumulated upon him. Much likewise may be more honourably ascribed to his personal character: he who, if he had claimed it, might have obtained the diadem, was not likely to be denied the laurel.

But time quickly puts an end to artificial and accidental fame; and Addison is to pass through futurity protected only by his genius. Every name which kindness or interest once raised too high is in danger lest the next age should, by the vengeance of criticism, sink it in the same proportion. A great writer has lately styled him "an indifferent poet, and a worse critic."

His poetry is first to be considered; of which it must be confessed that it has not often those felicities of diction which give lustre to sentiments, or that vigour of sentiment that animates diction: there is little of ardour, vehemence, or transport; there is very rarely the awfulness of grandeur, and not very often the splendour of elegance. He thinks justly, but he thinks faintly. This is his general character; to which, doubtless, many single passages will furnish exception.

Yet, if he seldom reaches supreme excellence, he rarely sinks into dullness, and is still more rarely entangled in absurdity. He did not trust his powers enough to be negligent. There is in most of his compositions a calmness and equability, deliberate and cautious, sometimes with little that delights, but seldom with anything that offends.

Of this kind seem to be his poems to Dryden, to Somers, and to the King. His ode on St. Cecilia has been imitated by Pope, and has something in it of Dryden's vigour. Of his *Account of the English Poets*, he used to speak as a "poor thing"; but it is not worse than his usual strain. He has said, not very judiciously, in his character of Waller:

> Thy verse could show ev'n Cromwell's innocence,
> And compliment the storms that bore him hence.
> O! had thy Muse not come an age too soon,
> But seen great Nassau on the British throne,
> How had his triumph glitter'd in thy page!—

What is this but to say, that he who could compliment Cromwell had been the proper poet for King William? Addison, however, never printed the piece.

The *Letter from Italy* has been always praised, but has never been praised beyond its merit. It is more correct, with less appearance of labour, and more elegant, with less ambition of ornament, than any other of his poems. There is, however, one broken metaphor, of which notice may properly b taken:

> Fir'd with that name—
> I bridle in my struggling Muse with pain,
> That longs to launch into a nobler strain.

To *bridle a goddess* is no very delicate idea; but why must she be *bridled?* because she *longs to launch;* an act which was never hindered by a *bridle:* and whither will she *launch?* into a *nobler strain.* She is in the first line a *horse,* in the second a *boat:* and the care of the poet is to keep his *horse* or his *boat* from *singing.*

The next composition is the far-famed *Campaign,* which Dr. Wharton has termed a "Gazette in Rhyme," with harshness not often used by the good nature of his criticism. Before a censure so severe is admitted, let us consider that War is a frequent subject of Poetry, and then inquire who has described it with more justness and force. Many of our own writers tried their powers upon this year of victory: yet Addison's is confessedly the best performance; his poem is the work of a man not blinded by the dust of learning; his images are not borrowed merely from books. The superiority which he confers upon his hero is not personal prowess, and "mighty bone," but deliberate intrepidity, a calm command of his passions, and the power of consulting his own mind in the midst of danger. The rejection and contempt of fiction is rational and manly.

It may be observed that the last line is imitated by Pope:

> Marlb'rough's exploits appear divinely bright—
> Rais'd of themselves their genuine charms they boast,
> And those who paint them truest, praise them most.

This Pope had in his thoughts; but, not knowing how to use what was not his own, he spoiled the thought when he had borrowed it:

> The well-sung woes will soothe my pensive ghost;
> He best can paint them who shall feel them most.

Martial exploits may be *painted;* perhaps *woes* may be *painted;* but they are surely not *painted* by being *well sung:* it is not easy to paint in song, or to sing in colours.

No passage in the *Campaign* has been more often mentioned than the simile of the Angel, which is said in *The Tatler* to be "one of the noblest thoughts that ever entered into the heart of man," and is therefore worthy of attentive consideration. Let it be first inquired whether it be a simile. A poetical simile is the discovery of likeness between two actions, in their general nature dissimilar, or of causes terminating by different operations in some resemblance of effect. But the mention of another like consequence from a like cause, or of a like performance by a like agency, is not a simile, but an exemplification. It is not a simile to say that the Thames waters fields, as the Po waters fields; or that as Hecla vomits flames in Iceland, so Ætna vomits flames in Sicily. When Horace says of Pindar, that he pours his violence and rapidity of verse, as a river swoln with rain rushes from the mountain; or of himself, that his genius wanders in quest of poetical decorations, as the bee wanders to collect honey; he, in either case, produces a simile; the mind is impressed with the resemblance of things generally unlike, as unlike as intellect and body. But if Pindar had been described as writing with the copiousness and grandeur of Homer, or Horace had told that he reviewed and finished his own poetry with the same care as Isocrates polished his orations, instead of similitude, he would have exhibited almost identity; he would have given the same portraits with different names. In the poem now examined, when the English are represented as gaining a fortified pass by repetition of attack and perseverance of resolution, their obstinacy of courage and vigour of onset is well illustrated by the sea that breaks, with incessant battery, the dikes of Holland. This is a simile; but when Addison, having celebrated the beauty of Marlborough's person, tells us that "Achilles thus was formed with every grace," here is no simile, but a mere exemplification. A simile may be compared to lines converging at a point, and is more excellent as the lines approach from greater distance: an exemplification may be considered as two parallel lines, which run on together without approximation, never far separated, and never joined.

Marlborough is so like the angel in the poem, that the action of both is almost the same, and performed by both in the same manner. Marlborough "teaches the battle to rage"; the angel "directs the storm": Marlborough is "unmoved in peaceful thought"; the angel is "calm and serene": Marlborough stands "unmoved amidst the shock of hosts"; the angel rides "calm in the whirlwind." The lines on Marlborough are just and noble; but the simile gives almost the same images a second time.

But perhaps this thought, though hardly a simile, was remote from vulgar conceptions, and required great labour of research or dexterity of application. Of this Dr. Madden, a name which Ireland ought to honour, once gave me his opinion. "If I had set," said he, "ten school-boys to write on the battle of Blenheim, and eight had brought me the Angel, I should not have been surprised."

The opera of *Rosamond*, though it is seldom mentioned, is one of the first of Addison's compositions. The subject is well chosen, the fiction is pleasing, and the praise of Marlborough, for which the scene gives an opportunity, is, what perhaps every human excellence must be, the product of good luck, improved by genius. The thoughts are sometimes great, and sometimes tender; the versification is easy and gay. There is doubtless some advantage in the shortness of the lines, which there is little temptation to load with expletive epithets. The dialogue seems commonly better than the songs. The two comic characters of Sir Trusty and Grideline, though of no great value, are yet such as the poet intended. Sir Trusty's account of the death of Rosamond is, I think, too grossly absurd. The whole drama is airy and elegant, engaging in its process, and pleasing in its conclusion. If Addison had cultivated the lighter parts of poetry, he would probably have excelled.

The tragedy of *Cato*, which, contrary to the rule observed in selecting the works of other poets, has by the weight of its character forced its way into the late collection, is unquestionably the noblest production of Addison's genius. Of a work so much read, it is difficult to say anything new. About things on which the public thinks long, it commonly attains to think right; and of *Cato* it has been not unjustly determined that it is rather a poem in dialogue than a drama, rather a succession of just sentiments in elegant language than a representation of natural affections, or of any state probable or possible in human life. Nothing here "excites or assuages emotion": here is "no magical power of raising fantastic terror or wild anxiety." The events are expected without solicitude, and are remembered without joy or sorrow. Of the agents we have no care; we consider not what they are doing, or what they are suffering; we wish only to know what they have to say. Cato is a being above our solicitude; a man of whom the gods take care, and whom we leave to their care with heedless confidence. To the rest neither gods nor men can have much attention, for there is not one amongst them that strongly attracts either affection or esteem. But they are made the vehicles of such sentiments and such expression that there is scarcely a scene in the play which the reader does not wish to impress upon his memory.

When *Cato* was shown to Pope, he advised the author to print it, without any theatrical exhibition, supposing that it would be read more favourably than heard. Addison declared himself of the same opinion, but urged the importunity of his friends for its appearance on the stage. The emulation of parties made it successful beyond expectation, and its success has introduced or confirmed among us the use of dialogue too declamatory, of unaffecting elegance, and chill philosophy.

The universality of applause, however it might quell the censure of common mortals, had no other effect than to harden Dennis in fixed dislike, but his dislike was not merely capricious. He found and showed many faults: he showed them indeed with anger, but he found them with acuteness, such as ought to rescue his criticism from oblivion, though at last it will have no other life than it derives from the work which it endeavours to oppress.

Why he pays no regard to the opinion of the audience he gives his reason, by remarking that:

"A deference is to be paid to a general applause, when it appears that the applause is natural and spontaneous; but that little regard is to be had to it when it is affected and artificial. Of all the tragedies which in his memory have had vast and violent runs, not one has been excellent, few have been tolerable, most have been scandalous. When a poet writes a tragedy, who knows he has judgment, and who feels he has genius, that poet presumes upon his own merit, and scorns to make a cabal; that people come coolly to the representation of such a tragedy without any violent expectation or delusive imagination, or invincible prepossession; that such an audience is liable to receive the impressions which the poem shall naturally make on them, and to judge by their own reason and their own judgments, and that reason and judgment are calm and serene, not formed by nature to make proselytes and to control and lord it over the imaginations of others. But that when an author writes a tragedy, who knows he has neither genius nor judgment, he has recourse to the making a party, and he endeavours to make up in industry what is wanting in talent, and to supply by poetical craft the absence of poetical art; that such an author is humbly contented to raise men's passions by a plot without doors, since he despairs of doing it by that which he brings upon the stage. That party, and passion, and prepossession are clamorous and tumultuous things, and so much the more clamorous and tumultuous by how much the more erroneous; that they domineer and tyrannise over the imaginations of persons who want judgment, and sometimes too, of those who have it, and, like a fierce and outrageous torrent, bear down all opposition before them."

He then condemns the neglect of poetical justice, which is always one of his favourite principles.

" 'Tis certainly the duty of every tragic poet, by an exact distribution of a poetical justice, to imitate the Divine dispensation and to inculcate a particular Providence. 'Tis true, indeed, upon the stage of the world the wicked sometimes prosper and the guiltless suffer. But that is permitted by the Governor of the world to show, from the attribute of his infinite justice, that there is a compensation in futurity, to prove the immortality of the human soul, and the certainty of future rewards and punishments. But the poetical persons in tragedy exist no longer than the reading or the representation; the whole extent of their entity is circumscribed by those; and therefore, during that reading or representation, according to their merits or demerits they must be punished or rewarded.

If this is not done, there is no impartial distribution of poetical justice, no instructive lecture of a particular Providence, and no imitation of the Divine dispensation. And yet the author of this tragedy does not only run counter to this in the fate of his principal character, but everywhere throughout it makes virtue suffer and vice triumph: for not only Cato is vanquished by Cæsar, but the treachery and perfidiousness of Syphax prevail over the honest simplicity and the credulity of Juba, and the sly subtlety and dissimulation of Portius over the generous frankness and open-heartedness of Marcus."—p. 16.

Whatever pleasure there may be in seeing crimes punished and virtue rewarded, yet, since wickedness often prospers in real life, the poet is certainly at liberty to give it prosperity on the stage. For if poetry has an imitation of reality, how are its laws broken by exhibiting the world in its true form? The stage may sometimes gratify our wishes, but, if it be truly the *"mirror of life,"* it ought to show us sometimes what we are to expect.

Dennis objects to the characters, that they are not natural or reasonable; but as heroes and heroines are not beings that are seen every day, it is hard to find upon what principles their conduct shall be tried. It is, however, not useless to consider what he says of the manner in which Cato receives the account of his son's death.

"Nor is the grief of Cato, in the fourth act, one jot more in nature than that of his son and Lucia in the third. Cato receives the news of his son's death not only with dry eyes, but with a sort of satisfaction, and in the same page sheds tears for the calamity of his country, and does the same thing in the next page upon the bare apprehension of the danger of his friends. Now, since the love of one's country is the love of one's countrymen, as I have shown upon another occasion, I desire to ask these questions: Of all our countrymen, which do we love most, those whom we know, or those whom we know not? And of those whom we know, which do we cherish most, our friends or our enemies? And of our friends, which are the dearest to us, those who are related to us, or those who are not? And of all our relations, for which have we most tenderness, for those who are near to us, or for those who are remote? And of our near relations, which are the nearest, and consequently the dearest to us, our offspring or others? Our offspring, most certainly; as Nature, or in other words Providence, has wisely contrived for the preservation of mankind. Now, does it not follow, from what has been said, that for a man to receive the news of his son's death with dry eyes, and to weep at the same time for the calamities of his country, is a wretched affectation and a miserable inconsistency? Is not that, in plain English, to receive with dry eyes the news of the deaths of those for whose sake our country is a name so dear to us, and at the same time to shed tears for those for whose sakes our country is not a name so dear to us?"—p. 39.

But this formidable assailant is less resistible when he attacks the probability of the action and the reasonableness of the plan. Every critical reader must remark that Addison has, with a scrupulosity almost unexampled on the English stage, confined himself in time to a single day, and in place to rigorous unity. The scene never changes, and the whole action of the play passes in the great hall of Cato's house at Utica. Much, therefore, is done in the hall for which any other place had been more fit, and this impropriety affords Dennis many hints of merriment and opportunities of triumph. The passage is long; but as such disquisitions are not common, and the objections are skilfully formed and vigorously urged, those who delight in critical controversy will not think it tedious.

"Upon the departure of Portius, Sempronius makes but one soliloquy, and immediately in comes Syphax, and then the two politicians are at it immediately. They lay their heads together, with their snuff-boxes in their hands, as Mr. Bayes has it, and feague it away. But, in the midst of that wise scene, Syphax seems to give a seasonable caution to Sempronius:

'*Syph.* But is it true, Sempronius, that your Senate
        Is call'd together? Gods! thou must be cautious;
        Cato has piercing eyes.'

"There is a great deal of caution shown, indeed, in meeting in a governor's own hall, to carry on their plot against him. Whatever opinion they have of his eyes, I suppose they had none of his ears, or they would never have talked at this foolish rate so near him:

> Gods! thou must be cautious.

Oh! yes, very cautious; for if Cato should overhear you, and turn you off for politicians, Cæsar would never take you; no, Cæsar would never take you."—p. 44. . . .

"When Cato, in the 23rd page, Act II., turns the senators out of the hall, upon pretence of acquainting Juba with the result of their debates, he appears to me to do a thing which is neither reasonable nor civil. Juba might certainly have better been made acquainted with the result of that debate in some private apartment of the palace. But the poet was driven upon this absurdity to make way for another, and that is, to give Juba an opportunity to demand Marcia of her father. But the quarrel and rage of Juba and Syphax, in the same act; the invectives of Syphax against the Romans and Cato; the advice that he gives Juba, in her father's hall, to bear away Marcia by force; and his brutal and clamorous rage upon his refusal, and at a time when Cato was scarce out of sight, and perhaps not out of hearing, at least some of his guards or domestics must necessarily be supposed to be within hearing; is a thing that is so far from being probable that it is hardly possible."—p. 45.

"Sempronius, in the second act, comes back once more in the same morning to the governor's hall, to carry on the conspiracy with Syphax against the governor, his country, and his family; which is so stupid that it is below the wisdom of the O——s, the Macs, and the Teagues; even Eustace Commins himself would never have gone to Justice-hall to have conspired against the Government. If any officers at Portsmouth should lay their heads together, in order to the carrying off J—— G——'s niece or daughter, would they meet in J—— G——'s hall to carry on that conspiracy? There would be no necessity for their meeting there, at least till they came to the execution of their plot, because there would be other places to meet in. There would be no probability that they should meet there, because there would be places more private and more commodious. Now there ought to be nothing in a tragical action but what is necessary or probable.

"But treason is not the only thing that is carried on in this hall. That, and love, and philosophy take their turns in it, without any manner of necessity or probability occasioned by the action, as duly and as regularly, without interrupting one another, as if there were a triple league between them, and a mutual agreement that each should give place to and make way for the other in a due and orderly succession.

"We now come to the *third act*. Sempronius, in this act, comes into the governor's hall, with the leaders of the mutiny; . . . but, as soon as Cato is gone, Sempronius, who but just before had acted like an unparalleled knave, discovers himself, like an egregious fool, to be an accomplice in the conspiracy:

> '*Semp.* Know, villains, when such paltry slaves presume
> To mix in treason, if the plot succeeds,
> They are thrown neglected by; but, if it fails,
> They're sure to die like dogs, as you shall do.
> Here, take these factious monsters, drag them forth
> To sudden death'—

"'Tis true, indeed, the second leader says there are none there but friends; but is that possible at such a juncture? Can a parcel of rogues attempt to assassinate the governor of a town of war, in his own house, in midday, and after they are discovered and defeated? Can there be none near them but friends? Is it not plain from these words of Sempronius,

> 'Here, take these factious monsters, drag them forth
> To sudden death'—

and from the entrance of the guards upon the word of command, that those guards were within ear-shot? Behold Sempronius then palpably discovered. How comes it to pass, then, that, instead of being hanged up with the rest, he remains secure in the governor's hall, and there carries on his conspiracy against the government, the third time in the same day, with his old comrade Syphax? who enters at the same time that the guards are carrying away the leaders, big with the news of the defeat of Sempronius, though where he had

his intelligence so soon is difficult to imagine. And now the
reader may expect a very extraordinary scene; there is not
abundance of spirit indeed, nor a great deal of passion, but
there is wisdom more than enough to supply all defects.

'*Syph*. Our first design, my friend, has prov'd abortive;
    Still there remains an after-game to play:
    My troops are mounted, their Numidian steeds
    Snuff up the winds, and long to scour the desert;
    Let but Sempronius lead us in our flight,
    We'll force the gate, where Marcus keeps his guard,
    And hew down all that would oppose our passage;
    A day will bring us into Cæsar's camp.
Semp. Confusion! I have fail'd of half my purpose;
    Marcia, the charming Marcia's left behind.'

Well! but though he tells us the half purpose he has failed of,
he does not tell us the half that he has carried. But what does
he mean by

'Marcia, the charming Marcia's left behind'?

He is now in her own house; and we have neither seen her nor
heard of her anywhere else since the play began. But now let
us hear Syphax:

'What hinders then, but that thou find her out,
    And hurry her away by manly force?'

But what does old Syphax mean by finding her out? They
talk as if she were as hard to be found as a hare in a frosty
morning.

'*Semp*. But how to gain admission?'

Oh! she is found out then, it seems. . . .

'But how to gain admission? for access
    Is giv'n to none but Juba and her brothers.'

But, raillery apart, why access to Juba? For he was owned
and received as a lover neither by the father nor by the daughter. Well! but let that pass. Syphax puts Sempronius out of

pain immediately, and, being a Numidian, abounding in wiles, supplies him with a stratagem for admission, that, I believe, is a nonpareil:

> '*Syph*. Thou shalt have Juba's dress, and Juba's guards;
> The doors will open when Numidia's prince
> Seems to appear before them.'

Sempronius is, it seems, to pass for Juba in full day at Cato's house, where they were both so very well known, by having Juba's dress and his guards; as if one of the marshals of France could pass for the Duke of Bavaria, at noon-day at Versailles, by having his dress and liveries. But how does Syphax pretend to help Sempronius to young Juba's dress? Does he serve him in a double capacity, as general and master of his wardrobe? But why Juba's guards? For the devil of any guards has Juba appeared with yet. Well! though this is a mighty politic invention, yet, methinks, they might have done without it; for, since the advice that Syphax gave to Sempronius was,

> 'To hurry her away by manly force,'

in my opinion the shortest and likeliest way of coming at the lady was by demolishing instead of putting on an impertinent disguise to circumvent two or three slaves. But Sempronius, it seems, is of another opinion. He extols to the skies the invention of old Syphax:

> '*Semp*. Heavens! what a thought was there!'

Now, I appeal to the reader if I have not been as good as my word. Did I not tell him that I would lay before him a very wise scene?"—p. 50.

"But now let us lay before the reader that part of the scenery of the fourth act, which may show the absurdities which the author has run into through the indiscreet observance of the unity of place. I do not remember that Aristotle has said anything expressly concerning the unity of place. 'Tis true, implicitly he has said enough in the rules which he has laid down for the chorus. For, by making the chorus an essential part of tragedy, and by bringing it on the stage immediately after the opening of the scene, and retaining it there till the very catastrophe, he has so determined and fixed the place of action that it was impossible for an author on the Grecian stage to break through that unity. I am of opinion that if a modern tragic poet can preserve the unity of place, without destroying the probability of the incidents, 'tis always best for him to do it, because, by the preservation of that unity, as we have taken notice above, he adds grace and cleanness and comeliness to the representation. But since there are no express rules about it, and we are under no compulsion to keep it, since we have no chorus as the Grecian poet had, if it cannot be preserved without rendering the greater part of the incidents unreasonable and absurd, and perhaps sometimes monstrous, 'tis certainly better to break it."—p. 51.

"And now comes bully Sempronius, comically accoutred and equipped with his Numidian dress and his Numidian guards. Let the reader attend to him with all his ears, for the words of the wise are precious:

'*Semp.* The deer is lodg'd—I've track'd her to her covert.'

"Now I would fain know why this deer is said to be lodged, since we have not heard one word, since the play began, of her being at all out of harbour: and if we consider the discourse with which she and Lucia begin the act, we have reason to believe that they had hardly been talking of such matters in the street. However, to pleasure Sempronius, let us suppose, for once, that the deer is lodged:

'The deer is lodg'd—I've track'd her to her covert.'

"If he had seen her in the open field, what occasion had he to track her, when he had so many Numidian dogs at his heels, which, with one halloo, he might have set upon her haunches? If he did not see her in the open field, how could he possibly track her? . . . If he had seen her in the street, why did he not set upon her in the street, since through the street she must be carried at last? Now here, instead of having his thoughts upon his business, and upon the present danger; instead of meditating and contriving how he shall pass with his mistress through the southern gate, where her brother Marcus is upon the guard, and where he would certainly prove an impediment to him, which is the Roman word for the *baggage*; instead of doing this, Sempronius is entertaining himself with whimsies:

> '*Semp.* How will the young Numidian rave to see
> His mistress lost! If aught could glad my soul,
> Beyond th' enjoyment of so bright a prize,
> 'Twould be to torture that young, gay barbarian.
> But hark! what noise? Death to my hopes! 'tis he,
> 'Tis Juba's self! There is but one way left!
> He must be murder'd, and a passage cut
> Through those his guards.'

"Pray, what are 'those his guards'? I thought at present, that Juba's guards had been Sempronius's tools, and had now been dangling after his heels."—p. 53.

"But now let us sum up all these absurdities together. Sempronius goes at noonday, in Juba's clothes, and with Juba's guards, to Cato's palace, in order to pass for Juba, in a place where they were both so very well known; he meets Juba there, and resolves to murder him with his own guards. Upon the guards appearing a little bashful, he threatens them:

> 'Hah! Dastards, do you tremble?
> Or act like men, or by yon azure heav'n!'

"But the guards still remaining restive, Sempronius himself attacks Juba, while each of the guards is representing Mr. Spectator's sign of the Gaper, awed, it seems, and terrified by Sempronius's threats. Juba kills Sempronius, and takes his own army prisoners, and carries them in triumph away to Cato. Now, I would fain know if any part of Mr. Bayes's tragedy is so full of absurdity as this?

"Upon hearing the clash of swords, Lucia and Marcia come in. The question is, why no men come in upon hearing the noise of swords in the governor's hall? Where was the governor himself? Where were his guards? Where were his servants? Such an attempt as this, so near the person of a governor of a place of war, was enough to alarm the whole garrison: and yet, for almost half an hour after Sempronius was killed, we find none of those appear who were the likeliest in the world to be alarmed; and the noise of swords is made to draw only two poor women thither, who were most certain to run away from it. Upon Lucia and Marcia's coming in, Lucia appears in all the symptoms of an hysterical gentlewoman:

> '*Luc.* Sure 'twas the clash of swords! My troubled heart
>   Is so cast down, and sunk amidst its sorrows,
>   It throbs with fear, and aches at every sound.'

"And immediately her old whimsy returns upon her.

> 'O Marcia, should thy brothers, for my sake—
>   I die away with horror at the thought.'

She fancies that there can be no cutting of throats but it must be for her. If this is tragical, I would fain know what is comical. Well! upon this they spy the body of Sempronius; and Marcia, deluded by the habit, it seems, takes him for Juba; for, says she,

> 'The face is muffled up within the garment.'

"Now, how a man could fight and fall with his face muffled up in his garment, is, I think, a little hard to conceive! Besides, Juba, before he killed him, knew him to be Sempronius. It was not by his garment that he knew this; it was by his face then: his face therefore was not muffled. Upon seeing this man with the muffled face, Marcia falls a-raving: and, owning her passion for the supposed defunct, begins to make his funeral oration. Upon which Juba enters listening, I suppose on tiptoe: for I cannot imagine how anyone can enter listening, in any other posture. I would fain know how it came to pass, that during all this time he had sent nobody, no, not so much as a candle-snuffer, to take away the dead body of Sempronius. Well! but let us regard him listening. Having left his apprehension behind him, he, at first, applies what Marcia says to Sempronius. But finding at last, with much ado, that he himself is the happy man, he quits his eaves-dropping, and discovers himself just time enough to prevent his being cuckolded by a dead man, of whom the moment before he had appeared so jealous; and greedily intercepts the bliss which was fondly designed for one who could not be the better for it. But here I must ask a question: how comes Juba to listen here, who had not listened before throughout the play? Or, how comes he to be the only person of this tragedy who listens, when love and treason were so often talked in so public a place as a hall? I am afraid the author was driven upon all these absurdities only to introduce this miserable mistake of Marcia, which, after all, is much below the dignity of tragedy, as anything is which is the effect or result of trick. . . .

"But let us come to the scenery of the *fifth* act. Cato appears first upon the scene, sitting in a thoughtful posture; in his hand Plato's treatise on the *Immortality of the Soul*, a drawn sword on the table by him. Now let us consider the place in which this sight is presented to us. The place, forsooth, is a large hall. Let us suppose that anyone should place himself in this posture in the midst of one of our halls in London; that he should appear *solus*, in a sullen posture, a drawn sword on the table by him; in his hand Plato's treatise on the *Immortality of the Soul*, translated lately by Bernard Lintot: I desire the reader to consider whether such a person as this would pass with them who beheld him for a great patriot, a great philosopher, or a general, or some whimsical person who fancied himself all these; and whether the people who belonged to the family would think that such a person had a design upon their midriffs or his own?

"In short, that Cato should sit long enough in the aforesaid posture, in the midst of this large hall, to read over Plato's treatise on the *Immortality of the Soul*, which is a lecture of two long hours; that he should propose to himself to be private there upon that occasion; that he should be angry with his son for intruding there; then, that he should leave this hall upon the pretence of sleep, give himself the mortal wound in his bed-chamber, and then be brought back into that hall to expire, purely to show his good breeding, and save his friends the trouble of coming up to his bed-chamber; all this appears to me to be improbable, incredible, impossible."—p. 56.

Such is the censure of Dennis. There is, as Dryden expresses it, perhaps "too much horse-play in his raillery"; but if his jests are coarse, his arguments are strong. Yet as we love better to be pleased than be taught, *Cato* is read, and the critic is neglected.

Flushed with consciousness of these detections of absurdity in the conduct, he afterwards attacked the sentiments of *Cato*; but he then amused himself with petty cavils and minute objections.

Of Addison's smaller poems, no particular mention is necessary; they have little that can employ or require a critic. The parallel of the princes and gods, in his verses to Kneller, is often happy, but is too well known to be quoted.

His translations, so far as I have compared them, want the exactness of a scholar. That he understood his authors cannot be doubted; but his versions will not teach others to understand them, being too licentiously paraphrastical. They are, however, for the most part, smooth and easy; and what is the first excellence of a translator, such as may be read with pleasure by those who do not know the originals.

His poetry is polished and pure; the product of a mind too judicious to commit faults, but not sufficiently vigorous to attain excellence. He has sometimes a striking line, or a shining paragraph; but in the whole he is warm rather than fervid, and shows more dexterity than strength. He was, however, one of our earliest examples of correctness.

The versification which he had learned from Dryden he debased rather than refined. His rhymes are often dissonant; in his *Georgic* he admits broken lines. He uses both triplets and Alexandrines, but triplets more frequently in his translation than his other works. The mere structure of verses seems never to have engaged much of his care. But his lines are very smooth in *Rosamond*, and too smooth in *Cato*.

Addison is now to be considered as a critic; a name which the present generation is scarcely willing to allow him. His criticism is condemned as tentative or experimental, rather than scientific; and he is considered as deciding by taste rather than by principles.

It is not uncommon for those who have grown wise by the labour of others, to add a little of their own, and overlook their masters. Addison is now despised by some who perhaps would never have seen his defects but by the lights which he afforded them. That he always wrote as he would think it necessary to write now, cannot be affirmed; his instructions were such as the characters of his readers made proper. That general knowledge which now circulates in common talk, was in his time rarely to be found. Men not professing learning were not ashamed of ignorance; and, in the female world, any acquaintance with books was distinguished only to be censured. His purpose was to infuse literary curiosity by gentle and unsuspected conveyance into the gay, the idle, and the wealthy: he therefore presented knowledge in the most alluring form, not lofty and austere, but accessible and familiar. When he showed them their defects, he showed them likewise that they might be easily supplied. His attempt succeeded; inquiry was awakened, and comprehension expanded. An emulation of intellectual elegance was excited, and from this time to our own, life has been gradually exalted, and conversation purified and enlarged.

Dryden had, not many years before, scattered criticism over his prefaces with very little parsimony; but though he sometimes condescended to be somewhat familiar, his manner was in general too scholastic for those who had yet their rudiments to learn, and found it not easy to understand their master. His observations were framed rather for those that were learning to write, than for those that read only to talk.

An instructor like Addison was now wanting, whose remarks being superficial might be easily understood, and being just might prepare the mind for more attainments. Had he presented *Paradise Lost* to the public with all the pomp of system and severity of science, the criticism would perhaps have been admired, and the poem still have been neglected; but by the blandishments of gentleness and facility, he has made Milton an universal favourite, with whom readers of every class think it necessary to be pleased.

He descended now and then to lower disquisitions; and by a serious display of the beauties of *Chevy-Chase* exposed himself to the ridicule of Wagstaff, who bestowed a like pompous character on *Tom Thumb*; and to the contempt of Dennis, who, considering the fundamental position of his criticism, that *Chevy-Chase* pleases, and ought to please, because it is natural, observes, "that there is a way of deviating from nature, by bombast or tumour, which soars above nature, and enlarges images beyond their real bulk; by affectation, which forsakes nature in quest of something unsuitable; and by imbecility, which degrades nature by faintness and diminution, by obscuring its appearances, and weakening its effects." In *Chevy-Chase* there is not much of either bombast or affectation, but there is chill and lifeless imbecility. The story cannot possibly be told in a manner that shall make less impression on the mind.

Before the profound observers of the present race repose too securely on the consciousness of their superiority to Addison, let them consider his *Remarks on Ovid*, in which may be found specimens of criticism sufficiently subtle and refined; let them peruse likewise his essays on Wit, and on the Pleasures of Imagination, in which he founds art on the base of nature, and draws the principles of invention from dispositions inherent in the mind of man with skill and elegance, such as his contemners will not easily attain.

As a describer of life and manners, he must be allowed to stand perhaps the first of the first rank. His humour, which, as Steele observes, is peculiar to himself, is so happily diffused as to give the grace of novelty to domestic scenes and daily occurrences. He never "outsteps the modesty of nature," nor raises merriment or wonder by the violation of truth. His figures neither divert by distortion, nor amaze by aggravation. He copies life with so much fidelity, that he can be hardly said to invent; yet his exhibitions have an air so much original, that it is difficult to suppose them not merely the product of imagination.

As a teacher of wisdom, he may be confidently followed. His religion has nothing in it enthusiastic or superstitious: he appears neither weakly credulous, nor wantonly sceptical; his morality is neither dangerously lax, nor impracticably rigid. All the enchantment of fancy, and all the cogency of argument, are employed to recommend to the reader his real interest, the care of pleasing the Author of his being. Truth is shown sometimes as the phantom of a vision; sometimes appears half veiled in an allegory; sometimes attracts regard in the robes of fancy; and sometimes steps forth in the confidence of reason. She wears a thousand dresses, and in all is pleasing.

Mille habet ornatus, mille decenter habet.

His prose is the model of the middle style; on grave subjects not formal, on light occasions not grovelling; pure without scrupulosity, and exact without apparent elaboration; always equable, and always easy, without glowing words or pointed sentences. Addison never deviates from his track to snatch a grace; he seeks no ambitious ornaments, and tries no hazardous innovations. His page is always luminous, but never blazes in unexpected splendour.

It was apparently his principal endeavour to avoid all harshness and severity of diction; he is therefore sometimes verbose in his transitions and connections, and sometimes descends too much to the language of conversation; yet if his language had been less idiomatical, it might have lost somewhat of its genuine Anglicism. What he attempted, he performed: he is never feeble, and he did not wish to be energetic; he is never rapid, and he never stagnates. His sentences have neither studied amplitude, nor affected brevity; his periods, though not diligently rounded, are voluble and easy. Whoever wishes to attain an English style, familiar but not coarse, and elegant but not ostentatious, must give his days and nights to the volumes of Addison.

JOHN HUGHES

1677 — 1719-20

Born at Marlborough in Wiltshire—Educated at a Private School—Early Appearance as a Poet—Addison's Opinion of his Talent—Joins in a Translation of Lucan —Writes *The Siege of Damascus*, a Tragedy—Death and Character.

John Hughes, the son of a citizen in London, and of Anne Burgess, of an ancient family in Wiltshire, was born at Marlborough, January 29, 1677. He was educated at a private school; and though his advances in literature are, in the *Biographia*, very ostentatiously displayed, the name of his master is somewhat ungratefully concealed.

At nineteen he drew the plan of a tragedy; and paraphrased, rather too profusely, the ode of Horace which begins "Integer Vitæ." To poetry he added the science of music, in which he seems to have attained considerable skill, together with the practice of design, or rudiments of painting.

His studies did not withdraw him wholly from business, nor did business hinder him from study. He had a place in the office of Ordnance; and was secretary to several commissions for purchasing lands necessary to secure the royal docks at Chatham and Portsmouth; yet found time to acquaint himself with modern languages.

In 1697 he published a poem on the *Peace of Ryswick*; and in 1699 another piece called *The Court of Neptune*, on the return of King William, which he addressed to Mr. Montague, the general patron of the followers of the Muses. The same year he produced a song on the Duke of Gloucester's birthday.

He did not confine himself to poetry, but cultivated other kinds of writing with great success; and about this time showed his knowledge of human nature by an *Essay on the Pleasure of being deceived*. In 1702 he published, on the death of King William, a Pindaric ode, called *The House of Nassau*; and wrote another paraphrase on the *Otium Divos* of Horace.

In 1703 his *Ode on Music* was performed at Stationers' Hall; and he wrote afterwards six cantatas, which were set to music by the greatest master of that time, and seem intended to oppose or exclude the Italian opera, an exotic and irrational entertainment, which has been always combated, and always has prevailed.

His reputation was now so far advanced, that the public began to pay reverence to his name; and he was solicited to prefix a Preface to the translation of Boccalini, a writer whose satirical vein cost him his life in Italy; but who never, I believe, found many readers in this country, even though introduced by such powerful recommendation.

He translated Fontenelle's *Dialogues of the Dead*; and his version was perhaps read at that time, but is now neglected; for by a book not necessary, and owing its reputation wholly to its turn of diction, little notice can be gained but from those who can enjoy the graces of the original. To the Dialogues of Fontenelle he added two composed by himself; and, though not only an honest but a pious man, dedicated his work to the Earl of Wharton. He judged skilfully enough of his own interest; for Wharton, when he went [1709] Lord Lieutenant to Ireland, offered to take Hughes with him, and establish him; but Hughes, having hopes or promises from another man in power, of some provision more suitable to his inclination, declined Wharton's offer, and obtained nothing from the other.

He translated the *Miser* of Molière, which he never offered to the stage; and occasionally amused himself with making versions of favourite scenes in other plays.

Being now received as a wit among the wits, he paid his contributions to literary undertakings, and assisted both the

Tatler, Spectator, and *Guardian.* In 1712 he translated Vertot's *History of the Revolution of Portugal;* produced an *Ode to the Creator of the World, from the Fragments of Orpheus;* and brought upon the stage an opera called *Calypso and Telemachus,* intended to show that the English language might be very happily adapted to music. This was impudently opposed by those who were employed in the Italian opera; and what cannot be told without indignation, the intruders had such interest with the Duke of Shrewsbury, then Lord Chamberlain, who had married an Italian, as to obtain an obstruction of the profits, though not an inhibition of the performance.

There was at this time a project formed by Tonson for a translation of the *Pharsalia,* by several hands; and Hughes Englished the tenth book. But this design, as must often happen where the concurrence of many is necessary, fell to the ground; and the whole work was afterwards performed by Rowe.

His acquaintance with the great writers of his time appears to have been very general; but of his intimacy with Addison there is a remarkable proof. It is told on good authority, that *Cato* was finished and played by his persuasion. It had long wanted the last act, which he was desired by Addison to supply. If the request was sincere, it proceeded from an opinion, whatever it was, that did not last long; for when Hughes came in a week to show him his first attempt, he found half an act written by Addison himself.

He afterwards [1715] published the works of Spenser, with his Life, a Glossary, and a Discourse on Allegorical Poetry; a work for which he was well qualified as a judge of the beauties of writing, but perhaps wanted an antiquary's knowledge of the obsolete words. He did not much revive the curiosity of the public; for near thirty years elapsed before his edition was reprinted. The same year produced his *Apollo and Daphne,* of which the success was very earnestly promoted by Steele, who, when the rage of party did not misguide him, seems to have been a man of boundless benevolence.

Hughes had hitherto suffered the mortifications of a narrow fortune; but in 1717, the Lord Chancellor Cowper set him at ease, by making him Secretary to the Commissions of the Peace, in which he afterwards, by a particular request, desired his successor Lord Parker to continue him. He had now affluence; but such is human life, that he had it when his declining health could neither allow him long possession, nor quick enjoyment.

His last work was his tragedy, *The Siege of Damascus*, after which *a Siege* became a popular title. This play, which still continues on the stage, and of which it is unnecessary to add a private voice to such continuance of approbation, is not acted or printed according to the author's original draught, or his settled mention. He had made Phocyas apostatise from his religion; after which the abhorrence of Eudocia would have been reasonable, his misery would have been just, and the horrors of his repentance exemplary. The players, however, required that the guilt of Phocyas should terminate in desertion to the enemy; and Hughes, unwilling that his relations should lose the benefit of his work, complied with the alteration.

He was now weak with a lingering consumption, and not able to attend the rehearsal, yet was so vigorous in his faculties, that only ten days before his death he wrote the dedication to his patron Lord Cowper. On February 17, 1719–20, the play was represented, and the author died. He lived to hear that it was well received; but paid no regard to the intelligence, being then wholly employed in the meditations of a departing Christian.

A man of his character was undoubtedly regretted; and Steele devoted an essay, in the paper called *The Theatre* [No. 15], to the memory of his virtues. His Life is written in the *Biographia* with some degree of favourable partiality; and an account of him is prefixed to his works, by his relation [brother-in-law] the late Mr. Duncombe, a man whose blameless elegance deserved the same respect.

The character of his genius I shall transcribe from the correspondence of Swift and Pope.

"A month ago," says Swift, "was sent me over, by a friend of mine, the works of John Hughes, Esquire. They are in prose and verse. I never heard of the man in my life, yet I find your name as a subscriber. He is too grave a poet for me; and I think among the Mediocribus in prose as well as verse."

To this Pope returns: "To answer your question as to Mr. Hughes: what he wanted as to genius, he made up as an honest man; but he was of the class you think him."

In Spence's *Collections* Pope is made to speak of him with still less respect, as having no claim to poetical reputation but from his tragedy.

JOHN SHEFFIELD
DUKE OF BUCKINGHAMSHIRE
1649—1720-21

Birth and Self-education—Summoned to Parliament—
Serves at Sea against the Dutch—Made Colonel of the
Grenadiers and K.G.—His Conduct at the Revolution—
Favours Lord Oxford's Administration—His three Wives
—Death and Burial in Westminster Abbey—Works and
Character.

John Sheffield, descended from a long series of illustrious
ancestors, was born in 1649, the son of Edmund [second]
Earl of Mulgrave, who died in 1658. The young Lord was put
into the hands of a tutor with whom he was so little satisfied,
that he got rid of him in a short time, and at an age not
exceeding twelve years resolved to educate himself. Such a
purpose, formed at such an age, and successfully prosecuted,
delights as it is strange, and instructs as it is real.

His literary acquisitions are more wonderful, as those years
in which they are commonly made were spent by him in the
tumult of a military life, or the gaiety of a court. When war
was declared against the Dutch, he went at seventeen on board
the ship in which Prince Rupert and the Duke of Albemarle
sailed, with the command of the fleet; but by contrariety of
winds they were restrained from action. His zeal for the King's
service was recompensed by the command of one of the independent troops of horse, then raised to protect the coast.

Next year he received a summons to Parliament, which, as
he was then but eighteen years old, the Earl of Northumberland censured as at least indecent, and his objection was allowed. He had a quarrel with the Earl of Rochester, which he

has perhaps too ostentatiously related, as Rochester's surviving
daughter, the Lady Sandwich, is said to have told him with
very sharp reproaches.

When another Dutch war (1672) broke out, he went again
a volunteer in the ship which the celebrated Lord Ossory commanded, and there made, as he relates, two curious remarks:

"I have observed two things, which I dare affirm, though
not generally believed. One was, that the wind of a cannon-
bullet, though flying never so near, is incapable of doing the
least harm; and indeed, were it otherwise, no man above deck
would escape. The other was, that a great shot may be sometimes avoided, even as it flies, by changing one's ground a
little; for, when the wind sometimes blew away the smoke, it
was so clear a sunshiny day, that we could easily perceive the
bullets (that were half-spent) fall into the water, and from
thence bound up again among us, which gives sufficient time
for making a step or two on any side; though, in so swift a
motion, 'tis hard to judge well in what line the bullet comes,
which, if mistaken, may by removing cost a man his life, instead of saving it."

His behaviour was so favourably represented by Lord Ossory, that he was advanced to the command of the *Katherine*,
the best second-rate ship in the navy.

He afterwards raised a regiment of foot, and commanded
it as colonel. The land-forces were sent ashore by Prince Rupert; and he lived in the camp very familiarly with Schomberg.
He was then appointed colonel of the old Holland regiment,
together with his own, and had the promise of a Garter, which
he obtained [April 23, 1674] in his twenty-fifth year. He was
likewise made gentleman of the bed-chamber.

He afterwards went into the French service, to learn the art
of war under Turenne, but stayed only a short time. Being by
the Duke of Monmouth opposed in his pretensions to the first
troop of foot-guards, he, in return, made Monmouth suspected
by the Duke of York. He was not long after, when the unlucky
Monmouth fell into disgrace, recompensed with the lieutenancy of Yorkshire and the government of Hull.

Thus rapidly did he make his way both to military and civil
honours and employments; yet, busy as he was, he did not

neglect his studies, but at least cultivated poetry; in which he must have been early considered as uncommonly skilful, if it be true which is reported, that, when he was yet not twenty years old, his recommendation advanced Dryden to the laurel.

The Moors having besieged Tangier, he was sent (June 13, 1680) with 2000 men to its relief. A strange story is told of danger to which he was intentionally exposed in a leaky ship, to gratify some resentful jealousy of the King, whose health he therefore would never permit at his table till he saw himself in a safer place. His voyage was prosperously performed in three weeks, and the Moors without a contest retired before him.

In this voyage he composed the *Vision*; a licentious poem, such as was fashionable in those times, with little power of invention or propriety of sentiment.

At his return he found the King kind, who perhaps had never been angry; and he continued a wit and a courtier as before.

At the succession of King James, to whom he was intimately known and by whom he thought himself beloved, he naturally expected still brighter sunshine; but all know how soon that reign began to gather clouds. His expectations were not disappointed; he was immediately admitted into the privy-council and made Lord Chamberlain. He accepted a place in the High Commission, without knowledge, as he declared after the Revolution, of its illegality. Having few religious scruples, he attended the King to mass, and kneeled with the rest; but had no disposition to receive the Romish faith, or to force it upon others; for when the priests, encouraged by his appearances of compliance, attempted to convert him, he told them, as Burnet has recorded, that he was willing to receive instruction, and that he had taken much pains to believe in God who made the world and all men in it; but that he should not be easily persuaded *that man was quits, and made God again.*

A pointed sentence is bestowed by successive transmission on the last whom it will fit; this censure of transubstantiation, whatever be its value, was uttered long ago by Anne Askew, one of the first sufferers for the Protestant religion, who in the time of Henry VIII. was tortured in the Tower; concerning which there is reason to wonder that it was not known to the historian of the Reformation.

In the Revolution he acquiesced, though he did not promote it. There was once a design of associating him in the invitation of the Prince of Orange; but the Earl of Shrewsbury discouraged the attempt, by declaring that Mulgrave would never concur. This King William afterwards told him, and asked what he would have done if the proposal had been made? "Sir," said he, "I would have discovered it to the king whom I then served." To which King William replied, "I cannot blame you."

Finding King James irremediably excluded, he voted for the conjunctive sovereignty, upon this principle, that he thought the titles of the Prince and his consort equal, and it would please the Prince their protector to have a share in the sovereignty. This vote gratified King William; yet, either by the King's distrust, or his own discontent, he lived some years without employment. He looked on the King with malevolence, and, if his verses or his prose may be credited, with contempt. He was, notwithstanding this aversion or indifference, made Marquis of Normanby (1694), but still opposed the Court on some important questions; yet at last he was received into the cabinet council, with a pension of 3000*l.*

At the accession of Queen Anne, whom he is said to have courted when they were both young, he was highly favoured. Before her coronation (1702) she made him Lord Privy Seal, and soon after Lord Lieutenant of the North Riding of Yorkshire. He was then named Commissioner for treating with the Scots about the Union; and was made next year, first, Duke of Normanby, and then of Buckinghamshire, there being suspected to be somewhere a latent claim to the title of Buckingham.

Soon after, becoming jealous of the Duke of Marlborough, he resigned the Privy Seal, and joined the discontented Tories in a motion extremely offensive to the Queen, for inviting the Princess Sophia to England. The Queen courted him back with an offer no less than that of the Chancellorship; which he refused. He now retired from business, and built (1703) that house in the Park which is now the Queen's, upon ground granted by the Crown.

When the ministry was changed (1710), he was made Lord Chamberlain of the Household, and concurred in all transactions of that time, except that he endeavoured to protect the Catalans. After the Queen's death [1714] he became a constant opponent of the Court; and, having no public business, is supposed to have amused himself by writing his two tragedies. He died February 24, 1720–21.

He was thrice married: by his two first wives he had no children; by his third, who was the daughter of King James by the Countess of Dorchester [d. 1717], and the widow of the Earl of Anglesea, he had, besides other children that died early, a son born in 1716, who died in 1735, and put an end to the line of Sheffield. It is observable, that the Duke's three wives were all widows. The Duchess died in 1742.

His character is not to be proposed as worthy of imitation. His religion he may be supposed to have learned from Hobbes; and his morality was such as naturally proceeds from loose opinions. His sentiments with respect to women he picked up in the Court of Charles; and his principles concerning property were such as a gaming-table supplies. He was censured as covetous, and has been defended by an instance of inattention to his affairs, as if a man might not at once be corrupted by avarice and idleness. He is said, however, to have had much tenderness, and to have been very ready to apologise for his violences of passion.

He is introduced into this collection only as a poet; and, if we credit the testimony of his contemporaries, he was a poet of no vulgar rank. But favour and flattery are now at an end; criticism is no longer softened by his bounties, or awed by his splendour, and, being able to take a more steady view, discovers him to be a writer that sometimes glimmers, but rarely shines, feebly laborious, and at best but pretty. His songs are upon common topics; he hopes, and grieves, and repents, and despairs, and rejoices, like any other maker of little stanzas; to be great, he hardly tries; to be gay, is hardly in his power.

In the *Essay on Satire* he was always supposed to have had the help of Dryden. His *Essay on Poetry* is the great work for which he was praised by Roscommon, Dryden, and Pope, and doubtless by many more whose eulogies have perished.

Upon this piece he appears to have set a high value; for he was all his lifetime improving it by successive revisals, so that there is scarcely any poem to be found of which the last edition differs more from the first. Amongst other changes, mention is made of some compositions of Dryden, which were written after the first appearance of the Essay.

At the time when this work first appeared, Milton's fame was not yet fully established, and therefore Tasso and Spenser were set before him. The two last lines were these. The Epic Poet, says he,

Must above Milton's lofty flights prevail,
Succeed where great Torquato and where greater Spenser fail.

The last line in succeeding editions was shortened, and the order of names continued; but now Milton is at last advanced to the highest place, and the passage thus adjusted:

Must above Tasso's lofty flights prevail,
Succeed where Spenser, and ev'n Milton fail.

Amendments are seldom made without some token of a rent: *lofty* does not suit Tasso so well as Milton.

One celebrated line seems to be borrowed. The Essay calls a perfect character

A faultless monster which the world ne'er saw.

Scaliger, in his poems, terms Virgil *sine labe monstrum*. Sheffield can scarcely be supposed to have read Scaliger's poetry: perhaps he found the words in a quotation.

Of this Essay, which Dryden has exalted so highly, it may be justly said that the precepts are judicious, sometimes new, and often happily expressed; but there are, after all the emendations, many weak lines, and some strange appearances of negligence; as, when he gives the laws of elegy, he insists upon connection and coherence; without which, says he,

'Tis epigram, 'tis point, 'tis what you will;
But not an elegy, nor writ with skill,
No Panegyric, nor a Cooper's Hill.

Who would not suppose that Waller's *Panegyric* and Denham's *Cooper's Hill* were elegies?

His verses are often insipid; but his memoirs are lively and agreeable: he had the perspicuity and elegance of an historian, but not the fire and fancy of a poet.

MATTHEW PRIOR

1664–1721

Born at Wimborne, in Dorsetshire—Educated at Westminster and Cambridge—Patronised by the Earl of
Dorset—Joins Montague in a Satire on *The Hind and
Panther*—Made Secretary to the English Embassy at the
Hague, and a Gentleman of the Bed-chamber to William
III.—Made Secretary to the Embassy at the Treaty of
Ryswick, Under-Secretary of State, and a Commissioner
of Trade—Collects his Poems—His future Advancement
stopped by the meanness of his Birth and the Accession
of the House of Hanover—His Intimacy with Harley, Earl
of Oxford—Is taken into custody and examined before
the Privy Council—Released—Retires on his Cambridge
Fellowship—Publishes his Poems by subscription—His
Deafness—Death, Burial, and Monument in Westminster
Abbey—Works and Character.

Matthew Prior is one of those that have burst out from
an obscure original to great eminence. He was born July 21,
1664, according to some, at Wimborne, in Dorsetshire, of I
know not what parents; others say that he was the son of a
joiner of London: he was perhaps willing enough to leave his
birth unsettled, in hope, like Don Quixote, that the historian
of his actions might find him some illustrious alliance.

He is supposed to have fallen, by his father's death, into
the hands of his uncle, a vintner, near Charing-cross, who sent
him for some time to Dr. Busby, at Westminster; but, not
intending to give him any education beyond that of the
school, took him, when he was well advanced in literature, to

his own house, where the Earl of Dorset, celebrated for patronage of genius, found him by chance, as Burnet relates, reading Horace, and was so well pleased with his proficiency, that he undertook the care and cost of his academical education.

He entered his name in St. John's College, at Cambridge, in 1682, in his eighteenth year; and it may be reasonably supposed that he was distinguished among his contemporaries. He became a Bachelor, as is usual, in four years; and two years afterwards wrote the poem on the Deity, which stands first in his volume.

It is the established practice of that college to send every year to the Earl of Exeter some poems upon sacred subjects, in acknowledgment of a benefaction enjoyed by them from the bounty of his ancestor. On this occasion were those verses written, which, though nothing is said of their success, seem to have recommended him to some notice; for his praise of the Countess's music, and his lines on the famous picture of Seneca, afford reason for imagining that he was more or less conversant with that family.

The same year he published *The Country Mouse and the City Mouse*, to ridicule Dryden's *Hind and Panther*, in conjunction with Mr. Montague. There is a story of great pain suffered, and of tears shed, on this occasion, by Dryden, who thought it hard that "an old man should be so treated by those to whom he had always been civil." By tales like these is the envy raised by superior abilities every day gratified: when they are attacked, every one hopes to see them humbled; what is hoped is readily believed, and what is believed is confidently told. Dryden had been more accustomed to hostilities than that such enemies should break his quiet; and if we can suppose him vexed, it would be hard to deny him sense enough to conceal his uneasiness.

The Country Mouse and the City Mouse procured its authors more solid advantages than the pleasure of fretting Dryden; for they were both speedily preferred. Montague, indeed, obtained the first notice, with some degree of discontent, as it seems, in Prior, who probably knew that his own part of the performance was the best. He had not, however, much reason to complain; for he came to London and obtained such notice, that (in 1691) he was sent to the Congress at the Hague as secretary to the embassy. In this assembly of princes and nobles, to which Europe has perhaps scarcely seen anything equal, was formed the grand alliance against Lewis, which at last did not produce effects proportionate to the magnificence of the transaction.

The conduct of Prior, in this splendid initiation into public business, was so pleasing to King William, that he made him one of the gentlemen of his bed-chamber; and he is supposed to have passed some of the next years in the quiet cultivation of literature and poetry.

The death of Queen Mary (in 1695) produced a subject for all the writers: perhaps no funeral was ever so poetically attended. Dryden, indeed, as a man discountenanced and deprived, was silent; but scarcely any other maker of verses omitted to bring his tribute of tuneful sorrow. An emulation of elegy was universal. Maria's praise was not confined to the English language, but fills a great part of the *Musæ Anglicanæ*.

Prior, who was both a poet and a courtier, was too diligent to miss this opportunity of respect. He wrote a long ode, which was presented to the King, by whom it was not likely to be ever read.

In two years he was secretary to another embassy at the treaty of Ryswick (in 1697); and next year had the same office at the court of France, where he is said to have been considered with great distinction.

As he was one day surveying the apartments at Versailles, being shown the Victories of Lewis, painted by Le Brun, and asked whether the King of England's palace had any such decorations; "The monuments of my master's actions," said he, "are to be seen everywhere but in his own house." The pictures of Le Brun are not only in themselves sufficiently ostentatious, but were explained by inscriptions so arrogant, that Boileau and Racine thought it necessary to make them more simple.

He was in the following year at Loo with the King; from whom, after a long audience, he carried orders to England, and upon his arrival became Under-Secretary of State in the

Earl of Jersey's office; a post which he did not retain long, because Jersey was removed; but he was soon made Commissioner of Trade.

This year (1700) produced one of his longest and most splendid compositions, the *Carmen Seculare*, in which he exhausts all his powers of celebration. I mean not to accuse him of flattery: he probably thought all that he writ, and retained as much veracity as can be properly exacted from a poet professedly encomiastic. King William supplied copious materials for either verse or prose. His whole life had been action, and none ever denied him the resplendent qualities of steady resolution and personal courage. He was really in Prior's mind what he represents him in his verses; he considered him as a hero, and was accustomed to say, that he praised others in compliance with the fashion, but that in celebrating King William he followed his inclination. To Prior gratitude would dictate praise, which reason would not refuse.

Among the advantages to arise from the future years of William's reign, he mentions a *Society for useful Arts*, and among them

> Some that with care true eloquence shall teach,
> And to just idioms fix our doubtful speech;
> That from our writers distant realms may know
>   The thanks we to our Monarch owe,
> And schools profess our tongue through every land
> That has invok'd his aid, or bless'd his hand.

Tickell, in his *Prospect of Peace*, has the same hope of a new academy:

> In happy chains our daring language bound,
> Shall sport no more in arbitrary sound.

Whether the similitude of those passages which exhibit the same thought on the same occasion proceeded from accident or imitation, is not easy to determine. Tickell might have been impressed with his expectation by Swift's *Proposal for ascertaining the English Language*, then [1712] lately published.

In the parliament that met in 1701 he was chosen representative of East Grinstead. Perhaps it was about this time that he changed his party; for he voted for the impeachment of those Lords who had persuaded the King to the Partition Treaty, a treaty in which he had himself been ministerially employed.

A great part of Queen Anne's reign was a time of war, in which there was little employment for negotiators, and Prior had therefore leisure to make or to polish verses. When the Battle of Blenheim called forth all the versemen, Prior, among the rest, took care to show his delight in the increasing honour of his country by an Epistle to Boileau.

He published, soon afterwards, a volume of poems, with the encomiastic character of his deceased patron the Earl of Dorset: it began with the *College Exercise* and ended with the *Nut-brown Maid*.

The Battle of Ramillies soon afterwards (in 1706) excited him to another effort of poetry. On this occasion he had fewer or less formidable rivals; and it would be not easy to name any other composition produced by that event which is now remembered.

Everything has its day. Through the reigns of William and Anne no prosperous event passed undignified by poetry. In the last war [1757–1763], when France was disgraced and overpowered in every quarter of the globe, when Spain, coming to her assistance, only shared her calamities, and the name of an Englishman was reverenced through Europe, no poet was heard amidst the general acclamation; the fame of our counsellors and heroes was intrusted to the Gazetteer.

The nation in time grew weary of the war, and the Queen [Anne] grew weary of her ministers. The war was burdensome, and the ministers were insolent. Harley and his friends began to hope that they might, by driving the Whigs from court and from power, gratify at once the Queen and the people. There was now a call for writers who might convey intelligence of past abuses, and show the waste of public money, the unreasonable "Conduct of the Allies," the avarice of generals, the tyranny of minions, and the general danger of approaching ruin.

For this purpose a paper called *The Examiner* was periodically published, written, as it happened, by any wit of the party, and sometimes, as is said, by Mrs. Manley. Some are owned by Swift; and one, in ridicule of Garth's verses to Godolphin upon the loss of his place, was written by Prior, and answered by Addison, who appears to have known the author either by conjecture or intelligence.

The Tories, who were now in power, were in haste to end the war; and Prior, being recalled (1710) to his former employment of making treaties, was sent (July 1711) privately to Paris with propositions of peace. He was remembered at the French court; and returning in about a month, brought with him the Abbé Gaultier, and M. Mesnager, a minister from France, invested with full powers.

This transaction not being avowed, Mackay, the master of the Dover packet-boat, either zealously or officiously, seized Prior and his associates at Canterbury. It is easily supposed that they were soon released.

The negotiation was begun at Prior's house, where the Queen's ministers met Mesnager (September 20, 1711) and entered privately upon the great business. The importance of Prior appears from the mention made of him by St. John in his Letter to the Queen:

"My Lord Treasurer moved, and all my Lords were of the same opinion, that Mr. Prior should be added to those who are empowered to sign; the reason for which is, because he, having personally treated with Monsieur de Torcy, is the best witness we can produce of the sense in which the general preliminary engagements are entered into: besides which, as he is the best versed in matters of trade of all your Majesty's servants who have been trusted in this secret, if you shall think fit to employ him in the future treaty of commerce, it will be of consequence that he has been a party concerned in concluding that convention, which must be the rule of this treaty."

The assembly of this important night was in some degree clandestine, the design of treating not being yet openly declared, and, when the Whigs returned to power, was aggravated to a charge of high treason; though, as Prior remarks in his imperfect answer to the *Report of the Committee of Secrecy*, no treaty ever was made without private interviews and preliminary discussions.

My business is not the history of the peace, but the Life of Prior. The conferences began at Utrecht on the 1st of January (1711–12), and the English plenipotentiaries arrived on the 15th. The ministers of the different potentates conferred and conferred; but the peace advanced so slowly, that speedier methods were found necessary: and Bolingbroke was sent to Paris to adjust differences with less formality; Prior either accompanied him or followed him; and after his departure had the appointments and authority of an ambassador, though no public character.

By some mistake of the Queen's orders the court of France had been disgusted; and Bolingbroke says in his Letter, "Dear Mat, hide the nakedness of thy country, and give the best turn thy fertile brain will furnish thee with to the blunders of thy countrymen, who are not much better politicians than the French are poets."

Soon after the Duke of Shrewsbury went on a formal embassy to Paris. It is related by Boyer that the intention was to have joined Prior in the commission, but that Shrewsbury refused to be associated with a man so meanly born. Prior therefore continued to act without a title till the Duke returned next year to England, and then he assumed the style and dignity of ambassador.

But, while he continued in appearance a private man, he was treated with confidence by Lewis, who sent him with a letter to the Queen, written in favour of the Elector of Bavaria. "I shall expect," says he, "with impatience, the return of Mr. Prior, whose conduct is very agreeable to me." And while the Duke of Shrewsbury was still at Paris, Bolingbroke wrote to Prior thus: "Monsieur de Torcy has a confidence in you; make use of it, once for all, upon this occasion, and convince him thoroughly, that we must give a different turn to our parliament and our people, according to their resolution at this crisis."

Prior's public dignity and splendour commenced in August 1713, and continued till the August following; but I am afraid that, according to the usual fate of greatness, it was attended with some perplexities and mortifications. He had not all that is customarily given to ambassadors: he hints to the Queen, in an imperfect poem, that he had no service of plate; and it appeared, by the debts which he contracted, that his remittances were not punctually made.

On the 1st of August, 1714, ensued the downfall of the Tories, and the degradation of Prior. He was recalled; but was not able to return, being detained by the debts which he had found it necessary to contract, and which were not discharged before March, though his old friend Montague was now at the head of the Treasury.

He returned then as soon as he could, and was welcomed on the 25th of March [1715] by a warrant, but was, however, suffered to live in his own house, under the custody of the messenger, till he was examined before a committee of the Privy Council, of which Mr. Walpole was chairman, and Lord Coningsby, Mr. Stanhope, and Mr. Lechmere were the principal interrogators; who, in this examination, of which there is printed an account not unentertaining, behaved with the boisterousness of men elated by recent authority. They are represented as asking questions sometimes vague, sometimes insidious, and writing answers different from those which they received. Prior, however, seems to have been overpowered by their turbulence; for he confesses that he signed what, if he had ever come before a legal judicature, he should have contradicted or explained away. The oath was administered by Boscawen, a Middlesex justice, who at last was going to write his attestation on the wrong side of the paper.

They were very industrious to find some charge against Oxford; and asked Prior, with great earnestness, who was present when the preliminary articles were talked of or signed at his house? He told them that either the Earl of Oxford or the Duke of Shrewsbury was absent, but he could not remember which; an answer which perplexed them, because it supplied no accusation against either. "Could anything be more absurd," says he, "or more inhuman, than to propose to me a question, by the answering of which I might, according to them, prove myself a traitor? And notwithstanding their solemn promise, that nothing which I could say should hurt myself, I had no reason to trust them: for they violated that promise about five hours after. However, I owned I was there present. Whether this was wisely done or no, I leave to my friends to determine."

When he had signed the paper, he was told by Walpole that the committee were not satisfied with his behaviour, nor could give such an account of it to the Commons as might merit favour; and that they now thought a stricter confinement necessary than to his own house. "Here," says he, "Boscawen played the moralist, and Coningsby the Christian, but both very awkwardly." The messenger in whose custody he was to be placed was then called, and very decently asked by Coningsby, "if his house was secured by bars and bolts?" The messenger answered, "No," with astonishment. At which Coningsby very angrily said, "Sir, you must secure this prisoner; it is for the safety of the nation: if he escape, you shall answer for it."

They had already printed their report, and in this examination were endeavouring to find proofs.

He continued thus confined for some time, and Mr. Walpole (June 10, 1715) moved for an impeachment against him. What made him so acrimonious does not appear: he was by nature no thirster for blood. Prior was a week after committed to close custody, with orders that "no person should be admitted to see him without leave from the Speaker."

When, two years after, an Act of Grace was passed, he was excepted, and continued still in custody, which he had made less tedious by writing his *Alma*. He was, however, soon after discharged.

He had now his liberty, but he had nothing else. Whatever the profit of his employments might have been, he had always spent it; and at the age of fifty-three was, with all his abilities, in danger of penury, having yet no solid revenue but from the fellowship of his college, which, when in his exaltation he was censured for retaining it, he said he could live upon at last.

Being, however, generally known and esteemed, he was encouraged to add other poems to those which he had printed, and to publish them [1718] by subscription. The expedient succeeded by the industry of many friends, who circulated the proposals, and the care of some, who, it is said, withheld the money from him lest he should squander it. The price of the volume was two guineas; the whole collection was four thousand; to which Lord Harley, the son of the Earl of Oxford, to whom he had invariably adhered, added an equal sum for the purchase of Down Hall, which Prior was to enjoy during life, and Harley after his decease.

He had now, what wits and philosophers have often wished, the power of passing the day in contemplative tranquillity. But it seems that busy men seldom live long in a state of quiet. It is not unlikely that his health declined. He complains of deafness; "for," says he, "I took little care of my ears while I was not sure if my head was my own."

Of any occurrences in his remaining life I have found no account. In a letter to Swift, "I have," says he, "treated Lady Harriot at Cambridge (Good God! a Fellow of a College treat!), and spoke verses to her in a gown and cap! What, the plenipotentiary, so far concerned in the damned peace at Utrecht! the man that makes up half the volume of terse prose, that makes up the report of the committee, speaking verses! *Sic est, homo sum.*"

He died [of a violent cholic occasioned by a cold] at Wimpole, a seat of the Earl of Oxford, on the 18th of September, 1721, and was buried in Westminster, where on a monument, for which, as the "last piece of human vanity," he left 500*l.*, is engraven this epitaph:

> Sui Temporis Historiam meditanti,
> Paulatim obrepens Febris
> Operis simul & Vitæ filum abrupit,
> Sept. 18. An. Dom. 1721. Ætat. 57.
> H. S. E.
> Vir Eximius
> Serenissimis
> Regi GULIELMO Reginæque MARIÆ
> In Congressione Fœderatorum
> Hagæ anno 1690 celebratâ,
> Deinde Magnæ Britanniæ Legatis
> Tum iis,
> Qui anno 1697 Pacem RYSWICKI confecerunt,
> Tum iis,
> Qui apud Gallos annis proximis Legationem obierunt:
> Eodem etiam anno 1697 in Hibernia
> SECRETARIUS;

Necnon in utroque Honorabili consessu
Eorum,
Qui anno 1700 ordinandis Commercii negotiis,
Quique anno 1711 dirigendis Portorii rebus,
Præsidebant,
COMMISSIONARIUS;
Postremo
Ab ANNA
Felicissimæ memoriæ Reginâ
Ad LUDOVICUM XIV. Galliæ Regem
Missus anno 1711
De Pace stabilienda,
(Pace etiamnum durante
Diuque ut boni jam omnes sperant duraturâ)
Cum summa potestate Legatus.
MATTHÆUS PRIOR Armiger;
Qui
Hos omnes, quibus cumulatus est, Titulos
Humanitatis, Ingenii, Eruditionis laude
Superavit;
Cui enim nascenti faciles arriserant Musæ.
Hunc Puerum Schola hic Regia perpolivit;
Juvenem in Collegio Sti. Johannis
Cantabrigia optimis Scientiis instruxit;
Virum denique auxit; & perfecit
Multa cum viris Principibus consuetudo;
Ita natus, ita institutus,
A Vatum Choro avelli nunquam potuit,
Sed solebat sæpe rerum Civilium gravitatem
Amœniorum Literarum Studiis condire:
Et cum omne adeo Poetices genus
Haud infeliciter tentaret,
Tum in Fabellis concinne lepideque texendis
Mirus Artifex
Neminem habuit parem.
Hæc liberalis animi oblectamenta:
Quam nullo Illi labore constiterint,
Facile ii perspexere, quibus usus est Amici;
Apud quos Urbanitatum & Leporum plenus

Cum ad rem, quæcunque forte inciderat,
Aptè variè copiosèque alluderet,
Interea nihil quæsitum, nihil vi expressum
Videbatur,
Sed omnia ultro effluere,
Et quasi jugi è fonte affatim exuberare,
Ita suos tandem dubios reliquit,
Essetne in Scriptis, Poeta Elegantior,
An in Convictu, Comes Jucundior.

Of Prior, eminent as he was, both by his abilities and station, very few memorials have been left by his contemporaries;
the account therefore must now be destitute of his private
character and familiar practices. He lived at a time when the
rage of party detected all which it was any man's interest to
hide; and as little ill is heard of Prior, it is certain that not
much was known. He was not afraid of provoking censure; for
when he forsook the Whigs, under whose patronage he first
entered the world, he became a Tory so ardent and determi-
nate, that he did not willingly consort with men of different
opinions. He was one of the sixteen Tories who met weekly,
and agreed to address each other by the title of *Brother*; and
seems to have adhered, not only by concurrence of political
designs, but by peculiar affection, to the Earl of Oxford and
his family. With how much confidence he was trusted, has
been already told.

He was, however, in Pope's opinion, fit only to make verses,
and less qualified for business than Addison himself. This was
surely said without consideration. Addison, exalted to a high
place, was forced into degradation by the sense of his own
incapacity; Prior, who was employed by men very capable of
estimating his value, having been secretary to one embassy,
had, when great abilities were again wanted, the same office
another time; and was, after so much experience of his knowledge and dexterity, at last sent to transact a negotiation in
the highest degree arduous and important; for which he was
qualified, among other requisites, in the opinion of Bolingbroke, by his influence upon the French minister, and by skill
in questions of commerce above other men.

Of his behaviour in the lighter parts of life, it is too late to get much intelligence. One of his answers to a boastful Frenchman has been related, and to an impertinent he made another equally proper. During his embassy, he sat at the opera by a man who, in his rapture, accompanied with his own voice the principal singer. Prior fell to railing at the performer with all the terms of reproach that he could collect, till the Frenchman, ceasing from his song, began to expostulate with him for his harsh censure of a man who was confessedly the ornament of the stage. "I know all that," says the ambassador, "mais il chante si haut, que je ne sçaurois vous entendre."

In a gay French company, where every one sung a little song or stanza, of which the burden was, "Bannissons la Melancholie"; when it came to his turn to sing, after the performance of a young lady that sat next him, he produced these extemporary lines:

> Mais celle voix, et ces beaux yeux,
> Font Cupidon trop dangereux,
> Et je suis triste quand je crie
> Bannissons la Melancholie.

Tradition represents him as willing to descend from the dignity of the poet and statesman to the low delights of mean company. His Chloe probably was sometimes ideal; but the woman with whom he cohabited was a despicable drab of the lowest species. One of his wenches, perhaps Chloe, while he was absent from his house, stole his plate, and ran away; as was related by a woman who had been his servant. Of this propensity to sordid converse I have seen an account so seriously ridiculous, that it seems to deserve insertion.

"I have been assured that Prior, after having spent the evening with Oxford, Bolingbroke, Pope, and Swift, would go and smoke a pipe, and drink a bottle of ale, with a common soldier and his wife, in Long-Acre, before he went to bed; not from any remains of the lowness of his original, as one said, but, I suppose, that his faculties,

> —— Strain'd to the height,
> In that celestial colloquy sublime,
> Dazzled and spent, sunk down, and sought repair."

Poor Prior! why was he so *strained*, and in such *want* of *repair*, after a conversation with men not, in the opinion of the world, much wiser than himself? But such are the conceits of speculatists, who *strain* their *faculties* to find in a mine what lies upon the surface.

His opinions, so far as the means of judging are left us, seem to have been right; but his life was, it seems, irregular, negligent, and sensual.

Prior has written with great variety, and his variety has made him popular. He has tried all styles, from the grotesque to the solemn, and has not so failed in any as to incur derision or disgrace.

His works may be distinctly considered as comprising Tales, Love-verses, Occasional Poems, *Alma* and *Solomon*.

His Tales have obtained general approbation, being written with great familiarity and great sprightliness: the language is easy, but seldom gross, and the numbers smooth, without appearance of care. Of these tales there are only four:—*The Ladle*, which is introduced by a Preface, neither necessary nor pleasing, neither grave nor merry; *Paulo Purganti*, which has likewise a Preface, but of more value than the Tale; *Hans Carvel*, not over decent; and *Protogenes and Apelles*, an old story, mingled, by an affectation not disagreeable, with modern images. *The Young Gentleman in Love* has hardly a just claim to the title of a "Tale." I know not whether he be the original author of any tale which he has given us. The adventure of *Hans Carvel* has passed through many successions of merry wits; for it is to be found in Ariosto's *Satires*, and is perhaps yet older. But the merit of such stories is the art of telling them.

In his amorous effusions he is less happy, for they are not dictated by nature or by passion, and have neither gallantry nor tenderness. They have the coldness of Cowley without his wit, the dull exercises of a skilful versifier, resolved at all adventures to write something about Chloe, and trying to be amorous by dint of study. His fictions therefore are mythological. Venus, after the example of the Greek Epigram, asks when she was seen *naked and bathing*. Then Cupid is *mistaken*; then Cupid is *disarmed*; then he loses his darts to

Ganymede; then Jupiter sends him a summons by Mercury. Then Chloe goes a-hunting, with an *ivory quiver graceful at her side;* Diana mistakes her for one of her nymphs, and Cupid laughs at the blunder. All this is surely despicable; and even when he tries to act the lover, without the help of gods or goddesses, his thoughts are unaffecting or remote. He talks not "like a man of this world."

The greatest of all his amorous essays is *Henry and Emma;* a dull and tedious dialogue, which excites neither esteem for the man nor tenderness for the woman. The example of Emma, who resolves to follow an outlawed murderer wherever fear and guilt shall drive him, deserves no imitation; and the experiment by which Henry tries the lady's constancy is such as must end either in infamy to her, or in disappointment to himself.

His occasional poems necessarily lost part of their value, as their occasions, being less remembered, raised less emotion. Some of them, however, are preserved by their inherent excellence. The burlesque of Boileau's *Ode on Namur* has, in some parts, such airiness and levity as will always procure it readers, even among those who cannot compare it with the original. The Epistle to Boileau is not so happy. The *Poems to the King* are now perused only by young students who read merely that they may learn to write; and of the *Carmen Seculare,* I cannot but suspect that I might praise or censure it by caprice, without danger of detection; for who can be supposed to have laboured through it? Yet the time has been when this neglected work was so popular, that it was translated into Latin by no common master.

His poem on the Battle of Ramillies is necessarily tedious by the form of the stanza: an uniform mass of ten lines thirty-five times repeated, inconsequential and slightly connected, must weary both the ear and the understanding. His imitation of Spenser, which consists principally in *I ween* and *I weet,* without exclusion of later modes of speech, makes his poem neither ancient nor modern. His mention of Mars and Bellona, and his comparison of Marlborough to the Eagle that bears the thunder of Jupiter, are all puerile and unaffecting; and yet more despicable is the long tale told by Lewis in his despair, of Brute and Troynovante, and the teeth of Cadmus, with his similes of the raven and eagle, and wolf and lion. By the help of such easy fictions, and vulgar topics, without acquaintance with life, and without knowledge of art or nature, a poem of any length, cold and lifeless like this, may be easily written on any subject.

In his epilogues to Phædra and to Lucius, he is very happily facetious; but in the prologue before the Queen, the pedant has found his way, with Minerva, Perseus, and Andromeda.

His epigrams and lighter pieces are, like those of others, sometimes elegant, sometimes trifling, and sometimes dull; among the best are the *Camelion* and the epitaph on *John and Joan*.

Scarcely any one of our poets has written so much, and translated so little: the version of Callimachus is sufficiently licentious; the paraphrase on *St. Paul's Exhortation to Charity* is eminently beautiful.

Alma is written in professed imitation of *Hudibras*, and has at least one accidental resemblance: *Hudibras* wants a plan, because it is left imperfect; *Alma* is imperfect, because it seems never to have had a plan. Prior appears not to have proposed to himself any drift or design, but to have written the casual dictates of the present moment.

What Horace said when he imitated Lucilius, might be said of Butler by Prior—his numbers were not smooth or neat: Prior excelled him in versification; but he was, like Horace, *inventore minor*; he had not Butler's exuberance of matter and variety of illustration. The spangles of wit which he could afford, he knew how to polish; but he wanted the bullion of his master. Butler pours out a negligent profusion, certain of the weight, but careless of the stamp. Prior has comparatively little, but with that little he makes a fine show. *Alma* has many admirers, and was the only piece among Prior's works of which Pope said that he should wish to be the author.

Solomon is the work to which he entrusted the protection of his name, and which he expected succeeding ages to regard with veneration. His affection was natural: it had undoubtedly been written with great labour; and who is willing to think that he has been labouring in vain? He had infused into it much knowledge and much thought; and often polished it to elegance, often dignified it with splendour, and sometimes heightened it to sublimity: he perceived in it many excellences, and did not discover that it wanted that without which all others are of small avail—the power of engaging attention and alluring curiosity.

Tediousness is the most fatal of all faults; negligences or errors are single and local, but tediousness pervades the whole; other faults are censured and forgotten, but the power of tediousness propagates itself. He that is weary the first hour, is more weary the second; as bodies forced into motion, contrary to their tendency, pass more and more slowly through every successive interval of space.

Unhappily this pernicious failure is that which an author is least able to discover. We are seldom tiresome to ourselves; and the act of composition fills and delights the mind with change of language and succession of images; every couplet when produced is new, and novelty is the great source of pleasure. Perhaps no man ever thought a line superfluous when he first wrote it, or contracted his work till his ebullitions of invention had subsided. And even if he should control his desire of immediate renown, and keep his work *nine years* unpublished, he will be still the author, and still in danger of deceiving himself: and if he consults his friends, he will probably find men who have more kindness than judgment, or more fear to offend than desire to instruct.

The tediousness of this poem proceeds not from the uniformity of the subject, for it is sufficiently diversified, but from the continued tenour of the narration, in which Solomon relates the successive vicissitudes of his own mind, without the intervention of any other speaker, or the mention of any other agent, unless it be Abra; the reader is only to learn what he thought, and to be told that he thought wrong. The event of every experiment is foreseen, and therefore the process is not much regarded.

Yet the work is far from deserving to be neglected. He that shall peruse it will be able to mark many passages to which he may recur for instruction or delight; many from which the poet may learn to write, and the philosopher to reason.

If Prior's poetry be generally considered, his praise will be that of correctness and industry, rather than of compass of comprehension, or activity of fancy. He never made any effort of invention: his greater pieces are only tissues of common thoughts; and his smaller, which consist of light images or single conceits, are not always his own. I have traced him among the French epigrammatists, and have been informed that he poached for prey among obscure authors. *The Thief and Cordelier* is, I suppose, generally considered as an original production; with how much justice this epigram may tell, which was written by Georgius Sabinus, a poet now little known or read, though once the friend of Luther and Melancthon:

De Sacerdote Furem consolante

Quidam sacrificus furem comitatus euntem
    Huc ubi dat sontes carnificina neci,
Ne sis mœstus, ait; summi conviva Tonantis
    Jam cum cœlitibus (si modo credis) eris.
Ille gemens, si vera mihi solatia præbes,
    Hospes apud superos sis meus oro, refert.
Sacrificus contra; mihi non convivia fas est
    Ducere, jejunans hac edo luce nihil.

What he has valuable he owes to his diligence and his judgment. His diligence has justly placed him amongst the most correct of the English poets; and he was one of the first that resolutely endeavoured at correctness. He never sacrifices accuracy to haste, nor indulges himself in contemptuous negligence, or impatient idleness; he has no careless lines, or entangled sentiments: his words are nicely selected, and his thoughts fully expanded. If this part of his character suffers any abatement, it must be from the disproportion of his rhymes, which have not always sufficient consonance, and from the admission of broken lines into his *Solomon;* but perhaps he thought, like Cowley, that hemistichs ought to be admitted into heroic poetry.

He had apparently such rectitude of judgment as secured him from everything that approached to the ridiculous or absurd; but as the laws operate in civil agency not to the excitement of virtue, but the repression of wickedness, so judgment in the operations of intellect can hinder faults, but not produce excellence. Prior is never low, nor very often sublime. It is said by Longinus of Euripides, that he forces himself sometimes into grandeur by violence of effort, as the lion kindles his fury by the lashes of his own tail. Whatever Prior obtains above mediocrity seems the effort of struggle and of toil. He has many vigorous but few happy lines; he has everything by purchase, and nothing by gift; he had no *nightly visitations* of the Muse, no infusions of sentiment or felicities of fancy.

His diction, however, is more his own than that of any among the successors of Dryden; he borrows no lucky turns or commodious modes of language from his predecessors. His phrases are original, but they are sometimes harsh; as he inherited no elegances, none has he bequeathed. His expression has every mark of laborious study: the line seldom seems to have been formed at once; the words did not come till they were called, and were then put by constraint into their places, where they do their duty, but do it sullenly. In his greater compositions there may be found more rigid stateliness than graceful dignity.

Of versification he was not negligent: what he received from Dryden he did not lose; neither did he increase the difficulty of writing by unnecessary severity, but uses triplets and Alexandrines without scruple. In his Preface to *Solomon* he proposes some improvements, by extending the sense from one couplet to another, with variety of pauses. This he has attempted, but without success; his interrupted lines are unpleasing, and his sense as less distinct is less striking.

He has altered the stanza of Spenser, as a house is altered by building another in its place of a different form. With how little resemblance he has formed his new stanza to that of his master, these specimens will show:

SPENSER

She flying fast from heaven's hated face,
And from the world that her discover'd wide,
Fled to the wasteful wilderness apace,
From living eyes her open shame to hide,

And lurk'd in rocks and caves long unespied.
But that fair crew of knights, and Una fair,
Did in that castle afterwards abide,
To rest themselves, and weary powers repair,
Where store they found of all that dainty was and rare.

PRIOR

To the close rock the frighted raven flies,
Soon as the rising eagle cuts the air:
The shaggy wolf unseen and trembling lies,
When the hoarse roar proclaims the lion near.
Ill-starr'd did we our forts and lines forsake,
To dare our British foes to open fight:
Our conquest we by stratagem should make:
Our triumph had been founded in our flight.
'Tis ours, by craft and by surprise to gain:
'Tis theirs, to meet in arms, and battle in the plain.

By this new structure of his lines he has avoided difficulties;
nor am I sure that he has lost any of the power of pleasing;
but he no longer imitates Spenser.

Some of his poems are written without regularity of measures; for, when he commenced poet, he had not recovered
from our Pindaric infatuation; but he probably lived to be
convinced that the essence of verse is order and consonance.

His numbers are such as mere diligence may attain; they
seldom offend the ear, and seldom soothe it; they commonly
want airiness, lightness, and vacility: what is smooth is not
soft. His verses always roll, but they seldom flow.

A survey of the life and writings of Prior may exemplify
a sentence which he doubtless understood well, when he read
Horace at his uncle's; "the vessel long retains the scent which
it first receives." In his private relaxation he revived the
tavern, and in his amorous pedantry he exhibited the college.
But on higher occasions and nobler subjects, when habit was
overpowered by the necessity of reflection, he wanted not wisdom as a statesman, or elegance as a poet.